JUNG IN CONTEXTS

A reader

Edited by Paul Bishop

London and New York

First published 1999
by Routledge
2 Park Square, Milton Park, Abingdon, Oxford, OX14 4RN

Simultaneously published in the USA and Canada
by Routledge
711 Third Avenue, New York, NY 10017

© 1999 Edited by Paul Bishop

Typeset in Times by
BC Typesetting, Bristol
Printed and bound in Great Britain by
the MPG Books Group

British Library Cataloguing in Publication Data
A catalogue record for this book is available from the British Library

Library of Congress Cataloging in Publication Data
Jung in Contexts: A reader/edited by Paul Bishop; foreword by
Anthony Storr.
p.   cm.
Includes bibliographical references and index.
1. Jungian psychology.   2. Psychoanalysis–History.
3. Psychoanalysis.   4. Jung, C.G. (Carl Gustav), 1875–1961.
I. Bishop, Paul, 1967–   .
BF173.J854   1999
150.19′54′092–dc21   98-45954 CIP

ISBN 978-0-415-20557-3 (hbk)

ISBN 978-0-415-20558-0 (pbk)

JUNG IN CONTEXTS

The current interest in Jung shows no sign of abating, with international controversy surrounding the origins of analytical psychology. *Jung in Contexts: A Reader* is a unique collection of the most important essays on Jung and analytical psychology over the past two decades.

A comprehensive introduction traces the growth and development of analytical psychology and its institutions. The nine essays which follow place Jung, the man and his work, in three important contexts: historical, literary and intellectual. In **historical** context, Jung's visions during his 'confrontation with the unconscious', his attitude towards National Socialism and the composition of his so-called 'autobiography' are examined. Next, in **literary** context, two essays investigate Jung's reading of E.T.A. Hoffman, and Thomas Mann's reception of Jungian ideas. Finally, in **intellectual** context, Jung's work is viewed in terms of the traditions of German and French thought from which it drew so many impulses: Schopenhauer, Nietzsche and Bergson.

Written by leading scholars on the history of Jungian psychology, *Jung in Contexts: A Reader* is an indispensable introductory text for students, both postgraduates and undergraduates, professionals and all those interested in Jung.

Paul Bishop teaches German at the University of Glasgow. Following the publication of *The Dionysian Self: C.G. Jung's Reception of Friedrich Nietzsche*, he has written various articles on Jung's intellectual affinities with Weimar Classicism, German philosophy and literature, the history of Jung's relationship with the Rascher Verlag, and the psychology of Hans Trüb.

Contributors: Paul Bishop; Stanley Grossman; Pete A.Y. Gunter; John Haule; James L. Jarrett; John Kerr; Richard Noll; Sonu Shamdasani.

But in the end, to inherit something one has to understand it; inheritance is, after all, culture.
Thomas Mann, letter to Klaus Mann, 22 July 1939

CONTENTS

CONTENTS

CONTRIBUTORS

Paul Bishop is a Senior Lecturer in German at the University of Glasgow. He has written *The Dionysian Self: C.G. Jung's Reception of Nietzsche* and is the author of various articles on the history of Jungian psychology and German literature.

Stanley Grossman is Professor Emeritus in the Department of History at Ball State University. His dissertation was entitled 'Neo-socialism: A Study in Political Metamorphosis'.

Pete A.Y. Gunter is Professor of Philosophy in the Department of Philosophy and Religious Studies at the University of North Texas. He is an authority on Bergson, Whitehead, and related subjects, and the author of *Henri Bergson: A Bibliography* and numerous articles on philosophy.

John R. Haule is an analyst and the author of various articles on Jungian psychology. He has written *Divine Madness: Archetypes of Romantic Love* and is a member of the International Association for Analytical Psychology.

James L. Jarrett is Professor of the Philosophy of Education at the University of California, Berkeley. He is the editor of Jung's *Seminar on Nietzsche's 'Zarathustra'*.

John Kerr was trained as a clinical psychologist at New York University and is associate editor of The Analytic Press. He has written *A Most Dangerous Method: The Story of Jung, Freud, and Sabina Spielrein*, and he is co-editor and contributor to *Freud and the History of Psychoanalysis*.

Richard Noll is a clinical psychologist and Lecturer in the History of Science at Harvard University. He has written *The Jung Cult*, which won the 1994 Best Book in Psychology Award, and *The Aryan Christ*.

Sonu Shamdasani is a research fellow at the Wellcome Institute for the History of Medicine. He has written *Cult Fictions* and various articles on analytical psychology, and is the editor of Jung's *Seminar on the Psychology of Kundalini Yoga* and the co-editor of *Speculations after Freud*.

Anthony Storr is a Fellow of the Royal College of Physicians, the Royal College of Psychiatrists, and the Royal Society of Literature, and an Emeritus Fellow of Green College, Oxford. His books include *Jung, The Dynamics of Creation, Freud, Feet of Clay*, and he is the editor of *The Essential Jung*.

FOREWORD

Anthony Storr

This collection of papers bears witness to Jung's fertility and originality, and also demonstrates that his thought is still influential in a variety of scholarly fields. Freud and Jung have both come under fire from psychologists and psychiatrists during the last three decades, and it may be that, in years to come, their ideas will be better remembered and acknowledged by philosophers and literary scholars than by psychiatrists. Since psychiatry became primarily concerned with biochemistry and genetics, no doctor specializing in psychiatry need read the works of Freud or Jung, and some young psychiatrists have hardly heard of either. It is therefore appropriate that a foreword to a collection of papers primarily concerned with Jung in historical, literary and intellectual contexts should remind the reader that his medical and psychiatric training and experience were the background from which his later views of the mind developed.

Jung started work at the Burghölzli mental hospital in Zurich in December 1900 and remained there until 1909 when he resigned his post in favour of his growing private practice. The Director of the Burghölzli was Eugen Bleuler whose monograph *Dementia Praecox or The Group of Schizophrenias* made him famous. Jung's first published work was his dissertation for his medical degree, *On the Psychology and Pathology of So-called Occult Phenomena*, which was based on his observation of a 15-year-old cousin, Hélène Preiswerk, who claimed to be a medium. She said that she received messages from the dead and other spirits who spoke through her; but Jung interpreted these voices as alternate personalities, aspects of the girl herself which had become dissociated from her normal ego.

Jung's interest in dissociation and splitting was reinforced by his daily encounters with chronic schizophrenics whose personalities, he concluded, were fragmented; that is, disintegrated into many parts rather than merely dissociated into two or three recognizable subsidiary personalities. John R. Haule's paper in the present collection demonstrates that Freud's idea that neurosis came about because the child's sexuality had become arrested at some immature stage was an attempt to replace the spatial metaphor of dissociation with the temporal metaphor of sexual stages. Freud's theories would have certainly developed differently if he had worked as a psychiatrist in a mental hospital, but Freud had virtually no experience with psychotic patients.

Jung's clinical observation of chronic schizophrenics convinced him that psychotic phenomena could not be explained, in Freudian fashion, as derivatives of infantile experience. He realized that the delusional systems of the insane were akin to myth, and this resemblance led him to conclude that there was a myth-making substratum of mind common to all people: a 'collective unconscious' which lay beneath the merely personal and which was responsible for the spontaneous production of myths, visions, religious ideas, and certain particularly impressive varieties of dream which were common to various cultures and different periods of history.

Jung was widely read in history, philosophy and comparative religion, and concluded that delusions could be interpreted as having a positive function. Pre-literate peoples depended on a variety of myths to account for the creation of the world and their own place in it. Myths were therefore adaptive, since they made sense of the world and gave meaning to the individual's existence. Perhaps delusional systems were positive attempts to make sense out of psychotic experience.

Freud, in his paper on Judge Schreber, had already suggested that 'The delusional formation, which we take to be the pathological product, is in reality an attempt at recovery, a process of reconstruction.'[1] Jung goes further.

> Closer study of Schreber's or any similar case will show that these patients are consumed by a desire to create a new world-system, or what we call a *Weltanschauung*, often of the most bizarre kind. Their aim is obviously to create a system that will enable them to assimilate unknown psychic phenomena and so adapt themselves to their own world. This a purely subjective adaptation at first, but it is a necessary transition stage on the way to adapting the personality to the world in general. Only, the patient remains stuck in this stage and substitutes his subjective formulations for the real world – which is precisely why he remains ill.[2]

For example, a paranoid delusional system which explains an individual's failure in life by alleging that he is the victim of malicious persecution preserves the subject's self-esteem and prevents him from regarding his life as futile. So does a religious conviction that he is a child of God in whom God takes a personal interest.

An account of her illness by a modern schizophrenic confirms Jung's interpretation. Elizabeth Farr had experienced hallucinations since she was 8 years old.

In high school I became engrossed in religion, the occult, and the arts as a possible way to help explain what was going on. The central driving feature in my behaviour was to understand my experiences.

The delusions started insidiously. I do not know where religion, the occult, and the arts left off and where the crazy ideas started. All I know was that I thought there had to be an explanation for my experiences and I had to be active in my pursuit of an Enlightenment to resolve the conflict between my reality and the reality that everybody else seemed to be experiencing. Everything had to be connected up somehow, I thought. I had to make sense out of it all and connect it up with what I was trying to do in my life.[3]

It is clear that Jung's experience with psychotic patients greatly influenced his later work. The patients who primarily interested him in his latter years were those who, having achieved success in the external world, found life meaningless and empty. In Jung's view, these patients had become cut off from the myth-making level of mind, and needed to regain contact with it by exploring their dreams and phantasies. The normal person, as well as the schizophrenic, needed a personal myth which would make sense out of experience, and restore a sense of meaning to life.

While working in the Burghölzli, Jung published his research into the nature of the psychoses as *The Psychology of Dementia Praecox* (1907). It was this book that led to his first meeting with Freud in March 1907. At Bleuler's suggestion, Jung employed word-association tests in the investigation of both psychotic and normal subjects. Word-association tests were originally devised in the hope that they would throw light upon different types of intelligence and upon the ways in which mental contents are linked by similarity, contrast and contiguity in space and time. In Jung's hands, they provided experimental proof that emotionally disturbing material can be banished from consciousness and yet continue to influence behaviour. For it often happens that subjects are quite unaware that their responses to emotionally significant words are delayed. And so the test became a means of investigating a subject's personal unconscious and gave experimental support to Freud's theory of repression.

Jung introduced the term *complex* to describe a collection of associations linked by the same feeling-tone, and went on to say, in his Tavistock Lectures of 1935:

a complex with its given tension or energy has the tendency to form a little personality of itself. It has a sort of body, a certain amount of its own physiology. It can upset the stomach. It upsets the breathing, it disturbs the heart – in short, it behaves like a partial personality. For instance, when you want to say or do

something and unfortunately a complex interferes with this intention, then you say or do something different from what you
intended.[4]

Jung never relinquished the idea that the mind could be divided into
partial personalities. In *Memories, Dreams, Reflections*, he reveals that he
thought of both his mother and himself as possessing at least two personalities. When, after his own mental illness during World War I, he came to
write *Psychological Types*, he concluded that the predominantly extra-
verted person had an introverted aspect which might be unconscious, and
vice versa. Neurosis was the consequence of an adaptation to life which
was exaggeratedly one-sided, and psychotherapy was a matter of revealing
and developing the hidden personality so that a better balance between
these two opposites could be achieved.

Jung's therapeutic efforts were always more directed toward reconciling
conflicting opposites within the mind than toward discovering the causal
roots of neurotic problems in childhood. This teleological emphasis on
achieving integration clearly originated from his clinical experience in the
Burghölzli. In addition, his medical training undoubtedly contributed to
his preoccupation with finding 'the middle path' between opposites to
which Paul Bishop refers in his Introduction.

The French physiologist Claude Bernard (1813–1878) had established
the principle that 'all the vital mechanisms, varied as they are, have only
one object: that of preserving constant the conditions of life'. For example,
Bernard discovered that the liver converted sugar into glycogen, a complex
substance which serves as a stored reserve of carbohydrates. When the
blood sugar drops for any reason, the liver reconverts glycogen into sugar,
thus keeping the sugar content of the blood at a more or less constant
level.

Bernard also discovered that the vasomotor nerves control the dilation
and constriction of blood vessels in response to external temperature
changes. In cold weather, the blood vessels contract in order to conserve
heat: in hot weather they expand to allow body heat to dissipate, thus
keeping the body temperature within acceptable limits. These self-
regulating functions are examples of what became known as *homeostasis*.

As a medical student, Jung studied physiology and became familiar with
the idea that the body was a self-regulating entity, always striving to find
the middle path between opposite extremes. Jung concluded that what was
true of the body was also true of the psyche. The principle of self-
regulation or homeostasis is a core concept in analytical psychology. It
governs Jung's view of dreams, his conception of neurosis, and his vision
of individuation.

Jung stated his position clearly when he wrote:

A psychological theory, if it is to be more than a technical make-shift, must base itself on the principle of opposition; for without this it could only re-establish a neurotically unbalanced psyche. There is no balance, no system of self-regulation without opposition. The psyche is just such a self-regulating system.[5]

We can take the theory of compensation as a basic law of psychic behaviour. Too little on one side results in too much on the other. Similarly, the relation betwen conscious and unconscious is compensatory. This is one of the best-proven rules of dream-interpretation. When we set out to interpret a dream, it is always helpful to ask: What conscious attitude does it compensate?[6]

In Jung's view, neurosis was not the consequence of being held up at some infantile stage of sexual development, but of a one-sided development which neglected the opposite within the psyche. The task of the analyst is to explore the subject's dreams and phantasies in the hope of bringing about a more balanced attitude.

Jung's concept of the self-regulating psyche which, as we have seen, was directly derived from his physiological studies, is also the basis for the central concept of his psychology, the process of individuation. Nearly all his later writings are devoted to this process. Returning to the subject of homeostasis, we can see that something within the body can be said to 'know better' than the conscious ego. We are accustomed to the fact that fatigue, hunger, or lack of sleep give rise to physical messages to which we are compelled to pay attention, which constitute restraints upon what we might wish to accomplish, and which therefore govern our behaviour. We are less sensitively attuned to the signals coming from within our minds. Jung was proposing that, just as there is a central control system which governs human physiology, so there is also a central control system which governs the individual's psyche. Neither control system is directly accessible to consciousness; but there is a wisdom of the psyche as well as a wisdom of the body. The process of individuation is a journey of personal psychological development which depends upon learning to pay attention to these signals, which manifest themselves both in dreams and in the kind of phantasies which come to people spontaneously when in a state of reverie.

Jung's own mental illness had taught him that, at the same time at which his mind appeared to be disintegrating, a healing process was proceeding which was striving to bring order to the chaos within and thus achieve a new integration. He found that he had to submit to being guided by something within himself which was independent of his conscious intention. Could this be the psychological equivalent of God – a kind of 'God within' rather than a 'God out there'? If so, Jung had found the answer to the problem which had plagued him ever since childhood: his loss of faith in the conventional God of Christianity in whom his pastor father had told him he ought to believe.

Jung wrote a paragraph which is so often quoted that it has become famous.

> Among all my patients in the second half of life – that is to say, over thirty-five – there has not been one whose problem in the last resort was not that of finding a religious outlook on life. It is safe to say that every one of them fell ill because he had lost what the living religions of every age have given to their followers, and none of them has really been healed who did not regain his religious outlook. This of course has nothing to do with a particular creed or membership of a church.[7]

Freud regarded psychoanalysis as 'draining the Zuider Zee' by disinterring repressed infantile sexual phantasies which, he was convinced, were causally implicated in the arrest of the neurotic's libidinal development. Nothing could be further removed from this concept of healing than Jung's proposition which has just been quoted. Yet Jung's ideas are actually more realistic. There is little evidence to support Freud's theoretical position, and a good deal of evidence to suggest that less laborious methods of psychotherapy are as effective, or more effective than psychoanalysis as Freud practised it. Jung's account has nothing to do with ridding patients of particular neurotic symptoms, and everything to do with bringing about a change in attitude to life, and this throws light on a problem which has perplexed many psychotherapists, including myself. Every psychotherapist has seen patients who have not been cured of all their neurotic symptoms, but who nevertheless claim that psychotherapy has transformed their lives. Perhaps changes in attitude to life are more important factors in healing than the cure of symptoms.

Jung describes how some of his patients, faced with what appeared to be an insoluble conflict, solved it by 'outgrowing it' through developing a new level of consciousness.

> Some higher or wider interest appeared on the patient's horizon, and through this broadening of his outlook the insoluble problem lost its urgency. It was not solved logically in its own terms, but faded out when confronted with a new and stronger life urge.[8]

> I had learned that all the greatest and most important problems of life are fundamentally insoluble. They must be so, for they express the necessary polarity in every self-regulating system. They can never be solved, but only outgrown.[9]

If you sum up what people tell you about their experiences, you can formulate it this way: They came to themselves, they could accept themselves, and thus were reconciled to adverse circumstances and events. This is almost like what used to be expressed by saying: He has made his peace with God, he has sacrificed his own will, he has submitted himself to the will of God.[10]

This is a very different view of healing from that put forward by Freud, but I believe that it faithfully reflects what actually happens in many patients undergoing long-term analytical therapy. Such patients are often more concerned with finding a way of living with themselves than they are with abolishing all their symptoms or achieving what Freudians call 'genitality'.

Jung's concept of the individuation process owes something to Schopenhauer's *principium individuationis*. But Schopenhauer's philosophy is governed by the ideal of deliverance from the bonds of individuality, whereas Jung's is ruled by the need to realize individuality. Jung may also have been influenced by Nietzsche's *Ecce Homo: How One Becomes What One Is*. It is evident that Jung and Nietzsche, both sons of clergymen, were equally bereft by their loss of faith in conventional Christianity. This deprivation led to their seeking a substitute, albeit in very different ways. But Jung's training as a doctor, and his experience with psychotic patients in the Burghölzli mental hospital were both important determinants of his thinking and must be taken into account when considering the origins of analytical psychology.

Notes

1 Sigmund Freud (1911) 'Psycho-Analytic Notes on an Autobiographical Account of a Case of Paranoia', *The Standard Edition of the Complete Psychological Works of Sigmund Freud*, translated by James Strachey, in collaboration with Anna Freud, assisted by Alix Strachey and Alan Tyson, vol. XII, p. 71, *The Case of Schreber, Papers on Technique and Other Works*, London: The Hogarth Press and The Institute of Psycho-Analysis, 1958.

2 C.G. Jung, *The Collected Works of C. G. Jung*, 21 volumes, edited by Sir Herbert Read, Michael Fordham and Gerhard Adler, executive editor William McGuire, translated by R.F.C. Hull (hereafter *Collected Works*), (1908/1914) 'On Psychological Understanding', in *Collected Works*, vol. 3, para. 416, p. 189, London: Routledge & Kegan Paul, 1960.

3 Ming T. Tsuang (1982) *Schizophrenia: The Facts*, Oxford: Oxford University Press, pp. 1–2.

4 C.G. Jung (1935) 'The Tavistock Lectures', in *Collected Works*, vol. 18, *The Symbolic Life*, para. 149, p. 72, London: Routledge & Kegan Paul, 1977.

5 C.G. Jung (1943) 'The Psychology of the Unconscious', 5th edition, in *Collected Works*, vol. 7, *Two Essays on Analytical Psychology*, para. 92, p. 60, London: Routledge & Kegan Paul, 1953.

6 C.G. Jung (1934) 'The Practical Use of Dream-Analysis', in *Collected Works*, vol. 16, *The Practice of Psychotherapy*, para. 330, p. 153, London: Routledge & Kegan Paul, 1954.
7 C.G. Jung (1932) 'Psychotherapists or the Clergy', in *Collected Works*, vol. 11, *Psychology and Religion*, para. 509, p. 334, London: Routledge & Kegan Paul, 1958.
8 C.G. Jung (1938) 'Commentary on "The Secret of the Golden Flower"', in *Collected Works*, vol. 13, *Alchemical Studies*, para. 17, pp. 14–15, London: Routledge & Kegan Paul, 1967.
9 C.G. Jung, ibid., para. 18, p. 15.
10 C.G. Jung (1937) 'The History and Psychology of a Natural Symbol', Terry Lecture 3, *Collected Works*, vol. 11, *Psychology and Religion*, para. 138, pp. 81–2, London: Routledge & Kegan Paul, 1958.

PREFACE

In the course of writing my doctoral dissertation on Jung, I found myself looking in various parts of the library for material from a wide variety of journals: psychology, philosophy, modern languages, and general humanities periodicals, in addition to specialist periodicals devoted to Jungian psychology. Or, once I had located the title of an article in a bibliography or a database, I then had to turn to inter-library loans to obtain a copy. Later on, while teaching a university course on Freud and Jung, I became aware of the need to have a part of the material that I had collected in this way made more easily available. Accordingly, this collection of essays is intended to fulfil a three-fold need.

First, *Jung in Contexts* is a collection of the most important essays on Jung and analytical psychology over the past two decades. It offers a selection of useful secondary literature on Jung to those interested in learning more about him from an historico-intellectual perspective. Previously published in specialist journals and academic periodicals, the material in this book, written by experts and scholars in the field of Jungian studies, is now made available to the wider audience it deserves.

Second, it reflects the trend in recent Jung scholarship away from hagiography to critical analysis. As a result, articles that were innovative in this respect have been chosen for inclusion. The collection will, it is hoped, prove useful to those interested in Jung not just from a clinical standpoint, but from a critical, historical and intellectual perspective.

Third, the current interest in Jung shows no sign of abating, and so this collection seeks to set Jung's insights, and the debates they have provoked, in context. In particular, it contextualizes the recent international controversy surrounding the origins of analytical psychology, and points up areas that require future research.

Jung's contribution to twentieth-century thought and culture has frequently been ignored by those within academic circles, abandoning serious work on Jung to the believers and the proselytizers. In this volume, however, notable examples of recent scholarly work have been brought together to open the way to a genuinely inter-disciplinary approach to Jung.

In his Foreword, Anthony Storr focuses on the clinical importance of Jung's psychology. After an extensive Introduction, which traces the growth and development of analytical psychology and its institutions, and the history of its reception, the nine essays place Jung, the man and his work, in three important contexts. First, in historical context, the composition of his so-called 'autobiography', Jung's visions during his 'confrontation with the unconscious', and his attitude towards National Socialism are examined. Next, in literary context, two essays investigate, in turn, Jung's reading of E.T.A. Hoffmann, and Thomas Mann's reception of Jungian ideas. Finally, in intellectual context, Jung's work is viewed in terms of the traditions of German, as well as French, thought from which it drew so many impulses: Schopenhauer, Nietzsche, Bergson.

By being alert to the historical roots of analytical psychology, we may become aware of the extent of Jung's significance in mediating the thought of previous centuries to our own, and the next. It is hoped that the papers collected in *Jung in Contexts* will contribute to that task.

Preparation of this volume has incurred a number of debts in a number of ways. First of all, I should like to thank Anthony Storr, for agreeing to write the foreword to this collection of essays. Then, my perspective on Jung has been deepened, yet my focus sharpened, by the opportunity to discuss his psychological writings with my colleagues in the Department of German at the University of Glasgow, particularly Bernard Ashbrook and Roger Stephenson, and with those students who have taken the course 'Modern German Thought II: Freud and Jung'. Equally, I am indebted to other Jung scholars, particularly Richard Noll and Sonu Shamdasani, among whom I find myself as *das Weltkind in der Mitten*. The idea for such a collection was first suggested to me by Richard Sheppard. At Routledge, Edwina Welham offered considerable assistance with this volume from proposal through to publication. Finally, for all her support, Jennifer Leeder deserves more thanks than I can ever express.

Paul Bishop

ACKNOWLEDGEMENTS

The essays reproduced in this volume were originally printed in the following journals:

Sonu Shamdasani, 'Memories, dreams, omissions', *Spring: A Journal of Archetype and Culture*, 57 (1995), 115–37.

Richard Noll, 'Jung the *Leontocephalus*', *Spring: A Journal of Archetype and Culture*, 53 (1994), 12–60.

Stanley Grossman, 'C.G. Jung and National Socialism', *Journal of European Studies*, 9 (1979), 231–59.

John Kerr, '*The Devil's Elixirs*, Jung's "Theology", and the dissolution of Freud's "Poisoning Complex"', *The Psychoanalytic Review*, 75 (1988), 1–34.

Paul Bishop, '"Literarische Beziehungen haben nie bestanden?" Thomas Mann and C.G. Jung', *Oxford German Studies*, 23 (1994), 124–72; '*Jung-Joseph*: Thomas Mann's Reception of Jungian Thought in the *Joseph* Tetralogy', *The Modern Language Review*, 91 (1996), 138–58.

James L. Jarrett, 'Schopenhauer and Jung', *Spring*, (1981), 193–204.

John R. Haule, 'From somnambulism to the archetypes: the French roots of Jung's split with Freud', *The Psychoanalytic Review*, 71 (1984), 635–59.

Pete A.Y. Gunter, 'Bergson and Jung', *Journal of the History of Ideas*, 43 (1982), 635–52.

I am grateful to these authors and journals for the permission to reprint.

1

INTRODUCTION

Paul Bishop

C.G. Jung: life and work

On 6 June 1961, C.G. Jung died in his house at Küsnacht, overlooking the Lake of Zurich, at the age of 86.[1] It is part of the legend which rapidly surrounded him that, shortly after his death, a violent thunderstorm broke, and a bolt of lightning struck the poplar tree by the lake where he used to sit.[2]

It is appropriate that an electrical phenomenon, a product of the tension between the negative pole and the positive, should apparently have been observed, for Jung's thinking itself was, in many respects, a development of the polaristic thought that he had found in Goethe and German *Naturphilosophie*.[3] For Jung, the psyche was best understood as an energic phenomenon, and his redefined concept of libido proposed the notion of psychic energy.[4] Although Jung claimed to have derived the notion from the Russian psychologist Nicolas von Grot (1852–1899), the German philosopher Theodor Lipps (1851–1914), and, significantly, the German poet, playwright and aesthetician Friedrich Schiller (1759–1805), he pointed out in his Seminar on Analytical Psychology (1925) that '[t]he idea of the pairs of opposites is as old as the world, and if we treated it properly, then we should have to go back to the earliest sources of Chinese philosophy'.[5] For Jung, the aim of psychology was to achieve a union of these opposites and, in his Seminar on *Thus Spake Zarathustra* (1934–1939), he suggested Nietzsche as a more recent source for this idea: '[Nietzsche] understands that the Self consists in pairs of opposites and that it is in a way a reconciliation of opposites.'[6] Indeed, Jung discovered a premonitory symbol of the 'reconciliation of opposites' in the union of the eagle and the serpent, representing the spirit and the body, at the end of the Prologue to *Zarathustra*: 'Zarathustra sees [the eagle and the serpent] together, representing pairs of opposites, because spirit is always supposed to be the irreconcilable opponent of the chthonic, eternally fighting against the earth.'[7] More colourfully, Jung turned to the alchemical tradition for examples of the *coniunctio oppositorum* or the *mysterium coniunctionis*.[8]

What are the opposites of which Jung so insistently speaks? They can be found throughout his work in many forms: the epistemological problem of the relation between extended substance and thinking substance; the psychosexual difference between masculine and feminine; Schiller's distinction between the formal drive and the material drive; Nietzsche's opposition of Apollo and Dionysos; or the broader categories of rationality/ rationalism vs. irrationality/irrationalism, the mind and the body, consciousness and the Unconscious. In his work *Psychological Types* (1921), Jung argued that the problem of types could be found in characterology (such as the work of Furneaux Jordan (1830–1911)), in poetry (in *Prometheus und Epimetheus* (1881) by Carl Spitteler (1845–1924), for example), in psychiatry (as shown by the work of Otto Gross (1877–1920)), in aesthetics (such as the differentiation by Wilhelm Worringer (1881–1965) between 'abstraction' and 'empathy'), as well as modern philosophy (particularly the distinction of William James (1842–1910) between 'tough-minded' and 'tender-minded') (*CW* 6). Indeed, in *Phaedrus*, Plato had spoken of the passions as being like horses which the charioteer, the ego, has to keep under control. The well-documented Platonic concept of mediating opposites would certainly have been known to the classically educated Jung. In 1921, Jung argued that it was the task of psychology to achieve a co-ordination of the opposites via 'the middle path', thus enhancing the flow of psychic energy and achieving 'the optimum of life':

> The natural flow of libido, this same middle path, means complete obedience to the fundamental laws of human nature, and there can positively be no higher moral principle than harmony with natural laws that guide the libido in the direction of life's optimum. . . . The optimum can be reached only through obedience to the tidal laws of the libido, by which systole alternates with diastole – laws which bring pleasure and the necessary limitations of pleasure, and also set us those individual life tasks without whose accomplishment the vital optimum can never be attained.
>
> (*CW* 6 §356)

As far as the history of the reception of Jung's thought is concerned, it has provoked a set of reactions and responses that may equally appropriately be characterized in terms of polar opposites.

Development of analytical psychology

Following his celebrated break with Freud, Jung was very quickly dismissed within Freudian circles as a heretic. No better example of the outright rejection of his position, mixed with *ad hominem* polemic, can be given than Freud's own view of Jung as expressed in 'On the History of the Psychoanalytic Movement' (1914):

> When one thinks of the inconsistencies displayed in the various public and private pronouncements made by the Jungian movement, one is bound to ask oneself how much of this is due to lack of clearness and how much to lack of sincerity. . . . For sexual libido an abstract concept has been substituted, of which one may safely say that it remains mystifying to wise men and fools alike.

Freud continued:

> It may be said lastly that by his 'modification' of psychoanalysis Jung has given us the counterpart to the famous Lichtenberg knife. He has changed the hilt, and he has put a new blade into it; yet because the same name is engraved on it we are expected to regard the instrument as the original one.[9]

An even more combative refutation of Jung was undertaken by Edward Glover in the 1950s,[10] whereas the more fair-minded approach of Robert Steele emphasized the hermeneutic differences between Freud and Jung.[11] But for every Freudian who attacked Jung, there was a Jungian who was prepared to defend him. For example, Liliane Frey-Rohn's *From Freud to Jung* is a veritable textbook of Jungian psychology,[12] and there is a host of uncritical and proselytizing accounts of Jung's life and works available from Jungian publishing houses. How did Jung come to achieve such fame, not to say notoriety? And what distinguishes 'analytical psychology' from 'psychoanalysis'?

Jung had first become well known through his pioneering experiments on word-association.[13] In an early psychoanalytic paper on word-association, Jung made use of Kant's distinction between analytic and synthetic judgments as proposed by Kant in his *Critique of Pure Reason* (1781) to differentiate two kinds of associative performance. Jung returned to this psychological version of the distinction between synthetic and analytic in his major work of 1911/1912 which marked his official break with Freud, *Wandlungen und Symbole der Libido*.[14] In an important footnote in this work, Jung not only defended himself against the charge of mysticism but also took up some of the implications of the earlier distinction between 'analytic' and 'synthetic' associations. Here he proposed that therapy should not just aim at psychological 'analysis' but instead should seek to realize what he called psychological 'synthesis'.[15]

As early as 1909, however, while starting work on 'Transformations and Symbols of the Libido', Jung had speculated in a letter to Freud of

2–12 April 1909 about the existence of 'some quite special complex, a universal one having to do with the prospective tendencies in man'. From this speculation, Jung developed the notion of a psychology that did not just look back to the past but also looked forward to the future: 'If there is a "psych[o]analysis" there must also be a "psychosynthesis" which creates future events according to the same laws.'[16] Thus the logical distinction between analytic and synthetic judgments as set out by Kant in the first *Critique* became, for Jung, the conceptual basis of the distinction between what he saw as two entirely different psychologies. One of them – Freud's – deals with the source of the neurosis (and hence, so Jung thought, says nothing new), whilst the other – Jung's own – would deal with the trajectory of the neurosis and its implications for the future development of the patient (and hence, so Jung thought, would show what it *meant*).[17] It remains unclear, however, why retrospective enquiry should be any less 'synthetic' than prospective enquiry. One might be forgiven for thinking that Jung merely presents the analogy between analytic/synthetic psychology and a concern with the past and with the future, rather than arguing for it. Yet the emphasis on 'synthesis' is intimately bound up with Jung's redefinition of libido, and the goal of Jungian therapy.

On the Freudian model, the life of the individual is largely predetermined by the resolution, successful or otherwise, of the Oedipal stage of psychosexual development. For Freud, the aim of psychotherapy was to take neurosis and turn it into ordinary misery.[18] Yet Freud once claimed that he was 'not basically interested in therapy',[19] and he drew attention to the allegedly wider explanatory power of psychoanalysis:

> I have told you that psychoanalysis began as a method of treatment; but I did not want to commend it to your interest as a method of treatment but on account of the truths it contains, on account of the information it gives us about what concerns human beings most of all – their own nature – and on account of the connections it discloses between the most different of their activities.[20]

For Jung, by contrast, the psychic development of the individual continues throughout his or her life, which was, as he suggested in a paper entitled 'The Stages of Life' (1930/1931), not just a question of biological but also cultural adaptation (*CW* 10 §750). And for Jung, the transformative power of therapy was much greater than Freud imagined it to be. As early as 11 February 1910, Jung had defined the cultural programme which he envisaged for psychoanalysis and which, by implication, became the goal of analytical psychology:

> I think we must give it [psychoanalysis] time to infiltrate into people from many centres, to revivify among intellectuals a feeling

4

for symbol and myth, ever so gently to transform Christ back into the soothsaying god of the vine, which he was, and in this way absorb those ecstatic instinctual forces of Christianity for the *one* purpose of making the cult and the sacred myth what they once were – a drunken feast of joy where man regained the ethos and holiness of an animal.[21]

If Freud and Jung were opposed on theoretical grounds, the organization and institutionalization of their respective psychologies were, however, remarkably similar.

In 1902, Freud and a small group of doctors began meeting on a regular basis in Berggasse 19 on Wednesday evenings, leading to the founding in 1906 of the Vienna Psychoanalytical Society. Four years later, the Society became the Vienna branch of the newly founded International Psycho-Analytical Association. As dissent within the analytic community, not least with Jung and his followers, grew, Freud convened the secret committee, whose members were given a gold ring.[22] Following his break with Freud in 1913, but still (in this respect, at least) taking his former mentor as a model, Jung had moved quickly to establish an organization in Zurich called the *Psychoanalytischer Verein* (*Verein für analytische Psychologie*), which would support and propagate his own views and beliefs. According to the minutes, the first recorded meeting of the *Psychoanalytischer Verein* was held on 17 January 1913 in the Restaurant Seidenhof in Zurich. As Friedel Elisabeth Muser has pointed out, Jung's concluding words during the second meeting on 31 January 1913 summarized what he saw as one of the main differences between him and Freud: 'The dream provides the answer by means of the symbol, and that must be understood. But you mustn't only see it as wish-fulfilment – otherwise the analyst is merely colluding with the imagination of the neurotic. The point is to uncover the goals of the Unconscious, which can never deceive a person.'[23]

By 30 October 1914, the club had decided to drop any mention of psychoanalysis from its title and to rename itself simply the *Verein für analytische Psychologie*. To acquire a more permanent residence, the *Verein* moved in 1916 into a magnificent house in Zurich (Löwenstraße 1, which no longer exists), donated by Edith Rockefeller McCormick, one of Jung's American patients. On 26 February 1916, the *Psychologischer Club Zürich* came into being, and in 1918 moved into another house, Gemeinde-strasse 25/27 (located, perhaps symbolically, at the intersection between the Minervastrasse and the Neptunstrasse), where the Club's library is still housed today. Although no formal inner circle was formed, such close associates as Aniela Jaffé (1903–1991), Liliane Frey-Rohn (1901–1993), and Jolande Jacobi (1890–1973) – collectively dubbed the 'Valkyries'[24] – stated that a dogmatic line of Jungian orthodoxy emerged from Küsnacht.

And although his followers did not have special rings, Jung owned and often wore a 'Gnostic' ring bearing an ancient motif.

In Jung's later works, the distinction between analysis and synthesis broadened out into a methodological dichotomy in the interpretation of dreams and became the basis of analytical psychology's claim to be superior to Freudian analysis. In the paper 'The Transcendental Function' (which Jung wrote in 1916 but which was not actually published until 1957), and in his much-revised book *On the Psychology of the Unconscious* (1917/1926/1943), Jung came to distinguish between Freud's 'analytic' (causal-reductive) interpretation of dreams and his own 'synthetic' interpretation (*CW* 7 §121–§140). Thirty years later, in *The Psychology of the Transference* (1946), to cite but one text, Jung, referring to the terminology of the ancient alchemists, would actually talk of the entire therapeutic process of analytical psychology in terms of the alchemical *opus* with its motto 'dissolve and coagulate' (*CW* 16 §353–§538).

So the choice of the phrase 'analytical psychology' as a label for the therapeutic approach and the set of ideas proposed by Jung misleadingly obscures his insistence on the superiority of his own 'synthetic' psychology as opposed to the merely 'analytic' psychoanalysis of Freud. Jung first used the term 'analytical psychology' in 'On the Doctrine of the Complexes', a paper delivered to the Ninth Australasian Medical Congress (1911) (*CW* 2 §1355), and again in 'General Aspects of Psychoanalysis', a lecture given to the London-based Psycho-Medical Society in 1913 (*CW* 4 §523). But on both occasions the expression was used synonymously with 'Depth Psychology' or *Tiefenpsychologie*, and early followers of Jung often preferred the term *Komplexe Psychologie*.[25]

On 24 April 1948, the C.G. Jung-Institut in Zurich was founded, and was officially opened on 11 October 1948. In 1948, its Curatorium consisted of Jung as President, Carl Alfred Meier (b. 1903) as Vice-President, Aniela Jaffé as Secretary, Kurt Binswanger as Treasurer, and Jolande Jacobi as Committee Member. In his address given on the occasion of the founding of the Institute in April 1948, Jung described its task as a continuation of his own research.[26] In the booklet prepared for the opening ceremony later that year, the Institute was described as 'a teaching and research institution for Complex Psychology in the form of a foundation': 'To realize these aims, teaching, research, and practical training should be taken equally into account. In addition, a lively exchange of ideas between the various groups interested in psychology should be fostered by the cultivation of personal contacts.'[27] Clearly, the Institute had high intellectual ideals, and was a substantially different kind of organization from the *Psychologischer Club*. The *Studies* of the Institute, to be published by the Rascher Verlag, were intended as works of scholarly acumen and analysis, as Jung's preface (written in September 1948) to C.A. Meier's *Ancient Incubation and Modern Psychotherapy* (1949) makes clear: 'The psychology of the unconscious is still a very young science which must first justify its existence before a critical public. This is the end which the publications of the Institute are designed to serve' (*CW* 18 §1164). By the time of the second edition of the Institute's *Ziele und Tätigkeit* in 1952, however, there is a small but significant change in the description of the Institute's aims – 'a training and research institution' – which introduces the less scholarly, more practical idea of training; the doctrinal sense of apprenticeship is replaced by a more pedestrian pedagogy, and research is relegated to the third position in the list of objectives: 'To realize the goals of the institute, there is tuition, practical training, and research.'

In the same year as the C.G. Jung-Institut was founded, plans for the *Collected Works* of Jung's writings began to take shape. In his extremely useful book on the history of the Bollingen Foundation – itself an organization imbued with Jungian ideals, founded in 1942 by the American entrepreneur, Paul Mellon (b. 1907), and his wife, Mary Conover Mellon (1904–1946), both followers of Jung – William McGuire devotes several pages to an account of the decisions surrounding the undertaking to publish Jung's collected works in both German and English and the editorial principles governing their composition.[28] With the creation of an informal network of clubs in London, New York, San Francisco, Los Angeles, Berlin, Rome, Paris and Basle; with the subsequent establishment of C.G. Jung Institutes in Zurich, and then in London, New York, San Francisco and Los Angeles; with the publication of his *Collected Works*; and with the regular production of secondary texts by such followers as Aniela Jaffé, Jolande Jacobi and Marie-Louise von Franz (b. 1915), Jung had transformed analytical psychology from a breakaway group of analysts into an international organization with a worldwide reputation. At the same time, Jung himself became transformed, at least in the eyes of many of his followers, into an incarnation of the archetype of the Wise Old Man, who offered advice on matters ranging from personal crises to the global political situation.[29]

Developments in analytical psychology

Following Jung's death, analytical psychology continued to develop and diversify in terms of theoretical complexity. In the wake of this development, several discrete directions in Jungian thought can be seen to emerge. Although there is reason to doubt his statement that Jung 'eschewed any ambition to start a school of psychology', Andrew Samuels, an analytical psychologist and the first Professor for Analytical Psychology in the UK, has helpfully summarized the various schools of Jungian psychology as classified by three other analysts and by himself.[30] First, according to the classification of Gerhard Adler (1904–1979), the analyst and co-editor of Jung's *Collected Works*, there are the orthodox Jungians (relying on such techniques as amplification[31] and active imagination,[32] pioneered by Jung), the 'neo-Jungians' (who imported concepts from such psychologists as Erik Erikson (b. 1902), Melanie Klein (1882–1960), and Donald Winnicott (1896–1971), stressing the importance of infantile material), and a 'middle group' that occupies the central ground, using not just the analysis of transference but also the interpretation of dreams and the method of active imagination.[33] Second, according to the classification of the Jungian analyst Michael Fordham (1905–1995), who also co-edited Jung's *Works*, there is a style of analysis found mainly in the C.G. Jung-Institut in Zurich (which emphasizes the mythological approach to clinical material), a style of analysis found in London (which corresponds roughly to Adler's 'neo-Jungians'), while in San Francisco and in London an emphasis was placed on typology and countertransference respectively.[34] Third, according to the classification of the scholar Naomi Goldenberg, post-Jungians can be divided into the second generation (as members of which both Adler and Fordham would be included) and the third generation (including such 'archetypal psychologists' as James Hillman, Wolfgang Giegerich, and Rafael Lopez-Pedraza).[35]

On the basis of these three classifications, Samuels developed a more sophisticated set of categories to distinguish between what he saw as three major post-Jungian schools. According to the importance given to three theoretical issues (1. the definition of the archetypal, 2. the concept of self, and 3. the development of personality) and to three clinical aspects (4. the analysis of the transference and the countertransference, 5. the emphasis placed on symbolic experiences of the self, and 6. the examination of highly differentiated imagery), Samuels distinguished three groups. Samuels classified these as the Classical school (which largely respected Jung's ordering of priorities, viz. 2,1,3, and 5,6,4 (or 5,4,6), and which resembles Adler's 'orthodox school' and Fordham's 'Zurich school'), the Developmental school (which orders its priorities as 3,2,1, and 4,5,6 (or 4,6,5), and which is similar to Adler's 'neo-Jungian school' and Fordham's 'London school'), and the Archetypal school (which would work with the ordering 1,2,3, and 6,5,4, and which is more or less identical to Goldenberg's 'third generation' of Jungians). Samuels adds the following important observation:

> We should note the extent to which post-Jungians have felt able to challenge or attack Jung's work, often arguing with him on the basis of stringent criticisms from non-Jungians, as well as adapting and integrating parallel developments in other approaches to psychology, and also from completely different disciplines. . . . Sometimes Jung anticipates, sometimes he influences, but sometimes he gets it wrong, and sometimes another thinker reaches a

broadly similar conclusion but does so in a more coherent or better documented way.[36]

In addition, Samuels highlights the broader differences between the models of the psyche proposed by Jung, his major influence (Freud), and one of his major successors (Hillman), with reference to their conception of the opposites. According to Samuels, Freud saw psychological activity in terms of pairs of conflicting opposites, whereas Jung saw it in terms of potentially reconcilable opposites, and Hillman in terms of the circularity and the identity of opposites.[37] As has often been observed, Jung demonstrated a remarkable passion in his psychology for the detection of opposites and their resolution through the constellation of quaternities.[38] Not only are there the four psychic functions of thinking, feeling, sensation and intuition, but he pointed to Empedocles' four elements, Hippocrates' four 'humours', the ascending quaternity of anima figures (Eve, Helen, Mary, Sophia), the three figures of the Trinity together with the Virgin Mary, and he frequently quoted the lines from the 'Cabiri Scene' of Goethe's *Faust II*: 'We've brought you three of them;/The fourth refused to come.'[39] In his discussion of the main shift in post-Jungian psychology, however, Samuels points out that '[s]chematic, hierarchical and classificatory approaches to psyche have been superseded by a neutral, functional ethos involving themes, patterns, behaviour, images, emotions, instincts', the key words of which are '*interaction* (of those elements), *relativity* (archetypes in the eye of the beholder) and *systemic*'. Above all, '[a]nalytical psychology seems no longer to march in fours (functions, stages of analysis, phases of life, forms of the feminine psyche), or in reliably computable patterns of opposites'.[40]

New ways in Jung studies

Just as there have been major changes within analytical psychology itself, so recent years have seen an important development in the attitude displayed towards Jung by scholars outside Jungian psychology in general and by intellectual historians in particular. Over the last two decades, and especially during the early 1990s, a turn of the tide in what might broadly be termed Jung studies has taken place. Up to that point, writers on Jung had displayed a worrying tendency to refrain from criticism of the master, and there was an almost total lack of interest in the question of the intellectual sources of Jungian psychology. More recently, however, there has been a move towards a more serious examination of the implications of his writings and the aporias in his thought.[41] In the words of Karin Barnaby and Pellegrino d'Acierno, '[t]he ideological ways in which Jung has heretofore come to be institutionalized and canonized will be replaced by historiographic and textual analyses that grasp the true dimension of his work'.[42] Indeed, one of the contributors to this volume has gone so far as to speak of 'the paradigm shift presently underway in the Jungian world', characterizing this shift as 'a movement from idealization to humanization, or from hagiography to critical history' (p. 77).

It is the purpose of this collection to reflect this shift, by offering a representative selection of some of the most important work that has been published over recent years and that reveals new aspects of the intellectual sources of Jung's thought and its reception. Many of these essays have appeared in specialist journals dedicated to Jungian psychology, philosophy, intellectual history or German studies, and so have not been easily available to a wider reading public, which is showing increasing interest in a more critical and less dogmatic approach to understanding Jung's works. Rather than being exercises in apologetics, these essays attempt to return Jung to a tradition of intellectual debate from which, very often thanks to his followers, he has been excluded, and to reinvest in Jung studies a scholarly rigour which has been all too lacking in the past. In some cases, this has led to a 'demasking' of Jung; in others, to a fresh attempt to appreciate the originality and significance of his work. In all cases, however – and this was the criterion for their choice – a genuinely new aspect of Jung's life and thought has been uncovered, which allows the reader to place Jung not just in one but in several contexts.

For the purposes of convenience, three major thematic contexts have been chosen: the historical and biographical background to Jung's psychology; the influence of literature upon Jung and his influence in turn upon a major German writer; and, finally, the intellectual sources of his psychology, and the philosophical context in which his work situates itself. This selection does not claim to be exhaustive, merely to offer an appreciation of the new areas in Jung studies that have been discovered.

Historical and biographical context

As recent studies have shown, an important element in the historico-cultural background to Jung's early intellectual development was the popularity of spiritualism.[43] As Jung has recounted in *Memories, Dreams, Reflections* (1962), he became interested in spiritualism during his time as a student at the University of Basle. At the end of the second semester, he made 'a fateful discovery' when, in the library of the father of one of his college friends, Jung came across a small book on spiritualism, dating from the 1870s. It is likely that the impact of this discovery would have been all the greater in the light of the recent death of his own father in spring 1896. The accounts of spiritualistic phenomena in this book reminded Jung of the tales and legends he had heard during his childhood, and he concluded that '[t]he material, without question, was authentic' (*MDR* p. 119). For Jung, these accounts were to be the first instance of what he came to regard as proof of 'objective psychic phenomena' (ibid.). Jung relates that, as a consequence, he began to read works by the astrophysicist and spiritist devotee Johann Karl Friedrich Zöllner (1834–1882), the English physicist and chemist Sir William Crookes (1832–1919), as well as the celebrated spiritist Baron Karl Ludwig August Friedrich Maximilian DuPrel (also known more simply as Carl DuPrel) (1839–1899), the philosophers Carl Adolph von Eschenmayer (1768–1852) and Joseph Görres (1776–1848), the medical doctor Johann Karl Passavant (1790–1857), the Romantic writer Justinus Christian Kerner (1786–1862), and the Swedish mystic Emanuel Swedenborg (1688–1772) (*MDR* pp. 119–20). *A propos* of these writers, Jung quite rightly remarked in his autobiography: 'I read virtually the whole of the literature on spiritualism available to me at the time' (*MDR* p. 120).

Of course, this is to say nothing of the various childhood experiences which may well have predisposed Jung towards spiritism. These include his dream of the man-eating ithyphallus, which he perceived to be 'a subterranean god, not to be named' (*MDR* p. 28); his strange visions of his mother who, at night, became 'strange and mysterious', and a powerful apprehension of 'frightening influences' from her bedroom door (*MDR* p. 33); nightmarish dreams (*MDR* p. 34); choking fits accompanied by visions (*MDR* p. 34); the secret manufacture of a small manikin (*MDR* p. 36); a sense of psychic splitting (*MDR* p. 50); a recurrent vision of God, sitting on his Heavenly throne, and dropping an enormous turd on the roof of Basle Cathedral, thereby destroying it (*MDR* pp. 52–6); and a strong intuition of the existence of 'Evil and its universal power' and a deep sense of 'the mysterious role it played in delivering Man from darkness and suffering', convictions confirmed by reading Goethe's *Faust* (*MDR* p. 78). Not surprisingly, Jung's contemporaries turned out to be unsympathetic towards his new-found interest but, from the evidence of his autobiography, the proportions of his personal investment in reading about spiritualism should not be underestimated: 'I had the feeling that I had pushed to the brink of the world' (*MDR* p. 120).

Soon, Jung was to experience occultism at close hand in the shape of his cousin, allegedly endowed with mediumistic powers. Even if Jung was able to reveal her as a fraud, he found in her evidence for the autonomy of the psyche that was to influence his later views on psychology. Jung first met Hélène Preiswerk in the summer of 1898, when he witnessed seances and table-rapping in the presbytery at Klein-Hüningen, where his father was the Protestant pastor (*MDR* p. 127). Having studied her during 1899 and 1900 (*CW* 1 §36), Jung recorded his observations of her in his MD dissertation, *On the Psychology and Psychopathology of So-Called Occult Phenomena* (1902).[44] Yet like some of Freud's most famous cases, including not just 'Anna O.' but also 'Little Hans' and Daniel Paul Schreber,

Jung's most elaborate and detailed analysis was to involve a patient whom he had never met.

The work originally called 'Transformations and Symbols of the Libido' is presented as a detailed commentary on the visions of an American actress and lecturer called Miss Frank Miller, which were originally published by Théodore Flournoy in an article in *Archives de psychologie* in 1906.[45] Flournoy, in whom Jung had discovered 'a fatherly friend' during the years in contact with Freud, had been an influence on Jung's study of Preiswerk; while working at the Burghölzli clinic, Jung had read Flournoy's *From India to the Planet Mars* (1899), an account of seances with an alleged medium in Geneva, Hélène Smith.[46] Presented by Flournoy and accepted by Jung as the phantasy products of a schizophrenic, Miss Miller's texts provided Jung with what he regarded as evidence for a universal mythology, in turn the basis for Jung's claims regarding the Collective Unconscious.

In many respects, 'Transformations and Symbols of the Libido' represents the Jungian equivalent of Freud's analysis of Schreber in 'Psychoanalytic Notes on an Autobiographical Account of a Case of Paranoia (Dementia Praecox)' (1911), but it is also regarded by many as Jung's most important book: 'In a different category altogether, (it) not only made the break with Freud, but also developed (Jung's) reputation as an original thinker in psychoanalysis.'[47] And Peter Homans summarizes the scope of the work in the following way: 'In writing *Symbols of Transformation*, Jung narcissistically and grandiosely attempted to fuse his own fantasies with the great myths of the past and, at the same time, repudiated traditional Christianity by interpreting it by the libido theory.'[48] More recently, John Kerr has summed up the contents of the work thus:

> The central motif was clearly Faustian: casting aside the constraints of Christianity, Jung meant to make a descent into the depths of the soul, there to find the roots of Man's being in the symbols of the libido which had been handed down from ancient times, and so to find redemption despite his own genial pact with the devil.[49]

Looking back on his book in his preface to the revised edition of 1950, Jung himself claimed that 'this book became a landmark, set up on the spot where two ways divided' (*CW* 5 p. xxiv).

So far, I have referred to Jung's 'autobiography' and been content to describe *Memories, Dreams, Reflections* as one of Jung's works. In fact, the status of this text is a highly problematic one, and the history of its composition and its publication is particularly complex. Because Jung's autobiography is questionable as an exact historical source, we need to read it for its gaps and silences, for what it fails to say as much as for what it does say. Reviewing the book in 1964, the paediatrician and psychoanalyst Donald Winnicott claimed that its publication provided analysts 'with a chance, perhaps the last chance they will have, to come to terms with Jung'.[50] The psychoanalyst Erich Fromm (1900–1980) argued that 'by revealing the man', the autobiography

> shows that Jung's emphasis on the Collective Unconscious and his opposition to Freud's personal Unconscious had the function of protecting him from becoming aware of his own repressed experiences by making his Unconscious part of a mythical entity that rules all men alike and knows no good or evil.[51]

Rightly, the sociologist Philip Rieff has described the book as 'at once (Jung's) religious testament and his science, stated in terms of a personal confession'.[52]

Yet the extent of the authenticity of the text is hard to establish. To begin with, there are three different manuscripts of the text: (i) a heavily copyedited MS of the initial English-language version, held in the C.G. Jung Oral Archive in the Countway Library of Medicine, Boston; (ii) a set of Jung protocols in the Bollingen Foundation Collection in the Library of Congress, Washington; (iii) an original German-language MS in the C.G. Jung Archive in the *Eidgenössische Technische Hochschule* (ETH), Zurich. To complicate matters further, access to both the Library of Congress and ETH versions is restricted. However, the following is clear.

In 1956, the German/American publisher, Kurt Wolff, who was responsible for publishing, among many others, works by Franz Kafka and Thomas Mann, and who had founded in New York a publishing house called Pantheon Books, suggested to Jung that he should write an autobiography. It was eventually agreed that Aniela Jaffé, his former secretary, would be put in charge of collating various autobiographical statements from Jung's seminars and private papers, together with material from interviews which she conducted with him. Jung himself contributed several handwritten chapters, too. As Aniela Jaffé's introduction indicates, Jung began work on the book in 1957 with Jaffé herself as chief collaborator; and it includes passages where it is evident that the line between remembering and vague reminiscing is a thin one. As befits a man for whom the psyche was a profound reality (*MDR* p. 9), Jung says that he can understand himself only in the light of the inner happenings of life: 'My life is a story of the self-realization of the Unconscious' (*MDR* p. 17). In fact, Jung had so little regard for his memoirs as a scientific work that he was content practically to attribute their authorship to Aniela Jaffé and expressly excluded them from the *Collected Works*. Nevertheless, he granted permission to publish *Memories, Dreams, Reflections*, thus spreading his message and a carefully cultivated image of himself while at the same time attempting to preserve some sort of scientific reputation. Despite the atmosphere of mystery which surrounds the book and its pretence to give us the 'authentic' Jung, there is good reason for studying, albeit critically, what *Memories, Dreams, Reflections* says, not least because they tell us what he wanted us to think about him, and because they represent a case-study of self-mythopoeisis.

Subsequent research has been largely concerned to determine which parts were written by Jaffé and which by Jung, as well as the extent to which the Jung family censored parts of the manuscript. The arguments between Aniela Jaffé, the Jung estate, the translators and the publishers intensified after Jung's death in 1961. One particularly controversial factor was Jung's decision to publish the work in English with the American publisher, Pantheon Books (which was bought by Random House in May 1960), rather than in German and with Rascher. Recent research has further drawn attention to the numerous discrepancies between the (Swiss) German version, the American edition of the English translation (1962) and the British one (1963).

In the first of the essays in the present collection, 'Memories, Dreams, Omissions' (1995), Sonu Shamdasani has drawn on R.F.C. Hull's unpublished account of the background to *Memories, Dreams, Reflections*, dated 27 July 1960 and entitled 'A Record of Events Preceding Publication of Jung's Autobiography', which is held in the Bollingen Foundation Collection in the Library of Congress,[53] as well as upon other archival sources. Yet despite the struggles surrounding the composition of the published text, not to mention what we now know to be the large omissions about, for example, Toni Wolff (Jung's intellectual companion and alleged 'mistress'), *Memories, Dreams, Reflections* remains an extremely powerful work.

Another major source of information about Jung's intellectual formation and own psychological experiences is his Seminar on Analytical Psychology, given in Zurich in 1925. Although most of Jung's seminars were held in the Psychological Club, his first proper seminars were, however, given not in Zurich but in England. In 1920, he held a seminar in Sennen Cove in Cornwall, which had been arranged by the analyst Dr Constance Long and was attended by, among others, Esther Harding, Eleanor Bertine and H.G. Baynes, all of whom would later become members of his Seminar on Nietzsche. In 1923, he held another seminar in Cornwall, at Polzeath, this time on 'Human Relationships in Relation to the Process of Individuation'. And from 23 March to 6 July 1925, he held his first set of sixteen seminars on analytical psychology to be recorded (by Cary F. de Angulo, who later married the English psychologist H.G. Baynes) and copied.[54] This series of seminars allowed Jung to unfold informally what had now become a more or less coherent system of ideas, which he called 'analytical psychology' (as distinct from 'psychoanalysis'). From 1928 to 1930, Jung gave a seminar on dream analysis in Zurich,[55] and from 1930 to 1934 the so-called Visions Seminar took place in Zurich, during which he analysed the visions of Christiana Morgan.[56] For his next seminar, Jung turned to Nietzsche's *Zarathustra*,[57] and finally, from 1936 to 1941, Jung held a series of seminars in Zurich on children's dreams, this time given in German as many of his Anglo-American followers left Switzerland during the War.[58] There were various other seminars,[59] but those mentioned above are the most important.

For Jung, a seminar meant a series of lectures with discussions, and an account of one of the lectures in Jung's Visions Seminar, published by Elizabeth Shepley Sergeant in *Harper's* of May 1931, captures something of the mood of these events:

> When, on Wednesday morning at eleven, at certain seasons of the Zurich year, Doctor Jung enters the long room at the Psychological Club where his Seminar is held, smiling with a deep friendliness at this or that face, the brown portfolio which he hugs to his side seems to be the repository of this joint account – the collective analytical account of a small international group whose common interest is the psyche. An involuntary hush falls on the room as Jung himself stands quiet and grave for a moment, looking down at his manuscript as a sailor might look at his compass, relating it to the psychological winds and waves whose impact he has felt on his passage from the door. The hush in the assembly means not only reverence but intense expectation.[60]

The significance of the seminars in terms of Jung's intellectual development has been emphasized by William McGuire, who rightly calls them 'an important feature of his working methodology', providing Jung with 'a means of trying out new ideas':[61] 'Jung's seminar colloquies are rich in material that is not to be found, or is only hinted at, in the published writings. For Jung they were germinative: he was often evolving ideas as he talked' (*Dream Seminar*, p. xvi). Yet Jung forbade the distribution of notes made during the seminars, and he did not lift the ban until 1957, since when they have begun appearing as supplementary volumes to the *Collected Works*.

Jung's 1925 Seminar on Analytical Psychology provides useful information on the background to the composition of 'Transformations and Symbols of the Libido'. For example, on 13 April 1925, Jung admitted that the work was, in essence, an exercise in self-analysis: '["Transformations and Symbols of the Libido"] can be taken as myself and . . . an analysis of it inevitably leads into an analysis of my own unconscious processes' (Seminar on Analytical Psychology, p. 27). More specifically, he cited Miss Miller as an example of what he had identified in 1911 as 'fantastic or passive automatic' (as opposed to 'intellectual or directed') thinking, and claimed that he had thereby been able to work through his own problematic relationship with the Unconscious:

> [Miss Miller] stood for that form of thinking in myself. She took over my fantasy and became stage director to it . . . she became an Anima figure, a carrier of an inferior function of which I was very little conscious . . . passive thinking seemed to me such a weak and perverted thing that I could only handle it through a diseased woman . . . in Miss Miller I was analyzing my own fantasy function, which because it was so repressed, like hers, was semi-morbid.
>
> (ibid., pp. 27–8)

Here, Jung is clearly admitting that one of his most important case-histories was in fact carried out in his own interest as much as that of the patient, and constituted an act of self-therapy. Thus, the ultimate source of the fundamental concepts of analytical psychology is Jung himself: 'I watched the creation of myths going on, and got an insight into the structure of the Unconscious. . . . I drew all my empirical material from my patients, but the solution of the problem I drew from the inside, from my observations of the unconscious processes' (ibid., p. 34).

The clinical psychologist Richard Noll has gone further and, on the basis of an episode related by Jung in his Seminar but omitted from *Memories, Dreams, Reflections*, argues in the second essay of this book, 'Jung the *Leontocephalus*' (1994), that the visions experienced by Jung during a psychotic breakdown from 1913 to 1916, frequently referred to in Jungian literature as 'the encounter with the Unconscious', provide evidence for what Jung interpreted as his 'self-deification'. For Noll, Jung's account of how, during one such vision, he assumed the posture of the crucified Christ and was squeezed by a large black snake, while his face was transformed into that of a lion, reveals the deep influence of the Mithraic mystery cult on Jungian psychology. This interpretation, together with a discussion of the interest in ancient mysteries in *fin-de-siècle* Germany, and a document found among the papers of one of Jung's followers, Fanny Bowditch Katz (purportedly the founding manifesto of the Psychological Club), formed the core of Noll's anti-Jungian bestseller, *The Jung Cult* (1995), which caused a flurry of controversy in Jungian circles and brought Jung, albeit polemically, to the attention of a wider public again.[62]

While these essays deal with Jung's early years, the third essay in this section deals with one of the charges that has been repeatedly levelled at Jung and that has, to a certain extent, stuck, namely that, during the 1930s and 1940s, he was a sympathizer with National Socialism, and that he was a racist and an anti-Semite. This accusation, made with particular force by Ernst Bloch (1875–1977), has recently been restated by another commentator working in the Frankfurt School tradition.[63] Indeed, as such Jungian commentators as Andrew Samuels and Aniela Jaffé, to mention just two, have recognized, Jung's relationship to National Socialism was an uncomfortable albeit distant one.[64]

In 'C.G. Jung and National Socialism' (1979), the main accusations against Jung have been clearly and objectively summarized by Stanley Grossman, in a way which permits a careful examination of the historical burden Jung has had to carry, under the following headings. First: Jung's alleged anti-Semitism and support for a Germanic (racial) psychotherapy; second, his ambivalent comments on Hitler and the Nazi regime; and third, his ties with the '*gleichgeschaltete*' General Medical Society for Psychotherapy (*Allgemeine Ärztliche Gesellschaft für Psychotherapie*). Jung's attitude to National Socialism is not unrelated to his reception of Nietzsche and the notion of the Dionysian (see Chapter 8), especially given the way in which the Nazis appropriated Nietzsche – an important source for right-wing thought and fascist ideology in the twentieth century, and not just in Germany – to support their doctrines.

Jung's analysis of the rise of National Socialism, offered in such essays as 'Wotan' (1936) and 'After the Catastrophe' (1945), is distinctive in its exclusive reliance on psychological factors, and could even be said to have similar roots in the occult beliefs and pagan mysticism that fed into the ideology of the National Socialists. While it may be true that Freud was also prepared to differentiate between 'Jewish' and 'Aryan' psychologies, what might have been permissible for Freud as a Jew to say in Austria before 1933 was not permissible for a non-Jew to publish in Germany after 1933, as Jung did in 'The State of Psychotherapy Today' (1934) (*CW* 10 §333–§370).[65] The renegade Hungaro-American psychologist Thomas Szasz comments on this aspect of the Freud/Jung dispute in the following words:

> Freud and the Freudians have deprived Jung of many of his best ideas and, to boot, have defamed him as an anti-Semite. Actually, Jung was far more candid and correct than Freud in identifying psychotherapy as an ethical rather than technical enterprise; and Freud was far more anti-Christian than Jung was anti-Semitic.[66]

Yet because, for Jung, the only collective that really counted was the unconscious one, Jungian therapy has been characterized by its lack of any sense of political engagement and by what might be termed its moral deficit.[67]

Literary context

It is true of both psychoanalysis in general and Jung's psychology in particular that they are rooted in the ideas and literary works of German Romanticism.[68] For example, the motif of the lost shadow, of which *The Wonderful Story of Peter Schlemihl* (1814) by Adalbert von Chamisso (1781–1838) is a notable example, provided the analyst Otto Rank (1884–1939) with a basis for his study of the Don Juan complex.[69] Then again, Sigmund Freud was extremely interested in *The Sandman* (1816), a short story by E.T.A. Hoffmann (1776–1822), in which he found an example of what he termed *das Unheimliche* ('the uncanny'). And it was another work by Hoffmann, his novel entitled *The Devil's Elixirs* (1815–1816), that played, as John Kerr has shown in '*The Devil's Elixirs*, Jung's "Theology", and the Dissolution of Freud's "Poisoning Complex"' (1988), a 'pivotal role' in the epistolary exchange of Freud and Jung. At the same time as Jung discovered this work, he was embroiled in an affair with one of his patients, Sabina Spielrein – the significance of which Kerr discussed in a later book-length study, published in 1994.[70] Kerr makes a strong case that, with 'the myriad juxtapositions of passion and lust on the one hand and pure transcendental love on the other', together with 'Hoffmann's handling of guilt in all its terrible ramifications: pride, posturing, self-destructiveness, and paranoia', this novel 'anticipated by forty years the doctrine of hereditary degeneration that was to dominate psychiatry for the second half of the nineteenth century' (p. 134–5). More specifically, Kerr believes it also anticipated at least four of Jung's theoretical pre-occupations: the possibility of psychosynthesis, the fraught notion of the 'meaningful coincidence' of intrapsychic and external physical events ('synchronicity'), and the second stage of psychological development Jung dubbed 'the afternoon of life', not to mention 'all the major archetypes discovered by Jung in his self-analysis' (p. 138).

In the twentieth century, the greatest German inheritor of the literary tradition of Romanticism was the novelist Thomas Mann (1875–1955),[71] who was born in the same year as C.G. Jung and, for a time, stayed in 33 Schiedhaldenstrasse in Küsnacht, not far away from Seestrasse 228 where Jung lived. Although Jung did not spend as many years as Mann did in Munich, he visited the city in its *fin-de-siècle* splendour in 1900, and he met Thomas Mann there in 1921 (see Chapter 6).

What did Jung make of his famous neighbour? There are no comments made about Mann in Jung's published writings or letters, and his library contains just two works by Mann, the short drama *Fiorenza* (1906, performed 1907) and the famous novella *Death in Venice* (*Der Tod in Venedig*) (1912). In an unpublished source written by one of Jung's female admirers, Hedy Wyss, we learn that she apparently gave Jung her copy of *Mario und der Zauberer* (*Mario and the Magician*) (1930) to read in August 1949. She records, however, that he never expressed an opinion about the work, but that he kept the copy, a first edition.[72]

For Thomas Mann, the problem of Romanticism – its seductive but dangerous over-idealization, its tendency to transform love into fetishism, and its obsession with darkness and death – could be approached through an understanding of its contribution to psychoanalysis. In 1925, he claimed that *Death in Venice* had been 'created under the immediate influence of Freud'. But he went on to say: 'As an artist I have to confess, however, that I am not at all satisfied with Freudian ideas; rather, I feel disquieted and reduced by them. The artist is being X-rayed by Freud's ideas to the point where it violates the secret of his creative art.'[73] Yet Mann went on to develop a more differentiated appreciation of Freud, expressed most notably in his lecture delivered on 16 May 1929 at the Auditorium Maximum in Munich and entitled 'The Position of Sigmund Freud in Modern Cultural History', which Mann described as 'a wide-ranging dissertation on the problem of revolution, with academic intentions and in fact serving the purposes of those who want the psychoanalytical movement to be recognised as the one manifestation of modern anti-rationalism – which offers no kind of handle to reactionary misuse',[74] and in a celebratory speech given on the occasion of Freud's 80th birthday, 'Freud and the Future', in which Mann described psychoanalysis as 'the greatest contribution to the art of the novel'.

Closer reading of 'Freud and the Future' reveals, however, that for Mann the future was not so much Freudian as Jungian, and that despite his reservations regarding Jung's anti-Semitism, this lecture is, in fact, a *plaidoyer* in favour of a Jungian, rather than a Freudian, understanding of myth. Nor is there any contradiction between Mann's Jungian use of myth and his distaste for Jung's politics, for as he once observed of another notorious anti-Semite, Wagner, 'I find an element of Nazism not only in Wagner's questionable literature; I find it also in his "music", in his work . . . albeit I have so loved that work that even today I am deeply stirred whenever a few bars of music from this world impinge on my ear.'[75] Mann's massive opus, *Joseph and his Brothers*, a huge achievement spanning nearly a decade of prodigious creativity (1933–1942), offers further evidence of Mann's artistic appropriation of Jungian themes, and is an important example of Jung's wider influence on twentieth-century culture, which has hitherto been overlooked.

What did Jung think of his famous neighbour, and why were the relations between them practically non-existent? An answer, albeit an extremely bizarre one, lies in one of the passages that never appeared in *Memories, Dreams, Reflections*.[76] Here, Jung is recorded as saying that he had deliberately shied away from Thomas Mann, because of Mann's sophisticated sense of culture, intellect and feeling. According to Jung, Thomas Mann had invited him into his circle, but he had been unable to accept; moreover, Jung said that he had felt the same about H.G. Wells. In this transcript of a conversation with Jaffé, Jung is reported as saying that he was afraid of Thomas Mann as of a South American vampire – that flies by night, sits at the feet of a sleeping man, and sucks blood from his toe . . .

Intellectual context

Jung frequently made the ultimately untenable assertion that there were no philosophical implications to his thought. One does not have to read far in Jung before coming across examples of such a denial, and his followers (as well as some of his detractors!) have frequently used them to avoid discussion of the metaphysical complexities of his system.[77] In *Memories, Dreams, Reflections*, however, Jung makes it clear that it was his intellectual labours in general and his study of mythology in particular which brought him to a new view of the psyche, thus enabling him to develop new therapeutic techniques: 'As early as 1909 I realized that I could not treat latent psychoses if I did not understand their symbolism. It was then that I began to study mythology' (*MDR* p. 153). Furthermore, Jung describes the early period of his life as his 'philosophical development' (*MDR* p. 89), recalling how he began, between the ages of 16 and 19, to read both early Greek philosophy – Heraclitus, Pythagoras, Empedocles, as well as Plato – and such medieval thinkers as Thomas Aquinas and Meister Eckhart. During his account of his schooling in Basle between 1881 and 1895, Jung mentions Immanuel Kant (1724–1804) three times (*MDR* pp. 89, 93–4) and, in the most important passage, he refers to him in the context of Arthur Schopenhauer (1788–1860), to whom he refers as 'the great find resulting from my researches' (*MDR* p. 88). In addition, he used Krug's *Allgemeines Handwörterbuch der philosophischen Wissenschaften* (second edition, 1832) (*MDR* p. 79), to which he would continue to refer as a student (*MDR* p. 184).

Jung explicitly drew a contrast between his own intellectual background and Freud's. Stressing, perhaps excessively, his own knowledge of 'the writers of the eighteenth and early nineteenth century', Jung notes sardonically of Freud: 'By contrast, I had the impression that Freud's intellectual history began with Büchner, Moleschott, du Bois-Reymond, and Darwin' (*MDR* p. 184). The common link between most of these writers – the German philosopher Ludwig Büchner (1824–1899), the Dutch physiologist and philosopher Jacob Moleschott (1822–1893), the German physiologist Emil Heinrich du Bois-Reymond (1818–1896) and the theorist of evolution Charles Darwin (1809–1882) – was their commitment to materialism.

Jung considered eighteenth- and nineteenth-century philosophy in general to be less interesting, and Hegel in particular was quickly dismissed.[78] Jung even wrote that 'for obvious reasons, the critical philosophy of the eighteenth century at first did not appeal to me at all' (*MDR* p. 87). To judge from the context, these 'obvious reasons' must have been the emphasis on logic and argumentation that Jung found so disagreeable about the 'the long-windedness of Socratic argumentation' and the 'Aristotelian intellectualism' of Thomas Aquinas which he described as 'more lifeless than a desert'. In contrast to his sharp dislike for Hegel, Jung was fascinated by the intellectual honesty and highly un-Leibnizean anti-Providentialism of Schopenhauer:

> He was the first to speak of the suffering of the world, which visibly and glaringly surrounds us, and of confusion, passion, evil – all those things which the others hardly seemed to notice and always tried to resolve into all-embracing harmony and comprehensibility. Here at last was a philosopher who had the courage to see that all was not for the best in the fundaments of the universe.
>
> (*MDR* p. 88)

Yet Jung was not completely content with Schopenhauer's analysis of the world. In particular, he was dissatisfied with Schopenhauer's concept of the Will, which he found highly problematic. The doctrine of the denial of the Will, with which the first volume of *The World as Will and Representation* (1819) concludes, and the high value which Schopenhauer placed on the power of the intellect, were the major stumbling blocks. Nor was Jung prepared to acquiesce in Schopenhauer's pessimism: 'Schopenhauer's sombre picture of the world had my undivided approval, but not his solution of the problem' (*MDR* p. 88). In order to understand *The World as Will and Representation* better, Jung turned to Schopenhauer's primary intellectual source, the critical philosophy of Kant. While admitting that he had found the *Critique of Pure Reason* difficult and that it had caused him much 'brain-racking', Jung believed that Kant had helped him discover the fundamental flaw in Schopenhauer's system. According to Jung, Schopenhauer had committed the 'deadly sin' of hypostatizing a metaphysical assertion and of talking about the noumenon or '*Ding-an-sich*' (*MDR* p. 89). Even if this is no more than a standard critique of Schopenhauer, Jung clearly believed that he had been able to overcome Schopenhauerian pessimism by using Kantian epistemology.

In the final section of this book, two essays examine the question of Jung's debt to the tradition of German philosophy. In 'Schopenhauer and Jung' (1981), James Jarrett investigates the intellectual affinities between the two thinkers. 'C.G. Jung and Nietzsche: Dionysos and Analytical Psychology' offers a reading of Jung's psychology in terms of a developing response to the concept of Dionysos in the work of Nietzsche (1844–1900).

There is, however, another intellectual tradition in the light of which Jung's psychology demands to be seen, and that is the French tradition of psychological investigation. In 'From Somnambulism to the Archetypes' (1984), John R. Haule investigates 'the French Roots of Jung's Split with Freud'. Jung was certainly familiar with the concept of the *ideé fixe subconsciente* developed by Pierre Janet (1859–1947), a pupil of Jean Martin Charcot (1825–1893), under whom Freud had studied at the Salpêtrière in Paris from October 1885 to February 1886. One of Janet's central concepts, the integration of the personality, is clearly central to the Jungian notion of the individuation process.[79] According to Haule, 'it is difficult to avoid the impression that the doctrine of the archetypes emerged in Jung's thought as a means to wed the best of Freud with the best of Janet' (p. 242). Another (to a certain extent, French-dominated) intellectual tradition to which Jung belongs is *Lebensphilosophie* or vitalism. Emphasizing the organic over the mechanical, the irrational over the rational, and Becoming over Being, the most important of the French vitalists was Henri Bergson (1859–1941). In 'Bergson and Jung' (1982), Pete A.Y. Gunter provides 'an extensive analysis of the parallels' between Bergsonian vitalism and analytical psychology (p. 265). To Gunter's essay, one might add that Jung's distinction in two papers, 'On Psychic Energy' (begun 1912 but not published until 1928) and 'On the Nature of the Psyche' (1946/1954), between the mechanistic (causal) standpoint and the energic (final) standpoint is reminiscent of an ancient typological difference in philosophy between, on the one hand, such mechanists as Democritus, Descartes, Lamettrie, and, on the other, such vitalists as Aristotle, the Romantic *Naturphilosophen*, Darwin – and Bergson. Even if Jung dissociated himself from the concept of a psychoid entelechy, found in the work of the German vitalist Hans Driesch (1867–1941), he none the less conceded the notion of a goal or *telos* – while simultaneously denying the possibility of ever attaining it – when he claimed that the psychic wholeness comprehended in the unity of consciousness is the ideal goal that cannot be reached (*CW* 8 §366). Opposites cannot be united so easily! In short, both Haule and Gunter open up the issue of continental influences beyond the mainly Germanic ones considered in recent years, and point the way to a new area of fruitful enquiry.

Moreover, the essays in this section offer convincing examples of the way in which Jung is proving increasingly useful in the elucidation of twentieth-century thinkers. For instance, Jung has been used to exemplify both phenomenology[80] in general and Heidegger[81] in particular, not to mention structuralism[82] and deconstruction,[83] to give just four examples. Thus there is good reason to hope that the search for intellectual sources, the analysis of affinities of thought, and the attempt at psycho-historical contextualization, far from diminishing the richness of Jungian psychology, will instead contribute to the very opposite: reinvigorating a body of thought that, for too long, has been rejected by the academy and grown stale by dint of mere restatement by over-enthusiastic followers and *ad hominem* sniping from ill-informed critics. Once seen in the contexts offered here, Jung's thought seems to be the very opposite of what it has often been held to be, and to deserve the fresh attention that, after a long and unjustified period of neglect, it is now beginning to receive.

Notes

Abbreviations

CW = C.G. Jung, *Collected Works*, London, Routledge & Kegan Paul, 1953–1983. Passages are referred to by volume and paragraph (§) number.

MDR = C.G. Jung, *Memories, Dreams, Reflections: Recorded and Edited by Aniela Jaffé*, tr. Richard and Clara Winston, London, Flamingo, 1983.

SE = Sigmund Freud, *The Standard Edition of the Complete Works*, London, Hogarth Press, 1953–1974.

1 Biographies of Jung fall into roughly three categories: hagiographical, hostile, and (in varying degrees) neutral. For examples of the first kind, see A. Jaffé, *From the Life and Work of Jung*, New York, Harper & Row, 1971; B. Hannah, *Jung: His Life and Work: A Biographical Memoir*, Boston, MA, Shambhala, 1976; Laurens van der Post, *Jung and the Story of Our Time*, London, Hogarth Press, 1976; and G. Wehr, *Carl Gustav Jung: Leben, Werk, Wirkung*, Munich, Kösel, 1985. For examples of the second kind, see P.J. Stern, *Jung: The Haunted Prophet*, New York, George Braziller, 1976; and R. Noll, *The Aryan Christ: The Secret Life of Carl Jung*, New York, Random House, 1997. For examples of the third kind, see V. Brome, *Jung*, London, Macmillan, 1978; C. Wilson, *Lord of the Underworld*, Wellingborough, Aquarian Press/ Thorson Publishing Group Ltd, 1984; A. Stevens, *On Jung*, London, Routledge, 1990; and F. McLynn, *Carl Gustav Jung: A Biography*, London, Bantam Press, 1996.
2 Brome, op. cit., p. 273.
3 For further discussion, see W. Willeford, 'Jung's Polaristic Thought in its Historical Setting', *Analytische Psychologie*, 1975, vol. 6, pp. 218–39. On the problem of opposites more generally, see P.F.M. Fontaine, *The Light and the Dark: A Cultural History of Dualism*, Amsterdam, Gieben, 1986–1997.
4 See his essay 'On Psychic Energy' (begun circa 1912 and completed in 1928) (especially *CW* 8 §26–§33).
5 C.G. Jung, *Analytical Psychology: Notes of the Seminar Given in 1925*, ed. W. McGuire, London, Routledge, 1990, p. 72.
6 C.G. Jung, *Nietzsche's Zarathustra: Notes of the Seminar Given in 1934–1939*, ed. J.L. Jarrett, London, Routledge, 1989, I, p. 433.
7 Ibid., I, pp. 18–19, 227. Jung is alluding to the following passage:

> Zarathustra said this to his heart as the sun stood at noon: then he looked inquiringly into the sky – for he heard above him the sharp cry of a bird. And behold! An eagle was sweeping through the air in wide circles, and from it was hanging a serpent, not like a prey but like a friend: for it was coiled around the eagle's neck. 'It is my animals!' said Zarathustra and rejoiced in his heart

(F. Nietzsche, *Thus Spake Zarathustra*, tr. R.J. Hollingdale, Harmondsworth, Penguin, 1969, pp. 52–3).

8 See *Psychology and Alchemy*, *Alchemical Studies*, and *Mysterium Coniunctionis* (volumes 12, 13 and 14 of Jung's *Collected Works*). In *Alchemy: An Introduction to the Symbolism and the Psychology*, Toronto, Inner City Books, 1980, based on a transcript of a lecture series presented by one of Jung's closest followers at the C.G. Jung-Institut, Zurich in 1959, M.-L. von Franz provides a summary of the Jungian understanding of alchemy.

9 Freud, 'On the History of the Psychoanalytic Movement' (*SE* XIV, pp. 60, 62, 66).

10 E. Glover, *Freud or Jung*, London, George Allen & Unwin, 1950.

11 R.S. Steele, *Freud and Jung: Conflicts of Interpretation*, London, Routledge & Kegan Paul, 1982.

12 L. Frey-Rohn, *From Freud to Jung: A Comparative Study of the Psychology of the Unconscious*, tr. F.E. Engreen and E.K. Engreen, Boston and Shaftesbury, Shambhala, 1974.

13 One of Jung's papers, entitled 'The Association of Normal Subjects' (*CW* 2 §1–§498), was co-written with his fellow Zurich psychologist Franz Riklin (1878–1938). It was first published in the *Journal für Psychologie und Neurologie*, III (Leipzig, 1904) and IV (1905), and subsequently republished in *Diagnostische Assoziationstudien: Beiträge zur experimentellen Psychopathologie*, I (Leipzig, 1906), which Jung himself edited.

14 This work, whose title literally means 'Transformations and Symbols of the Libido', was translated by one of his followers, Beatrice Hinkle, as *Psychology of the Unconscious* (London, Kegan Paul, Trench, Trubner & Co., 1915). This translation has been recently reissued with an introduction by W. McGuire (London, Routledge, 1991).

15

> But just so little as the science of history concerns itself with the combinations for the future, which is the function of politics, so little, also, are the psychological combinations for the future the object of analysis; they would be much more the object of an infinitely refined psychological synthesis, which attempts to follow the natural current of the libido.
>
> (*Psychology of the Unconscious*, p. 493, n. 17)

16 W. McGuire (ed.), *The Freud/Jung Letters: The Correspondence between Sigmund Freud and C.G. Jung*, tr. R. Manheim and R.F.C. Hull, Cambridge MA, Harvard University Press, 1974, p. 216. Later, the notion of psychosynthesis was taken up by the psychologist Hans Trüb (1889–1949), while the Italian psychologist Roberto Assagioli (1888–1974) founded his own school of therapy on the term 'psychosynthesis'.

17 Furthermore, there may also be a Goethean influence here. In 'Analysis and Synthesis', Goethe remarked: 'The analytical thinker ought to begin by examining (or rather, by noting) whether he is really working with a hidden synthesis, or something of the sort' (Goethe, *Scientific Studies*, ed. and tr. D. Miller (*Works*, Suhrkamp Edition, vol. 12), New York, Suhrkamp, 1988).

18 Freud, 'The Psychotherapy of Hysteria', in *Studies on Hysteria* (with Josef Breuer) (1893–1895) (*SE* II, p. 305).

19 Quoted by A. Kardiner in 'Freud – The Man I Knew, The Scientist and His Influence', in B. Nelson (ed.), *Freud and the 20th Century*, London, Allen & Unwin, 1958, pp. 46–58 (p. 51).

20 Freud, *New Introductory Lectures on Psycho-Analysis* (1932), Lecture 34, 'Explanations, Applications and Orientations' (*SE* XXII, p. 156).

21 Jung, letter to Freud of 11 February 1910 (*Freud/Jung Letters*, p. 294).

22 For further discussion, see P. Grosskurth, *The Secret Ring: Freud's Inner Circle and the Politics of Psychoanalysis*, London, Jonathan Cape, 1991.

23 Quoted in F.E. Muser, *Zur Geschichte des Psychologischen Clubs Zürich von den Anfängen bis 1928* (Zurich, Psychologischer Club, 1984), p. 4. For a more general discussion of the function of the Psychological Club, see A. Samuels, 'The Professionalization of Carl G. Jung's Analytical Psychology Clubs', *Journal of the History of the Behavioral Sciences*, 1994, vol. 30, pp. 138–47.

24 See M. Anthony, *The Valkyries: The Women Around Jung*, Longmead, Element Books, 1990.

25 As Arië Sborowitz has remarked: 'The analytic schools . . . sought in different ways to grasp the life of the soul from the complexes of the psyche. In this respect basically all analytic schools, not just that of Jung, deserve to be called 'complex psychology' (*Beziehung und Bestimmung: Die Lehren von Martin Buber und C.G. Jung in ihrem Verhältnis zueinander*, Darmstadt, H. Gentner, 1955, p. 87).

26 'Address on the Occasion of the Founding of the C.G. Jung Institute, Zurich, 24 April 1948' (*CW* 18 §1129–§1141).

27 See *C.G. Jung-Institut Zürich: Ziele und Tätigkeit*, Zurich, 1948.

28 W. McGuire, *Bollingen: An Adventure in Collecting the Past*, Princeton NJ, Princeton University Press, 1982, pp. 106–12 and 123–30. See also his 'Firm Affinities: Jung's Relations with Britain and the United States', *Journal of Analytical Psychology*, 1995, vol. 40, pp. 301–26.

29 For an informative and entertaining collection of Jung's interviews with a variety of individuals and journalists, see W. McGuire and R.F.C. Hull (eds), *C.G. Jung Speaking: Interviews and Encounters*, Princeton NJ, Princeton University Press, 1977.

30 A. Samuels, *Jung and the Post-Jungians*, London and New York, Routledge & Kegan Paul, 1985, pp. 2, 11–21.

31 'Elaboration and clarification of a dream-image by means of *directed* association and of parallels from the humane sciences (symbology, mythology, mysticism, folklore, history of religion, ethnology, etc.)' ('Glossary', in *MDR*, p. 410).

32 Jung defined 'active imagination' as a technique of 'intense concentration on the background of consciousness, that is perfected only after long practice' (*CW* 7 §366). See also C.G. Jung, *Jung on Active Imagination*, London, Routledge, 1997; as well as B. Hannah, *Encounters with the Soul: Active Imagination as Developed by C.G. Jung*, Santa Monica CA, Sigo Press, 1981.

33 G. Adler, 'Methods of Treatment in Analytical Psychology', in *Psychoanalytical Techniques*, ed. B. Wolman, New York, Basic Books, 1967.

34 M. Fordham, *Jungian Psychotherapy: A Study in Analytical Psychology*, Chichester, Wiley, 1978.

35 N. Goldenberg, 'Archetypal Theory After Jung', *Spring*, 1975, pp. 199–220.

36 Samuels, 1985, op. cit., p. 1.

37 Ibid., p. 115.

38 For example, see McLynn, pp. 474–5.

39 Goethe, *Faust II*, tr. D. Luke, Oxford and New York, Oxford University Press, 1994, p. 114.

40 Samuels, 1985, op. cit., p. 266.

41 Two collections of essays in particular exemplify this 'new' approach to Jung: R.K. Papadopoulos and G. Saayman (eds), *Jung in Modern Perspective*, Hounslow, Wildwood House, 1984; and K. Barnaby and P. d'Acierno (eds), *C.G. Jung and the Humanities: Towards a Hermeneutics of Culture*, London, Routledge, 1990. For a wide-ranging anthology of essays on Jung, see the four-volume collection: R.K. Papadopoulos (ed.), *Carl Gustav Jung: Critical Assessments*, London and New York, Routledge, 1992. More recently, P. Young-Eisendrath and T. Dawson (eds), *The Cambridge Companion to Jung*, Cambridge, Cambridge University Press, 1997, has been published, but this largely ignores the recent shift in Jung studies.

42 'Preface', Barnaby and d'Acierno, op. cit., p. xxvi.

43 See F.X. Charet, *Spiritualism and the Foundations of C.G. Jung's Psychology*, Albany NY, State University of New York Press, 1993.

44 See W.B. Goodheart, 'C.G. Jung's First "Patient": On the Seminal Emergence of Jung's Thought', *Journal of Analytical Psychology*, 1984, vol. 29, pp. 1–34; H. Ellenberger, 'C.G. Jung and the Story of Helene Preiswerk: A Critical Study with New Documents', in Mark S. Micale (ed.), *Beyond the Unconscious: Essays of Henri F. Ellenberger in the History of Psychiatry*, Princeton NJ, Princeton University Press, 1993, pp. 291–305. Josef Breuer described the treatment of Anna O. as 'the germ cell of the whole of psychoanalysis' (Josef Breuer to August Forel, 21 November 1907, quoted in P.F. Cranefield, 'Josef Breuer's Evaluation of his Contribution to Psycho-Analysis', *International Journal of Psycho-Analysis*, 1958, vol. 39, pp. 319–22 (p. 320)).

45 On the identity of Miss Miller, see S. Shamdasani, 'A Woman Called Frank', *Spring*, 1990, vol. 50, pp. 26–56.

46 For further discussion, see J. Witzig, 'Théodore Flournoy – A Friend Indeed', *Journal of Analytical Psychology*, 1982, vol. 27, pp. 138–41. See also the section on 'Théodore Flournoy' in the appendix of the German edition of *Memories, Dreams, Reflections* (not included in the English edition). See the recent republication of Flournoy, *From India to the Planet Mars: A Case of Multiple Personality with Imaginary Languages*, ed. S. Shamdasani, Princeton NJ, Princeton University Press, 1996.

47 Brome, op. cit., p. 155.

48 P. Homans, *Jung in Context: Modernity and the Making of a Psychology*, Chicago and London, Chicago University Press, 1979, p. 129.

49 J. Kerr, *A Most Dangerous Method: The Story of Jung, Freud, and Sabina Spielrein*, London, Sinclair-Stevenson, 1994, p. 326.

50 D. Winnicott, book review of *Memories, Dreams, Reflections*, *International Journal of Psychoanalysis*, 1964, vol. 45, pp. 450–55.

51 E. Fromm, 'C.G. Jung: Prophet of the Unconscious', *Scientific American*, 1963, vol. 209, pp. 283–90 (p. 283).

52 P. Rieff, *The Triumph of the Therapeutic: Uses of Faith after Freud*, London, Chatto & Windus, 1966, p. 139.

53 See also A.C. Elms, 'The Auntification of C.G. Jung', in *Uncovering Lives: The Uneasy Alliance of Biography and Psychology*, New York and Oxford, Oxford University Press, 1994, pp. 51–70.

54 See note 5 above. For further bibliographical information on the Seminars, see *Collected Works*, vol. 19 (*General Bibliography*), pp. 209–15.

55 C.G. Jung, *Dream Analysis: Notes of the Seminar given in 1928–1930*, ed. W. McGuire, London, Routledge & Kegan Paul, 1984.

56 Excerpts from the Seminar on *Interpretation of Visions*, selected and edited by Jane A. Pratt, appeared in ten instalments of *Spring*, 1960–1969. Together with

three concluding instalments, edited by Patricia Berry, and a postscript by Henry A. Murray, these texts were republished as *The Vision Seminars: From the Complete Notes of Mary Foote*, Zurich, Spring Publications, 1976. For further information on Christiana Morgan, see C. Douglas, *Translate this Darkness: The Life of Christiana Morgan, the Veiled Woman in Jung's Life*, New York, Simon & Schuster, 1993.

57 See note 6 above.
58 C.G. Jung, *Kinderträume*, ed. L. Jung and M. Meyer-Grass, Olten/Freiburg im Breisgau, Walter, 1987.
59 Four lectures of Jung's 'Psychological Commentary on the Kundalini Yoga' (delivered at the Eidgenössische Technische Hochschule, Zurich, in 1932, were published in *Spring*, 1975, pp. 1–32. The full text was recently published as C.G. Jung, *The Psychology of Kundalini Yoga: Notes of the Seminar given in 1932*, ed. S. Shamdasani, London, Routledge, 1996. Excerpts from the lectures on the 'Exercitia Spiritualia of St Ignatius of Loyola', translated by Barbara Hannah, were published in *Spring*, 1977, pp. 183–200 and *Spring*, 1978, pp. 28–36.
60 E.S. Sergeant, 'Doctor Jung: A Portrait in 1931', in W. McGuire and R.F.C. Hull (eds), op. cit., pp. 50–8 (pp. 52–3).
61 McGuire, 1982, op. cit., pp. 14–15. As for Jung's style in the seminars, McGuire has characterized it as follows:

> Altogether, the seminars give us a Jung who was self-confidently relaxed, uncautious and undiplomatic, disrespectful of institutions and exalted personages, often humorous, even ribald, extravagantly learned in reference and allusion, attuned always to the most subtle resonances of the case in hand, and true always to himself and his vocation.
>
> (*Dream Seminar*, p. xvi)

62 R. Noll, *The Jung Cult: Origins of a Charismatic Movement*, Princeton NJ: Princeton University Press, 1994. See also note 1 above.
63 E. Bloch, 'Imago as Appearance from the "Depths"', in *Heritage of Our Times* [1962], tr. N. and S. Plaice, Cambridge, Polity Press, 1991, pp. 312–18; and H. Gess, *Vom Faschismus zum Neuen Denken: C.G. Jungs Theorie im Wandel der Zeit*, Lüneburg, zu Klampen, 1994.
64 See the essays collected in A. Maidenbaum and S.A. Martin (eds), *Lingering Shadows: Jungians, Freudians, and Anti-Semitism*, Boston and London, Shambhala, 1991.
65 See T. Evers, *Mythos und Emanzipation: Eine kritische Annäherung an C.G. Jung*, Hamburg, Junius, 1987, p. 141.
66 T. Szasz, *Heresies*, Garden City NY, Anchor Press, 1976, p. 139.
67 For an attempt to make good this deficit, see Andrew Samuels, *The Political Psyche*, London and New York, Routledge, 1993.
68 See V. Hubbs, 'German Romanticism and C.G. Jung: Selective Affinities', *Journal of Evolutionary Psychology*, 1983, vol. 4, pp. 8–20; and C. Douglas, 'The Historical Context of Analytical Psychology', *The Cambridge Companion to Jung*, pp. 17–34.
69 See R. Cardinal, *German Romantics in Context*, London: Studio Vista, 1975, p. 25.
70 See note 49.
71 See T.E. Apter, *Thomas Mann: The Devil's Advocate*, London and Basingstoke, Macmillan, 1978.

72 I am grateful to Paul A. Frasca and Hedy Wyss for permission to quote from this document. And I am indebted to Richard Noll for bringing its existence to my attention.
73 Thomas Mann in *La Stampa* of June 1925, quoted in *Internationale Zeitschrift für Psychoanalyse*, 1925, vol. 11, p. 247.
74 Thomas Mann, letter to Charles du Bos of 3 May 1929, quoted in R. Hayman, *Thomas Mann: A Biography*, London, Bloomsbury, 1996, pp. 376–7.
75 'To the Editor of Common Sense' [1940], in T. Mann, *Wagner und unsere Zeit: Aufsätze, Betrachtungen, Briefe*, Frankfurt am Main, S. Fischer, 1963, p. 158.
76 This is a paraphrase from the Jung–Jaffé transcripts in the Jung collection, Library of Congress. I am indebted to Sonu Shamdasani for bringing this passage to my attention.
77 Two examples of works that do, however, approach Jung from an avowedly philosophical perspective are M. Nagy, *Philosophical Issues in the Psychology of C.G. Jung*, Albany NY, State University of New York Press, 1991; and J.J. Clarke, *In Search of Jung: Historical and Philosophical Enquiries*, London and New York, Routledge, 1992.
78 In his letter of 27 April 1959 to Dr Joseph F. Rychlak about the possible influence of Hegel on his thought, Jung wrote: 'The philosophical influence that has prevailed in my education dates from Plato, Kant, Schopenhauer, Ed[uard] v[on] Hartmann, and Nietzsche' (Jung, *Letters*, ed. G. Adler and A. Jaffé, London, Routledge, 1973–1976, II, pp. 500–1). Jung then went on in the same letter to launch a bitter attack on Hegel – 'who in my very incompetent opinion is not even a proper philosopher but a misfired psychologist' – and to deny any traces at all of dialectical thought in his work. In the same letter, Jung admitted that he had 'never studied Hegel properly'. Nevertheless, Jung still felt qualified to describe Hegel as '*un psychologue raté*' and to claim that there was 'a remarkable coincidence between certain tenets of Hegelian philosophy and my findings concerning the Collective Unconscious' (p. 502). 'On the Nature of the Psyche' (1947/1954) contains the following remark: 'Hegel was a psychologist in disguise who projected great truths out of the subjective sphere into a cosmos he himself had created' (*CW* 8 §358). For further discussion of Jung and Hegel, see F. Seifert, *Seele und Bewußtsein: Betrachtungen zum Problem der psychischen Realität*, Munich and Basle, Ernst Reinhardt, 1962; B. Eckman, 'Jung, Hegel, and the Subjective Universe', *Spring*, 1986, pp. 88–99; W. Giegerich, 'The Rescue of the World: Jung, Hegel, and the Subjective Universe', *Spring*, 1987, pp. 107–14; H. Solomon, 'The Transcendent Function and Hegel's Dialectical Vision', *Journal of Analytical Psychology*, 1994, vol. 39, pp. 77–100; and S.M. Kelly, *Individuation and the Absolute: Hegel, Jung, and the Path towards Wholeness*, New York and Mahwah NJ, Paulist Press, 1993.
79 'I use the term "individuation" to denote the process by which a person becomes a psychological "in-dividual", that is, a separate, indivisible entity or "whole"' (*CW* 9 §490).
80 R. Brooke, *Jung and Phenomenology*, London and New York, Routledge, 1991. For a critique of Jung's phenomenology, see Jef Dehing, who cites a passage (*CW* 11 §308) from Jung's 'Transformation Symbolism in the Mass' (1941) and comments as follows: 'Something very strange has happened here: on the one hand Jung insinuates that the reality of the statement of belief is in fact a psychological one; on the other hand, whilst criticising the hypostasis of a metaphysical statement, he boldly hypostasises psychic reality' ('Jung and

Knowledge: From Gnosis to Praxis', *Journal of Analytical Psychology*, 1990, vol. 35, pp. 377–96 (p. 382)).

81 For further discussion of Heideggerian perspectives on Jung, see J.R. Haule, *Imagination and Myth: A Heideggerian Interpretation of C.G. Jung* (Ph.D. diss., Temple University, Philadelphia, 1973); R.S. Avens, 'Heidegger and Archetypal Psychology', *International Philosophical Quarterly*, 1982, vol. 22, pp. 184–202; and R. Capobianco, 'Heidegger, Opposites, and the Jungian Unconscious', *Phenomenological Inquiry*, 1990, vol. 14, pp. 126–36. On the few occasions that Jung discusses Heidegger, his remarks are always highly negative. In his letter to Josef Meinertz of 3 July 1939, Jung accused Heidegger of 'juggling with words' (Jung, *Letters*, I, p. 273). Then again, in his letter to Arnold Künzli of 13 February 1943, Jung contrasted Kant's use of long-accepted philosophical terminology – 'Even Kant, for all his critiques, constantly employs the concepts that were current in his century' – with another sort of criticism that only leads to 'the mastery of complicated banalities, the Platonic exemplar of which', Jung jokingly added, 'is embodied for me in the philosopher Heidegger' (*Letters*, I, p. 330). And in his next letter to Künzli of 28 February 1943, Jung went so far as to say that 'Heidegger's *modus philosophandi* is neurotic through and through and is ultimately rooted in his psychic crankiness' (p. 331). As Jung's letters to Medard Boss of 27 June 1947 and 5 August 1947 (*Letters*, II, pp. xl–xlv) and to Gerhard Zacharias of 24 August 1953 (*Letters*, II, p. 121) show, Jung had a strong dislike of Existential Psychology, which used concepts derived from Heidegger. But Capobianco is concerned to demonstrate structural parallels, not influence, in the thought of Jung and Heidegger.

82

> The structures of structuralism and the images of analytical psychology alike precede and prestructure the human persons who exist in their ambience and by their means. The 'outside' of such structures and such images is a very different outside from that which figures into the early modern notion of sensory experience and its imitation in iconic signs. It belongs to a world or cosmos that is the source of symbols, just as it is the origin of the psyche itself – indeed, of the 'objective psyche' as Jung came to call it.

(E.S. Casey, 'Jung and the Postmodern Condition', in Barnaby and Acierno (eds), *C.G. Jung and the Humanities*, pp. 319–24 (p. 322)). For a comparison of the structuralism of Claude Lévi-Strauss and Jung's theory of the archetypes, see E. d'Aquili, 'The Influence of Jung on the Work of Claude Lévi-Strauss', *Journal of the History of the Behavioral Sciences*, 1975, vol. 11, pp. 41–8; M.J. Chang, 'Jung and Lévi-Strauss: Whose Unconscious?', *Mankind Quarterly*, 1984, vol. 25, pp. 101–14; and R.J. Werblowsky, 'Struktur und Archetyp', *Analytische Psychologie*, 1989, vol. 20, pp. 19–31. For a Jungian critique of Lacanian structuralist psychology, see S.M. Joseph, 'Fetish, Sign and Symbol Through the Looking-Glass: A Jungian Critique of Jacques Lacan's Ecrits', *The San Francisco Jung Institute Library Journal*, 1987, vol. 7, no. 2, pp. 1–16.

83

> Jung's dualism is undeniably the structuring principle of his theories. All the major concepts are arranged in antagonistic pairs such as: conscious/unconscious, eros/logos, ego/self, introversion/extr(a)version, image/instinct, anima/animus etc. Yet, like Derrida, Jung is aware

of the violence inherent in oppositional thinking, using words like 'aggressive' and 'hostile', and claims that these opposites are a kind of likeness, a metaphor, their property is to be reversible: they are ready to deconstruct, 'their reversibility proves their validity'. Indeed, Jung deconstructs Freud's priority over the dream image. To Freud, the conscious/unconscious hierarchy was paramount and dream images are to be deciphered by the ego or at least contained by a concept. Jung asserted that most dream images were archetypal, they were *about* the unconscious which in adult life would attempt to dissolve ego dominance, to dismember consciousness and re-member it as subject to unconscious archetypes. This was individuation, an essentially deconstructive process. Of course, like Derrida, he found the abolition of hierarchy, here between conscious and unconscious, a near inconceivable goal and its reversibility difficult. Indeed, conscious priorities would creep into his attempt to privilege unconscious images because his individuation narratives, of many patients, are generically similar, and [do] not coincidentally resemble what he believed to be his own story. However, it is fair to say that Jung aimed at a deconstructive system of 'oppositions' rather than the absolute rigidity of separation depicted by Freud.

(S. Rowland, 'The Body's Sacrifice: Romance and Sacrifice in Religious and Jungian Narratives', *Literature and Theology*, 1996, vol. 10, pp. 160–70 (p. 161)).

Part I

JUNG IN HISTORICAL CONTEXT

2

MEMORIES, DREAMS, OMISSIONS[1]

Sonu Shamdasani

Source: Spring: A Journal of Archetype and Culture, 57, 1995.

This is such an important and intensely original book – I think it will have an enormous success and become a classic!
Richard Hull, 1960[2]

Memories, Dreams, Reflections is commonly regarded as Jung's most important work, as well as being the most widely known and read. It has been taken as his final testament, for, as Gerhard Adler notes, "Nowhere else has the man Jung revealed himself so openly or testified to his crises of decision and the existence of his inner law."[3] Since Jung's death, it has been the preeminent source on his life and has spawned a plethora of secondary literature. In this study, my first omission will be the vast majority of this secondary literature, for reasons that will become clear. I hope to show that through a process that has had disturbing implications for the understanding of Jung, and his rightful location in twentieth-century intellectual history, *Memories, Dreams, Reflections* is by no means Jung's autobiography.

The existence of *Memories, Dreams, Reflections* has significantly delayed scholarly work on Jung. In her preface to her biographical memoir, which was one of the first to appear, Barbara Hannah writes that "Jung's children were very much against anything biographical being written about their father, since they feel that all that is necessary has been said in his own *Memories, Dreams, Reflections*."[4] When Jung biographies came to be written, without exception they all relied heavily on the book, not only as a source of information, but also as the fundamental narrative structure of Jung's life. Thus Hannah writes of *Memories* that it "will always remain the deepest and most authentic source concerning Jung."[5] So much has the prevalent understanding of Jung relied on this text that it is unlikely such understanding could change without a radical rereading of it.

From the outset, the significance of an autobiography by Jung was entailed by his own understanding of the nature of the psychological

33

enterprise. Jung claimed as one of his central insights the notion of the "personal equation." He writes: "philosophical criticism has helped me to see that every psychology – my own included – has the character of a subjective confession."[6] Regardless of whether one agrees with this notion, it is crucial in understanding Jung's psychology, for it clearly indicates how Jung understood his own psychology – and meant it to be understood.

Aside from a tantalizing glimpse in a private seminar in 1925,[7] however, Jung did not publicly present his life story. From his own understanding of the significance of the theorist's biography, this lacuna presented perhaps the major impediment for an understanding of his work. In that same seminar, he candidly provides one rationale for this lacuna:

> All of this is the outside picture of the development of my book on the types. I could perfectly well say that this is the way the book came about and make an end of it there. But there is another side, a weaving about making mistakes, impure thinking, etc., etc., which is always very difficult for a man to make public. He likes to give you the finished product of his directed thinking and have you understand that so it was born in his mind, free of weakness. A thinking man's attitude towards his intellectual life is quite comparable to that of woman toward her erotic life.
>
> If I ask a woman about the man she has married, "How did this come about?" she will say, "I met him and loved him, and that is all." She will conceal most carefully all the little meannesses, and squinting situations that she may have been involved in, and she will present you with an unrivalled perfection of smoothness. Above all she will conceal the erotic mistakes she has made . . .
>
> Just so with a man about his books. He does not want to tell of the secret alliances, the *faux pas* of his mind. This it is that makes lies of most autobiographies. Just as sexuality is in women largely unconscious, so is this inferior side of his thinking largely unconscious in man. And just as a woman erects her stronghold of power in her sexuality, and will not give away any of the secrets of its weak side, so a man centers his power in his thinking and proposes to hold it as a solid front against the public, particularly against other men. He thinks if he tells the truth in this field it is equivalent to turning over the keys of his citadel to the enemy.[8]

In this remarkable statement, what Jung sees as the near impossibility of honesty, which "makes lies of most autobiographies," proves to be the major contraindication for entering upon such an endeavour. Clearly, Jung hadn't the slightest intention of 'turning over the keys of his citadel' to his enemies. In the years following this seminar, Jung consistently held to this position. In 1953, Henri Flournoy, the son of Jung's mentor, the

Swiss psychologist, Théodore Flournoy, relayed to Jung the question of a Dr Junod as to whether he had written an autobiography or intended to do one.[9] Jung replied:

> I have always mistrusted an autobiography because one can never tell the truth. In so far as one is truthful, or believes one is truthful, it is an illusion, or of bad taste.[10]

When it came to *Memories*, had Jung latterly succumbed to an illusion, or to a severe lapse in taste? In a letter to his lifelong friend Gustave Steiner, Jung expressed his continued resistance to undertaking an autobiography, despite continued pressure:

> During the last years it has been suggested to me on several occasions to give something like an autobiography of myself. I have been unable to conceive of anything of the sort. I know too many autobiographies and their self-deceptions and expedient lies, and I know too much about the impossibility of self description, to give myself over to an attempt in this respect.[11]

Jung was no less sanguine concerning the possibility of a biography of his life. In reply to J.M. Thorburn, who had suggested that Jung should commission a biography of his life, Jung states:

> if I were you I shouldn't bother about my biography. I don't want to write one, because quite apart from the lack of motive I wouldn't know how to set about it. Much less can I see how anybody else could disentangle this monstrous Gordian knot of fatality, denseness, and aspirations and what-not! Anybody who would try such an adventure ought to analyze me far beyond my own head if he wants to make a real job of it.[12]

How then did *Memories* come about? It initially arose out of the suggestion of a remarkable publisher, Kurt Wolff. At that time, Jung already had exclusive contracts with Routledge and Kegan Paul and the Bollingen Foundation. That another publisher managed to publish Jung's "autobiography" was quite a coup, though clearly one that Kurt Wolff was up to. In an article entitled "On luring away authors," Wolff writes:

> Every country in the world has strict laws about white-slave traffic. Authors, on the other hand, are an unprotected species and must look after themselves. They can be bought and sold, like girls for the white-slave trade – except that in the case of authors it is not illegal.[13]

To Richard Hull, Jung's translator, Kurt Wolff described how:

> for several years he had tried to persuade Jung to write it [an auto-biography], how Jung had always refused, and how finally he (Kurt) hit on the happy idea of an "Eckerfrau" to whom Jung could dictate at random, the Eckerfrau being Aniela Jaffé.[14]

In a letter to Herbert Read, Kurt Wolff wrote that in the last analysis it was Aniela Jaffé who persuaded Jung to undertake this task.[15] Due to the involvement of another publisher, the book did not go down the same editorial channels as the rest of Jung's work, which was to have significant consequences for what ensued.

In her introduction to *Memories*, Aniela Jaffé writes:

> We began in the spring of 1957. It had been proposed that the book be written not as a "biography" but in the form of an "auto-biography," with Jung himself as the narrator. This plan determined the form of the book, and my first task consisted solely in asking questions and noting down Jung's replies.[16]

When the book was published, its significance for the understanding of Jung was perceptively pointed out by Henri Ellenberger. He writes:

> Few personalities of the psychological and psychiatric world have been as badly understood as Carl Gustav Jung. . . . It is precisely the interest of his *Autobiography* that it permits us to unify in a plausible fashion the disparate images which one made up till now of the life, personality and work of the founder of Analytical Psychology.[17]

However, as I shall argue, its very plausibility by no means diminished the misunderstandings surrounding the work of Jung, but escalated them to unforeseen proportions.

From the beginning, much was made of Jung's omissions. On the one hand, Jung was much criticized for the absence of any mention of his life-long extramarital affair with Toni Wolff, of figures such as Eugen Bleuler and Pierre Janet, and the vexed issue of his alleged collaboration with the Nazis. It has been argued that Jung's omissions, for a psychologist who made the issue of subjective confession into the cornerstone of his psychology, were the mark of bad faith and intellectual dishonesty. Seriously, this charge continues to be used as an indictment of the Jungian movement.

On the other hand these self-same omissions have not only been defended but given a profound rationale. Aniela Jaffé writes:

In Jung's memoirs the personalia are almost entirely lacking, to the disappointment of many readers. . . . This criticism and the charge of Jung's "unrelatedness" were beside the point. His eye was always turned to the impersonal, the hidden archetypal background which he was willing to reveal only so far as it concerned his own life.[18]

Some have argued that such omissions are justified because *Memories* inaugurated nothing less than a new chapter in the history of autobiography and of Western self-understanding – that of the new, "inner" form of modern psychological autobiography, and that *Memories* is historically as significant as the *Confessions* of St Augustine or of Rousseau.[19]

This reading, which can be conveniently called the canonization of Jung, is brought out by Kathleen Raine in her review, "A Sent Man," in which she simply states:

Jung's life, even so fragmentarily revealed, invites comparison not with profane autobiography, but with the lives of Plotinus and Swedenborg, the lives of the saints and sages, interwoven with miracle.[20]

Raine was not the only one to make the comparison with the lives of saints. The same analogy was made by the psychologist Hans Eysenck, though with a characteristically different slant. In his review, he writes:

Acolytes writing hagiographies are seldom fortunate enough to have the assistance of the saint himself in their endeavours; Aniela Jaffé had the benefit of extensive discussion with Jung. . . . It may therefore be regarded as representing the kind of picture Jung wished to give of himself.[21]

In the prologue to *Memories*, Jung writes: "I have now undertaken . . . to tell my personal myth [den Mythus meines Lebens]." Thus the text itself was taken as a paradigmatic example of what such a myth might look like. In this way, it was not only taken as the definitive account of Jung's life, but also of the form that a psychologically individuated life should take. Edward Edinger comments:

just as Jung's discovery of his own mythlessness paralleled the mythless condition of modern society, so Jung's discovery of his own individual myth will prove to be the first emergence of our new collective myth. . . . Almost all the important episodes of Jung's life can be seen as paradigmatic of the new mode of being which is the consequence of living by a new myth.[22]

In her introduction to the book, Aniela Jaffé states that its genesis determined its eventual form. Hence a word or two is necessary concerning Aniela Jaffé and her relationship with Jung. Jaffé first encountered Jung in 1937 and subsequently went into analysis with him. Twenty years later, she became his secretary. It was a job she would be well suited to, as she had already worked as a freelance secretary for Professors Gideon and von Tsharner.[23] In 1947 she became Secretary of the Jung Institute in Zürich.

In an interview, she recalled that after his wife's death, Jung did not feel like answering his correspondence, and that she answered many letters in his name, reading him her replies, to which he at times made minor corrections.[24] This astonishing statement leaves unclear precisely how many of Jung's letters during this period were written in this fashion. Jung's late letters, which make up the bulk of the second volume of his selected letters, which Aniela Jaffé edited with Gerhard Adler, are commonly held to have his wisest and most humane statements. How many of these were actually the work of Aniela Jaffé?

This working arrangement shows the initial level of trust that Jung showed in Jaffé, allowing her to "write in his name." It further helps us understand how *Memories* was composed. At the outset, Jung trusted her ability to "assume his 'I,'" and to represent it to the outer world.

In her introduction to *Memories*, Aniela Jaffé states, "Jung read through the manuscript of this book and approved it."[25] Hence it has generally been taken that Jung was ultimately responsible for any omissions in the text. However, from the start, there were rumours of another order of omissions. This question was put to Jaffé in an interview with Suzanne Wagner which took place in 1977:

> Wagner: I heard that there were parts of his autobiography that were not allowed to be published – ideas about reincarnation for example.
> Jaffé: No, we published everything I thought could be published. What I cut were parts of the chapter he had written on Africa. It was simply too long. It would have taken the whole book. But I discussed it with him and he was very glad.[26]

The only significant omission in the text would thus seem to be a book-length account of Jung's travels in Africa, which would be a lost continent of Jung's work, which has subsequently never surfaced. Be that as it may, what is crucial here is her statement that Jung approved of the changes that were made.

In a conversation in 1988 with Michael Fordham that was the instigation of my research, he spoke of his impressions of an early draft of *Memories* that he had read. He stated that the early chapters were greatly different and "far madder" than the published version. I subsequently located an editorial typescript at the Countway Library of Medicine at Harvard, and found not only whole chapters that were not published – such as an account of Jung's travels in London and Paris, and a chapter on William James – but also significant editing on almost every page.[27] I then contacted Aniela Jaffé concerning my research project. She informed me that not all of the material upon which the book was based went into the published text, and that she had planned to use some of the further material at a later date, but that permission was denied by the Jung heirs.[28] She informed me that the transcripts of the interviews were at the Library of Congress, which I subsequently consulted.[29]

I will first deal with some general features of the texts. While the Countway manuscript is recognizable as an extended version of the published text, the same is not true concerning the unpublished transcripts. Jaffé herself deals with the difference between the published texts and the actual interviews. Some had claimed that as she had been Jung's secretary, her task in compiling *Memories* had simply been to take down Jung's dictation. This claim incensed her, and led her to reveal the active role she had in fact had. In a letter, Jaffé noted that it was completely ridiculous to claim, as many did, that Jung had merely dictated to her. She noted that Jung spoke in something like a Freudian free association, and that his mode of speaking was not suitable for print. She noted that she had to do a great deal of work untangling these associations into a coherent narrative. Hence the view that the text was simply dictated represented a great compliment to her work.[30]

This statement reveals her active hand in the text, and suggests that the whole narrative structure of the book, which has been taken not only as the quintessence of Jung's life, but the exemplar of the new myth of individuation that the latter represented, was largely her construction. The typescripts themselves give a completely different impression. They usually begin with Jaffé posing specific questions and Jung associating freely in reply, following no chronological pattern. In a passage from the Countway typed manuscript that was omitted, Jung said that the frequent repetitions in the text were an aspect of his circular mode of thinking. He described his method as a new mode of peripatetics.[31] This suggests that in terms of narrative structure at least, something rather central to Jung's self-understanding landed up on the cutting floor.

In the published version, the paucity of any mention of figures in Jung's life is taken by some as the mark of his individuation or self-realization, and by others as a symptom of a quasi-autistic withdrawal from the world, or of an extreme degree of narcissism. However, in the typescripts of the interviews, there are many passages on figures as varied as Adolf Hitler, Billy Graham, Eugen Bleuler and Sabina Spielrein, not to mention a lengthy passage on the uncanny and suggestive resemblance between Jung's sister and Goethe's sister. I will first take up one such omission, as an example.

Many have waited with bated breath concerning Jung's lifelong extra-marital affair with Toni Wolff; and yes, the transcripts do indeed contain material on this affair. Laurens van der Post justifies its omission as follows:

> She [Toni Wolff] is not mentioned in Jung's *Memories*, and one understands the omission in measure, because the book is a record only of quintessence. Jung's own personal relationships are deliberately not a part of it.[32]

Van der Post provides the following account of her role in his life:

> She was the only person capable of understanding, out of her own experience and transfiguration, what Jung was taking upon himself. This world of the unconscious which he was entering as a man, she had already endured as a woman. Thanks to Jung's guidance she had re-emerged, an enlarged and re-integrated personality.[33]

In this view, she plays the role of Beatrice in the Dantesque *Vita Nuova* that was Jung's myth. In the transcripts of Jaffé's interviews with Jung, he said that at the beginning of her analysis, Toni Wolff had incredible wild and cosmic fantasies, but because he was so preoccupied with his own, he was unable to deal with hers.

He said that he was faced with the problem of what to do with Toni Wolff after her analysis, which he ended, despite feeling involved with her. A year later, he dreamt that they were together in the Alps in a valley of rocks, and that he heard elves singing in a mountain into which she was disappearing, which he dreaded. After this, he contacted her again, as he knew that it was unavoidable, and because he felt in danger of his life. On a later occasion, while swimming, he found himself with a cramp, and vowed that if it receded, and he survived, he would give in to the relation-ship – which he then embarked upon. He said that he had infected her with his experience, which was awful and terrible, and that she got drawn into it and was equally helpless. He said that he became her centre, and through his insights, she found her centre. However, she needed him to play this role too much, which meant that he couldn't be himself, and she got lost. He felt as if he were being torn apart and often had to hold onto the table to keep together.

In this instance, one perhaps can understand the omission for reasons of propriéty, but this is by no means so concerning the following omission. To contextualize it, I will address some critical differences between the published version and the Countway manuscript. In *Memories* the only section that is named after an individual is that on Freud, leaving the impression that the two most important figures in Jung's life were Freud and God, which has left commentators disputing which of these two came first. This impression is strengthened in the American and English editions, as the appendices on Théodore Flournoy and Heinrich Zimmer which are in the German edition are absent.[34] This strengthens the Freudocentric reading of Jung, which to date has been the prime manner that Jung and the development of Analytical Psychology have been understood.

The Countway manuscript presents a radically different organization. This version shows variant chapter arrangements that considerably alter the structure of the narrative. The section following the chapter on Freud is headed "Memories. Flournoy – James – Keyserling – Crichton-Miller – Zimmer." This heading is then crossed out by hand, and replaced by "Théodore Flournoy and William James."[35] These variations in arrangement alone show the contingency of the arrangement in *Memories*. Further, in this arrangement, the tributes to Flournoy and James directly follow the section on Freud.

In the chapter on Freud in *Memories*, Jung diagnoses Freud as suffering from a serious neurosis and claims that his followers have not grasped the significance of their founder's neurosis. For Jung, the universal claims made by Freud's psychology are invalid due to Freud's neurosis. The chapter that immediately follows portrays Jung's heroic "confrontation with the unconscious" and his discovery of archetypes, and through the discovery of his own myth, a means for "modern man to find his soul." *Memories* furthers the myth of Jung's heroic descent and self-generation, after he has freed himself from the shackles of Freudian psychology (founding a foundling psychology, without antecedents, with no prior model to follow, only counter exemplars).

The Countway typed manuscript presents a very different version. In the sections on Flournoy and James, which immediately follow the chapter on Freud, the problems as to how one could found a non-neurotic psychology, on which Jung claims Freud foundered, already appear to have been answered in the affirmative before Freud, by Flournoy and James. Further, Jung portrays the positivity of the mentoring relationship, through which no breaks were necessary. Jung credits their significance in helping him to formulate his criticisms of Freud and furnish the methodological presuppositions for his formulation of a post-Freudian psychology.[36]

In the chapter on James, Jung gives an account of their contact and attempts to spell out his intellectual debt to James. Jung recounts that he met James in 1909 and paid him a visit the following year. He said that James was one of the most outstanding persons that he ever met. He found him aristocratic, the image of a gentleman, yet free of airs and graces. He spoke to Jung without looking down on him; Jung felt that they had an excellent rapport. He felt that it was only with Flournoy and James that he could talk so easily, that he revered James' memory, and that he was a model. He found that both of them were receptive and of assistance with his doubts and difficulties, which he never found again. He esteemed James' openness and vision, which was particularly marked in his psychical research, which they discussed in detail, as well as his seances with the medium Mrs Piper. He saw the far-reaching significance of psychical research as a means of access to the psychology of the unconscious. Jung said that he was also very influenced by James' work on the psychology of religion, which also became for him a model, in particular by the way in which he managed to accept and let things stand, without forcing them into a theoretical bias.

These two omissions concern the large scale deletion of several critical figures in Jung's life. The third omission consists simply in a small detail, yet its implications for the understanding of the genesis of Jung's thought is perhaps no less significant. In a passage in *Memories* that has attracted much attention, Jung describes his experience of hearing the voice of a female patient speak within him, informing him that his activities were in fact art, and which he famously christened as the voice of the anima. Subsequent to the publication of Aldo Carotenuto's *A Secret Symmetry*, it has generally been assumed that this patient was none other than Sabina Spielrein.

The most extended argument for this occurs in John Kerr's *A Most Dangerous Method*, where it forms a crucial part of a thesis that the most important intellectual and emotional influences on Jung were Freud and Spielrein. Kerr states: "The first mention of the 'anima' to occur in Jung's writings came in his 1920 tome *Psychological Types*."[37] (However, as noted long ago by the editors of the collected works, Jung had already treated of the anima in his 1916 "The Structure of the Unconscious"[38] and *Psychological Types* was actually published in 1921.) Kerr claims that Jung "immortalised" Spielrein under the name of the anima, arguing that two clues Jung gave as to the woman's identity – that he had been in correspondence with her, and that he broke with her in 1918–19, point to Spielrein. However in the transcripts, where he actually speaks of Spielrein by name, Jung simply implies that he lost touch with her when she went to Russia. Kerr claims that: "Perhaps the biggest clue . . . is the debate on science versus art."[39] However, to make this last clue point to Spielrein, Kerr claims, without any textual support, that the voice had actually said, "It is not science. It is poetry."[40] Kerr's supposition that the voice was Spielrein leads him to "correct" the historical record so that it supports his claim, forming a circular argument. Kerr also claims that Jung's stone carving at Bollingen of a bear rolling a ball represents Spielrein, and concludes that "Jung's 'anima,' the 'she who must be obeyed' finished her career as a Freudian,"[41] thus substantiating his Freudocentric reading of the genesis of Jung's psychology. However, there are grounds for asserting that the stone carving does not represent Spielrein. Roger Payne notes that "Franz [Jung] said that the often discussed bear which 'sets the ball rolling' in his Bollingen carving was actually Emma [Jung]."[42]

In the transcripts, Jung adds a small but telling detail – that the woman in question was Dutch. The one Dutch woman in Jung's circle at this time was Maria Moltzer.[43] The closeness of her relationship to Jung is attested to by Freud. On 23 December 1912, in reply to Jung's letter of 18 December in which Jung claimed that he had been analyzed, and hence was not neurotic, unlike Freud who hadn't been,[44] Freud wrote to Ferenczi: "The master who analyzed him could only have been Fräulein Moltzer, and he is so foolish as to be proud of this work of a woman with whom he is having an affair."[45] Freud's claim is substantiated by Jolande Jacobi, who claimed in an interview: "I heard from others, about the time before he met Toni Wolff, that he had had a love affair there in the Burgholzli with a girl – what was her name? Moltzer."[46] In an unpublished letter of 1 August 1918, Moltzer wrote to Fanny Bowditch Katz, who had been her patient:

> Yes, I resigned from the Club. I could not live any longer in that atmosphere. I am glad I did. I think, that in time, when the Club really shall become something, the Club shall be thankful I did. My resignation has its silent effects. Silent, for it seems that it belongs to my path, that I openly don't get the recognition or the appreciation for what I do for the development of the whole analytic movement. I always work in the dark and alone. This is my fate and must be expected.[47]

Jung subsequently made an acknowledgement to her, tucked away in a footnote in *Psychological Types*, where he states: "The credit for having discovered the existence of this type [the intuitive] belongs to Miss M. Moltzer."[48] Given that Jung regarded himself as of this type, this statement is telling. Taken together, I would claim that the case for the voice having been that of Moltzer is significantly stronger than for it having been Spielrein's.

At the current time, it is unclear who in a particular instance was responsible for a specific omission.[49] However, one might counter, that if Jung approved the changes, as Jaffé leads us to believe, these questions are not of great import. Crucial light on Jung's attitude to the text is shed by an unpublished memo written by Richard Hull, entitled, "A record of Events preceding Publication of Jung's Autobiography, as seen by R.F.C. Hull." Hull narrates that in February 1960, Jaffé informed him that Jung wanted to see him at the end of the month. Hull writes:

The old man turned up . . . said he wanted to talk, and talked solidly for over an hour about the autobiography. I gathered that there was some controversy going on as to the "authentic" text. (At this time I had seen no text at all.) He impressed upon me, with the utmost emphasis, that he had said what he wanted to say in his own way – "a bit blunt and crude sometimes" – and that he did not want his work to be *tantifiziert* ("auntified" or "old-maidified," in Jack's felicitous phrase). "You will see what I mean when you get the text," he said. As he spoke at some length about the practice of "ghost-writing" by American publishers, I inferred that the "Tantifierung" would be done by Kurt. I thereupon asked Jung whether I would have the authority to "de-oldmaidify" the text supplied to me by Kurt. "In those cases," he said, "the big guns will go into action," pointing to himself. I found all this rather puzzling, because Kurt had said earlier that, especially in the first three chapters, the impact lay precisely in the highly personal tone and unorthodox outspokenness, which should at all costs be preserved.[50]

Hull then read the text and began revising the translation. He recounts:

It soon became apparent that the alterations were all of a kind which toned down and "old-maidified" Jung's original written text. As some of the deleted passages seemed to me extremely important for a proper understanding of the subsequent narrative, I restored them from Winston's version, together with a number of critical references to Jung's family, and some remarks which couldn't shock anyone, except the Swiss bourgeoisie, including a highly dramatic use of the word "shit." I suspected that the "auntie" was to be found not at the Hotel Esplanade in Locarno but nearer home in Küsnacht, and that it was Aniela Jaffé.[51]

It seems that before Jung, the "big gun," could go into action, he died. After his death, Hull took up this issue directly with Jaffé. In reference to a proposed excision, he writes:

I would call the excision – and I choose my word very carefully – censorship, a thing that Jung would have despised and detested. . . . Four times you have said that you are no longer capable of being objective. In a matter of such vital importance, dear Mrs. Jaffé, it is your duty to regain your objectivity: it was in your hands and no one else's, that Jung entrusted the responsibility for the final version of his life's testimony. . . . Do you imagine that if Pantheon are compelled to bring out an expurgated edition, all this explosive evidence is going to lie idle? . . . All my arguments pale and diminish beside the one dominant thought: why did the old man take the trouble to come to see me, and talk so earnestly about the book, and why did he entrust it into your hands? I must leave you to find the answer.[52]

However, Hull himself was reticent in how far he was willing to go to "de-auntify" the text. In one section, Jung diagnosed his mother as hysterical. This was omitted. In a letter to Gerald Gross, Hull writes:

Aniela wrote that Mrs. Niehus would insist on its removal, and that this was Mrs. N.'s condition for Aniela's final placet. . . . I felt that it would be a blunder to antagonize her by fighting for the word "hysterical." To be frank, I am not willing to jeopardize my relations with her, as regard future work, for its sake. I therefore suggested "nervous" by way of a compromise, and Aniela gladly accepted this. At the same time, I have pointed out yet again that this little piece of family censorship will in all probability come to light in the end. . . .[53]

The significance of these changes is that they concern the manuscripts of the sections of *Memories* that Jung actually wrote – and which have been the basis of an endless stream of psychobiographies.

The final issue is that of the book's billing as Jung's autobiography. Hull highlighted the significance of this issue:

there is all the difference in the world between a book advertised as "The Autobiography of C. G. Jung" and a book of Jung's memoirs edited by Aniela Jaffé (of whom few have heard). One is an automatic bestseller, the other is not.[54]

As one would expect, Jung's English publisher, Routledge, clearly wanted to publish the book. In a letter of 18 December 1959, Cecil Franklin wrote to Jung:

I believe that the history of this book is that it started as a work by Aniela Jaffé which she would have written with your close help; but that it grew out of that and far beyond it until it became in fact your autobiography. . . . We have looked into our agreement for 1947 and find that if this is indeed your autobiography . . . publishing rights would be with us. . . . We have looked forward to the time when we might publish your autobiography. . . . It would worry us very much and might harm our reputation over here to be considered the publishers only of your more strictly technical books. . . .[55]

However, Jung never regarded the book as his autobiography. On 5 April 1960, Jung wrote to Walter Niehus-Jung, his son-in-law and literary executor:

> I want to thank you for your efforts on behalf of my so-called "Autobiography" and to confirm once more that I do not regard this book as my undertaking but expressly as a book which Frau A. Jaffé has written. . . . The book should be published under her name and not under mine, since it does not represent an auto-biography composed by myself.[56]

On 25 May 1960, Herbert Read wrote to John Barrett concerning the book:

> It now appears it will have some such title as:
>
> Aniela Jaffé
> "Reminiscences, Dreams, Thoughts"
> with contributions from C.G. Jung.[57]

Following these negotiations, a resolution of the Editorial Committee of the Collected Works of Jung was drawn up, allowing the book to be published outside of the exclusive contracts with the Bollingen Foundation and Routledge and Kegan Paul. It contains the following statement:

> C.G. Jung has always maintained that he did not consider this book as his own enterprise but expressly as a book written by Mrs. Jaffé. The chapters written by C.G. Jung were to be considered as his contributions to the work of Mrs. Jaffé. The book was to be published in the name of Mrs. Jaffé and not in the name of C.G. Jung, because it did not represent an autobiography composed by C.G. Jung (letter of C.G. Jung to Walter Niehus dated 5th April 1960).
>
> On a conference held on the 26th August between Prof. C.G. Jung, Mr. John Barrett, Miss Vaun Gillmor, Sir Herbert Read, Mr. and Mrs. W. Niehus-Jung and Mrs. Aniela Jaffé, C.G. Jung confirmed again that he did strictly consider this book as an undertaking of Mrs. A. Jaffé to which he had only given his contributions. . . . The Editorial Committee decides hereby formally that it will not approve any decision of the Executive

Subcommittee which would add the book of Mrs. A. Jaffé to the Collected Works.[58]

From this, it appears that it was a precondition for the contractual release of the book that it appeared as Aniela Jaffé's biography of Jung, rather than as Jung's autobiography. In July, 1960, Kurt Wolff resigned from Pantheon, which was subsequently bought by Random House. On 6 June 1961, Jung died. The following year, extracts from *Memories* appeared in *Die Weltwoche* and the *Atlantic Monthly*. The first extract in *Die Weltwoche* was simply titled, "The Autobiography of C.G. Jung." The book itself appeared in 1962 in English and German. In October of that year, Kurt Wolff died in a car crash. A French edition appeared in 1966, entitled, *My Life: Memories, Dreams and Thoughts.*[59]

What was indeed a remarkable biography has been mistakenly read as an autobiography. Unfortunately, it seems that when some grasped the significance of the confession of Jung's "personal equation," their efforts were in part directed towards determining the form it should take, and which of his memories and dreams to omit – fashioning Jung in their own likeness, making him the bearer of their "personal myths." Might it now be time for a de-auntification?

Notes

1 I am grateful to Michael Whan for this title.
2 Richard Hull to John Barrett, 4 May 1960, Bollingen Archive, Library of Congress. Hull's letters have been cited with the permission of Mrs Birte-Lena Hull.
3 Gerhard Adler, "The Memoirs of C.G. Jung," *The Listener*, 18 July 1963, p. 85.
4 Barbara Hannah, *Jung: His Life and Work, A Biographical Memoir* (London: Michael Joseph, 1976) p. 7.
5 Ibid., p. 8.
6 Jung, "Freud and Jung: Contrasts," *CW* 4, p. 336.
7 Jung, *Analytical Psychology: Notes of the Seminar Given in 1925*, *CW* Supplementary Volume.
8 Ibid., pp. 32–3.
9 Henri Flournoy to Jung, 8 February 1953, Jung archives, E.T.H., Zürich.
10 Jung to Henri Flournoy, *C.G. Jung Letters*, vol. 2: 1951–1961, ed. Gerhard Adler and Aniela Jaffé (London: Routledge and Kegan Paul, 1976), p. 106, translation modified. In a dedicatory note to a collection of his offprints for Jürg Fierz, Jung simply wrote: "I myself have a distaste for autobiography." 21 December 1945, *C.G. Jung Letters*, vol. 1: 1906–1950 (London: Routledge and Kegan Paul, 1973), p. 404.
11 Jung to Gustave Steiner, 30 December 1957, *C.G. Jung Letters*, vol. 2: 1951–1961, p. 406, trans. modified.
12 Jung to J.M. Thorburn, 6 February 1952, *C.G. Jung Letters*, vol. 2: 1951–1961, pp. 38–9.

13 Kurt Wolff, "On Luring Away Authors, or How Authors and Publishers Part Company," *Kurt Wolff: A Portrait in Essays and Letters*, ed. M. Ermarth (Chicago: University of Chicago Press, 1991), p. 21.

14 Richard Hull, "A record of events preceding the publication of Jung's autobiography, as seen by R.F.C. Hull," 27 July 1960, Bollingen archive, Library of Congress. Cited with permission, Mrs Birte-Lena Hull. In her introduction to *Memories*, Aniela Jaffé states that it was Jolande Jacobi who suggested her for this role. The Eckermann–Goethe analogy was not lost on Jung; in a letter to Kurt Wolff, he wrote, "God help me, when I read Eckermann's *Conversations* even Goethe seemed to me like a strutting turkey-cock." Jung to Kurt Wolff, 1 February 1958, *C.G. Jung Letters*, vol. 2: 1951–1961, p. 453.

15 Kurt Wolff to Herbert Read, 27 October 1959, Bollingen archive, Library of Congress.

16 Jung, *Memories, Dreams, Reflections* (London: Flamingo, 1983), p. 7.

17 Henri Ellenberger, "La Psychologie de Carl Gustav Jung: à Propos de son Autobiographie," *L'Union Médicale du Canada*, vol. 93, August 1964, p. 993, trans. mine.

18 Aniela Jaffé, *From the Life and Work of C.G. Jung* (Einsielden: Daimon, 1989), p. 133.

19 One of the first to make these analogies was Arthur Calder-Marshall, in his review, "Jung: the Saint of Psychology," *Time and Tide*, 11–17 July 1963, in which he stated: "This volume . . . is destined to be as much a classic as Rousseau's *Confessions*" (p. 24).

20 Kathleen Raine, "A Sent Man," *The Listener*, 22 August 1963, p. 284.

21 Hans Eysenck, "Patriarch of the Psyche," *The Spectator*, 19 July 1963, p. 86.

22 E. Edinger, *The Creation of Consciousness: Jung's Myth for Modern Man* (Toronto: Inner City Books, 1984), pp. 12–13.

23 Aniela Jaffé, interview with Gene Nameche, Jung oral history archive, Countway Library of Medicine, Harvard Medical Library, Boston, p. 11.

24 Ibid.

25 Jung, *Memories, Dreams, Reflections*, p. 9.

26 Suzanne Wagner, "Remembering Jung: Through the Eyes of Aniela Jaffé," *Psychological Perspectives*, vol. 26, 1992, p. 109.

27 Dr Richard Wolff, whom I would like to thank for facilitating my research, informed me that one of the editors involved in the publication sold it to a bookseller. It was then purchased by Dr James Cheatham and donated to the Harvard Medical Library in May 1979. It bears corrections by several hands, some of which were identified by Alan Elms: Gerald Gross, Aniela Jaffé (through Richard Winston), Richard Hull, Wolfgang Sauerlander, Richard Winston, together with notes labelled 'CGJ,' though not in Jung's hand.

28 Aniela Jaffé to the author, letter dated January 1991. All statements from her letters and from the manuscripts, drafts and transcripts are given in paraphrase, as permission to quote has not been granted by the executor of the Jaffé estate.

29 The transcripts, together with some correspondence concerning their fate, were officially restricted until 1993; I thank William McGuire and Princeton University Press for allowing me to consult them in the Easter of 1991.

30 Aniela Jaffé to William McGuire, 1981, Bollingen archive, Library of Congress.

31 Countway ms., p. 1.

32 Laurens van der Post, *Jung and the Story of our Time* (London: Penguin, 1976), p. 172.

33 Ibid., p. 176.
34 Jung's tribute to Flournoy is published in English in Théodore Flournoy, *From India to the Planet Mars: A Case of Multiple Personality with Imaginary Languages*, ed. Sonu Shamdasani (Princeton: Princeton University Press, 1996). Jung's tributes to Flournoy and Zimmer were also published in the French edition of *Memories*.
35 Countway ms., p. 197.
36 For Jung's relation to James, see Eugene Taylor, "William James and C.G. Jung," *Spring*, 1980; for a complementary critique of the Freudocentric reading of Jung, see his "Jung in his Intellectual Setting: The Swedenborgian Connection," *Studia Swedenborgiana*, vol. 7, 1991.
37 John Kerr, *A Most Dangerous Method: The Story of Jung, Freud and Sabina Spielrein* (New York: Knopf, 1993), p. 503. It is curious that Kerr did not draw upon Spielrein's case history, despite the fact that it has been in the public domain since 1992 in Bernard Minder's "Sabina Spielrein: Jungs Patientin am Burghoelzli," (Ph.D., University of Bern, 1992). (I thank Han Israëls for alerting me to this, and supplying a copy.) Needless to say, this material, together with the letters between Bleuler, Jung and Spielrein's family that Minder has retrieved, occasions a complete re-evaluation of the Jung–Spielrein relationship. The draft letter of referral from Jung to Freud concerning Spielrein in 1905 that Minder has retrieved ("Jung an Freud 1905: Ein Bericht über Sabina Spielrein," *Gesnarus*, vol. 50, 1993), brilliantly confirms Peter Swales's reconstruction in "What Jung *Didn't* Say," *Harvest: Journal for Jungian Studies*, vol. 38, 1992. For further new material on Spielrein, see my "Spielrein's Associations: A Newly Identified Word Association Protocol," *Harvest: Journal for Jungian Studies*, vol. 39, 1993.
38 *CW* 7, p. 295, n. 21.
39 Op. cit., p. 506.
40 Op. cit., p. 507.
41 Ibid.
42 Roger Payne, "A Visit to 228 Seestrasse," *Harvest: Journal for Jungian Studies*, vol. 39, 1993, p. 137.
43 William McGuire provides the following biographical information on Moltzer: "Mary or Maria Moltzer (1874–1944), daughter of a Netherlands distiller, became a nurse as a protest against alcoholic abuse. Had Psycho-analytic training with Jung and after 1913 continued as an analytical psychologist." Ed. William McGuire, *The Freud/Jung Letters* (London: Hogarth/Routledge, 1974), pp. 351–2. For Moltzer's role as Jung's assistant, see Eugene Taylor, "C.G. Jung and the Boston Psychopathologists, 1902–1912," *Voices*, vol. 21, 1985.
44 Ibid., p. 535.
45 Ed. E. Brabant, E. Falzeder and P. Giampieri-Deutsch, *The Correspondence of Sigmund Freud and Sándor Ferenczi*, vol. 1, 1908–1914 (Cambridge, Mass.: Harvard University Press, 1993), p. 446.
46 Jolande Jacobi, interview with Gene Nameche, Jung oral history archive, Countway Library of Medicine, Harvard Medical Library, Boston, Box 3, p. 110.
47 Maria Moltzer to Fanny Bowditch Katz, 1 August 1918, Countway Library of Medicine, Harvard Medical Library, Boston, cited with permission.
48 *CW* 6, p. 454.
49 This issue has been explored in an excellent piece by Alan Elms, "The Auntification of Jung," in *Uncovering Lives: the Uneasy Alliance of Biography and*

Psychology (New York and Oxford: Oxford University Press, 1994, pp. 51–70), which complements the discussion here.

50 Hull, "A record of events," pp. 1–2.

51 Ibid., p. 2.

52 Richard Hull to Aniela Jaffé, 9 September 1961, Bollingen archive, Library of Congress.

53 Richard Hull to Gerald Gross, Bollingen archive, Library of Congress.

54 Hull, "A record of events," p. 4.

55 Cecil Franklin to C.G. Jung, 19 December 1959, Bollingen archive, Library of Congress.

56 Jung to Walther-Niehus Jung, 5 April 1960, *C.G. Jung: Letters*, vol. 2: 1951–1961, p. 550, trans. modified.

57 Herbert Read to John Barrett, 25 May 1960, Bollingen archive, Library of Congress.

58 "Resolution of the Editorial Committee for 'The Collected Works' of Prof. C.G. Jung," Bollingen archive, Library of Congress, signed by Jung on 29 November 1960, and by John Barrett on 13 December 1960.

59 "Die Autobiographie von C.G. Jung," *Die Weltwoche*, 31 August 1962. The German title differs from the English: *Erinnerungen, Träume, Gedanken von C.G. Jung*, aufgezeichnet und herausgegeben von [recorded and edited by] Aniela Jaffé (Olten: Walter Verlag, 1988). Other items in the German edition that were missing in the English editions were a letter by Jung to a 'young student,' Jung's postscript to his *Red Book* and "Details about C.G. Jung's family" by Aniela Jaffé. The latter item was published in English in *Spring*, 1984. There are many discrepancies between the German and English editions, notably numerous passages in the former that are missing from the latter. Some, but by no means all, were published in English by Shoji Muramoto, "Completing the Memoirs: The Passages Omitted or Transposed in the English and Japanese Versions of Jung's Autobiography," *Spring*, 1987. However, given that the text was being translated into English as it was being compiled, it is not possible to consider one or the other as the original version. The French edition was *Ma vie. Souvenirs, rêves et pensées*, recueillis et publiés par Aniela Jaffé (Paris: Gallimard, 1966), trans. Roland Cahen and Yves Le Lay. Details concerning Kurt Wolff are from William McGuire, *Bollingen: An Adventure in Collecting the Past* (Princeton: Princeton University Press, 1982), pp. 273–4 (I thank Charles Boer for recalling this to my attention).

3

JUNG THE *LEONTOCEPHALUS*

Richard Noll

Source: *Spring: A Journal of Archetype and Culture*, 53, (1994), 12–60.

> Awe surrounds the mysteries, particularly the mystery of dei-
> fication. This was one of the most important of the mysteries;
> it gave the immortal value to the individual – it gave certainty
> of immortality. *One gets a peculiar feeling from being put
> through such an initiation . . .*
>
> C.G. Jung, 8 June 1925

There is a significant, *deliberate* omission from Jung's alleged autobiography. We will perhaps never know why its primary author, Aniela
Jaffé, left it out of *Memories, Dreams, Reflections*, but given the incredu-
lous response the reader initially experiences upon finally reading these
long withheld, deeply personal confessions from Jung, a safe bet is that she
knew this material would be misunderstood and was protecting him and
his widely idealized public image from any further devaluation by his
detractors. This missing information is crucial to understanding Jung, the
metaphors he chose for his method of psychotherapy, and the early development of analytical psychology. Indeed, it forms the core of his "personal
myth," elements of which he himself kept secret but which can now be
revealed with a contextual analysis of this important new material.

What did Aniela Jaffé omit from the "official" version of Jung's myth?
We know from her own words that she based the chapter in *Memories,
Dreams, Reflections* known as "Confrontation with the Unconscious" on
"a number of passages from a seminar delivered in 1925 in which Jung
spoke for the first time of his inner development."[1] The complete version
of this famous 1925 Seminar on Analytical Psychology was finally published only in 1989 after decades of existence in mimeographed form in
limited circulation. What is missing from the posthumously published
"official" biography prepared by Jaffé (in collaboration with the editors of
its publishing house, the Jung family, and only with "contributions" by
Jung himself to the project he consistently referred to as "Jaffé's book"

and *not* his own) is an entire episode from Jung's famous December 1913 visionary descent into the unconscious during which, among other things, Jung meets the figures of Elijah and a blind Salome, is encircled and squeezed by a large black snake, himself assumes the stance of the crucified and suffering Christ *which restores sight to Salome, and then experiences his face transforming into that of a lion.* We are familiar with this image of the metamorphosed Jung from the famous frontispiece photograph of a statue of this ancient therioanthropic deity in the book by Jung that bears its assumed name – *Aion*.

Jung was, by his own account, "deified" when he transformed into the *Deus Leontocephalus*, the lion-headed god whose image is found in the sanctuaries of the mystery cult of Mithras of the ancient Roman world (first to fourth centuries C.E.). It is noteworthy that Jung gives his 1951 book on the "phenomenology of the self" – *Aion* – the name of his own secret god-image as revealed to him during this 1913 active imagination, which Jung refers to as his "initiation." Jung must have been haunted by the fact that he was the *Leontocephalos*. He devoted his life to trying to understand this essential epiphany. It was the revelation of the great and unspeakable mystery of the *imago Dei*.

Jung's frequent use of root metaphors derived from the ancient mysteries (especially early in the development of his psychology) has not, to my knowledge, been explored in any detail to date. This is surprising considering the vast number of references to the "mysteries" in general in the *Collected Works*, and in particular those even more frequent ones to Mithras and Mithraism.[2]

I will not attempt a comprehensive review of all of Jung's references to the ancient mysteries, nor will I offer psychodynamic or psychopathological interpretations of Jung's dreams and visions, but instead I will focus on how Jung tried to make sense of his inner experiences, *how he interpreted himself to himself.* Indeed, a careful reading of Jung's remarks reveals that he felt he had undergone a direct initiation into the Mithraic mysteries. It is my opinion that Jung turned to the ancient Greco-Roman mysteries in general and Mithraism in particular as a core symbolic system that provided external grounding for his inner experiences with its corresponding historical material, thus supporting his notion – in his mind – of the "phylogenetic" or (later) "collective unconscious." Later, Jung abandoned his reliance upon the mysteries and Mithraism as historical parallels for analytical psychology and adopted the symbolic metaphors of Gnosticism and alchemy to validate his work. However, it is clear from the seminars on analytical psychology that in 1925, despite his familiarity with Gnosticism and the stirring of interest in alchemy, Jung was still immersed within a Mithraic/ancient mysteries "initiation" model of analytical psychology.

PART I

The ancient mystery cults: Jung and the classical scholars

How and when did Jung become interested in the mysteries? And who provided Jung with these *fin de siècle* imaginings about the classical world?

Jung's self-admitted "obsession" with mythology – perhaps one should say his *possession* by this material – seized him directly after returning from his famous seven-week trip in autumn of 1909 with Sigmund Freud and Sándor Ferenczi to the conference at Clark University in the United States. "Archeology or rather mythology has got me in its grip," he writes to Freud on 14 October 1909 (157 J), just two weeks after returning home to Switzerland. Jung had initially wanted to become an archeologist, and so from a young age he had an active interest in the classical world that would have made him aware of the existence of the ancient mystery cults, at the very least, perhaps, that devoted to the myth of Demeter and Persephone at Eleusis. "All my delight in archeology (buried for years) has sprung into life again" he writes to Freud on 8 November 1909 (159 J), perhaps giving the first indication of a psychotherapeutic return to the fantasies of his childhood that so occupied the initial stages of his confrontation with the unconscious. He first read Friedrich Creuzer's four-volume *Symbolik und Mythologie der alten Völker* (Leipzig, 1810–1823), and then subsequently put special emphasis on the (then) new scholarship documenting the Mithraic mysteries. Apparently his first public presentation of a psychological interpretation of mythological material, including Mithraic iconography, was at a meeting of Swiss psychiatrists in Herisau, Switzerland, in May, 1910.

From 1910 onwards[3] Jung repeatedly makes impassioned references to the ancient mysteries of classical Greece and Rome in his correspondence, lectures and publications. Indeed, such references are frequent in his psychological interpretation and mythological amplification of the fantasies of the unusual and talented American woman Miss Frank Miller, *Wandlungen und Symbole der Libido*, which was published initially in two parts in the *Jahrbuch für psychoanalytische und psychopathologische Forschungen* in the autumns of 1911 and 1912, and in book form in 1912.[4] It was this mammoth effort which, in his mind, decisively severed his allegiance to Sigmund Freud and his ideas.

His new passion for mythology was stimulated by a dream he had during his voyage with Freud. In the dream Jung finds himself descending layer by layer – spatially and temporally – into the foundations of an old house, a dream which Jung later credits for giving him his first conception of the "collective unconscious."[5] In the dream he leaves a "rococo style salon" on the top floor for a fifteenth- or sixteenth-century dwelling on the ground floor, then descends a stone stairway that leads to a room from

"Roman times," and then further down from this level through a "low cave cut into the rock" where, at the lowest levels he found the remnants of a primitive culture, with pottery and scattered human bones and "two human skulls."

This descent (*katabasis*) into an eternal subterranean realm is significant because the candidate for initiation into the Roman world's mysteries of Mithras, the *mystes*,[6] was led down through an underground cave (natural or carved into rock) or structures that resembled caves for the (usually) nocturnal rites of passage. Jung's references to the "cave cut into the rock" in "Roman times" is an exact description of a typical Mithraeum, and perhaps indicates this dream may have been, in his mind, the actual beginning of his initiatory experiences into the Mithraic mysteries which culminated in his December 1913 experiences. Indeed, human skulls have sometimes been found in these Mithraeums, a fact which Jung also knew at some point after this dream supposedly occurred.[7] In any event, such subterranean *loci* of initiations were also part of most of the mystery cults of the ancient world.

Jung's imaginings about the rituals of mystery cults, which had become extinct at least 1,400 years before his own birth, were constructed from elements in the work of primarily three scholars, all of whom were his contemporaries. Two of them are now distinguished for providing the impetus for a century of scholarship on the mysteries of ancient Greece and Rome: the Belgian classicist Franz Cumont, who inspired this new scholarly trend with his researches into the mysteries of Mithras; and the German scholar Richard Reitzenstein, who had a broader interest in all the mysteries of the Hellenistic world.

Cumont was the very first to gather all of the primary evidence of Mithraism in his magisterial two-volume *Textes et monuments figurés relatifs aux mystères de Mithra*, published in 1896 and 1899. It is a comprehensive descriptive and interpretive collection of all of the archeological monuments, inscriptions and texts and references relating to Mithraism from antiquity. A more popular edition of the "Conclusions" of the first volume of Cumont's *magnum opus* was published in French in 1900 and later in German as *Die Mysterien des Mithra*.[8] Jung's library contains the 1911 edition of the latter book as well as Cumont's two-volume set.

Reitzenstein's classic work of 1910, *Die hellenistischen Mysterionreligionen nach ihren Grundgedanken und Wirkungen*,[9] explored the mysteries of the ancient world as "Oriental" (Iranian, Egyptian, Anatolian) spirituality in a Hellenized form. Reitzenstein's work inspired a definitive school of thought in the history of religions which mainly explored the Iranian influence on Gnosticism.[10] Jung cites both Cumont and Reitzenstein in *Wandlungen*. Thus, Jung was well-acquainted with this new trend in classical scholarship and avidly absorbed the details of Cumont's version of Mithraism. He referred to Cumont's volumes repeatedly in his own works from 1911 onwards.

The third scholar whose work is approvingly and repeatedly mentioned by Jung is Albrecht Dieterich. Dieterich's *Eine Mithrasliturgie* (Leipzig: 1st edition, 1903; 2nd edition, 1910) posited that certain key passages from the famous Greek magical papyri[11] were parts of an authentic Mithraic ritual, named by Dieterich the "Mithras Liturgy."[12] (Although this interpretation was rejected by Cumont, it has been supported, in part, by three noted modern scholars of Mithraism – Roger Beck, R.L. Gordon, and David Ulansey – although still doubted by classicist Walter Burkert.)[13] This particular section of the Greek magical papyri begins with an announcement that it is a revelation from "the great god Helios Mithras." It then goes on to describe the celestial ascent of the initiate and a series of prayers of invocation which results in the appearance of, among other entities, Mithras: "a god immensely great, having a bright appearance, youthful, golden-haired, with a white tunic and golden crown and trousers, and holding in his right hand a golden shoulder of a young bull." The "Mithraic Liturgy" ends with some advice from Zeus which Jung scribbled in the upper margin of a famous letter of 31 August 1910 to Sigmund Freud, suggesting it should be adopted as a "motto for psychoanalysis: Give what thou hast, then thou shalt receive."[14] Jung's playful appeal to Freud for a Mithraic credo for psychoanalysis indicates his increasingly strong identification with the Mithraic mysteries.

The "Mithraic Liturgy" is important in the development of Jung's later psychology for another reason: it is the source of the mythological material regarding a phallic "tube hanging down from the sun" which "produces the wind" that matched the delusion of a male patient with paranoid schizophrenia Jung claims (at least in the 1930s) that he met in 1906. (The first version of this story in *Wandlungen* credits his younger associate J.J. Honegger with the discovery – a fact which was changed in later revisions of this book after Honegger's suicide in March 1911, and never mentioned again by Jung.)[15] Jung considered this remarkable story of the "Solar Phallus Man" (as he has been named by Sonu Shamdasani) important independent evidence of the collective unconscious and referred to it often throughout his life, since he believed that the "Mithraic Liturgy" had first appeared in print in 1910 and therefore the patient could not have had access to this particular cluster of symbols. Apparently, however, it wasn't until some time after 1936 (when his fullest account of the case appeared in his paper on "The Concept of the Collective Unconscious") that Jung found out a 1903 first edition of Dieterich's book existed. Jung never admitted (or had forgotten) that the mythological motif of a "solar phallus" (*Sonnenphallus*) was discussed by Creuzer in the third volume of his widely read mythological works that were first published between 1810 and 1823 (see the discussion in note 15). Besides this striking correspondence between the paranoid delusions of a modern man and Mithraic imagery, Jung noted that this patient "thought he was God and Christ in one person." This corresponded to the "ritual transformation into the deity" found in the mysteries of Isis and Mithras, as well as to Jung's interpretation of the "Mithraic Liturgy" as describing "a kind of initiation into mystic experience of the Deity".[16] Perhaps Jung told and retold this story throughout his life because it reminded him so much of something he had experienced himself.

The mysteries and rites of passage

What were the ancient mysteries of pagan antiquity? Modern scholars have added much to our knowledge of these special cults from antiquity and many of the theories that Jung cites about them – particularly those concerning Mithraism – have been revised extensively.[17] Bold assertions about the beliefs and practices of these cults have not been supported by the more conservative scholarship of modern researchers, and so many statements about the mysteries that Jung makes in his works would not be considered supportable today. Perhaps the best single modern treatment of this topic that fascinated Jung so much is Walter Burkert's *Ancient Mystery Cults*, described as a "comparative phenomenology of the ancient mysteries."

According to Burkert, "Mysteries were initiation rituals of a voluntary, personal, and secret character that aimed at a change of mind through experience of the sacred." Also: "Mysteries are a form of personal religion, depending on a private decision and aiming at some form of salvation through closeness to the divine." Participation in the mysteries was not obligatory or unavoidable, unlike participation, for example, in organized "religions" as we commonly think of the concept. Even within the polytheistic world of ancient Greece and Rome regular ritual sacrifices were obliged and were considered a civic duty in some cases (such as making offerings at the temples of the imperial cults of Rome). Burkert explains, "Mysteries are to be seen as a special form of worship offered in the larger context of religious practice. Thus the use of the term 'mystery religions,' as a pervasive and exclusive name for a closed system, is inappropriate. Mystery initiations were an optional activity within polytheistic religion, comparable to, say, a pilgrimage to Santiago de Compostela within the Christian system."

Again, in another passage Burkert notes: "mysteries are initiation ceremonies, cults in which admission and participation depend on some personal ritual to be performed on the initiand. Secrecy and in most cases a nocturnal setting are concomitants of this exclusiveness."[18]

Although the mysteries conveyed to the initiates a sense of "better hopes" or of a "better life," particularly in the underworld, the ancient mysteries were not "religions of salvation" because they were not "religions" in the first place as we know them. Burkert insightfully notes that "the constant use of Christianity as a reference system when dealing with the so-called mystery religions leads to distortions as well as partial clarification, obscuring the often radical difference between the two."[19] Both of Jung's main sources of information, Cumont and Reitzenstein, were particularly guilty of this form of distortion. Cumont once referred to the loss of the "liturgical books of paganism" as the most regrettable one in the metaphoric "great shipwreck" that lost so much of the literature of antiquity. Reitzenstein likewise believed that these "oriental religions" were bound together by shared, systematized articles of faith, a Credo. Although each of the mystery cults was based on a central myth, or *hieros logos*, perhaps even kept in written form along with the sacred ritual instruments in the *cista mystica* ("secret casket"), there is no evidence that such binding Credos or theological works were ever in existence.[20]

The mystery cults of the classical world practiced initiatory rituals which match, in some respects, those "rites of passage" long described by anthropologists. Another contemporary of Jung's, Arnold van Gennep, introduced the concept of "rites of passage" in 1908 in his *Les rites de passage*. They have unique structures and dynamics, he argues, which distinguish them from other forms of ritual. Van Gennep notes that rites of passage are marked by three stages: (1) *separation*, in which some form of symbolic behavior signifies the detachment of the individual or group from an earlier fixed point in the social structure, or from a set of cultural or existential conditions; (2) *margin*, a threshold or "liminal" period during which the characteristics of the initiate are ambiguous (he or she may pass through a cultural realm which has few or none of the attributes of the past or coming state); and (3) *aggregation*, or "reincorporation," in which the passage is complete. The initiate is in a relatively stable state again, and, by virtue of this, has rights and obligations vis-à-vis others of a clearly defined type.[21]

In preliterate cultures, this novel status attained at the stage of reincorporation is an obvious result of those "life crisis" rituals surrounding birth, puberty, illness, and death. However, in the mystery cults of the classical world, the transformation, in our terms, was often more *psychological* than sociological. The individual's status vis-à-vis a particular deity was changed, not his or her social position (unless of course it was within the subculture of the mystery cult, especially the highly structured Mithraic organizations). Furthermore, in many instances (Eleusis, and the many centers of the mysteries of Dionysus) the initiations could be repeated. In the mysteries of Mithras there was a series of grades of initiation, perhaps indicating that within this subculture the "liminal period" could last a period of some years.

Thus, through having the mysteries revealed to one (mysteries are referred to as "seen" by the ancients) the passage is made from one state of being to another. Or, in the words of an individual who had seen the mysteries of Eleusis (an *epoptes*, "one who had seen"), "I came out of the mystery hall feeling like a stranger to myself."[22]

The lost Jungian liturgy washes up on shore

Let us return to the spring of 1925, when Carl Jung "spoke for the first time of his inner development."

He was 49 years old, awaiting the completion of his first half-century of life on 26 July. When the year began he was in the United States and visited the Taos Pueblo Indians of New Mexico. On the 23rd of March of that year he began a weekly seminar in Zürich – his first in English – in which he revealed the personal experiences of his life that formed the foundation for the basic concepts of his psychology. We know many of them from Jaffé's edited version of Jung's remarks in *Memories, Dreams, Reflections*. Let us now consider the full story, finally available to us all in *Analytical Psychology: Notes of the Seminar Given in 1925*.[23]

Jaffé's version of Jung's story in *MDR*[24] is taken largely from the brief remarks made at the end of the lectures Jung gave on 11 May and 1 June 1925.[25] A middle lecture given on 25 May dealt primarily with the problem of opposites and typology. In this familiar version, Jung uses active imagination to make a "descent" into the unconscious, the "land of the dead," where he meets an old man with a white beard and a beautiful young girl, who is blind. The old man introduces himself as "Elijah" and Jung is then "shocked" to learn the girl is Salome. Elijah assures him that this couple "had been together since eternity." With them was a large black snake which had an affinity for Jung. "I stuck close to Elijah because he seemed to be the most reasonable of the three, and to have a clear intelligence. Of Salome I was distinctly suspicious."[26]

In the 1925 seminars Jung then amplifies these figures with references to motifs in mythology and symbolism. He explains that the snake is associated with hero myths. Salome is "an anima figure, blind because, though connecting the conscious and unconscious, she does not see the operation of the unconscious."[27] In *MDR*, Salome is blind because "she does not see the meaning of things."[28] Elijah represents "the wise old prophet," a "factor of intelligence and knowledge." Elijah and Salome are, furthermore, personifications of Logos and Eros, says Jung, but, he adds, "it is very much better to leave these experiences as they are, namely as events, experiences."[29]

One point on which these two versions depart is the important figure of Philemon, Jung's imaginal "guru." In *MDR*, Jung reveals that this figure, "a pagan" with "an Egypto-Hellenistic atmosphere with a Gnostic coloration,"[30] developed out of the Elijah figure in subsequent fantasies. Philemon is not mentioned in the 1925 seminars.

During the lecture Jung delivered on 8 June 1925 (which contains the material not in *MDR*), he further amplifies these figures according to his own typology: "As I am an introverted intellectual my anima contains feeling [that is] quite blind. In my case the anima contains not only Salome, but some of the serpent, which is sensation as well." He describes Salome as an "evil" figure, and confesses: "When Elijah told me he was always with Salome, I thought it was almost blasphemous for him to say this. I had the feeling of diving into an atmosphere that was cruel and full of blood."[31]

This initial voyage into the underworld was followed by a second: the long ignored (suppressed?) story of Jung's deification. Jung tells his audience that, "a few evenings later, I felt that I should continue; so again I tried to follow the same procedure, but *it* would not descend. I remained on the surface."[32] He felt it was an "inner conflict" which prevented him from going down. He imagines "a mountain ridge, a knife edge, on one side a sunny desert country, on the other side darkness." He then sees a white snake on the light side and a dark snake on the dark side, and a fight ensues, but Jung feels it is a fight between 'two dark principles." When the head of the black snake turned white and was defeated, Jung felt he could go on.

He then sees Elijah on a rocky ridge, a ring of boulders, which he interprets as a "Druidic sacred place." Inside, the old man climbs up on a mounded Druidic altar, and then both Elijah and the altar begin to shrink in size while the walls get larger. He sees a tiny woman, "like a doll," who turns out to be Salome. A miniature snake and a house are also seen. Jung then realizes, as the walls keep growing, "I was in the underworld." When they all reach bottom Elijah smiles at him and says, "Why, it is just the same, above or below."[33]

Jung then completes the tale of his second descent into the unconscious with the following remarkable paragraph:

> Then a most disagreeable thing happened. Salome became very interested in me, and she assumed I could cure her blindness. She began to worship me. I said, "Why do you worship me?" She replied, "You are Christ." In spite of my objections she maintained this. I said, "This is madness," and became filled with skeptical resistance. Then I saw the snake approach me. She came close and began to encircle me and press me in her coils. The coils reached up to my heart. I realized as I struggled, that I had assumed the attitude of the Crucifixion. In the agony and the struggle, I sweated so profusely that the water flowed down on all sides of me. Then Salome rose, and she could see. While the snake

was pressing me, I felt that my face had taken on the face of an animal of prey, a lion or a tiger.[34]

Jung then offers rather predictable interpretations of the fight of the snakes, the setting of the descent, and Elijah's Gnostic comment. He also says that, "Salome's approach and her worshipping of me is obviously that side of the inferior function which is surrounded by an aura of evil. I felt her insinuations as a most evil spell."[35]

In a meaningful shift of focus that must have taken only a couple of minutes during the spoken lecture, *Jung then compares his experience with the experience of the ancient mysteries*: "You cannot get conscious of these unconscious facts without giving yourself to them. . . . These images have so much reality that they recommend themselves, and such extraordinary meaning that one is caught. They form part of the ancient mysteries; in fact it is such figures that made the mysteries."[36]

What then follows is the quote that began this essay, in which Jung speaks of the "mystery of deification" which gave "certainty of immortality." It is a remarkable statement of Jung's own "deification." As he interprets it (without, interestingly, ever addressing his *imitatio Christi*):

> One gets a peculiar feeling from being put through such an initiation. The important part that led up to the deification was the snake's encoiling of me. Salome's performance was deification. The animal face which I felt mine transformed into was the famous [Deus] *Leontocephalus* of the Mithraic mysteries, the figure which is represented with a snake coiled around the man, the snake's head resting on the man's head, and the face of the man that of the lion. This statue has only been found in the mystery grottoes (the underchurches, the last remnants of the catacombs). The catacombs were not originally places of concealment, but were chosen as symbolical of a descent into the underworld.[37]

Furthermore, after presenting a few historical details concerning Mithraism as he knew it from the scholarship of his day, Jung tells his audience, "It is almost certain that the symbolical rite of deification played a part in these mysteries." He then proceeds to identify the *Leontocephalus* as "Aion, the eternal being" which is derived from a Persian deity whose name means "the infinitely long duration." He interprets the image of a Mithraic amphora with a flame arising from it that depicts a lion on one side and a snake on the other as "opposites of the world trying to come together with the reconciling symbol between them." Significantly, "The lion is the young, hot, dry July sun in culmination of light, the summer. The serpent is humidity, darkness, the earth, winter."[38]

In closing this astounding lecture, Jung once again returns to his theme of the deification initiation in the ancient mysteries: "In this deification mystery you make yourself into the vessel, and are a vessel of creation in which the opposites reconcile."[39]

An unidentified person then asks Jung the date of this "dream," and he replies: "December 1913. All this is Mithraic symbolism from beginning to end."[40] However, near the end of his life, Jung no longer acknowledged the "Mithraic/ancient mysteries initiation model" of analytical psychology and its origins in the period of his tumultuous "confrontation with the unconscious" (the source of Jung's "personal myth"). For he notes in *MDR* that after the publication of *Psychology and Alchemy* in 1944, "Thus I had at least reached the ground which underlay my own experiences of the years 1913 to 1917; for the process through which I had passed at that time corresponded to the process of alchemical transformation discussed in that book."[41]

Summary of Part I

Let us pause for a moment and look at this material again. In light of this newly revealed episode in Jung's life, what conclusions can be drawn from our discussion so far?

1 His intensive reading in archeology and mythology concerning the mystery cults of Ancient Greece and Rome, and especially in the scholarship on Mithraism (*circa* 1910), gave form to the symbolism of his dreams and visions. "I had read much mythology before this fantasy came to me, and all of this reading entered into the condensation of these figures,"[42] he explains at the very beginning of his landmark 8 June 1925 lecture. Is Jung admitting here that *cryptomnesia* played a role in generating the content of his visionary experiences and dreams? If so, this admission detracts somewhat from the alternative hypothesis that he promoted throughout his life to interpret the source of such experiences – the existence of a *collective unconscious*. Archeology and mythology also gave form to the *interpretation* of psychological phenomena through the (later) hypothesis of the collective unconscious.

2 His fascination with the (then) new scholarship on Mithraism led him to an increasing self-identification with Mithraic images and ideas. His increasing emotional connection with Mithraism induced him to attempt to merge it with psychoanalysis – the matrix of images and ideas that helped form his self-identity and interpret his own and others' psychic life until that time.

3 Two key pieces of evidence that led Jung to develop his concept of the collective unconscious are imbued with Mithraic influences (his 1909 dream of descending temporally and spatially in an old house, and the

correspondences between the delusions of a psychotic patient – the "Solar Phallus Man" – and the Mithraic Liturgy).

4   Jung viewed his *second* visionary descent into the unconscious in December 1913 as an "initiation." Furthermore, since Jung felt "all of this is Mithraic symbolism," it is clear from the flow of the text of his talk that Jung felt this experience was an initiation into the mysteries of Mithras. It was almost as if Jung felt he could enter the timeless realm of the collective unconscious and experience directly *exactly* the same transformative initiation process as the ancients. Sometime after 1925 Jung abandoned Mithraic interpretations and metaphors derived from the mysteries and adopted Gnostic and alchemical ones.

5   The key aspect of Jung's initiation was his "deification." He first imitated the crucified Christ and then transformed into the lion-headed god of Roman Mithraism. He is "certain" that the "rite of deification" played a part in the Mithriac mysteries. This is also the key element of Jung's story which his detractors might interpret as the grandiosity of a paranoid psychotic episode and may have added to the secrecy surrounding the 1925 seminars.

6   Given these observations, it is clear, furthermore, that Jung must have identified with the paranoid schizophrenic patient who was likewise deified as Christ in the context of Mithraic symbolism. Jung may have viewed this patient as someone who had also independently gone through the deification initiation into the Mithraic mysteries, thus validating Jung's experience and his assumptions about the independent existence of the collective unconscious.

7   The blind Salome – despite her corrupt nature – is healed and her sight is restored. This new element to Jung's saga has important implications for Jung's interpretation of his experience as a Mithraic initiation (to be discussed in detail below) as well as for the speculative literature of analytical psychology that pathologizes Jung's life and work based on this single striking symbol.[43]

Did Jung experience a genuine Mithraic initiation as he believed? Are all of the symbols of his visionary initiation "Mithraic from beginning to end?" The answer to this question may lead to a secret that Jung hinted at but never fully revealed.

PART II

Imagining Mithras

Jung's view of Mithraism was largely Cumont's Christianized one: Mithras was an ancient Iranian solar god (like Helios) and a god of correct behavior and order (like Apollo). He is referred to in inscriptions as *Sol*

Invictus, the "invincible sun." Mithraism was a survival of the old dualist Mazdaen religion of ancient Persia, but adapted to the world of the Roman empire. Despite the fact that only men could participate in these mysteries, its wide geographical spread "from the banks of the Black Sea to the mountains of Scotland and to the borders of the great Sahara Desert"[44] was interpreted to mean that Mithraism was the main rival to Christianity, especially since both rose in prominence at about the same time (first to fourth centuries C.E.). Indeed, Cumont argues, if historical events had gone a little differently, the Western world would be Mithraic and not (Judeo-) Christian today. There was even perhaps a voluminous "Mithraic liturgy" akin to that of the Christian Church, but it did not survive antiquity.

There were seven grades of initiation. Mithraic mystery initiations involved "sacramental" feasts at which bread and water were consecrated and at which blood was offered as a sacrifice in ceremonies involving priests in robes who offered prayers, sang hymns, and rang bells[45] – as in the Roman Catholic Church – at the holiest moment of the ritual: the unveiling of the ubiquitous image of Mithras killing a bull, the *tauroctony*. Indeed, practically all of these basic elements of Mithraism – which Jung refers to repeatedly – can be found in a single chapter of Cumont's book on *The Mysteries of Mithra* entitled "The Mithraic Liturgy, Clergy and Devotees."[46]

The problem is that recent scholars have called into question almost all of Cumont's basic assumptions about the Iranian origins and "sacramental" ceremonies of Mithraism. Using the same archeological and textual evidence that Cumont was the first to compile, and hunting down new evidence and deducing new theories in a manner that would rival Sherlock Holmes, Mithraic scholars now offer very different interpretations of the mysteries. The main difficulty is simple: although there is a wealth of archeological material which is well-preserved because the Mithraeums were built underground, there is not one single recorded account of the central myth (*hieros logos*) of Mithraism. Nor does Mithraic iconography provide us with the story.[47] Any attempted interpretation of the myth of Mithras, then, is an imagining, a reconstruction, and indeed the incomplete archeological and textual evidence provides a wonderfully ambiguous hook for the projections of modern scholars and their particular "personal equations."

If Jung did indeed break through to the eternal realm of the collective unconscious and experienced, as an archaic vestige, an actual Mithraic process of transformation, then non-Cumontian elements should appear in the structure of these two December 1913 visions that are supported by the revisionists. My review of the old and new scholarship on Mithraism does not support this hypothesis: all of the elements in Jung's "initiation" can be derived from Cumont and his reading of other scholars. This once again raises the issue of whether all of his experiences were *not* from collective unconscious sources but instead were derivatives of individual or personal unconscious ones – cryptomnesia. If this latter hypothesis is so, the "collective unconscious" may still yet be said to exist – but only on the shelves of Jung's personal library.

However, a review of the aspects of Mithraism that touch upon Jung's personal "symbols of transformation" sheds new light on secrets that Jung never publicly acknowledged, secrets so personally profound that he only hinted at them in public.

The sacrifice: killing the bull

It has been noted that Jung followed the standard position of his day and interpreted Mithras as a "solar deity." More recent interpretations of Mithras and the Mithraic symbolism of the tauroctony, the bull-slaying, suggest an even greater role for Mithras: that of *kosmokrator*, ruler of the entire cosmos, a deity powerful enough indeed to shift the structure of the stars, constellations and planets. This is the interesting theory of Mithraic scholar David Ulansey, who persuasively argues for an astronomical and astrological interpretation of Mithraic iconography in his fascinating book, *The Origins of the Mithraic Mysteries*. According to Ulansey[48] in his section on "Mithras and Helios," Mithras was thus a greater power than the sun, and indeed Mithraic iconography contains many so-called "investiture" scenes in which the sun-god Helios is bowing before Mithras on one knee. However, there are also many images of Mithras and Helios dining or riding a chariot together, and since in the greater Greco-Roman world the role of "cosmic ruler" was more often attributed to the sun, Mithras and Helios might be equals in a sense as *kosmokratores*.

Jung was aware of this relationship between Mithras and Helios, and compares their relationship to that between "Christ and Peter"[49] or as that between a divine father and his son, who are one.[50] The Mithras/Helios distinction has interesting implications for Jung's *katabasis*. Marie-Louise von Franz, Jung's close collaborator and classical language scholar (who must surely have known all of the details of Jung's December 1913 active imagination episodes and their Mithraic implications, although, to my knowledge, she never devoted any single work to Mithraism in depth), mentions in a provocative passage that Elijah "was even identified with the sun-god Helios (from which the word "Elijah" was supposedly derived)."[51] Given the absence of references to "Elijah" in the Mithraic evidence, was the Elijah of Jung's visions in actuality the Mithraic Helios?

A survey of Jung's references to Elijah in the *Collected Works* suggests, instead, that the figure of Elijah in Jung's vision may have been interpreted by him as an epiphany of Mithras himself. Jung's most extensive amplification of Elijah can be found in a November 1953 letter to Père Bruno. Jung says, most emphatically, "Elijah is a *living archetype*." Indeed, Elijah is another manifestation of the Anthropos, "more human than Christ himself," and indeed "more universal in that he included even the pre-Yahwist pagan deities like Baal, El-Elyon, Mithras, Mercurius, and the personification of Allah, al-Khadir."[52]

Thus Jung makes an Elijah/Mithras/Christ/Mercurius equation. Indeed, Jung already made the connection between Elijah and Mithras in his *Wandlungen* in 1911–1912, noting that both are depicted as ascending in a fiery chariot, and he repeated Cumont's speculation that "early Christian paintings of the ascension of Elijah are based partly on the corresponding Mithraic representations."[53] But why would Jung's Mithraic "initiation" include the Hebrew figure of Elijah and not the classical image of Mithras, or perhaps even a replay of the slaying of the bull, the tauroctony?

In his closing paragraph in his letter to Père Bruno Jung gives us an answer:

> To complete the establishment of a living archetype, the historical proofs do not wholly suffice, since one can explain the historical documentation by tradition (whose beginnings, however, always remain unexplained). That the archetype also manifests itself spontaneously outside tradition needs to be added to the evidence.

In Jung's visions Elijah acts as an advisor and sage but only acts as a *kosmokrator* when he guides Jung through a rapid descent to the bottom of the world. Perhaps the famous "Red Book" which contains Jung's illustrated account of these fantasies can shed more light on the Elijah/Mithras identity. We must await further evidence of what Jung himself (or perhaps his imaginal spirit guide or guru, Philemon?) privately thought about this issue to confirm this hypothesis.

And what of the tauroctony? Of what significance could the image of Mithras slaying the bull have to Jung and his secret Mithraic identity?

Let us first describe the classical tauroctony – the only universally found image in Mithraic cult sites and the central icon of Mithraism. Mithras is typically depicted as wearing a Phrygian cap (a felt cap that would have represented someone from the eastern outreaches of the Roman empire, or even beyond). His left knee is on the back of a bull, pinning it down. With his left hand he is pulling the head of the bull back by its nostrils, and with his right hand he is slaying the bull by plunging a dagger or a sword in its neck. Mithras' cape is usually billowing out in a curved shape behind him and on its interior are sometimes depicted seven stars – the seven planets known to the ancient world. A scorpion is generally depicted attacking the bull's testicles, but other figures are also implicated in images of the tauroctony, namely, a snake, a dog, a raven, and sometimes a lion and a cup. The tip of the bull's tail takes on the form of an ear of grain. Two torchbearers dressed like Mithras, Cautes and Cautopates, are included in the tauroctony, holding torches alternately pointed up and pointed down, respectively.

The most intriguing theory of the meaning of the tauroctony is Ulansey's astronomical interpretation of Mithraic symbolism. The key component of this interpretation concerns the fact that the spring and autumn equinoxes occur within the period of one of the twelve zodiacal constellations, and that they proceed backward through the zodiac every 2,500 years or so. From about 4000 B.C.E. the precession of the spring equinoxes has moved from Taurus to Aries to Pisces and, soon, to the Age of Aquarius. In brief, the discovery of the precession of the equinoxes by the Greek astronomer and astrologer Hipparchus around 128 B.C.E. – a major event in the history of science – led Stoics in Tarsus (the capital of Cilicia, a place mentioned by the ancients as an origin of Mithraism) to "hypothesize the existence of a new divinity responsible for this new cosmic phenomenon, a divinity capable of moving the structure of the entire cosmos and thus a divinity of great power."[54] Mithras was this deity, and he is seen killing the bull because it symbolizes the ending of the cosmic age – the Age of Taurus – just prior to the age in which Mithraism was born.

A thriving cult of Perseus in the region of Tarsus may have given rise to Mithraism. Mithras is depicted with a Phrygian cap and is slaying a beast with his face averted just as Perseus is represented when killing the Gorgon, and indeed, the constellation of Perseus is just above that of Taurus in the heavens. Ulansey[55] further interprets the tauroctony by demonstrating that when the spring equinox was in Taurus, a western progression across the celestial equator goes through the following constellations known to the ancients and accounts for the rest of the figures found in the tauroctony (except the Lion): Taurus the Bull, Canis Minor the Dog, Hydra the Snake, Crater the Cup, Corvus the Raven, Scorpius the Scorpion. Indeed, Ulansey's astronomical argument is compelling.

The Mithraic tauroctony is repeatedly explored in Jung's fateful chapter on "The Sacrifice" in *Wandlungen*. This image obviously held deep significance for Jung. His interpretation was that Mithras was the "sacrificer and the sacrificed," but "it is only his animal nature that Mithras sacrifices, his instinctuality."[56] Yet, there is another layer of meaning within this text.

In *Memories, Dreams, Reflections*, Jung reports that he waited two months before writing this chapter because he knew that his new ideas on the nature of the libido would cost him his relationship with Freud. At the time of writing this chapter Jung had been deeply immersed in mythology and right from the start had tried to make sense of the tauroctony. *A disagreement over the tauroctony between Freud and Jung is a telling sign of the dominance of Mithraism over psychoanalysis in Jung's own personal symbolic system.*

In June 1910, a month after Jung's first public lecture on the psychological interpretation of mythological (and Mithraic) material, Jung rejects Freud's interpretation of the Mithraic bull-slaying as "the killing of the animal ego by the human ego, as the *mythological projection of repression*, in which the sublimated part of the human being (the conscious ego) sacrifices (regretfully) its vigorous drives."[57] Instead Jung tells Freud, "there must be something very typical in the fact that the symbol of fecundity, the useful and generally accepted (not censored) *alter ego* of Mithras (the bull), is slain by another sexual symbol. The self-sacrifice is voluntary and involuntary at once (the same conflict as in the death of Christ)."[58] Here we see the beginnings of Jung's firm but polite rejection of Freud, dismissing the psychoanalytic role of an unconscious censor that keeps the instincts out of awareness and putting forth instead a more pagan interpretation that views the Mithraic bull as an accepted alter ego of Mithras.

There is yet another more poignant meaning of the tauroctony for Jung, and indeed, I would venture to say it forms part of a secret encased in the *cista mystica* of Jung's life and work that can only be unlocked with a Mithraic key. Jung notes in this same letter of 26 June 1910 to Freud that "the Mithras myth has undergone an adaptation to the calendar," revealing to us that he has read Cumont and has likewise noted the astronomical and *astrological* basis of Mithraic symbolism.[59]

My personal guess is that Jung initially took up the study of astrology to decipher Mithraic symbolism. "My evenings are taken up largely with astrology," he writes to Freud on 12 June 1911, further reporting that, "I make horoscopic calculations in order to find a clue to the core of psychological truth."[60] Aware of the great differences in psychological temperament between himself and Freud, and disturbed by the growing tensions between them during this time, it is highly probable that Jung constructed and analyzed Freud's astrological chart. Jung of course knew that Freud, born on 6 May 1857, had as his astrological sun sign Taurus, the Bull.

The centrality of the Mithraic tauroctony in "The Sacrifice" now takes on new meaning: *it symbolizes the triumph of Jung's broader concept of libido over the strictly instinctual (sexual or venereal) libido theory of Freud.* More importantly, it symbolized Jung's sacrifice of Freud himself. His final break with Freud is therefore heralded repeatedly with every reference to the "killing of the bull" in the chapter on "The Sacrifice."

We know that in 1911 Antonia Wolff had entered Jung's life as his assistant, and it is thought that it was she who taught astrology to Jung. We know for certain that while writing "The Sacrifice" in early 1912 Jung connected the Mithraic tauroctony with the astrological sign Taurus and with sexuality in a very revealing footnote (number 30 in the original) to the section where the tauroctony is discussed in detail: "Taurus is astrologically the Domicilium Veneris."[61] This was no doubt yet another hint from Jung to his readers that this chapter contained veiled references to his knowing sacrifice of his relationship with Freud and Freud's sexual theory of libido.

Freud's fears of patricide are well known. It is not known how well Freud knew astrology, but surely he must have at least known his own sun sign was Taurus. Did Jung's fascination with the Mithraic image of the slaying of the bull feed into Freud's fears that Jung had a "death-wish" against him? Freud was a master at the language of symbolism and would cast an analytic glance at the obsessions of anyone – and especially those of a trusted disciple who may have harbored secret desires to slay the father.

Leonticha: Jung the Leo, Jung the Leontocephalus

There is yet another secret awaiting us.

I have documented the evidence for Jung's personal belief that his transformative December 1913 active imagination sessions were an "initiation" into the ancient mysteries of Mithras. What he certainly knew, but did not share with his amazed audience that spring in 1925, was that the initiation he underwent was of a very specific type: the achievement of a very special status within the Mithraic mysteries. Let us now look closer at the initiatory process in Mithraism and thereby reveal a fact about Jung's life which has been hidden for eighty years.

Based on some remarks by the Christian apologist Jerome (circa 342–420 C.E.) and on archeological evidence (primarily from the Mithraeum of Felicissimus at the Roman sea port at Ostia), we know that there were seven grades of initiation into the Mithraic mysteries. They were, in ascending order, *corax* (raven), *nymphus* (embryo), *miles* (soldier), *leo* (lion), *perses* (Persian? Or, the name of the son of Perseus?), *heliodromus* (sun-runner), and *pater* (father). Most of the references that survive from antiquity concern the grades *leo* and *pater*, and we know next to nothing about the grades of *perses* and *heliodromus*. According to the ancient observer Pallas (cited by Porphyry), while the members of the *corax* level of initiates were called "servants," those initiates of the grade *leo* – known as the *leones* – were acknowledged as "participants." Thus it has been posited that members of the first three grades of initiation were not yet allowed to partake of the extraordinary experience that would mark one as a full initiate into the mysteries of Mithras. This apparently only happened to those who made it to the grade of initiation known as *leo*. Indeed, as Mithraic scholar R.L. Gordon observes in his fascinating structural analysis of Mithraic initiation, the grade *Leo* marked a very important moment in the initiate's progress, indeed a "large shift in status, from some stage of preparation to 'membership.'"[62]

The conclusion I have reached in light of this new information is this: As late as 1925, twelve years after his first experiments with active imagination, Jung continued to interpret those experiences as *an initiation into a specific grade of the Mithraic mysteries – that of "leo."* This special level of initiation into the Mithraic mysteries was referred to as the *Leonticha.* However, he never publicly admitted this fact. To further verify that Jung had prior knowledge of the significance of the grade of *leo*, we need look no further than Jung's primary source for inspiration, Franz Cumont. In *The Mysteries of Mithra*, a book Jung owned and cited repeatedly, Cumont writes: "We may conclude from a passage in Porphyry that the taking of the first three degrees did not authorize participation in the mysteries. . . . Only the mystics that had received the Leontics became Participants . . . and it is for this reason that the grade of *Leo* is mentioned more frequently in the inscriptions than any other."[63] Jung only admits his knowledge of the grade of *Leo* in the Mithraic mysteries in two places in the *Collected Works*, a footnote in *Wandlungen*[64] and much later in his life in *Mysterium Coniunctionis* when comparing them to stages in the alchemical *opus*: "Each of these stages stands for a new degree of insight, wisdom, and initiation, just as the Mithraic eagles, lions, and sun-messengers signify grades of initiation."[65]

What did it mean to become one of the *leones* in the mysteries of Mithras? *And what did his status as leo mean to Jung?*

The objects associated with the grade of *leo* depicted on the mosaic floor of the Mitreo di Felicissimo at Ostia give us some clues: a fire-shovel, a *sistrum* (a "sacred rattle," which in the Greco-Roman world was associated with Egypt and was imported as part of the ritual instruments of the cult of Isis), and a thunderbolt. Fire is associated with the grade *leo*, as it is with the astrological sign of Leo, which was Jung's sun sign (he was born on 26 July 1875). The thunderbolt was a symbol of Zeus, and in the classical world the constellation Leo was under the tutelage of Zeus.[66] In the Greco-Roman world, lions held a special status among animals. Gordon[67] notes that it was believed that lions could be divided into two other categories, as human beings with intelligence and moral acumen, and as gods who could mete out divine retribution. Furthermore, lions were thought of as "fire-filled and as intimately associated with the sun," and their powerful fiery-breath was a vehicle of divine punishment, for fire purifies. The initiate who attains the status of *leo*, therefore, would assume powers attributed to lions in the ancient world.

This is borne out by the literary references to the *leonticha*. In *On the Cave of the Nymphs in the Odyssey*, Porphyry states that "the *leo* is an initiate of fire, which purifies."[68] In the Mithraic mysteries the *leones* were responsible for burning incense and other aromatics, which in the ancient world were also substances associated with the sun.[69] The *sistrum*, or sacred rattle, was used to ward off malevolent influences and to purify the sacred ritual site.

Therefore, the cluster of symbols associated with the status of *leo* mirrored those of lions: sun/fire/purity/mediation (between men and gods)/ the constellation Leo. Jung reveals his knowledge of this symbolic cluster in his amplification of the leonine qualities of the lion-headed god and a special Mithraic amphora in the 1925 Seminars.[70] And as we know from Jung's later work, these symbols – especially those of fire and of lions – form part of the transformation process in the alchemical *opus* as well.[71]

Jung knew these descriptions by ancient authors of the special status of *leo* through Cumont's works. He may have also known a passage found in Pliny's *Natural History* (an encyclopaedic work which he cites in *Wandlungen*) which states, according to a paraphrase by Gordon, "Man-eating lions in Libya were crucified as though they were human malefactors."[72] Recall that in his December 1913 active imagination Jung assumed the stance of the crucified Christ and then transformed into the lion-headed god. *Could these passages from his readings in archeology and mythology have provided Jung with the necessary elements that were cryptomnestically "condensed," as he put it, into his visionary "deification"?*

The mystery of deification

In Jung's pivotal episode in his confrontation with the unconscious he reports that he transformed into the *Deus Leontocephalus*, the lion-headed god of the Mithraic mysteries. He interpreted this as the climax of his initiation, and, as he knew *and kept secret*, it was his initiation into the very special grade of *leo* in these mysteries. We do not know enough about the rituals of Mithraic initiation or their associated beliefs, so it is impossible to conclusively state that the culmination of the *leonticha* was the transformation of initiate into the *Deus Leontocephalus*. But it is clear from Jung's reading of Cumont and the archeological research he did in preparing *Wandlungen* that he believed the process of "becoming-one-with-god" was the climax of the initiation process in the Mithraic mysteries. To Jung this would mean becoming one with Mithras or donning a lion's mask (as Cumont describes) and becoming one with the *Deus Leontocephalus*.

The lion-headed god of Mithraism has remained a perplexing figure. Mithraic scholar Howard Jackson's 1985 paper on "The Meaning and Function of the Leontocephaline in Roman Mithraism"[73] provides the best review of the literature on the *Deus Leontocephalus*, and so readers desiring a fuller treatment of this figure are referred to that source. Jung, following Cumont, thought he was the Hellenistic deity known as *Aion*, although only human-headed figures, not lion-headed ones, seemed to represent this deity. Indeed, as Jackson cautions, "the early identification of the god . . . as [Aion] . . . certainly reflects the deity's person, though it may not correctly express the name by which the Mithraists knew him."[74] However, whatever the name of this deity, Jackson concludes:

> there is general agreement among scholars that many of its most common attributes which the deity possesses suffice to identify it as what late antique texts often term a [*kosmokrator*], an astrologically conditioned embodiment of the world-engendering and world-ruling Power generated by the endless revolution of all wheels of the celestial dynamo.[75]

Thus, what we may possibly have in the *Deus Leontocephalus* is a therioanthropic version of Mithras,[76] an animal version of his human form, or, given the specifically solar qualities of the lion, perhaps a manifestation of Mithras' companion and fellow *kosmokrator*, Helios. According to Ulansey, "the Mithraic *leo's* initiation, then, made him the companion of Mithras-as-Helios."[77]

Let us now return to the *leonticha*. Jackson tells us that, "One can scarcely doubt that the leontocephaline had some bearing on the Mithraic mysteries, and specifically for the Mithraic grade *leo*.[78] He notes that, as supporting evidence, there is a portrait of a lion-headed human being who specifically represents the grade *leo* on the Konjica relief from Dalmatia. The lightning bolt of Zeus is also found on some leontocephaline figures as well as in the Mithraeum at Ostia as a representation of the grade *leo*. Furthermore, Jackson notes, the leontocephaline is also associated with fire and fire-breathing or blowing, and fire-kindling is one of its attributes, and that "the text from Porphyry shows that the lion-headed figure represents that into knowledge of which the candidates were being initiated."[79]

What is this knowledge revealed to the *leo*? Jung knew: "it gave the immortal value to the individual – it gave certainty of immortality."[80] Becoming a "participant" in the mysteries at the grade of *leo* probably conferred an eternal status on the individual. This may be conjectured from the specific form the lion-headed god took – as a variant of the Hellenistic god of eternity, Aion.[81] In the Tavistock Lectures of 1935 Jung gives an accurate description of this deity:

> In the cult of Mithras there is a peculiar kind of god, the key god Aion, whose presence could not be explained; but I think it is quite understandable. He is represented with the winged body of a man and the head of a lion, and he is encoiled by a snake which rises up over his head. . . . He is Infinite Time and Long Duration; he is the supreme god of the Mithraic hierarchy and creates and destroys all things. . . . He is a sun-god. Leo is the zodiacal sign where the sun dwells in summer, while the snake symbolizes the

winter or wet time. So Aion, the lion-headed god with the snake round his body, again represents the union of opposites, light and dark, male and female, creation and destruction.

The god is represented as having his arms crossed and holding a key in each hand. He is the spiritual father of St. Peter, for he, too, holds the keys. The keys which Aion is holding are the keys to the past and future.[82]

As Jackson notes, the "crucial attributes" of the lion-headed god are "the serpent-entwined body, the wings, the clutched keys."[83] Jung's deification experience did not include the wings or clutched keys, but these aspects were part of the very first manifestation of the imaginal figure that evolved out of Elijah: Philemon.

Philemon, as has been noted, is not mentioned by Jung in the 1925 seminar. We do know that Philemon formed a living part of Jung's life for quite some time, and that he was painting Philemon's portrait at Bollingen in the 1920s. In *MDR* Jung reports that at some point after December 1913, the figure of Philemon first appeared to him in a dream of a "winged being sailing across the sky." He was an "old man with the horns of a bull," perhaps indicating once again a Mithraic influence. "He held a bunch of four keys, one of which he clutched as if he were about to open a lock. He had the wings of the kingfisher with its characteristic colors."[84]

It is now clear that Philemon is an Aion figure that combines Mithraic and Gnostic elements. We know that Jung describes Philemon as "a pagan" with "an Egypto-Hellenistic atmosphere with a Gnostic coloration."[85] It is interesting to note that there was a thriving cult of Aion in Egypt, specifically, in Ptolemaic Alexandria[86] – a major center of Gnosticism, which Jung studied intensively from 1916 onwards. By 1916 Jung began to link his self-identity and personal destiny with Gnosticism, and even took on the pseudonym (and literary voice) of the second-century Gnostic leader Basilides of Alexandria when (automatically) writing his mediumistic *Septem Sermones Ad Mortuos*. Thus, the elements of mythological and archeological knowledge concerning Mithraism and Gnosticism that became important to Jung are "condensed" into Philemon, another symbol of the self for Jung, a transformed *imago dei* which became dominant when he began to move from a fascination with one ancient tradition (the Mithraic mysteries, circa 1910–1914) to another (Gnosticism, circa 1916).[87]

"Mithras . . . detested the race of women"

There is one more aspect of the missing visionary journey from Jung's official "autobiography" that requires comment. It is the role of Salome in Jung's initiation into the Mithraic mystery of deification.

The Mithraic mysteries were strictly a male society. The membership was largely comprised of Roman soldiers, merchants and some male slaves. The Mithraeums of the ancient world – large enough for only about twenty to forty or so initiates – contain no images of women, nor do they contain any inscriptions concerning women. Mithras himself is depicted as being born from a stone – *not* from a woman. A legend concerning the genesis of a mountain in Armenia named after a figure named Diorphos also involves Mithras in a *petra genetrix* (birth stone): "Mithras wished to have a son, but detested the race of women; and so he masturbated onto a rock. The stone became pregnant and when the proper time had come it produced a child named Diorphos."[88] In addition, as Gordon explained and as Luther Martin so succinctly puts it, even "the names of the Mithraic initiation grades all have in common the systematic exclusion or suppression of the feminine."[89]

If all of this is true about Mithraism, then what is the female figure of Salome doing in Jung's process of transformation that he himself says is "Mithraic symbolism from beginning to end"?

I propose that Jung's experience of Salome is quite consistent with the Mithraic perspective, which Jung certainly absorbed through his reading. Jung mistrusts Salome, who is initially blind. She is an "evil" figure, and what's more she is "surrounded by an aura of evil" and produces "an atmosphere that was cruel and full of blood." He feels "her insinuations [that he is Christ] as a most evil spell." Thus we have here the notion of the feminine as an evil, corrupting, polluting, dangerous force that is not to be trusted.

The very structure of Mithraism implies it was a mystery cult based on a series of rites of passage that necessitated *separation from women* before the transformative, liminal stage could be entered and successfully completed. Furthermore, the apex of the initiatory process, the achievement of the status of *pater* ("father"), signified the end of the long liminal period. No further transformation need occur, for *pater* was the ideal end of the initiation process, in a sense *a state of being outside of the initiation grades themselves*.[90] The very name chosen for this exalted state of being – "father" – implies "not mother," "never mother," "never will be mother." It is profoundly akin to the role of the hero-myth that was so important to Jung at the time of these visions and which forms the basis of his *Wandlungen*: the triumph over the urge to regress or return to the mother. From Jung's point of view, the achievement of the status of *pater* in the mysteries of Mithras – and Jung knew about the initiatory grade of *pater* and its significance from Cumont – would be equivalent to the successful outcome of the challenges of the hero, the triumph of the whole personality over the "infantile personality" that wishes to regress.

As Gordon points out, the only reference to women in connection with the Mithraic mysteries refers to them as "hyenas." Porphyry quotes Pallas as saying: "Those responsible for initiations in the Mysteries typically allegorized our common nature with the animals by imagining us in the form of animals; thus they called the initiates who had been fully admitted into their Mysteries 'lions,' women 'hyenas,' and the underlings 'ravens.'"[91] This passage is discussed in an 1896 volume by Cumont, and thus may have attracted Jung's attention.[92]

In his article Gordon tries to understand the nature of Mithraic symbolism by reconstructing the images of these various terms (lions, ravens, etc.) as they would have appeared in the minds of the average person in the Hellenistic world. Ravens and particularly lions have primarily positive attributes, many of which link humankind with the gods. As he documents,[93] hyenas have a peculiarly malevolent, corrupting and polluting aspect to them. They are associated with "human witches or sorceresses," indeed the *lamia* of ancient Greek folklore that, among other things, was "wont to remove its eyes."[94] Most importantly to the ancients, the *eyes* of the hyena had a special significance: "the hyena is the only animal in the Greco-Roman 'encyclopedia' proper which possessed the evil eye."[95]

Pliny's *Natural History* – which, as mentioned above, was familiar to Jung and is cited in his 1912 book – is the source of much of this information about the characteristics of hyenas. Pliny says hyenas have the "highest regard" of magicians for their power to "snare men whom [they have] driven out of their minds."[96] He also says that hyenas can paralyze any creature it looks at three times, "by magic, I suppose." The same source – Pliny – also tells us that in the Hellenistic world it was believed that *women* possess the evil eye, the power to bewitch and fascinate men. Gordon's final statement of his conclusions regarding this issue deserves to be cited in full: "I would argue that the evil eye is another of the links between the hyena and the 'race of women', and intimately connected with the ability of both to derange men."[97]

Did Jung "condense" (through cryptomnesia?) in the figure of Salome the systematic Mithraic denial of women – of which Jung was certainly well aware – with the information Jung read in Pliny regarding the cluster of meanings connecting women/hyenas/malevolent magic/the evil eye/the power to destroy the minds of men? The most striking attributes of Salome in Jung's account are her "evilness" and her eyes, which are not "evil" but are special because they are "blind." In this way many of the Hellenistic attitudes towards both women and hyenas are represented in the figure of Salome. I will leave speculation about the symbolic significance of Jung's curing her blindness through his deification to others. In this discussion I am only interested in demonstrating how the figure of Salome is consistent with Mithraic symbolism and with Jung's own incorporation of this system of meaning into his "personal myth" – the *hieros logos* or sacred text of analytical psychology.

Summary

In "Late Thoughts," one of the chapters of *MDR* that Jung wrote by hand himself, Jung launches into a cryptic discussion of the importance of "secrets" (the ancients would refer to this as *mysteria*). Clearly Jung is hinting at something about himself in these passages, but what? "There is no better means of intensifying the treasured feeling of individuality than the possession of a secret which the individual is pledged to guard,"[98] he counsels. And more significantly:

> Like the initiate of a secret society who has broken free from the undifferentiated collectivity, the individual on his lonely path needs a secret which for various reasons he may not or cannot reveal. Such a secret reinforces him in the isolation of his individual aims. A great many individuals cannot bear this isolation. . . . Only a secret which the individual cannot betray – one which he fears to give away, or which he cannot formulate in words, and which therefore seems to belong to the category of crazy ideas – can prevent the otherwise inevitable retrogression.[99]

It is my opinion that the "secret" Jung kept throughout his life was the fact that his increasing fascination with Mithraism from about 1910 onward led – as he interpreted it – to his December 1913 initiation into the Mithraic mysteries, and what's more, it was an initiation into the special grade of those mysteries, the grade of *leo*. I have used a "Mithraic key" to unlock possible secrets hidden in Jung's life and work. The climax of his attainment of *leo* status was his self-proclaimed "deification" as the *Deus Leontocephalus*, the Mithraic lion-headed god perhaps known as Aion, and that this gave the initiate Jung the "certainty of immortality." In 1925 it is still clear from his seminar lectures that Jung was using metaphors from his readings on the ancient mysteries, and Mithraism in particular,[100] to ground his discoveries in historical parallels. Alchemy later took the place of the mysteries and Mithraic symbolism in his work. Key experiences that convinced Jung of the collective unconscious (his dreams and visions and the delusions of a psychiatric patient, the "Solar Phallus Man") are imbued with Mithraic influences. I believe Jung probably took up astrology as a way to unlock the secrets of Mithraic symbolism. His frequent references to the Mithraic tauroctony in "The Sacrifice" in *Wandlungen und Symbole der Libido* cry out his anguish over sacrificing his relationship with Freud, astrologically characterized by Taurus the bull. The blind Salome in his 1913 "initiation" fits well into Jung's interpretation of his experiences as "Mithraic" from beginning to end, as she represents the necessary separation from women through devaluation that was needed before the transformation process could develop in the male initiates of the Mithraic mysteries. In Jung's later experiments with active imagination, the Mithraic Aion transformed into the Gnostic Philemon.

To open now the first pages of *Aion* (1951) is to realize that the frontispiece photograph is Jung the *Leontocephalus*, Jung's secret experience of the self, his revealed *imago dei*.

Notes

1 "Introduction," in C.G. Jung, *Memories, Dreams, Reflections*, vii.
2 The lack of scholarship in the literature of analytical psychology on the figure of Mithras is astounding. Even James Hillman, who has otherwise attempted to amplify the implicit mythology of analytical psychology with his paper on Dionysus in Jung's work and in many other publications, has neglected Mithras. This fact is even more curious since even a quick check of the *General Index* of the *Collected Works* lists more than twice as many references to Mithras than to Dionysus. Perhaps even more surprising, given his unquestioned erudition, Hillman neglects to mention the important scholarship on the mysteries and on Mithras and their subterranean initiations in his book, *The Dream and the Underworld* (New York: Harper & Row, 1979) which is directly concerned with such Hades-metaphors.

A fuller treatment of the considerable influence of the ancient mystery cults of the classical world on Jung and the early development of analytical psychology was to have been explored in a book I prepared (but which was never published) on the subject, *Mysteria: Initiation, Transformation and the Ancient Mysteries in the Psychology of C.G. Jung*. Such influences are many. For example, the famous first dream of childhood that Jung could remember as an adult (and which he kept secret until 1940 when he was 65 years old) could very well have been interpreted by him as an initiation into the ancient mysteries of Dionysus. In the dream the child Jung enters a stone-lined underground chamber beneath a meadow and is terrified when he sees a giant phallus on a throne, and then hears his mother's voice call out to him, "Yes, look at him, that is the man-eater!" Jung acknowledges in *Memories, Dreams, Reflections* that, years later, he realized that a "ritual phallus" had been revealed to him in this dream. However, he diverts the discussion to his conflicts with Christianity and does not mention any connection with the Dionysian mysteries which involved underground initiations in which, as far as we can tell, a ritual phallus in a basket (*liknon*) was uncovered and shown to the initiate. The orgiasts of Dionysus were known as the *homophagoi* or "man-eaters," and Jung's mother's instructions for him to "look" at the ritual phallus is consistent with the "revealed" nature of the ancient mysteries, for the mysteries were "seen."

Jung's anguished attempt to understand this dark, phallic, subterranean God in light of the image of Jesus Christ of his early childhood religious education echoes *the* major historical conflict of the fourth century A.D., for the primary threat to early Christianity was probably not Mithraism, but instead, the cult of Dionysus. As the classicist G.W. Bowersock notes, "In late antiquity, the preeminent pagan god seems to have been Dionysus" (*Hellenism in Late Antiquity*, Ann Arbor: University of Michigan Press, 1990, p. 41). A wonderful discussion of this dream and related imagery in Jung's life can be found in Daniel Noel, "Veiled Kabir: C.G. Jung's Phallic Self-Image," *Spring* 1974, pp. 224–242, although no connection is made to the Dionysian mysteries.

I wish to thank the following members of the informal "mystery cult" that has formed through their repeated attendance at a series of seminars on these and related topics which I led in the summer and fall of 1991 and the spring and summer of 1992 for the Aion Society and the C.G. Jung Center of Philadelphia (2008 Chancellor Street, Philadelphia, PA 19103): Barbara Crawford (resident *soror mystica*), Don Zenner, Pam Donleavy, Mary Stamper, Jeanie Jaffe, Marsha Pilz, Bill Halter, Marcia Kapps, Scott Stehle, Dawn Stehle, Jack Giegerich, Jack Roddy, Jean Ritzke, Virginia Loftus, Anne Yarnall, Margetty Coe, Virginia Muhlenberg, George Bernato, Dorothy Reichardt, Mac Fleming, Kate Barcus, Robert A. Clark, M.D. (an early translator of Jung), Jack Light, Thorpe Feidt and Ken Ford. Thanks also go to Anne Malone and Leonard George for their contributions to my knowledge of Mithraism and for keeping me sane, and to Regina Cudemo, Dolores Brien, James Hillman, John Beebe, Charles Boer, David Ulansey, John Kerr and Sonu Shamdasani for reading earlier versions of this paper and improving it with their comments and criticisms as it developed.

This paper is intended to be a contribution to the paradigm shift presently underway in the Jungian world. In essence, this shift may be characterized as a movement from idealization to humanization, or from hagiography to critical history. I join a growing number of other scholars in this project: Peter Homans, Eugene Taylor, Claire Douglas, and especially Sonu Shamdasani and John Kerr. The examination of the historical record of Jung's life and work – rarely before conducted in a non-hagiographic manner by "Jungians" themselves – has led to new insights into the development of Jung's ideas and character. This new historical research has profound implications for the theory and practice of Jungian psychology as it is known today. The eventual publication of Aniela Jaffé's early, unexpurgated version of *MDR* under her own authorship would be a great help to presenting Jung to the world in the way he apparently wanted to be presented: warts and all. I have read the unexpurgated version of *MDR* in the archives of the Countway Library of Medicine, Harvard Medical School, in Boston and feel that the omitted material (such as the chapters on Toni Wolff [not at the Countway], and on William James and Théodore Flournoy, etc.,) could only contribute to the humanization of Jung. We all owe a great debt to Sonu Shamdasani for discovering those materials and drawing our attention to the controversy over *MDR*.

3 The first published mention of the Mithraic mysteries is in Jung's letter to Sigmund Freud dated 26 June 1910 (200 J). All references to specific letters between Freud and Jung will follow the coding in W. McGuire (ed.), *The Freud–Jung Letters* (London: The Hogarth Press and Routledge & Kegan Paul, 1974).

4 For exemplary scholarship on Miss Frank Miller and her importance to Jung's own psychological development, her influence on his later psychological method, and the factors involved in Jung's development of *Wandlungen und Symbole der Libido*, see Sonu Shamdasani, "A Woman Called Frank," *Spring* 50 (1990), and John Kerr, "Freud, Jung and Sabina Spielrein," in Paul Stepansky (ed.), *Freud: Appraisals and Reappraisals*, vol. 3 (Hillsdale, NJ: The Analytic Press, 1988).

5 C.G. Jung, *MDR*, 158–159.

6 *Mystes* as a word for the candidate for an initiation (*myesis*) can be traced back to Mycenean Greek. *Mysteria* is derived from the same root, *myeo* ("to initiate"). The Latin translation of *mysteria*, *myein*, *myesis* is *initia*, *initiare*,

initiatio. A word family more commonly used in Greek that provided much of the same sacred vocabulary is derived from the verb *telein,* "to accomplish," "to celebrate," "to initiate." Related terms are *telestes* for "initiation priest," *telete* for "ritual" or "initiation" or "festival," and *telesterion* for "initiation hall" or "mystery hall." At Eleusis, the main building is the *Telesterion,* and the ritual events were referred to as *Mysteria.* The mysteries of Dionysus were referred to using variants of the *telein* root. Thus, *Dionysoi telesthenai* means "to be initiated into the mysteries of Dionysus." The "mysteries of Mithras" was the usual designation in the classical world, although they were also referred to as *teletai.* W. Burkert, *Ancient Mystery Cults* (Cambridge: Harvard University Press, 1987) provides these clarifications and many others in the introduction to his exemplary volume.

7 This fact is reported in Franz Cumont's *Textes et monuments figurés relatifs aux mystères de Mithra,* vol. II, 44 (Brussels: H. Lamertin, 1896 [I], 1899 [II]), a two-volume set which Jung owned (see the discussion below) and probably purchased in 1909 or 1910. Since antiquity some Christian apologists have suggested that some sort of ritual murder or human sacrifice may have been part of the rituals of some Mithraic cults, although the evidence for this is sketchy.

8 The work appeared in English rather quickly as well. See Franz Cumont, *The Mysteries of Mithra* (New York: Open Court, 1903).

9 R. Reitzenstein, *Die hellenistischen Mysterienreligionen nach ihren Grundgedanken und Wirkungen* (Leipzig, 1910).

10 The hypothesized Iranian influences on Gnosticism by Reitzenstein and his school have been largely discarded by modern scholars, a growing number of whom argue against any pre-Christian origins of Gnosticism at all (see the persuasive volume in this vein by Simone Pétrement, *A Separate God: The Christian Origins of Gnosticism,* San Francisco: HarperSanFrancisco, 1984). Cumont's main thesis, which has come under attack in recent years, is that Mithraism is of Iranian origin. His view – and those of scholars who did not challenge it until 1971, when the First International Congress of Mithraic Studies was held at Manchester University in England – is that since "Mithras" is the Latin and Greek equivalent of the ancient Iranian god Mithra, and because the Romans believed that the mysteries were associated with Persia, Mithraism was a survival or continuation of this ancient Iranian religion. Cumont's life's work was devoted to making the archeological evidence fit this theory point by point, even to the exclusion of disconfirming information. For a summary of the scholarship on "Mithraism since Franz Cumont" see the comprehensive review article by R. Beck in *Aufstieg und Niedergang der römischen Welt* (New York: Walter de Gruyter, 1984). It is interesting to speculate on whether Jung's fascination with Zarathustra – also of Iranian origin – is related to his interest in Mithras.

11 The "Greek magical papyri" is the commonly known label for the large collection of papyri from Greco-Roman Egypt that date from the second century B.C.E. to the fifth century C.E. They were acquired in an unknown manner and sold to European museums by Jean d'Anastasi (1780?–1857), a consular representative of Sweden to Egypt. The collection of magical spells, hymns and rituals that comprise the content of these papyri apparently came from a single collection in Thebes, and possibly from an authentic *magus* and scholar who actually used these magical spells for his own ends. Albrecht Dieterich was the first to suggest that all of these papyri should be collected together and translated in a single authoritative edition, an idea that emerged

when he taught a graduate seminar on the magical papyri in 1905 at the University of Heidelberg. Although Dieterich's death in 1908 and the First World War delayed the collaborative project that arose to accomplish this end, the two volumes of the *Papyri Graecae Magicae* (often abbreviated to the *PGM*) appeared in 1928 and 1931 under the editorship of one of Dieterich's former pupils, Karl Preisendanz. Hans Dieter Betz, the editor of the even more comprehensive English translation, *The Greek Magical Papyri in Translation* (Chicago: University of Chicago Press, 1986), xlii, asserts that "Their discovery is as important for Greco-Roman religions as is the discovery of the Qumran texts for Judaism or the Nag Hammadi library for Gnosticism." Jung considered this material to be extremely important and makes repeated references to the Preisendanz edition in his works after 1928.

Jung's fascination with the Greek Magical Papyri is notable for the similarity of its suggested magical procedures with Jung's "descent into the unconscious" and his techniques of "active imagination" which allowed him to meet with imaginal beings such as Philemon. As Hans Dieter Betz documents in "The Delphic Maxim 'Know Yourself' in the Greek Magical Papyri," *History of Religions* 21 (1981), 156–171, the ancients believed that, in practice, "self-knowledge can be obtained by some kind of consultation of the 'personal daimon'" (p. 160) rather than through the outcome of philosophical self-examination. Betz (p. 159) cites some maxims of Epictetus, all variations on this particular Delphic maxim, in support of this:

> Take council very carefully,
> know yourself,
> consult your personal daimon,
> without God undertake nothing.

Furthermore, as Betz (p. 160) explains,

> In a different frame of reference, however, the magicians will interpret mantic language on their own terms. For them, therefore, "consult your personal diamon" implies that the Delphic maxim orders them to conjure up their personal diamon and get control of it by magical procedures; when that daimon appears, the magician can then submit questions and receive answers. This type of interpretation and procedure is what we find in the *PGM*.

James Hillman ("The Pandaemonium of Images: Jung's Contribution to Know Thyself," in J. Hillman, *Healing Fiction*, Dallas: Spring, 1983) lucidly interprets Jung's psychological method along similar lines, arguing that, "Know Thyself in Jung's manner means to become familiar with, to open oneself to and listen to, that is, to know and discern, daimons" (p. 55). Such experiences seem to be uniquely human and are universally reported, regardless of cultural complexity or epoch. Viewing Jung's psychological method in this manner makes it a twentieth-century version of ancient Hellenistic theurgy, and Jungian psychology a great multidimensional magical system that shares kinship with the millennia-old occult sciences of Europe.

There are many formulae in the *PGM* for animating statues for the purposes of divination and self-knowledge, a practice known as *telestikei* (cf. E.R. Dodds' appendix on "Theurgy" in his *The Greeks and the Irrational* (Berkeley: University of California Press, 1951) and his exemplary "Supernormal Phenomena in Classical Antiquity," in *Proceedings of the Society for*

Psychical Research 55 (1971), 189–237). There is some anecdotal evidence that Sigmund Freud may have engaged in this practice. Freud owned a large collection of ancient Greek, Roman, Oriental and Egyptian antiquities. A sample of his most important pieces made an international tour of various museums in the United States and Europe in 1989 (see I. Gamwell and R. Wells, *Sigmund Freud and Art: His Personal Collection of Antiquities.* Binghamton, NY: The State University of New York Press, 1989). On his desk were arranged three rows of statuettes, a pantheon of ancient deities, as well as a tiny toy porcupine, all of whom stared at Freud with ancient eyes as he wrote. On a small table to the right of the desk sat an antique statue of a Chinese scholar. According to the Freud family's housekeeper, Paula Fichtl, Freud – the paragon of the triumph of reason over the irrational – would verbally greet this Chinese statue each day as he came into his study to write (see the captions, p. 64, by R. Ransohoff in Edmund Engelman, *Berggasse 19: Sigmund Freud's Home and Offices, Vienna 1938*, Chicago: University of Chicago Press, 1976). Furthermore, at about the time of the opening of the Freud Museum, one of its associates, John Harrison, revealed a more intimate relationship between Freud and his statues in an interview with a reporter from *The Philadelphia Inquirer* (2 August 1986): "The artifacts weren't only decorative. He used some of them to help him to write," Harrison explained in hushed tones as he stood near the desk. "He used to hold one in his hand and sometimes, when it was time to go and eat dinner, he would take the artifact with him to the table. He used it as an inspiration, to help him develop and retain a train of thought." Whether Freud engaged in such imaginal dialogues with his statuettes with an awareness of their ancient magical implications is uncertain.

12 The English translation of the "Mithraic Liturgy" can be found in H.D. Betz, *The Greek Magical Papyri in Translation*, 48–54. All quotations of the "Mithras Liturgy" in this paper are from this source.

13 W. Burkert, *Ancient Mystery Cults*, 68–69.

14 McGuire (ed.), *The Freud–Jung Letters*, 210 J.

15 It is dismaying to note that so many of Jung's closest collaborators also repeated this story as a way of offering dramatic evidence for the collective unconscious without mentioning that Honegger was the original source or the fact that the Dieterich book existed before the patient's delusions were discovered. Both M.L. von Franz (in *C.G. Jung: His Myth in Our Time*, Boston: Little Brown & Co., 1975, 124) and C.A. Meier (*Soul and Body: Essays on the Theories of C.G. Jung*, Santa Monica: The Lapis Press, 1986, 78) continue to repeat this incident without correction, although after all this time they certainly must have known the true circumstances. A footnote added to the *Collected Works* admits that Jung later (assumedly after 1936) became aware of the 1903 edition of Dieterich's book, but Honegger's role in the matter is not mentioned.

In the 1916 English translation by Beatrice Hinkle, *The Psychology of the Unconscious* (New York: Moffat, Yard, & Co., 1916) there are two explicit references to Honegger that were removed by Jung in later editions:

Honegger discovered the following hallucination in an insane man (paranoid dement): The patient sees in the sun an 'upright tail' similar to an erected penis. When he moves his head back and forth, then, too, the sun's penis sways back and forth in a like manner, and out of that the wind arises. This strange hallucination remained unintelligible to us for a long time until I became acquainted with the Mithraic liturgy and its visions (pp. 108–109).

After giving Honegger credit (in one of only the two places in the twenty volumes of the *Collected Works* where he is mentioned) for first recording the delusion of a paranoid psychotic patient about the earth being a flat disk over which the sun rotates, Jung adds in parentheses in a passage omitted in later editions, "I am reminded of the sun-phallus mentioned in the first part of this book, for which we are also indebted to Honegger" (154).

However, in 1936, Jung (in "The Concept of the Collective Unconscious," *CW* 9i, §105) relates this tale changing many of the critical details: "About 1906 I came across a very curious delusion in a paranoid schizophrenic who had been interned for many years . . ." Which story is correct?

Honegger's first clinical experience with institutionalized psychiatric patients began only in the winter of 1909 at the Burghölzli under Eugen Bleuler. If Honegger *is* the one who reported this psychotic patient's delusion to Jung, can we trust *him*? As Jung's devoted student during the exact period when Jung was immersed in his study of mythology (the winter of 1909 and the spring of 1910), he must surely have been aware of the Mithraic Liturgy and of the main elements of Mithraism even if the institutionalized patient could not have been. Jung's letters during this period are filled with mythological references, and in one case with references to Honegger and Mithraism in the same letter to Freud (200 J, of 26 June 1910).

Perhaps most damaging to the credibility of Jung for his reliance upon the "Solar Phallus Man" story throughout his career for his first conclusive "proof" of the existence of a "collective unconscious" is the fact that *published mythological material regarding the motif of a "solar phallus" (Sonnenphallus) was in print in a major scholarly work on mythology several decades before Jung, Honegger or the Solar Phallus Man were even born.* This work went through several editions and was widely read in German Europe in the nineteenth century. Henri Ellenberger points this out in an obscure but vitally important footnote in his *The Discovery of the Unconscious* (New York: Basic Books, 1970, 743, no. 140) by noting that Creuzer includes a section on this motif in his *Symbolik und Mythologie der alten Völker* (3rd edition, 1841, III, 335). Given Jung's admiration for this work, it is almost certain that he had Creuzer's books read by the three assistants (Honegger, Sabina Spielrein, and Jan Nelken) whom he assigned to compile evidence for the phylogenetic layer of the unconscious that was exposed in psychotic states of mind. Hypothetically, the "Solar Phallus Man" could have read Creuzer as well.

Did the devoted pupil Honegger (who may have been under considerable stress for some time, considering his suicide in 1911, and perhaps may have experienced lapses in judgment or honesty) present his idealized master Jung with a "gift" that may have undergone considerable "wrapping"? Did the story truly come out of the mouth of an institutionalized patient, or is it Honegger's creation? And if so, and if Jung suspected the veracity of the details surrounding the source of this tale after Honegger's suicide threw him into doubt about so many other aspects of his relationship with his younger pupil, is this why Honegger's name was removed from later editions of Jung's works in which this story is recounted?

The story of the correspondence between the delusions of an institutionalized psychotic patient and a second-century C.E. mythological text, if true, is striking if one is to consider the evidence for the hypothesis of the collective unconscious. Jung may have felt that rather than retracting the story, he would eliminate any doubts about it instead by failing to mention Honegger's stigmatizing name ever again in connection with it. At best, this discrepancy in the 1912 and 1936 tellings of the tale is a distortion in Jung's memory; at worst, it calls Jung's integrity into question.

Why aren't the true circumstances more openly discussed by Jungians? As Jung's protégé and "Crown Prince" equivalent with whom he intended to share a private practice in Zürich, Honegger left a deep wound in Jung with his suicide and, for whatever reason, Jung dealt with this by removing references to him in his public lectures and in his continually revised published works. Jung's inner circle and subsequent generations of Jungians have followed suit and remained silent for the most part on the significance of Honegger in Jung's life, except, that is, for an article in *Spring* 1974 by Hans Walser, "An Early Psychoanalytic Tragedy: J.J. Honegger and the Beginnings of Training Analysis," 243–255. Indeed, in a footnote on p. 248, the author cites speculation by Herman Nunberg, who was on staff at the Burghölzli at the time, that *Honegger himself was the Solar Phallus Man*. The assertion here is that Honegger experienced a psychotic episode with delusions that had Mithraic influences. If this is true – and no corroborating evidence has come to light to support this – Jung's "deification" was an imitation (replication?) of Honegger's psychotic experiences, but with a crucial difference: Jung survived his grandiose, inflationary initiation into the male brotherhood of the Mithraic mysteries while his "son" Honegger did not.

The tragedy of J.J. Honegger (along with those tales of Jung's experience as the victim of a sexual assault by a male mentor while Jung was an 18-year-old youth, his erotic relationships with Sabina Spielrein and Toni Wolff and the omission of material regarding them from *Memories, Dreams, Reflections*, his self-reported December 1913 *imitatio Christi* and leontocephaline deification in the ancient mysteries of Mithras, etc.) seems to be one of the many "family secrets" hidden by the shadow of the Jungian community. Its often unconscious social norms perhaps inhibit the telling of such tales because such an act would be a "breach of taboo," and thus risk the perception of publicly devaluing, through greater awareness of his humanity, the person and work of Jung.

16 C.G. Jung, "The Concept of the Collective Unconscious" (1936), *CW* 9i, §107, 106.

17 See Roger Beck, "Mithraism since Franz Cumont," in *Aufstieg und Niedergang der römischen Welt* (New York: Walter de Gruyter, 1984); R.L. Gordon, "Franz Cumont and the Doctrine of Mithraism," in J. Hinnells (ed.), *Mithraic Studies*, vol. 1 (Manchester: Manchester University Press, 1975); R.L. Gordon, "Reality, Evocation and Boundary in the Mysteries of Mithras," *Journal of Mithraic Studies* 3 (1982), 19–99; and David Ulansey, *The Origins of the Mithraic Mysteries: Cosmology and Salvation in the Ancient World* (New York: Oxford University Press, 1989).

18 The four passages cited in the above two paragraphs can be found in W. Burkert, *Ancient Mysteries*, 11; 12; 10; and 8.

19 Ibid., 3.

20 Burkert (ibid., 69) is particularly incisive on this point: "It could be held that the quest for mystery texts is essentially futile for more basic reasons: no Nag Hammadi library of mysteries will ever be discovered because it never existed, and there was not even a shipwreck as imagined by Cumont."

21 The leading figure in symbolic anthropology, Victor Turner (*The Ritual Process: Structure and Anti-Structure*, Ithaca: Cornell University Press, 1969) has devoted considerable attention to the middle stage of "liminality" as he terms it and the special attributes to persons in that stage. Turner says they are bonded together in a sacred community, a state which he terms *communitas* and which is the antithesis of "structure," the realm of conventional social norms. "Communitas," as Turner describes it is directly applicable to the initiates of the Eleusinian and Mithraic mysteries as we know them. We have less information about the "before" and "after" status of the Dionysian mystery initiates. Other useful books on rites of passage are the classic by Mircea Eliade, *Rites and Symbols of Initiation: The Mysteries of Birth and Rebirth* (New York: Harper, 1958), and a volume edited by L.C. Mahdi, S. Foster, and M. Littel, *Betwixt and Between: Patterns of Masculine and Feminine Initiation* (La Salle, IL: Open Court, 1987), which is uneven in quality.

22 Cited in W. Burkert, *Ancient Mysteries*, 90.

23 (Princeton: Princeton University Press, 1989.) For decades these lectures existed only in selected Jungian analytic training centers in mimeographed form. Only Jungian analysts, trainees, and certain approved members of the "laity" who had a preapproved number of hours of psychotherapy with a certified Jungian analyst could read these documents until they were openly published in 1989. Thus, the text of the 1925 seminars was, in a sense, forbidden to those deemed "uninitiated" in some formal manner. However, there is nothing potentially dangerous or destabilizing to the reader of the 1925 seminars. After decades of mystery such a judgment is disappointing to the seeker of forbidden fruit.

The emphasis on the maintaining of secrets privy only to the select few is a sociological phenomenon found in organizations that operate within the same model as mystery cults and secret societies. It allows those in more privileged positions in the social hierarchy to have more *perceived* power in the eyes of novices who hope to attain such knowledge and power by completing the requirements of their formal initiation and rising in the ranks. It is ironic that a psychological movement such as the Jungian analytic community which constantly professes greater consciousness, individual responsibility and individuation as desired goals continues to follow this mystery cult/secret society model in many formal respects. The stake in the unconsciousness of the "uninitiated" (the general public, patients, et al.) is high in analytic communities of all types (Jungian, Freudian, etc.) as they tend to operate as twentieth-century, formalized and bureaucratized versions of ancient mystery cults or secret societies.

24 C.G. Jung, *MDR*, 181–184.

25 C.G. Jung, *Analytical Psychology: Notes of the Seminar Given in 1925* 63–64, 88–89.

26 C.G. Jung, *MDR*, 181.

27 C.G. Jung, *Analytical Psychology*, 89.

28 C.G. Jung, *MDR*, 182.

29 C.G. Jung, *Analytical Psychology*, 89.

30 C.G. Jung, *MDR*, 182.

31 C.G. Jung, *Analytical Psychology*, 93.

32 Ibid., 95.

33 Ibid., 96.

34 Ibid.

35 Ibid., 97.

36 Ibid.
37 Ibid., 98.
38 Ibid.
39 Ibid., 99.
40 Ibid.
41 C.G. Jung, *MDR*, 209.
42 C.G. Jung, *Analytical Psychology*, 92. Early in his psychiatric career Jung was fascinated with the operation of *human memory* and in the phenomena of *memory disorders*. For example, Volume 1 of his *Collected Works* contains such scientific papers as "On Hysterical Misreading" (1904), and "Cryptomnesia" (1905), and Volume 2 contains his "Experimental Observation on the Faculty of Memory" (1905) along with his other experimental studies in word association (1904–1907) which also focus on the operation of human memory. At some point after the autumn of 1909 Jung made the fateful leap of faith that interpreted some of the phenomena of dreams and visions as emerging from phylogenetic or racial sources (the collective unconscious). The alternative was to envision a novel – but unconscious – repackaging of *individual* memories of events and information that had long been forgotten. Cryptomnesia – "hidden memories" which later resurface in a new form and which are perceived as novel creations and not old memories – is a plausible alternative hypothesis to the collective unconscious. It is also almost as difficult to "prove" conclusively in a scientific sense, for it is impossible to determine each element in a lifetime of individual experience that may be stored and reprocessed in long-term memory.
   Jung knew that cryptomnesia was a logical alternative hypothesis to the collective unconscious and points this out in many places in the *Collected Works* in which he either ignores the implications of it or simply dismisses them (e.g., "The Psychological Foundations of a Belief in Spirits" (1920/ 1948) *CW* 8, §599; "The Relations Between the Ego and the Unconscious" (1928) *CW* 7, §219; "The Concept of the Collective Unconscious" (1936), *CW* 9i, §92; "The Philosophical Tree" (1945/1954), *CW* 13, §352n.; "Synchronicity: An Acausal Connecting Principle" (1952), *CW* 8, §845.). It has been argued by Sonu Shamdasani that J.J. Honegger's "Solar Phallus Man" (see note 15 above) "carried on his shoulders the weight and burden of proof of the Collective Unconscious" ("A Woman Called Frank," *Spring* 50 [1990], 40) as the primary argument against the alternative hypothesis of cryptomnesia, and indeed this seems to be the case. In "The Structure of the Psyche" (1928/1931, §319) Jung offers as evidence the observation, "The vision of my patient in 1906, and the Greek text first edited in 1910, should be sufficiently far apart to rule out the possibility of cryptomnesia on his side and of thought-transference on mine." Yet we know that the facts cited by Jung here are incorrect and open to serious dispute. Is the information Jung offered as the strongest independent evidence for the collective unconscious faulty?
   Jung was fascinated by the problem of cryptomnesia until the very end of his life. Cryptomnesia in a sense has always been the "shadow" of the collective unconscious, and this was a fact that haunted Jung. In the very last essay Jung ever wrote, "Symbols and the Interpretation of Dreams" (1961) *CW* 18 (completed shortly before his death in June 1961), Jung reproduces a section demonstrating the unconscious operation of cryptomnesia in the work of Nietzsche that he included in his doctoral dissertation of 1902 ("On the Psychology and Pathology of So-Called Occult Phenomena" *CW* 1, §138–

§146) – thus closing the circle of his intellectual career. Cryptomnesia was an intellectual problem for Jung for more years (since 1902) than the phylogenetic (circa late 1909) or collective unconscious (circa 1918) ever was. For the best and most readable summary of scientific knowledge about cryptomnesia, see Robert A. Baker, *Hidden Memories: Voices and Visions from Within* (Buffalo, NY: Prometheus Books, 1992).

43 In *The Woman in the Mirror* (Boston: Sigo Press, 1990) Claire Douglas makes much of the image of Jung's blind Salome in her book on the feminine in analytical psychology. Despite the superb literature review that makes this book so valuable, her tendency to moralize about how Jung should have conducted himself with women and with his internal anima-images (the blind Salome), her criticism (p. 50) of Jung for his "deep but ambivalent connection with the potent feminine" (whatever that phrase means), and her rather idiosyncratic interpretation of the black serpent as a monstrous Baucis/Baubo figure (which Douglas suggests could have healed and completed Jung) borders on an unfortunate excursion into pathography that is increasingly to be found in Freudian and feminist critiques of Jung and his psychology. Admittedly, this may be indicative of a necessary stage in the development of the Jungian movement in which idealization is followed by devaluation, which in turn will (it is to be hoped) lead to more balanced visions of Jung the man versus Jung the myth. Jung was human, had difficulties in his relationships with women and men, can certainly be judged by us to be ambivalent about both sexes, and by his own admission had difficulty with his feeling function. Now we learn that Salome was cured of her blindness after all. Let the romantic speculations begin!

44 Franz Cumont, *The Mysteries of Mithra* (New York: Open Court, 1903), 43.

45 During the 1925 seminars Jung maintained the Christianized version of Mithraism as he had thirteen years before in *Wandlungen*, especially the notion that certain features of ritual had later been incorporated into the Christian Church – an assumption that is viewed more critically by scholars today. According to his view in 1925, the "Mithraic religion" had "churches" built above the underground initiation caves. "Bells were used in the ceremony, and bread marked with a cross. We know that they celebrated a sacramental meal where this bread was eaten with water instead of wine" (C.G. Jung, *Analytical Psychology* [1989], 98). None of these features has found support during subsequent analyses of the Mithraic evidence. See J.P. Kane, "The Mithraic Cult Meal in its Greek and Roman Environment," in J. Hinnells (ed.), *Mithraic Studies*, vol. 2 (Manchester: Manchester University Press, 1975) for a review of the evidence and a new interpretation of the Mithraic cult meal, and Samuel Laeuchli, *Mithraism in Ostia: Mystery Religion and Christianity in the Ancient Port of Rome* (Evanston, IL: Northwestern University Press, 1967) for a discussion of the problems of the relationship between Mithraism and Christianity. Cumont's influence is also seen in a dream Jung reports during this seminar that is recorded nowhere else: "In 1910 I had a dream of a Gothic cathedral in which Mass was being celebrated. Suddenly the whole side wall of the cathedral caved in, and herds of cattle, with ringing bells, trooped into the church. You may remember that Cumont remarked that if something had happened to disrupt Christianity in the third century, the world would be Mithraic today" (C.G. Jung, *Analytical Psychology* [1989], 99).

46 Franz Cumont, *The Mysteries of Mithra* (1903), 150–174.

47 Luther Martin explains the problem in his extremely useful book, *Hellenistic Religions: An Introduction* (New York: Oxford University Press, 1987), 114–115: "Unlike the myths of other mystery deities, no received myth of Mithras survives, nor does the iconographic evidence seem to reflect any such official narrative of the deity's life. Mithraic iconography seems rather to depict isolated scenes of Mithraic activity from which modern attempts to reconstruct a mythic narrative have been made. Even these scenes, with several exceptions, seem to express regional variations of the cult expression."

48 David Ulansey, *The Origins of the Mithraic Mysteries: Cosmology and Salvation in the Ancient World* (New York: Oxford University Press, 1989), 103–112.

49 C.G. Jung, *The Psychology of the Unconscious* (B. Hinkle, trans., New York: Moffat, Yard, & Co., 1916), 222. Also: C.G. Jung, *Symbols of Transformation*, CW 5 (1911/1912/1952), §289.

50 C.G. Jung, *Symbols of Transformation*, CW 5 (1911/1912/1952), §596.

51 M.-L. von Franz, *C.G. Jung: His Myth in Our Time* (Boston: Little, Brown & Co., 1975), 214.

52 C.G. Jung, "Letter to Père Bruno" (1953), CW 18, §1529.

53 C.G. Jung, *Symbols of Transformation*, CW 5, §158.

54 David Ulansey, *The Origins of the Mithraic Mysteries* (1989), 93.

55 Ibid., 46–52.

56 C.G. Jung, *Symbols of Transformation*, CW 5, §668.

57 W. McGuire (ed.), *The Freud–Jung Letters*, 199a F.

58 Ibid., 200 J.

59 Following generations of scholars until the 1970s, Jung probably did not construct a detailed astrological interpretation of Mithraic symbolism because Cumont didn't, even though Cumont was an acknowledged expert on the use of astrology in antiquity. Cumont was obsessed with tracing the Iranian correspondences of each and every Mithraic symbol, especially those in the tauroctony. However, Mithraism seems to have been more astronomical than astrological in nature, at least according to one prominent Mithraic scholar (R.L. Gordon, "Franz Cumont and the Doctrine of Mithraism," in J. Hinnells (ed.), *Mithraic Studies*, vol. 1, Manchester: Manchester University Press, 1975) and a classicist who is a leading expert on the history and significance of astrology (S.J. Tester, *A History of Western Astrology*, Woodbridge, Suffolk, England: Boydell & Brewer, 1987).

60 C.G. Jung, *Letters*, vol. I (Princeton: Princeton University Press, 1973), 24.

61 C.G. Jung, *The Psychology of the Unconscious* (B. Hinkle, trans., New York: Moffat, Yard, & Co., 1916), 557.

62 R.L. Gordon, "Reality, Evocation, and Boundary in the Mysteries of Mithras," *Journal of Mithraic Studies* 3 (1980), 32.

63 Franz Cumont, *The Mysteries of Mithra* (New York: Open Court, 1903), 155.

64 C.G. Jung, *Symbols of Transformation*, CW 5, §89n.

65 C.G. Jung, *Mysterium Coniunctionis*, CW 14 (1955–1956), §168.

66 H. Jackson, "The Meaning and Function of the Leontocephaline in Roman Mithraism," *Numen* 32 (1985), 29.

67 R.L. Gordon, "Reality, Evocation, and Boundary in the Mysteries of Mithras," *Journal of Mithraic Studies* 3 (1980), 35.

68 See the fuller citation in H. Jackson, "The Meaning and Function of the Leontocephaline in Roman Mithraism," *Numen*, 32 (1985), 17–45.

69 R.L. Gordon, "Reality, evocation . . ." (1980), 36–37.

70 C.G. Jung, *Analytical Psychology* (1989), 98.

71 Although such a connection is very tenuous, it is difficult not to notice the similarities between the qualities of the *leo* and that of classical Eurasian shamans. Both take on animal identities, are associated with fire and its transformative effects (both spiritual and material), are in mediatory roles between the sacred and the profane, and are associated with the use of sacred rattles (and other percussion instruments) in rituals. Are there proto-Indo-European roots common to shamanism and the *leonticha* of the Mithraic mysteries? Such roots have been posited for the European folklore tradition concerning fairies and witches by Carlo Ginzburg (*Ecstasies: Deciphering the Witches' Sabbath*, New York: Pantheon, 1992), and the continuing influence (linguistic, mythic, etc.) of our long-forgotten tribal origins for those of us of Eurasian descent has been richly documented by J.P. Mallory (*In Search of the Indo-Europeans*, London: Thames & Hudson, 1989). If so, and if Jung had made this connection, would Jung instead have interpreted his experiences as his initiatory training (or "sickness") as a shaman?

   Although he makes about forty references to shamanism throughout the twenty volumes of his *Collected Works*, no single substantive discussion of Jung's interpretation of this magico-religious tradition can be found. This may very well be due to the fact that the first comprehensive comparative volume on the subject did not appear until Jung was 76 years old and after he had already spent decades revisioning his initiatory experiences and his subsequent psychology and its methodology in terms of alchemical metaphors (and not those that could be found in the vast ethnographic literature on shamanism). This historic volume on shamanism was Mircea Eliade's *Le Chamanisme et les techniques archaïques de l'extase* (Paris: Librairie Payot, 1951). A critical note on modern romantic speculations about shamanism can be found in my "Comment on 'Individuation and Shamanism'", *Journal of Analytical Psychology* 35 (1990), 213–217. For the role of imagination, imaginal beings and the *ars memoria* in shamanism, see also my "Mental Imagery Cultivation as a Cultural Phenomenon: The Role of Visions in Shamanism," *Current Anthropology* 26 (1985), 443–461.

72 R.L. Gordon, "Reality, Evocation . . ." (1980), 33.

73 *Numen* 32 (1985), 17–45.

74 Ibid., 19. A statue with its head missing and without the usual serpent found at York has been tentatively identified as the Mithraic leontocephalus, and it is one of the few to bear an inscription. This inscription mentions the key word *ARIMANIV*. When a final interpretation is made, it may indicate that this deity's name was Arimanius, a Romanized form of the Zoroastrian deity Ahriman, the great Evil One. Jackson, who claims that this is an "admittedly shaky identification of the leontocephaline," notes that even if the deity's name is Arimanius it is depicted as benign in so many instances that it could not be identical with the malevolent Persian deity.

75 Ibid., 19.

76 I therefore disagree with Ulansey's (pp. 116–124) logic in interpreting the lion-headed god as a "Gorgon." Ulansey argues that early representations of the Gorgon resemble monstrous animal- or lion-headed deities, and since Mithras is turning his head away from the bull which he is slaying in the same way that Perseus is depicted turning from the Gorgon which he is decapitating, the lion-headed god "most likely represents a power subdued by Mithras, just as the Gorgon was subdued by Perseus" (p. 117). This makes no sense to me as there are no images of Mithras slaying a lion or a lion-headed figure.

77 Ibid., 31.

78 Ibid., 29.

79 Ibid., 31.

80 C.G. Jung, *Analytical Psychology* (1989), 97. In part I of *Wandlungen* published in 1911 Jung discusses the deification process of "becoming-one-with-god" (see Hinkle's translation, *The Psychology of the Unconscious*, 96–98) in the ancient mysteries. Jung explains that, "The identification with God necessarily has as a result the enhancing of the meaning and power of an individual. That seems, first of all, to have been really its purpose: a strengthening of the individual against his all too great weakness and insecurity in real life. The great megalomania thus has a genuinely pitiable background" (p. 98). The tragic irony of this paragraph is apparent to us only now when we consider that Jung's "deification" in December 1913 followed the bitter cessation of his emotionally wrenching relationships with Sabina Spielrein and Sigmund Freud. For a sensitive and masterfully written telling of this tale, read John Kerr, *A Most Dangerous Method: The Story of Jung, Freud, and Sabina Spielrein* (New York: Alfred A. Knopf, 1993).

81 For the best interpretive review of the archeological evidence on this figure, see the exemplary treatment by Doro Levi, "Aion," *Hesperia* 13 (1944), 269–314.

82 C.G. Jung, "The Tavistock Lectures" (1935), *CW* 18.

83 H. Jackson, "The Meaning and Function . . .", 34.

84 C.G. Jung, *MDR*, 182–183.

85 Ibid., 182.

86 See G.W. Bowersock, *Hellenism in Late Antiquity* (Ann Arbor, Michigan: University of Michigan Press, 1990), 21–28. Also: Peter M. Fraser, *Ptolemaic Alexandria*, 2 volumes (Oxford: Oxford University Press, 1972).

87 It is important to note that, from the point of view of Jung's revered mentor, the Swiss psychologist Théodore Flournoy (1854–1920) of Geneva, imaginal figures such as Elijah, Salome, Philemon, and (perhaps) Basilides that Jung encountered in visions and other altered states of consciousness *do not* have an independent existence of their own. According to Flournoy in his important volume *Spiritism and Psychology* (H. Carrington, trans., New York and London: Harper & Brothers, 1911), Jung's imaginal colleagues are nothing more than *teleological automatisms*, "symbolic personifications" constituted from an amalgam of forgotten memories of Jung's previous experiences and research – i.e., *cryptomnesia*, a term which Flournoy coined and masterfully used as an explanatory principle for the source material of the "romances" and "planetary voyages" of a spiritualist medium in *From India to the Planet Mars* (New York and London: Harper & Brothers, 1901; original French edition, 1900). Jung used *From India to the Planet Mars* as a model for his 1902 doctoral dissertation study of his mediumistic cousin.

In *Spiritism and Psychology*, in the chapter on "Beneficent Spirits," Flournoy states:

> In the tradition and the popular language of the spiritists they carry all sorts of names – spirit protectors, angel guardians, good geniuses, familiar demons, spiritual guides, etc. In our scientific jargon, barbarous and pedantic, we call them *teleological automatisms*; or, more exactly, they represent events psychologically superior to teleological automatisms, since they form, often, a secondary personality, more or less complete, which includes everything from happy inspirations to simple reflexes (p. 96).

The intervention of teleological automatisms – alias "beneficent spirits" – is not limited to the extreme cases which prevent an unfortunate man from taking his life. It manifests itself, also, to protect the individual against dangers of which he has no knowledge – imminent, distant, or only probable; more often still, to inform him and guide him to his advantage in the little occurrences of life. As for psychic facts, scarcely noticed, we could hardly tell whether or not they were willed by ourselves, so completely is their origin lost in the marginal regions of our personality, and which, when we reflect upon it, astonish us by their admirable adaptation to circumstances. Forgotten memories, returning at a favorable moment, repartees which are *à propos*, and which surprise us ourselves, suppressed after-thoughts, inexplicable hesitations preventing us from action, or, on the contrary, obscure impulses which we are glad we have followed, good ideas, illuminating thoughts, inspirations of genius which flash into our heads and bring us unexpected help; in fact, all that we call "tact," "presence of mind," "inspiration," or "intuition;" all that is at the basis of teleological automatisms and fill our whole lives – the study of all this is well worth the most painstaking research and analysis.

(p. 115)

Jung surely knew the position of his "revered and fatherly friend" (see James Witzig, "Théodore Flournoy – A Friend Indeed," *Journal of Analytical Psychology* 27 [1982], 131–148) but chose later to construct a psychology that purposely downplayed the personal and resurrected the role of transcendental forces – all in direct opposition to Flournoy's careful analysis and critique of a transcendental hypothesis of a related sort, "spiritism," in favor of ubiquitous, intrapersonal psychological processes. Given their relationship (Jung made many visits to Flournoy in Geneva during the period of his break with Freud), Jung knew that in his 1910 book, *Spiritism and Psychology*, Flournoy offers all of the most devastating psychological arguments and evidence against Jung's later (circa 1918) theory of "archetypes" and the "collective unconscious" that have ever been made.

In the 1925 seminars (p. 92) Jung reveals about his December 1913 visionary descent into "the land of the dead" (the collective unconscious) that, "I had read much mythology before this fantasy came to me, and all of this reading entered into the condensation of these figures." Contrast this with Flournoy's explanation that only points to the operation of cryptomnesia in the *personal* unconscious:

Everyone knows with what facility descriptions which we read or hear set on fire the visual imagination, and are translated into representations more or less vivid. These concrete representations once born may subsist in latent memory and reappear, even when one can no longer remember the occasion which first of all provoked them.

(p. 122)

From Flournoy's point of view as stated in 1910 (a time of increasing contact between him and Jung), Jung's later interpretations of his visions as due to the agency of autonomous archetypes of the collective unconscious ("the land of the dead") may have been interpreted as an attempt to inject spiritism into psychology. (For related information, see Sonu Shamdasani, "Automatic Writing and the Discovery of the Unconscious," *Spring* 54, 1993, 100–103.) Jung continued to look over his shoulder at the disapproving gaze of his mentor, for Jung's many offhand dismissals of cryptomnesia in many of his works that follow the development of his archetypal theory may be viewed as an ongoing imaginal dispute with Flournoy.

Although I did not intentionally begin this article in November 1991 with an awareness of "cryptomnesia" or even of Flournoy, it is clear to me now that I have applied the same method – and arrived at the same conclusions – to and about Jung's mythic visionary "confrontation with the unconscious" that Flournoy used and also concluded about the "planetary voyages" of medium Hélène Smith, i.e., that there is no reason to posit transcendental explanations whose contents can be so decisively traced to prior individual experience (especially previously read published sources).

88 R.L. Gordon, "Reality, Evocation . . ." (1980), 55.

89 Luther H. Martin, *Hellenistic Religions: An Introduction* (New York: Oxford University Press, 1987), 118.

90 We can learn much about the Jungian movement of the twentieth century and its modern mystery cult attributes from the hierarchical initiation structure of the Mithraic mysteries. If examined with the eyes of a sociologist or cultural anthropologist who has dropped in on the "island of Jungians" to conduct fieldwork, one would find that there are no recognized roles other than (1) interested nonpatient, (2) patient of a certified Jungian analyst or trainee, (3) trainee (essentially an elevated status of patienthood), and (4) certified Jungian analyst. As in other cultures, the linear progression of these social roles in the hierarchy of the Jungian community imply that community values and core Jungian concepts (Jungian cultural shared beliefs, especially in "individuation") are reflected in the very social structure of the community. The perceived status of one's level of individuation, healing ability, wholeness, completeness, power, knowledge, spirituality, compassion, etc., flow upwards from "interested nonpatient" to "analyst" in this four-fold system of levels of Jungian initiation.

As in the Mithraic mysteries, the modern Jungian is obsessed with the "fantasy of being a Jungian analyst" much in the same way the ancient Mithraist was obsessed with the "fantasy of being a *pater*."

91 Cited in R.L. Gordon, "Reality, Evocation . . ." (1980), 57.

92 Franz Cumont, *Textes et monuments figurés relatifs aux mystères de Mithra* (Brussels: H. Lamertin, 1896), I, 42, n. 2.

93 R.L. Gordon, "Reality, Evocation . . ." (1980), 57–63.

94 Ibid., 60.

95 Ibid., 61.

96 Ibid., 60.

97 Ibid., 61.

98 C.G. Jung, *MDR*, 342.

99 Ibid., 343–344.

100 As it is abundantly clear that Jung was highly influenced by the new scholarship on Mithraism that appeared at the turn of the century, a fuller exploration of the integration of Mithraic symbolism into twentieth-century culture needs to be explored. For example, the novel *Les Bestiaires* (Paris: Mornay, 1926), by Henry de Montherlant (English translation by Peter Wiles, *The Matador*, London: Elek Books, 1957) contains incantatory passages addressed to Mithras, and the protagonist, matador Alban de Bricoule, openly attempts

to syncretize Christianity and Mithraism through the cult of bullfighting (very much in accord with the picture of Mithraism constructed by Franz Cumont). For more detailed information on the work of Montherlant, see Robert Johnson, *Henry de Montherlant* (New York: Twayne, 1968). Also, the symbolism of the "Rider" tarot deck that was devised by Arthur Waite and which appeared in 1910 contains imagery that is associated with Mithraism (see, e.g., the card for the "Two of Cups").

4

C.G. JUNG AND NATIONAL SOCIALISM

Stanley Grossman

Source: *Journal of European Studies* 9 (1979), 231–59.

With the recent resurgence of interest in the occult, the intuitive wisdom of the East, and ethnic history, it is small wonder that, in addition to its intrinsic merits, the work of C.G. Jung continues to find a substantial audience. There are Jungians, however, who evidently feel that he has not received the full measure of praise due to him because his views on National Socialism have been distorted; one of Jung's advocates has pointed out that a critic had even gone so far as to call the Swiss psychiatrist a "psychoanalyst foaming with fascism".[1] Another supporter claims that despite numerous rebuttals, the "legend of Jung's Nazi sympathies persists". This perseveration is attributed, in part, to the archetypal father–son relationship, and encounter between Jew and gentile inherent in Jung's association with Freud. In contrast, the absence of similar motifs from the career of someone like Heidegger, it is claimed, has made it relatively easy for the public to brush aside the latter's open support of Nazism.[2] Has Jung been unjustly treated or was he, in fact, sympathetic to the Nazis? Can we ignore Jung's claim to have given prophetic forewarning of the German tragedy?[3] It will be the purpose of this chapter to show (1) that though he was no Nazi fanatic, the "legend" of Jung's National Socialist sympathies contains a kernel of truth, and (2) that his attitude towards the Hitler regime was not only the result of circumstances, but also the product of currents embedded in his thought. We will begin by examining his activities during the 1930s, then seek to show the roots of these actions in his theories and elsewhere – a task facilitated by the publication of much of Jung's basic correspondence during the past few years – and finally we will consider the extenuating circumstances that can be mustered in Jung's defence, thus attempting to evaluate the situation in a broader perspective. First, however, we must examine Jung's activities during the 1930s.

These actions fall into three main categories: (1) his alleged anti-

Semitism and support for a German psychotherapy, (2) his comments on Hitler and the Nazi regime, and (3) his ties with the General Medical Society for Psychotherapy.

In the spring of 1933 Jung acceded to the presidency of the General Medical Society for Psychotherapy – an organization which was not only subject to Nazi influence, but one which had also just lost its previous president Ernst Kretschmer, who resigned because of its political affiliations.[4] When Jung became president, he also assumed the editorship of the organization's *gleichgeschaltet* publication, the *Zentralblatt für Psychotherapie.*

Another category of actions centres on the comments Jung made during the 1930s on Hitler and the Nazi regime. In a speech delivered to the *Kulturbund* at Vienna in November 1932, Jung remarked:

> Education to personality has become a pedagogical ideal that turns its back upon the standardized – the collective and normal – human being. It thus recognizes the historical fact that the great liberating deeds of world history have come from the leading personalities and never from the inert mass that is secondary at all times and needs a demagogue if it is to move at all. The paean of the Italian nation is addressed to the personality of the Duce, and the dirges of other nations lament the absence of great leaders.

When publishing the text of this lecture in 1934, Jung added a footnote to the above, eliminating any doubt that Hitler was the kind of leader or personality he meant to indicate in his *Kulturbund* lecture of November 1932. "Since then", he wrote, "Germany too has found its leader . . .".[5]

Also characteristic of the outstanding personality, in Jung's opinion, was a Luciferian quality which might be dangerous, though the evil it contained often turned out to be superficial – a case of the good making way for the better – as well as an indispensable aid. One had to risk absorbing some of the apparent evil if the development of personality were to progress. Things could not be left as they were indefinitely; there came a point where change became a necessity. It was the leader, the hero or the saviour, who discovered a new way to greater certainty.[6] Evidently Jung had someone like the Duce or Hitler in mind when writing this and apparently was making excuses for the less palatable side of their reputations.

Equally characteristic of the liberating personality was an ability to listen to his own unconscious, his inner voice, rather than the dictates of convention.

> It is what is commonly called vocation: an irrational factor that destines a man to emancipate himself from the herd and its well-worn paths. . . . But his vocation acts like a law of God from

which there is no escape. . . . Who has vocation hears the voice of
the inner man: he is *called*.[7]

This voice came from the collective unconscious and belonged fundamentally to all, though it manifested itself in the individual. Hence seemingly
possessed, the outstanding personality was a man of vocation who
answered the callings of the collective unconscious.

In February 1933 Jung again delivered this lecture, this time at Essen,
under the title of "The Development of Personality", the title it bore when
published in 1934. Whether or not Jung remarked, as he did in the 1934
version, that Germany too had found its leader is not clear from the newspaper accounts.[8] Nevertheless his insistence on the importance of liberating leadership would very likely have been interpreted as support for the
Hitler regime which had just inaugurated a crucial election campaign to
establish a total dictatorship.

However, Jung showed some hesitations later in 1933 when he wrote,
"So-called leaders are the inevitable symptoms of a mass movement",[9] and
by 1936 he was even more critical when in an apparent reference to Hitler
he noted that "one man, who is obviously 'possessed', has infected a whole
nation to such an extent that everything is set in motion and has started
rolling on its course towards perdition".[10]

Still, this essay of 1936 entitled "Wotan" after the Nordic god did not
focus on criticism of National Socialism, but sought a causal hypothesis
for Nazism in the German psyche rather than in the world of economics
and politics.

> Apparently everyone had forgotten that Wotan is a Germanic
> datum of first importance, the truest expression and unsurpassed
> personification of a fundamental quality that is particularly
> characteristic of the Germans.[11]

Jung also remarked in this essay that:

> The Hitler movement literally brought the whole of Germany to
> its feet, from five-year-olds to veterans, and produced the spectacle
> of a nation migrating from one place to another. Wotan the
> wanderer was on the move.[12]

The link between the Hitler movement and a fundamental component of
the German mind seemed to indicate a unanimous acceptance of National
Socialism by the German people, and the use of a figure from Nordic
mythology to describe the Nazis lent them a certain epic stature. Indeed,
the Wotan essay winds up being as ambivalent as the archetype it
describes.

If interviews granted to journalists are to be trusted – Jung issued no disclaimers – his attitude also showed its more positive side in the later 1930s. He stated clearly that he supported a form of aristocracy which resembled the *comitatus* organization of the primitive teutonic tribes. Of tribal institutions carried on in his own time, he said:

> They are healthy because they are good for the unconscious. When the old tribal institutions – the small duchies and princedoms of Germany and Italy – are broken up, then comes the upheaval, before a new tribal order is created. It is always the same, the tribe has a personal ruler. He surrounds himself with his own particular followers, who become an oligarchy.[13]

Evidently, Jung believed in something resembling a *comitatus* theory of history. "The S.S. men", he said, "are becoming transformed into a caste of knights ruling sixty million natives."[14] There is little doubt that Jung looked on this development favourably. "A decent form of oligarchy – call it aristocracy if you like – is the most ideal form of government."[15]

Many of the references Jung made to Hitler prior to World War II tended to support the latter's claim to messianic leadership. "If he is not their true Messiah, he is like one of the Old Testament prophets; his mission is to unite his people and lead them to the Promised Land."[16] In a 1937 interview Jung said of Hitler: "He is a medium, German policy is not made; it is revealed through Hitler. He is the mouthpiece of the Gods of old. . . . Hitler is the Sybil, the Delphic oracle."[17] Any layman having contact with such statements must certainly have concluded that Jung gave his benediction to Hitler.

In a 1939 interview in which Jung spoke on behalf of appeasement, his statements betrayed an admixture of admiration and wariness. "Let the wolf lame himself", he argued in support of an appeasement policy which was to lead to Hitler's attacking Russia.[18] If Hitler was described as a wolf, he was nonetheless depicted as having extraordinary capabilities. There were strong indications that the Swiss psychotherapist saw Hitler as a case in which the outstanding personality, described in the *Kulturbund* speech (subsequently published under the title of "The Voice Within"), had gone astray. The Führer had that prime requisite of personality, the ability to listen to his inner voice. "He himself has referred to his voice. His voice is nothing other than his own unconscious, into which the German people have projected themselves. . . ." Evidently, Hitler was a man with a vocation, a man able to tap the resources of the collective unconscious. "He is the loud-speaker which magnifies the inaudible whispers of the German soul until they can be heard by the German's unconscious ear." On this basis, "Hitler", in Jung's opinion, "had perceived the true balance of political forces at home and in the world; he has so far been infallible. The source of his success lay in the fact that he had exceptional access to his unconscious and that he permitted himself to be moved by it; he listened to his inner voice. The true leader is always led."[19] In Jung's opinion, then, Hitler seemed to be an embodiment of the collective will able to tap the resources of the collective unconscious, a man of vocation who had nonetheless given way to some of the destructive elements contained in the unconscious – if the term "wolf" is any indication – instead of integrating them into his personality.

Dictators could be dangerous, but Jung's attitude in the later 1930s is probably best summarized in the following statement of 1937: "The dictatorships . . . may not be the best form of government, but they are the only possible form of government at the moment." Given the contemporary economic and political disorder, these regimes, he felt, were a necessary reaction.[20]

Thus while he showed some hesitations, the overall impression conveyed by the statements Jung made during the 1930s on the National Socialist regime show that he was relatively sympathetic.

The final category encompassing Jung's relation to National Socialism is that of an alleged anti-Semitism and support for the regime's desire to establish a specifically German psychotherapy. When Jung became editor of the *Zentralblatt* in 1933, he declared that the magazine's new policy would be to differentiate between Germanic and Jewish psychologies:

> The differences which actually do exist between Germanic and Jewish psychologies and which have long been known to every intelligent person are no longer to be glossed over, and this can only be beneficial to science.[21]

This, he claimed, did not constitute anti-Semitism, but the objective establishment of existing differences. In the next issue of the *Zentralblatt*, Jung not only indicated differences in racial psychology, but the superiority of the Aryan mind as well. Differences between psychological schools of thought, he believed, could be explained on the basis of differing racial characteristics. The Jewish psychologies of Adler and Freud, in particular, were positively harmful to the idealistic Aryan soul. Jung granted that all aspects of mental life could ultimately be reduced to the lower impulses. In reference to Freud, he said,

> this [reduction] will never prove that the symbol or symptom so explained really has that meaning; it merely demonstrates the adolescent smutty-mindedness of the explainer . . . if he degrades everything to the level of a 'dirty joke' psychology, then we must not be surprised if the patient becomes spiritually blighted and compensates for this blight by an incurable intellectualism.

Again, Jung remarked of the Freudians:

> The psychoanalyst's every second word is "nothing but" – just what a dealer would say of an article he wanted to buy on the cheap. In this case it is man's soul, his hope, his boldest flight, his finest adventure.[22]

Thus we are given an image of the psychoanalysts and their supposedly damaging reductive technique in terms evoking the image of a huckster.

Jung maintained that such far-reaching differences of interpretation required an explanation beyond that of mere scientific error. Men such as Freud and Adler were not guilty of any naive self-deception – the problem ran much deeper, to the very nature of the thought processes themselves.

> Freud and Adler have beheld very clearly the shadow that accompanies us all. The Jews have this peculiarity in common with women; being physically weaker, they have to aim at the chinks in the armour of their adversary, and thanks to this technique which has been forced on them through the centuries, the Jews themselves are best protected where others are most vulnerable.[23]

The Jews, according to Jung, were under the influence of their ancestral experience just as the other historical collectivities on the European continent. But the Jews were at a special disadvantage:

> The Jew, who is something of a nomad, has never yet created a cultural form of his own and as far as we can see never will, since all his instincts and talents require a more or less civilized nation to act as host for their development.[24]

The Jew, then, was nomadic, materialistic, lacking in a valid cultural form of his own; he did, in fact, bear striking resemblance to the Jews described and stereotyped in nineteenth-century German literature.[25] Part of the reason for the peculiar characteristics of the Jew was his lack of roots in the soil. As a result, there could be no deeply felt correspondence with nature, and consequently no genuine creativity. Jung seemed to imply there would always be sharp differences between the Jews and the German *Volk*; since, as nomads, the Jews would never be subject to the influence of the German soil.[26]

By complementing this negative view of the Jewish psyche with a positive view of the Aryan mind, Jung seemed to serve the purposes of the regime. So different were the unconscious experiences of Aryans and Jews that he claimed they could receive only conditional comparison, one in fact that was dangerous to make at all if Freudian categories were used.

The 'Aryan' unconscious, on the other hand, contains explosive forces and seeds of a future yet to be born, and these may not be devalued as nursery romanticism without psychic danger. The still youthful Germanic peoples are fully capable of creating new cultural forms that still lie dormant in the darkness of the unconscious of every individual – seeds bursting with energy and capable of mighty expansion.[27]

Unfortunately this new cultural form turned out to be the modern totalitarian state.

Initially, at least, Jung identified National Socialism with the creative forces in the German unconscious.

Where was that unparalleled tension and energy while as yet no National Socialism existed? Deep in the Germanic psyche, in a pit that is anything but a garbage-bin of unrealizable infantile wishes and unresolved family resentments. A movement that grips a whole nation must have matured in every individual as well. That is why I say that the Germanic unconscious contains tensions and potentialities which medical psychology must consider in its evaluation of the unconscious.[28]

Thus it would be difficult to deny that Jung contributed to the attempt to formulate a Germanic psychotherapy which recognized the unique and dynamic aspects of the Aryan mind, a task which the Nazis sought to foster.

This brings us to the more basic question of how Jung arrived at such a stance. Here his earlier notions on racial psychology were a critical element. As far back as 1912, he indicated an interest in racial psychology when he wrote:

And since we, in the present day, have the power to decipher the symbolism of dreams and thereby surmise the mysterious psychology in the history of the development of the individual, so a way is here opened to the understanding of the secret springs of influence beneath the psychological development of races.[29]

In Jung's opinion, the myth was the collective dream of the race. Just as Freudian psychology used the individual dream as the *via regia* to the individual unconscious, so Jung tried to use myth to gain access to the racial unconscious. The interest in, and use of, mythology which was distinctive of Jung's psychology was, in the final analysis, linked with the notion of race.

It was not, however, a static conception of race.

The greatest experiment in the transplantation of a race in modern times was the colonization of the North American continent by a predominantly Germanic population. As the climatic conditions vary very widely, we would expect all sorts of variations of the original racial type. The admixture of Indian blood is increasingly small, so it plays no role. . . . At all events, the 'Yankee' type is formed, and this is so similar to the Indian type that on my first visit to the Middle West, while watching a stream of workers coming out of a factory, I remarked to my companion that I should never have thought there was such a high percentage of Indian blood.[30]

Jung later realized that their Indian appearance was the product of the soil. He believed "there [was] an 'X and a Y' in the air and in the soil of a country, which slowly permeate and assimilate him to the type of the aboriginal inhabitant, even to the point of slightly remodelling his physical features". The original racial type was subject to local influences, and this produced a collective attitude or *spiritus loci*.[31] In effect Jung's ideas on race prior to 1933 were broadly commensurate with the Nazi emphasis on soil and blood.

Another factor which must be considered in accounting for the stance Jung assumed in the 1930s derives from his conflict with Freud, a conflict which combined differences over race and professional enmities. Explaining his differences with Freud and Adler, Jung remarked in 1918:

As a rule, the Jew lives in amicable relationship with the earth, but without feeling the power of the chthonic. His receptivity to this seems to have weakened with time. This may explain the specific need of the Jew to reduce everything to its material beginnings; he needs these beginnings in order to counterbalance the dangerous ascendancy of his two cultures. A little bit of primitivity does not hurt him; on the contrary, I can understand very well that Freud's and Adler's reduction of everything psychic to primitive sexual wishes and power-drives has something about it that is beneficial and satisfying to the Jew, because it is a form of simplification. For this reason, Freud is perhaps right to close his eyes to my objections. But these specifically Jewish doctrines are thoroughly unsatisfying to the Germanic mentality; we still have a genuine barbarian in us who is not to be trifled with, and whose manifestation is no comfort for us and is not a pleasant way of passing time.[32]

Thus, Jung clearly found the root of his theoretical differences with Freud in race, though the tone of this essay is somewhat more balanced than the statement cited above from the 1933 *Zentralblatt*. For example, in the earlier essay, there was the threat from the "blond Beast" – meaning the primitive European in general. There was the Jew lacking in the quality that rooted one to the strengthgiving earth, but "this chthonic quality [was also] found in dangerous concentration in the Germanic peoples".[33] Nonetheless the image of the rootless materialistic Jew fitted the stereotype later fostered by the Nazis.

Freud and some of his supporters classified Jung as a racist twenty years before the advent of the Hitler regime. In his "On the History of the Psycho-Analytic Movement", Freud remarked that Jung "seemed ready to enter into a friendly relationship with me, and for my sake to give up certain prejudices in regard to race which he had previously permitted himself".[34] Whatever preconceptions Jung may have had in respect to race, they did not prevent him from becoming an ardent supporter of Freud's theories, one who was expected at one time to succeed his Viennese mentor. On the other hand, Ernest Jones, Freud's biographer and an early participant in the Psycho-Analytic Movement, also felt that some racial prejudice distorted Jung's judgment.[35] The Englishman [in fact, Welshman – ed.], having failed to vote for Jung's reelection as president of the Society at the Munich Congress of 1913, recalled Jung's rebuking him with the phrase, "I thought you were a Christian."[36] This may be testimony from hostile witnesses. Still, Jung's reputed anti-Semitism probably contributed to Nazi willingness to allow him to act as the editor of a journal published in Germany.

In turn, the professional rivalry with Freud and the hopes of propagating his own doctrine also made the Nazis more acceptable to Jung and were important in his decision to accept the presidency of the International General Medical Society for Psychotherapy and the editorship of the politically controlled *Zentralblatt*. In 1933 Jung complained, "Unfortunately, it is only in Germany that I am not known."[37] Yet, like Freud, Jung believed the fate of psychotherapy would be decided in Germany; thus his eagerness to retain contacts with the Germans even under difficult circumstances.[38] If for the moment Jung was obliged to concentrate on differentiating a Germanic psychology in the *Zentralblatt*, it fitted well in the framework of his racial theories and had the advantage of clearing the two major rivals, both Jewish, from his path. The International General Medical Society for Psychotherapy might well, indeed, for the moment, have had to rival Freud's International Psychoanalytic Association.

Another factor which made him sympathetic toward the German regime as well as making him acceptable to it was a current of romanticism that was deeply embedded in his work: that is, an emphasis on the emotional and irrational, on fantasy, symbol and myth; a belief in the merits of synthesis over those of the dissecting intellect; and a reverence for nature and the organic. In examining the romantic features of Jung's work, we will look at the notion of the collective unconscious, the source of symbol and fantasy, because it is one of the distinctive elements most often associated with his theories, because it will help us understand the structure of the psyche as he conceived it, and because it will clarify his views on myth and symbol.

The structure of the psyche, for Jung, contained three major levels: the conscious mind, the personal unconscious, and the collective unconscious. In order to emphasize its universal aspect, Jung sometimes referred to the latter as the objective psyche; everyone possessed these unconscious traits. In contradistinction, the personal unconscious was the result of individual experience; therefore it was largely subjective, and nearer the surface of mind. It was sharply distinguished from the unconscious repressed, and was, moreover, a potentiality carried from the ancient past in the form of mnemonic images which were inherited as part of the anatomy of the brain. Just as physical organs provided functional adaptations to environmental conditions, the mind had developed organs or functions that reflected regular physical events.[39] The psyche, however, did not register constantly repeated or impressive physical events directly; instead, it registered the human effect which the event produced. These effects, in turn, excited fantasies in the mind which humanized or personified the forces of nature in the form of archetypes or primordial images. The archetypes were merely the forms that the instincts had assumed.[40] These were not innate ideas, but the innate possibilities of ideas. They were transcendental categories whose presence was to be inferred from their effects.[41] The figures or primordial images constantly recurred through the ages wherever fantasy was used freely. These were the most ancient and universal thought-forms of humanity. Hence they were called archetypes, and these inherited categories constituted the collective unconscious. The inherited patterns in the collective unconscious were adaptations to, as well as means of transcending, the environment; fantasy thinking, therefore, was of elemental importance in understanding human nature, a position common to both Jung and the romantics.

Possessing universal images on the more basic levels, the structure of the psyche was nevertheless the product of a lengthy evolution, developing from a vague *participation mystique* to a clearly defined consciousness. In the course of a slow process, consciousness emerged from this primitive identification with the natural surroundings to a collective identification with more clearly defined groups, and, ultimately, to an identification with the individual. In the course of evolution, Jung felt, various levels of collective experience were established. The unconscious contents of various nations bore different traits in the form of primordial images. And it was due to the influence of these unconscious images that the behaviour of nations took on its specific character; in the case of Germany, one of these archetypal patterns might be described as Faust, or, alternatively, as

101

Wotan.[42] The Faust image was biologically inherited along with the brain of every German, and predisposed him to react to events in a characteristic manner.

> Thus there must be typical myths which are really the instruments of a folk-psychological complex treatment. Jacob Burckhardt seems to have suspected this when he once said that every Greek of the classical era carried in himself a fragment of Oedipus, just as every German carries a fragment of Faust.[43]

There was a national psychology as well as an individual psychology. There was, in other words, a *Volk*-soul quite similar to the one revered by the German romantics.

Moreover, Jung, like the romantics, had a rather positive orientation toward the contents of the *Volk*-soul and the unconscious as the depository of the wisdom of the ages. Whoever could tap this source of knowledge, he believed, would be "an incomparable prognosticator".[44] Similarly, he felt that all effective art had its roots in the collective unconscious, here paralleling Herder's notion of good literature as the product of the *Volk*-soul. During the creative process there was, Jung felt, an unconscious reanimation of the archetype which the artist developed and shaped. The individual artist played the role of educator. By shaping the primordial image, he translated that image into contemporary form; thus making it possible "to find our way back to the deepest springs of life".[45] Like his romantic forebears, Jung found a source of illumination in the typical myths of a folk-psychological complex, or *Volk*-soul, as indeed in the archetypes in general.

Nature, too, was a basic reality for Jung as for the romantics.

> The peasant's alternating rhythm of work secures his unconscious satisfaction through its symbolical content – satisfactions which the factory workers and office employees do not know and can never enjoy. What do we know of his life with nature, of those grand moments. . . . From all this we city-dwellers, we modern machine-minders are far removed.[46]

This Swiss physician, who had so profound an appreciation for the importance of symbols and myths, felt that science, which was synonymous with the intellect, should not be an end in itself. Life was the criterion, and not intellect alone.[47] Practical psychology, he believed, was superior to science in that it transcended the limits of a specialized discipline. Rather than disdaining the use of creative fantasy, Jung found this faculty often solved the problem raised by external reality for which reason could find no answer. Thus, he saw himself as having surpassed the intellectual limitations of the Enlightenment and of its offspring, nineteenth-century science. Too much concentration in the latter sphere caused distortion. The historical situation, he believed, required emphasis on the irrational. "We ought to be particularly grateful to Bergson for having broken a lance in defence of the irrational."[48] Thus, Jung in line with the romantic tradition, frankly espoused the benefits of the irrational.

Similarly, Jung was alienated by what he considered to be the materialism and hedonism of the Enlightenment. He considered Freud to be a descendant of Enlightenment thinkers, a descendant who had the negative view of religion which had flowered in the materialistic and rationalistic scientists of the nineteenth century. The originator of psychoanalysis, he maintained, had many of the same failings as the men of the Enlightenment, taking for example Voltaire's *Ecrasez l'infâme* as one of his favourite quotations.[49] In contrast, Jung always attached the greatest importance to reinforcing a religious attitude in the psyche. He believed that reason stifled the natural forces which nonetheless would seek their revenge one day and try to overwhelm consciousness. Religion was developed to help protect humanity against this danger, and to cope with any damage that might be done: "religions are systems of healing for psychic illness."[50] Conversely, in his view, analysis retained a religious nature of its own. One could interpret the transference as an attempt to free a vision of God from the individual person of the doctor. One could find the truest meaning of the transference, perhaps, by seeing it as a "little bit of real *Gottesminne*" which had departed from consciousness since the end of the Middle Ages.[51] Indeed, Jung originally envisioned a religious mission for psychoanalysis.

> I think [he wrote to Freud] we must give it time to infiltrate into people from many centres, to revivify among the intellectuals a feeling for symbol and myth, ever so gently to transform Christ back into the soothsaying god of the vine, which he was, and in this way absorb those ecstatic instinctual forces of Christianity for this *one* purpose of making the cult and the sacred myth what they once were – a drunken feast of joy where man regained the ethos and holiness of an animal. That was the beauty and purpose of classical religion, which from God knows what temporary biological needs has turned into a Misery Institute.[52]

Freud wrote back that he did not want to be thought of as the founder of a religion.[53] Jung, however, always continued to feel the need for what he called "the eternal truths of myth" as did other romantics before him, and like them, he, too, found that this impulse ran counter to what he conceived of as the materialism and hedonism of the Enlightenment.[54]

This basic attitude was also reflected in the different roles attributed to sexual drives in the psychic development. It was in the unconscious fastening of libido to certain infantile fantasies and habits, according to Jung, that Freud found the aetiology of the neurosis; a strong attachment to the Oedipus complex, for example, was characteristic of many neurotics.[55] While this fixation, Jung thought, explained those cases which were neurotic from infancy, it did not account for those which showed no very noticeable traces of neurosis until the actual onset of the illness. He believed that the origins of the neurosis were only partially traceable to infantile predisposition, and that an inability to adjust to the demands of the present were equally important. The infantile fantasies to which the neurotic was attached occurred often in normal individuals without necessarily bringing neurotic behaviour with them. In short, it was the unusual utilization of these fantasies rather than the fact of fixation which was most significant. For Freud, the real cause of regression to the Oedipus complex was incestuous desires. Jung denied the special intensity of these incestuous desires which would have made them determinative. He maintained that the incest taboo among primitives was not the result of a great desire in that direction, but simply one of the numerous taboos and superstitious fears typical of primitives, the expression of a large quantity of free-floating anxiety.[56] In childhood, as in primitive humanity, there were no particularly strong incestuous desires; the reason for regression was not to be sought in sexual desires. Hence the sexual aetiology of the neurosis was too narrow a conception. It was also too hedonistic a view for a romantic temperament like Jung's. Consequently, he sought an alternative explanation.

Instead of assuming a strictly sexual perspective, Jung proposed what he termed the energic view which involved a redefinition of the nature of the libido. He came to see all psychological phenomena as manifestations of energy just as physical manifestations were to be conceived as expressions of energic phenomena under the law of the conservation of energy. Subjectively and psychologically, these manifestations appeared as desire, though not limited to sexual desire. Indeed this definition of libido corresponded to Schopenhauer's idea of the Will, a continuous life impulse, or to vital energy in general, to Bergson's *élan vital*.[57]

Moreover, according to Jung, the nature of the libido was historically determined. In what he termed the genetic conception of libido, it was viewed as the product of a lengthy evolution: from a primitive sexual instinct, the libido developed many complicated functions, which today lacked any sexual character. Many modifications of the procreative instinct took place during the ascent through the animal kingdom. Instead of producing a large number of eggs and sperma, the energy which would have been used in their production was transferred into the creation of mechanisms of allurement, and protection of the young. In this way, the survival of the individual as well as the genus reached a higher degree of certainty. Jung found an example of this development in the nest-building activities of birds. Here the energy which might have been expended in the production of larger numbers of offspring was transferred to the protection of a relatively small number. But in the process, the libido had been desexualized; the energy used in the building of the nest might have been sexual in origin, but its nature had been completely altered. The original sexual character of these biological institutions became lost in their *organic* fixation and functional independence.[58]

Both ontogenetically and phylogenetically, the libido increasingly adapted itself to the external world. This conception of the libido allowed Jung to find a nonsexual aetiology for neuroses. When an insurmountable obstacle blocked the libido, it returned to more primitive modes of adaptation; if the obstacles were removed, on the other hand, the system of infantile fantasies would lose its grip on the individual.[59] The cause of the neurosis was in the present, not in the past. It consisted of the life task, the duties imposed by existence, which the patient was unable to accomplish. It was not to be found in the infantile fantasies which had been swollen by a regressive libido unable to find a normal path of development in adjusting to reality. He admitted that infantile fantasies determined the form and further development of the neurosis, but that did not mean they were causative.[60] True enough, the neurosis was characterized by infantile attitudes or the predominance of infantile fantasies and desires. Infantile desires, however, were important for both neurotics and normal people; but they were not significant aetiologically. Instead they were reactions, secondary and regressive phenomena. Infantile sexual fantasies did not cause the neurosis.[61] The fantasies themselves were not primary phenomena based upon a perverted sexual proclivity. Instead they were a consequence of not successfully applying accumulated libido to reality. Jung realized this was a very old view, but he believed it was true nonetheless.[62] The aetiology of the neurosis, then, was not to be found in the different expressions of infantile sexual development and their accordant fantasies which merely became prominent in the neurosis through the agency of dammed-up and regressive libido. In keeping with a romantic predisposition, Jung did not emphasize the negative role of fantasy. Indeed, as we shall see, he accorded it a very positive function.

Soon after the rupture with Freud, Jung began to refer to his own method of therapy as a constructive or synthetic method. In explaining his position, he often chose to use the Latin terms *causa* and *fines*. The causal standpoint sought to reduce everything to its elements, to trace them back to their *causae*. A *reductio ad causam*, however, could never adequately grasp the psyche, in Jung's opinion, because change was viewed as nothing but the sublimation of the basic factors – in reality another form of the same thing.[63] There was no apparent reason to regard the psyche as a mere epiphenomenon of the brain, any more than life was an epiphenomenon of the chemistry of carbon compounds. The Cathedral of Cologne was something radically different from the stones of which it was composed; it was not to be explained in terms of mineralogy merely because it was constructed of rocks. Similarly a plant was not merely a product of the soil.[64] In the same way, an organic entity required special treatment beyond the grasp of reductive rational analysis, as romantics have generally agreed.

To grasp an organic entity like the psyche, the mind as becoming, one had to make use of the constructive standpoint, that is one had to elaborate its elements into something higher and more complex; one had to judge subjectively the *fines* or goals towards which, for example, neurotic or psychotic symptoms were tending. Jung realized his constructive method corresponded to Bergson's intuitive method, though he limited himself to the psychological aspect and to practical work.[65] A mental manifestation had to be interpreted not only causally – Jung admitted that almost all things could be reduced to the procreative instincts – but anagogically as well. Analytical psychology, as Jung called his method, or constructive comprehension, analysed but it did not reduce.[66] Psychic phenomena were treated as symbols. Contrary to the common use of the word, a *symbol* was not just a sign for something else which everyone knew, nor was it, as Freud and Adler would have had it, a veil disguising primitive tendencies or desires. It was rather an attempt to elucidate, by means of analogy, something that was yet to be. In this way, our imagination revealed to us, in the form of a cogent analogy, what was in the process of becoming. When we reduced this by analysis to something else, we destroyed the real value of the symbol: "they [symbols] were the best possible expressions for something unknown – bridges thrown out towards an unseen shore." It was "the intimation of a meaning beyond the level of our present powers of comprehension".[67] This conception of the symbol was in keeping with the romantic attitude toward synthesis.

This had a fundamental impact on the principles of treatment. Reductive procedure, according to Jung, was useful only when a morbid structure, taking the place of natural accomplishment, had to be broken down. In neurotics, the symbol-forming powers were relatively purposeless. The libido was not converted into effective work, but flowed into archaic sexual phantasies. These symbols had to be split or reduced until the libido flowed back into natural channels. But reducing everything exclusively to causes reinforced the primitive trends of the personality and might lead to resignation and hopelessness. Only if, at the same time, the primitive tendencies were balanced by recognition of the symbolic values, would the original reduction be valuable. Once freed from morbid structures, the libido had to find a more favourable outlet. At that point, the symbol-forming tendency was to be reinforced in a synthetic direction.[68]

Instead of purely reductive analysis, Jung advocated an approach which resembled the ancient science of hermeneutics, that is successively adding other analogies to the analogy given in a symbol. Initially, the subjective analogies of the patient, gathered at random, were added; later those objective analogies discovered by the analyst in the course of his erudite research were included. By this method, the initial symbol was widened and enriched, so that the outcome was a complex structure in which certain lines of psychological development stood out as possibilities.[69] As with the romantics, the meaning of life was to be found in the symbol – a symbol that led to synthesis.

One of romanticism's characteristic desires was to treat nature organically: hence the emphasis on synthesis. Reduction destroyed the force that made the organic whole a living unity. J.G. Fichte's theory of science, for example, set synthesis as a counter ideal to mechanistic analysis.[70] Over one hundred years later, a similar emphasis could still be discerned in the psychology of C.G. Jung.

Without attempting to evaluate Jung's use of symbol and myth and without insisting that Jung was purely a romantic, I think we have demonstrated that the influence of romanticism on his work cannot be ignored. Nor did his contemporaries ignore it. Indeed the elements of romanticism in his work helped make him acceptable to a nationalist regime in Germany where romanticism was deeply embedded in the nation's cultural heritage. In the first issue of the *Zentralblatt* published under his editorship, one of the contributors expressed the following opinion:

> His [Jung's] encompassing work and spirit avoided the extremes of Scylla and Charybdis to renew the old, interrupted work of the romantics who created poetry and philosophized. In this he showed a good German style. . . .[71]

That is precisely our point.

The final important factor influencing Jung's behaviour during the 1930s was his fear of socialism, a fear that made him willing to make his peace with contemporary dictatorships.

> Communistic or Socialistic democracy is an upheaval of the unfit against attempts at order. Consider the stay-in-strikes in France, the former socialistic upheavals in Germany and Italy. The state of disorder called democratic freedom or liberalism brings its own reactions – enforced order. Inasmuch as the European nations are incapable of living in a chronic state of disorder, they will make attempts at enforced order, or Fascism. . . . The dictatorships . . . may not be the best form of government, but they are the only possible form of government at the moment.[72]

Jung, then, felt that the threatening disorders on the Continent made the dictatorships necessary. From this vantage point, one can understand his willingness to countenance the activities of National Socialism even when it might have been less than perfect.

Such were the factors which moulded Jung's relationship to National Socialism, a relationship which has laid him open to criticism. We can now examine this criticism and the responses to it, again employing our initial division of Jung's activities into three categories – anti-Semitism and support for Germanic psychotherapy, comments on the Hitler regime, and ties with the General Medical Society for Psychotherapy – as a frame of reference. One advocate sought to clarify the situation by pointing out that Jung had already been a vice-president of the Society for several years when, in April 1933, he acceded to the presidency.[73] In his own defence, Jung maintained that the problem was to avoid the destruction of the Society, whose membership was predominantly German, and still prevent the Society's complete subordination to the Nazi regime. He felt that he helped to promote an ingenious compromise. The Germans, who were to conform politically, formed a separate group of their own in September 1933. In the meantime Jung helped to organize an International General Medical Society for Psychotherapy in which the conformed German group was to be only one among a number of unconformed national groups. Eventually Dutch, Danish, Swedish, Austrian, and Swiss groups were formed. Moreover, the defence of Jung continued, the statutes of the International Society which were accepted by a Constituent Congress held at Bad-Nauheim in May 1934 also made provision for those individuals who wished to affiliate with the International Society directly. In this way, Jung argued, he hoped German Jews would be able to retain some professional membership. One must point out, however, that he realized the political authorities might prevent such a development.[74] Still this reorganization could be credited with protecting the professional interests of the German society's membership by retaining some international contacts.

It has been maintained that Jung has been unjustly criticized for serving as editor of a *gleichgeschaltet* periodical, the *Zentralblatt für Psychotherapie*. One of his disciples even contends that it was not a *gleichgeschaltet* magazine.[75] Interestingly enough, Jung himself explicitly admitted that *all* German periodicals were *gleichgeschaltet*.[76] Moreover as Jung admitted to a prospective colleague, who he hoped would write the book reviews for this journal, the contributors would be engaged in a veritable "egg balancing dance". Hence it would be preferable to have a German national direct the editorial staff so that those who submitted articles would have a better idea of what they were permitted to say.[77]

M.H. Göring, a family relation of Hermann Göring, and the head of the German branch of the International General Medical Society for Psychotherapy, inserted a political programme in the December issue of this journal without Jung's knowledge. The latter, in an article published in the Swiss *Neue Zürcher Zeitung*, saw that action as so serious a step as to call his own editorship into question.[78] But he did not resign; indeed he retained his post until 1940. Instead he protested to C.W. Cimbal, the managing editor of the *Zentralblatt*. In the same letter, however, Jung expressed an understanding of the political necessities which occasioned such a step. Moreover at the same time that he demanded the *Zentralblatt* remain separate from any political programme, he reassured Cimbal that he would say nothing in that journal which would be politically inappropriate. In other words, he would not insist on inserting a disclaimer of Göring's statement to mark off his own position.[79] The German authorities, then, did not have complete freedom to run the *Zentralblatt* as a propaganda organ, but neither did the authors who published in this periodical have the freedom due to scholars.

Jung always maintained that his actions as president were altruistically motivated. Admittedly a moral conflict arose within him when he assumed the presidency of the General Medical Society for Psychotherapy and the editorship of its publication: was he to hide himself as a prudent citizen of a neutral country or, as he was well aware, "expose myself to the inevitable misunderstandings [from] which no one escapes who, from [a] higher necessity, has to make a pact with the existing political powers in Germany"?[80]

Seeking to vindicate himself with a historical precedent, Jung cited the case of Galileo's recantation. Faced with the choice of the stake or retraction of his scientific views before the Inquisition, Galileo chose the latter. In this situation Jung implied an analogy to his own acceptance of the limitations imposed by National Socialism. But this was a very loose analogy, for Galileo had no other options while Jung, as a Swiss citizen, was under no real duress to accept National Socialist supervision. After commending Einstein for having the prudence to bask on the beaches of Los Angeles, and asserting that Galileo would have been well-advised, in a similar circumstance, to follow the same course, Jung proclaimed his own willingness to face the situation out of a higher necessity.[81]

We in Switzerland can hardly understand such a thing, but we are immediately in the picture if we transport ourselves back three or four centuries to a time when the Church had totalitarian presumptions. Barbed wire had not been invented then, so there were probably no concentration camps; instead, the Church used large quantities of faggots.[82]

Understanding the nature of the German government, or of higher necessities, may not have been granted to the Swiss, but Jung certainly understood it quite well. His reference to the concentration camps and barbed wire can leave no doubts as to the fullness of his knowledge where National Socialism was concerned.

After such an admission, it is difficult to justify Jung's invocation of the biblical injunction to "render unto Caesar". By cooperating with a totalitarian regime, he rendered not only those things which were Caesar's but those which had a good claim to an existence free of state intervention.

Jung's attempt to justify himself by claiming that he was adapting to the inevitable is equally unconvincing. He argued:

> they must learn to adapt themselves. To protest is ridiculous – how protest against an avalanche: It is better to look out. Science has no interest in calling down avalanches; it must preserve its intellectual heritage even under changed conditions.[83]

The avalanche for which he wanted to make way had barely won control over the German government; the Nazi party itself never did win an absolute majority in a free election. However popular it may have been subsequently, the fact remains that in the crucial year of 1933, the avalanche could have used some added support, and that is precisely what Jung, in his capacity as editor of the *Zentralblatt*, gave it. No one will argue that it is the business of science to defy avalanches; on the other hand, it is even less decorous to help them down the mountain.

Moreover, Jung's defence continues, he hoped to preserve a young and insecure science. It was his duty as a doctor to make psychotherapeutic help available to the afflicted, his duty to practice medicine regardless of the form of government. In addition, the ties of friendship with many German physicians, and the link of their common German culture forbade his withdrawal.[84] Jung thus pleaded altruism as well as necessity.

His actions in the second category, that of comments on the Hitler regime, might also be defended, though in this area no reply to criticisms was launched until after the Second World War. At that time the emphasis of his defence was upon a pretended prescience concerning National Socialism's disastrous consequences, and a forthright condemnation of the regime after its demise.

Prior to 1945 Jung never published anything that unequivocally advised opposition to the Hitler regime. Such prewar statements as indicated any criticism of National Socialism were generally mild and counter-balanced by more positive assessments. It was not until Germany's fate had already been decided that Jung published several essays containing statements very different from some of those he made in the 1930s. No longer was Hitler referred to as the Sybil or the Delphic oracle.

> A more accurate diagnosis of Hitler's condition would be *pseudo-logia phantastica*, that form of hysteria which is characterized by a peculiar talent for believing one's own lies.[85]

Indeed Hitler's followers were psychopaths – not knights – and National Socialism was a mass psychosis. His prewar and postwar comments on Hitler and the Nazi regime formed a decided contrast, and belied a pretended forewarning.

Only on the eve of the war did Jung counsel any organized attempt to control the regime, albeit through the indirect route of appeasement. This followed from the statement: "You must keep away from the craze, avoid the infection." But the advice offered Western statesmen immediately thereafter was, in effect, to permit Hitler to carry out his plans for eastward expansion.

> You may try to divert him but to stop him will be impossible without the Great Catastrophe for all. . . . Germany in her present mood . . . is much too dangerous. . . . Let her go to Russia. There is plenty of land there – one sixth of the surface of the earth.[86]

This advice fitted well with Hitler's original desire for an Aryan domain in Eastern Europe as well as with Jung's anti-socialist sentiments. In any case, clear public comments on the danger came rather late in the game. An apparent confusion in Jung's memory in regard to a key text lends credence to the belief that, in fact, his initial evaluation of National Socialism was much more positive. He cited a passage seemingly critical of dictators – quoted above – from a lecture which he claimed to have delivered at Essen and Cologne in February 1933. These words, however, were not in all probability pronounced at Essen in February 1933, but appeared only as part of the essay, "The Meaning of Psychology for Modern Man", published in the summer of 1933.[87] Though I have been unable to find any newspaper reports of the speech given in Cologne, a check of the newspaper archive in Dortmund revealed that the lecture actually given at Essen in February 1933 was a repeat of the *Kulturbund* lecture on the development of personality.[88] Whether or not the lecture as delivered in Essen contained the passage "The paean of the Italian nation is addressed to the personality of the Duce, and the dirges of other nations lament the absence of other great leaders" or the comment subsequently appended by Jung in 1934 to the effect that Germany too had found her leader cannot be determined from the newspaper accounts. In any case this lecture was far more likely to have been construed as support for the Hitler regime. Perhaps it is significant that he originally delivered the *Kulturbund* lecture in November 1932 – a date which Jung claimed marked the year in which Germany's fate was decided.[89] An election took place in

Germany in November 1932 (though the speech was delivered in Austria), and when he repeated this lecture in Germany in February 1933, the Nazis were again engaged in an electoral battle, this time one designed to permit Chancellor Hitler to impose a complete dictatorship. One is tempted to ask if this correlation is accidental or if these talks had a political as well as a scientific purpose? It is a tribute to the pioneering efforts of Jung, the results of which appeared in his *Studies on Word Association*, that we can pause here to pose some other questions: Did Jung's misdating of texts cited in his defence result from the unconscious constellation of forces interfering with the functioning of consciousness, that is from a complex? Why was it precisely the repeat of the *Kulturbund* lecture rather than another that was involved in the confusion? Or, to draw upon the popularized terminology of his former associates and fellow pioneers in the study of the psychopathology of everyday life, was this a Freudian slip?

Actually Jung did a better job of defending himself when he admitted an initial uncertainty as to the outcome of the National Socialist phenomenon:

> When Hitler seized power it became evident to me that a mass psychosis was boiling up in Germany. But I could not help telling myself that this was after all Germany, a civilized European nation with a sense of morality and discipline. Hence the ultimate outcome of this unmistakable mass movement still seemed to me uncertain, just as the figure of the Führer at first struck me as being merely ambivalent.[90]

He maintained that his attitude toward the Nazis at that point was determined by a therapeutic view which sought to integrate archetypal elements emerging from the unconscious. Since archetypes could produce directly opposite results, he explained,

> [m]y medical attitude towards such things counselled me to wait . . . to give things a 'fair trial'. . . . The therapist's aim is to bring the positive, valuable, and living quality of the archetype . . . into reality and at the same time to obstruct as far as possible its damaging and pernicious tendencies. It is part of the doctor's professional equipment to summon up a certain amount of optimism even in the most unlikely circumstances, with a view to saving everything that it is still possible to save . . . even if this means exposing himself to danger.[91]

His argument that therapeutic considerations determined his reactions in 1933 is the most favourable interpretation of his conduct that can be made. It has the unfortunate effect, however, of contradicting his claim to having warned against mass psychoses, at least where the Nazis were concerned.

In reality, as we have seen, Jung was originally more positively oriented toward National Socialism. It is true, however, that by 1936 his assessment of the Nazis showed some public hesitations. No doubt this ambivalence resulted in part, at least, from his therapeutic outlook. Jung regarded religions as systems for preventing psychic illness. Consequently, he encouraged Wotan-worship and did not merely describe it, as one of his postwar defenders, Philip Wylie, has maintained.[92] The Swiss psychiatrist did, in fact, say:

> I would therefore advise the German Faith Movement to throw aside their [sic] scruples. Intelligent people will not confuse them with the crude Wotan-worshippers whose faith is a mere pretence. There are people in the German Faith Movement who are intelligent enough not only *to believe* but to know that the God of the *Germans* is Wotan and not the Christian God.[93]

Moreover Wylie has asserted: "Jung explained the idiocy of it [Wotan-worship] but the claim that he advocated it was silly."[94] Such a statement simply was not true. On the contrary, Jung encouraged an organization which maintained that the religious renaissance of the nation would flow from the hereditary origins of the German race – in part, at least, through the worship of Wotan. However efficacious this encouragement of a religious attitude in the psyche may be in a therapeutic situation, describing the irrational elements associated with National Socialism in terms of Nordic mythology during the 1930s and accepting these elements as manifestations of a valid religious experience was more likely to encourage irrationalism than to integrate such elements into consciousness.

It is true that Jung probably intended some criticism of Hitler when he said: "what a so-called Führer does with a mass movement can plainly be seen if we turn our eyes to the north or south of our country." Wotan, however, was also identified with a broader phenomenon, with the nationalist god, "German Faith" or the state.[95] Utilization of the knowledge of mythology which went along with his method of constructive comprehension led Jung to view the Wotan phenomenon in a relatively optimistic fashion. Wotan, he believed, had an ecstatic and mantic side so that National Socialism could be viewed as a *reculer pour mieux sauter*.[96] In seeking the prospective tendencies involved in the reanimating of the Wotan archetype, Jung remained true to his general approach. Just as the reflux of libido into the mother image was not simply a regression but an attempt to find a solution to the patient's problem, so Wotan *redivivus* was also a hopeful sign. Indeed Jung closed this essay on the optimistic note of predicting the imminent realization of Wotan's ecstatic and mantic qualities.

After the Second World War, Jung claimed to have ended the 1936 essay with a quote from the Voluspa (Poetic Edda) that predicted the coming catastrophe.[97] This was a distortion of the facts. The original text closed with the statement, "Then at last we shall know what Wotan is saying when he murmurs with Mimir's head."[98] Coming as it did immediately after a sentence in which Wotan was referred to as a *reculer pour mieux sauter*, it was evident that Jung originally intended to conclude on a positive note. The supplementary, explanatory quotation from the Voluspa which seemed to predict dire events was only added after World War II. Unfortunately the reader has not been notified of this change, not even in the *Collected Works* edition.

In the postwar era Jung insisted that by 1937 he had become convinced that the end of National Socialism would be even bloodier than he had previously anticipated. Indeed, we can detect some change in his views at that time. Back in 1934 he had pleaded for understanding in regard to German censorship and totalitarianism, alleging, at that time, that it was "only consistent with the logic of history that after an age of clerical *Gleichschaltung* the turn should come for one practised by the secular state".[99] By 1937, in contrast, he condemned "the amazing spectacle of states taking over the age-old totalitarian claims of theocracy, which are inevitably accompanied by suppression of free opinion". Jung also claimed that as a result of these remarks which appeared in German translation in 1940, he was blacklisted by the Gestapo.[100] This claim, however, has not been substantiated; no one has been able to publish such a list with Jung's name on it. Nonetheless, there was a clear shift in his opinions by 1937.

After examining the defence which could be made in favour of Jung in regard to his comments on the Hitler regime, and after reviewing the justification for his ties with the General Medical Society for Psychotherapy, we must look at the remaining category, that of the retorts that could be made to criticism of Jung's views on Germanic psychotherapy and race. During the 1930s he defended his comments on racial psychology by maintaining that not only were they demanded by the necessities of the hour, but they were scientifically based as well. Everything in Germany, he insisted, including psychotherapy, had to be German; thus he considered it a "cheap jibe" to poke fun at Germanic psychotherapy. Here, however, he was somewhat inconsistent; while he objected when a Swiss colleague, Dr V. Gustav Bally, published a newspaper article critical of Jung's work as a *deutschstämmige Psychotherapie*, he never objected to the comments of C.W. Cimbal, the managing editor of the *Zentralblatt*. Cimbal wrote: "The Congress, as the introduction of the editor of the *Zentralblatt* announced, will similarly serve the shaping of a teutonic-racial (germanic) [*deutschstämmigen (germanischen)*] psychology and psychotherapy."[101] If the use of such terminology by Bally was objectionable, it should have been almost as objectionable coming from Cimbal, even allowing for political necessity. Bally's characterization of Jung's work as *deutsch-stämmige Psychotherapie* was not far off the mark.

Indeed Jung defended the medical and psychological validity of distinctions between Germans and Jews. He was aware that he would probably be misunderstood, but he saw a positive value in bringing certain questions to the fore immediately.

> I tabled the Jewish question. This I did deliberately. . . . The Jewish problem is a regular complex, a festering wound, and no responsible doctor could bring himself to apply methods of medical hush-hush in this matter.[102]

When criticized for not having supported his opposition to Freud with the express differences between Christian-Germanic and Semitic psychology in his scientific writings at the time of the split, and only taking an interest in them recently, Jung replied that he had noted the importance of racial psychology well before.[103] And as we have shown above this was certainly true. One may, however, question the wisdom of raising the issue in a periodical subject to German censorship, and consequently unable to present more than one side – the one favoured by the Nazis.

Was Jung, then, a racist? According to the *Dictionary of the Social Sciences* racism is "the doctrine that there is a connection between racial, and cultural traits, and that some races are inherently superior to others".[104] As Jung once said, "so intimate is the intermingling of bodily and psychic traits that not only can we draw far-reaching inferences as to the constitution of the psyche from the constitution of the body, but we can also infer from psychic peculiarities the corresponding bodily characteristics".[105] In his younger days he felt he was following in the footsteps of such men as Franz Joseph Gall and Lavater, placing his work in their tradition.[106] Later in his career he was less sanguine about the immediate feasibility of the project, but continued to believe in the importance and ultimate possibility of correlating physical and mental characteristics.[107] Thus Jung's statements fit the first part of the definition of racism.

Some of his ideas also seemed to fit the second part of the definition, that is, that some races are superior. Jung himself claimed that he had not gone beyond the first element, that he merely distinguished between German and Jewish psychologies, and that this did not constitute any form of denigration. Thus when he said, "The Aryan unconscious has a higher potential than the Jewish; that is both the advantage and disadvantage of a youthfulness not yet weaned from barbarism", it was meant as accurate observation, and not one which was flattering to the Germans to whom the term *barbarism* was applied.[108] The use of this term did not, however, raise any objections from the German authorities, and the word *barbarian* which could be equated with vigour and virility was not necessarily taken as pejorative by National Socialist enthusiasts. Similarly Jung maintained that he was not slighting the Jews when he argued:

> In my opinion it has been a grave error in medical psychology up till now to apply Jewish categories – which are not even binding on all Jews – indiscriminately to Germanic and Slavic Christendom. Because of this the most precious secret of the Germanic peoples – their creative and intuitive depth of soul – has been explained as a morass of banal infantilism.[109]

He pointed out that he had been careful to say these categories were not even binding on all Jews.[110]

In actual fact Jung's published characterization of the Jewish psyche as it appeared in 1933–34 did bear the marks of denigration: lack of contact with the strength-giving soil, an inability to create a cultural form of its own, a penchant to reduce everything to its material origins – in contrast to the idealistic Aryan – and a quality held in common with women which sought the weak points of others; this was more than mere distinction. His delineation of the Negro mentality was also a rather negative one. In a description of life in the United States the Negroes were depicted as a primitive influence, and the image of the Negro which he presented was that of an inferior group.

> The expression of religious feeling, the revival meetings, the Holy Rollers and other abnormalities are strongly influenced by the Negro. The vivacity of the average American, which shows itself not only at baseball games but quite particularly in his extraordinary love of talking – the ceaseless gabble of American papers is an eloquent example of this – is scarcely to be derived from his Germanic forefathers, but is more like the chattering of a Negro village.[111]

On the other hand Jung could express feelings of amity for his "African brother".[112] Still, in the dreams of his American patients as interpreted by Jung, the Negro often expressed the inferior side of their personality. While Jung described the primitive influence of the local environment on the predominantly Germanic population, there was little consideration of the inverse process; a rise in the cultural level of the Negroes was not discussed. Thus Jung's descriptions of Negroes and Jews did combine biologically determined cultural traits with inferiority and could have been termed racist.

But his ideas on race were not to be isolated from the rest of his work. While he maintained some racist notions which are of significance in understanding his work, particularly in grasping the manner in which he viewed the differences between himself and Freud, there was also a more universal element in Jung's theories, and this element was in the last resort more important. If Jung was interested in racial archetypes, he was even more interested in exploring the archetypes which were common to all of humanity; his ideas on race were a significant but secondary feature of his work. As far as race is concerned it would be more accurate to say that there were some racist components in his thought rather than to characterize its orientation as racist.

Ostensible racial differences did not prevent Jung from treating Jewish patients nor from retaining ties with Jewish pupils of his throughout the 1930s, one of whom, E. Neumann, eventually settled in Israel. Some were concerned over the *Zentralblatt* statements, but were subsequently reassured. One may surmise that his pupils did not agree with some of his conclusions on racial character even if they believed in the efficiency of Jung's methodology; a projected book on Jewish psychology which he planned to coauthor with a Jewish pupil never appeared.[113] The continued loyalty and support of these people could be cited as a refutation of Jung's anti-Semitism. This would be to miss the point; Jung was not a petty anti-Semite, and quite probably not a conscious one either. The racial categories he employed were so widely disseminated in the German cultural milieu of the early twentieth century as to make them appear objective and impersonal. As a part of that milieu he tried to find an explanation for certain differences in terms of race, a fact which helped to make him willing to give National Socialism a "fair trial" where those who found this form of explanation antipathetic would have been more inclined to condemn the regime from the outset.[114]

Thus a broader view of Jung's relation to National Socialism shows it to be the product of his racial presupposition, of the romantic tendencies in his psychological theories, of his personal and professional conflict with Freud, and of his own wariness of socialism: these were the elements which led him to respond to the Hitler regime with initial optimism, these were the elements which made him ready to give up hope of meeting what he saw as an impasse in Western civilization with grand economic and political schemes; instead he recommended seeking direction from the archetypes of the collective, and in the case of Wotan, racial unconscious.[115] It was not until after the start of the Second World War, in 1940, that Jung resigned as president of the International General Medical Association for Psychotherapy and as editor of the *Zentralblatt*. It was not until 1946, however, that he published any open denunciation of the Nazi regime. Even then he never publicly admitted to any original error in judgement. His experience with National Socialism, however, did not alter the basic tenor of his work which continued to seek guidance from the collective unconscious, and to hold scientific rationalism largely responsible for psychological mass-mindedness.[116]

Notes

1 Quoted in Gerhard Wehr, *Portrait of Jung*, trans. by W.A. Hargreaves (New York, 1970), 191.
2 Aniela Jaffé, *From the Life and Work of C.G. Jung*, trans. by R.F.C. Hull (New York, 1971), 92, 93.
3 Because of their accessibility I have tried to cite the *Collected Works* in most cases (C.G. Jung, *The Collected Works of C.G. Jung* (hereafter cited as *CW*; [reference is by volume and page number – ed.]), trans. by R.F.C. Hull (New York, 1953–1979)). C.G. Jung, *Civilization in Transition* (*CW*, x, 1964), 194.
4 *CW*, x, 535.
5 C.G. Jung, *The Integration of Personality*, trans. by Stanley Dell (New York, 1939), 295, 305. The German text of Jung's footnote reads: "Seitdem dieser Satz geschrieben wurde, hat auch Deutschland seinen Führer gefunden." C.G. Jung, *Wirklichkeit der Seele* (Zürich, 1934), 180. This is translated as follows in the *Collected Works*: "Since then Germany too has turned to a Führer" (C.G. Jung, *The Development of Personality*, *CW*, xvii, 1954, 185). The original Dell translation is clearly more accurate.
6 *The Integration of Personality*, 303–5. See also Albert D. Parelhoff, "Dr. Carl G. Jung – Nazi Collaborationist. I", *Protestant*, vii (June–July, 1946), 23 for the interpretation of this passage as referring to Hitler. In *Freud or Jung* (New York, 1950), 143 ff., Edward Glover roundly criticized Jung's theories in general. In particular the validity of the Jungian notion of individuation was challenged by maintaining that this idea implied a *Führer-prinzip* and predisposed the Swiss psychotherapist to a favourable impression of Hitler in the 1930s. Glover also sought to discredit Jung's notions on group psychology, in part by pointing to the unscientific nature of the latter's racial theories.
7 *The Integration of Personality*, 291 (italics in the original).
8 "Vom Werden der Persönlichkeit", *Essener Anzeiger*, 8 February 1933; "Vom Werden der Persönlichkeit", *Essener Allgemeine Zeitung*, 7 February 1933.
9 *CW*, x, 154.
10 *CW*, x, 185.
11 *CW*, x, 186.
12 *CW*, x, 180.
13 "Psychology of Dictatorship: An Interview with Dr. C.G. Jung", *Living Age*, ccccli (September 1936–February 1937), 341.
14 Ibid.
15 Ibid.
16 H.R. Knickerbocker, "Diagnosing the Dictators – An Interview with Dr. Jung", *Cosmopolitan*, cvi (January, 1939).
17 "Psychology of Dictatorship".
18 Knickerbocker, "Diagnosing the Dictators".
19 Ibid.
20 "Psychology of Dictatorship".
21 *CW*, x, 533.
22 *CW*, x, 167, 168, 170.
23 *CW*, x, 165.
24 *CW*, x, 165–6.
25 See George L. Mosse, *Germans and Jews* (New York, 1970), 35ff.
26 In a letter to a Jewish pupil of his, Erich Neuman, written in December 1939, he seems to take a contradictory position in saying that he found the arche-

type Wotan occurring among German Jews. *C.G. Jung: Letters*, ed. by Gerhard Adler and Aniela Jaffé (Princeton, 1973), i, 280.

27 *CW*, x, 165.

28 *CW*, x, 166.

29 C.G. Jung, *Psychology of the Unconscious*, trans. by Beatrice M. Hinkle (New York, 1944), 40–1. This passage does not appear in the *Collected Works* which uses Jung's 1952 revision of the original text.

30 *CW*, x, 45–6.

31 *CW*, x, 510, 511.

32 *CW*, x, 14.

33 *CW*, x, 13, 227.

34 Sigmund Freud, "On the History of the Psycho-Analytic Movement", *Collected Papers*, ed. by Ernest Jones, trans. by Joan Riviere (London, 1953), i, 329.

35 Ernest Jones, *The Life and Work of Sigmund Freud: Years of Maturity 1901–1919* (New York, 1957), 33–4.

36 Jones, *Freud*, 102.

37 "Jung to Christian Jenssen 29 May 1933", *Letters*, i, 122.

38 "Jung to Max Guggenheim 28 March 1934", *Letters*, i, 156.

39 C.G. Jung, *The Structure and Dynamics of the Psyche* (*CW*, viii, 1960), 153.

40 C.G. Jung, *Two Essays on Analytical Psychology* (*CW*, vii, 1953), 68–9.

41 C.G. Jung, *The Spirit in Man, Art, and Literature* (*CW*, xv, 1966), 80–1.

42 *CW*, x, 186, 187.

43 Jung, *Psychology of the Unconscious*, 40–1.

44 *CW*, viii, 350.

45 *CW*, xv, 82.

46 *CW*, vii, 255.

47 C.G. Jung, *Psychological Types* (*CW*, vi, 1971), 57–61.

48 *CW*, vii, 283.

49 Jung, *Wirklichkeit*, 121.

50 C.G. Jung, *Psychological Reflections: A Jung Anthology*, ed. by Jolande Jacobi (New York, 1953), 224.

51 *CW*, vii, 130, 131.

52 "Jung to Freud 11 February 1910", *The Freud/Jung Letters*, ed. by William McGuire, trans. by Ralph Manheim and R.F.C. Hull (New York, 1974), 294 (italics in the original).

53 "Freud to Jung 13 February 1910", *Freud/Jung Letters*, 295.

54 "Jung to Freud 11 February 1910", *Freud/Jung Letters*, 294.

55 C.G. Jung, *Freud and Psychoanalysis* (*CW*, iv, 1961), 245.

56 *CW*, iv, 247.

57 *CW*, vii, 263; C.G. Jung, *Symbols of Transformation* (*CW*, v, 1956), 136; *CW*, iv, 246, 248.

58 *CW*, v, 136 (italics mine).

59 *CW*, iv, 248.

60 *CW*, iv, 249.

61 *CW*, iv, 249–50.

62 *CW*, iv, 250.

63 *CW*, viii, 19.

64 *CW*, v, 136; *CW*, xv, 72.

65 C.G. Jung, *Collected Papers on Analytical Psychology*, trans. by Constance Long (2nd edn, London, 1920), 351. This passage does not appear in the *Collected Works*.

66 C.G. Jung, *The Psychogenesis of Mental Disease* (*CW*, iii, 1960), 183–7.
67 *CW*, xv, 76.
68 *CW*, viii, 58.
69 *CW*, vii, 287–8.
70 Peter Viereck, *Metapolitics, The Roots of the Nazi Mind* (New York, 1961), 31.
71 G.R. Heyer, "Die Polarität, ein Grundproblem der deutschen Psychotherapie", *Zentralblatt für Psychotherapie und ihre Grenzgebiete*, vii (Leipzig, 1934), 17–23, p. 18. For the pervasive influence of romanticism on German nationalism see Hans Kohn, *The Mind of Modern Germany* (New York, 1960), 49ff.
72 "Psychology of Dictatorship" (ref. 13).
73 Jaffé, *From the Life*, 78.
74 "Jung to J.H. van der Hoop 12 March 1934", *Letters*, i, 150.
75 Jaffé, *From the Life*, 78, 83.
76 *CW*, x, 536.
77 "Jung to Rudolf Allers 23 November 1933", *Letters*, i, 132.
78 *CW*, x, 538.
79 "Jung to C.W. Cimbal 2 March 1934", *Letters*, i, 145, 146.
80 *CW*, x, 536.
81 *CW*, x, 537.
82 Ibid.
83 *CW*, x, 538.
84 *CW*, x, 536.
85 *CW*, x, 203–4.
86 Knickerbocker, "Diagnosing the Dictators".
87 *CW*, x, 230, 134. Cf. the original shorter version of the essay, "Ueber Psychologie", *Neue Schweizer Rundschau*, n.s., i (May, July 1933), 21–8, 98–106.
88 *The Integration of Personality*, 281; "Vom Werden der Persönlichkeit", *Essener Anzeiger*, 8 February 1933; "Vom Werden der Persönlichkeit", *Essener Allgemeine Zeitung*, 7 February 1933.
89 *CW*, x, 235.
90 *CW*, x, 236.
91 *CW*, x, 237.
92 Philip Wylie, "A Misunderstood Man", *Saturday Review of Literature*, xxxii (30 July, 1949), 8.
93 *CW*, x, 191.
94 Wylie, "A Misunderstood Man", 8.
95 *CW*, x, 190.
96 *CW*, x, 192.
97 *CW*, x, 194.
98 C.G. Jung, "Wotan", *Neue Schweizer Rundschau*, n.s., iii (March, 1936), 669; cf. *CW*, x, 192.
99 *CW*, x, 537.
100 *CW*, x, 204, 231, 232.
101 *CW*, x, 538; "Aktuelles", *Zentralblatt*, vi (Leipzig, 1933), 144.
102 *CW*, x, 539.
103 *CW*, x, 543.
104 *Dictionary of the Social Sciences*, ed. by Julius Gould and William L. Kolb (London, 1964).
105 *CW*, vi, 524–5.

106 C.G. Jung, *Analytical Psychology*, trans. by Constance Long (New York, 1916), 297. This passage does not appear in the *Collected Works*.

107 *CW*, vi, 525.

108 "Jung to C.E. Benda 19 June 1934", *Letters*, i, 167.

109 *CW*, x, 166.

110 "Jung to Gerhard Adler 9 June 1934", *Letters*, i, 164.

111 *CW*, x, 46.

112 *CW*, x, 504.

113 "Jung to Gerhard Adler 9 June 1934", *Letters*, i, 164; "Jung to James Kirsch 26 May 1934", *Letters*, i, 161.

114 *CW*, x, 237.

115 *CW*, x, 154, 149.

116 *CW*, x, 253.

Part II

JUNG IN LITERARY CONTEXT

5

THE DEVIL'S ELIXIRS, JUNG'S "THEOLOGY" AND THE DISSOLUTION OF FREUD'S "POISONING COMPLEX"

John Kerr

Source: *The Psychoanalytic Review*, 75 (1988), 1–34.

Psychoanalysis and literature have from the beginning stood in the uneasy relationship of half-brothers unsure of their shares in a single estate. These half-brothers have at times acted as though their own claims were best served by invoking ties of the closest kinship between them. Then again, at other times, they have abruptly reversed themselves and each has insisted, with renewed vigor, that his lineage needs to be distinguished from the other's, that his is a different paternity. Accordingly, one enters into any arrangement with the two brothers with a certain apprehension. What was gladly agreed to today may be tomorrow's point of contention.

Let us begin, then, with the gentlest of discriminations. One of these half-brothers is clearly the elder, and though the younger may protest his greater acuity, the claims of the first-born should be heard first. Thus, we should note, with Ellenberger (1970), Holt (1978), and Rudnytsky (1987), that the literature and philosophy of the Romantic movement, both in Germany and elsewhere, provided the first dynamic psychiatry with many of its themes and issues, and that these then subsequently made their way into psychoanalysis. The literary motif of the *Doppelgänger*, to take but one example, appears to have rematerialized in French psychopathology as "multiple personality," and to have subsequently come down to us in the form of "splitting," that most disturbing concept which has lately been seen haunting the clinical imagination.

In what follows, I shall focus on the impact exerted on the history of psychoanalysis by a single work from the Romantic tradition, E.T.A. Hoffmann's *The Devil's Elixirs* (1816). Owing to the wealth of historical documents now available, it is possible to state with considerable precision how this particular novel came to be one of the foci of the dialogue between Freud and Jung, this moreover at a particularly critical point in the evolution of their friendship. Principally, I propose to argue that the novel had a formative role in shaping both Jung's incipient disaffection with the Freudian paradigm and his own later theories. As well, I will offer a tentative suggestion concerning the novel's impact on Freud's ongoing theorizing both at the time and subsequently.

A difficult time

To understand the pivotal role of *The Devil's Elixirs* in the dialogue between Freud and Jung, we first have to grasp the unusual circumstances in which Jung read the book during the first week of March, 1909. The early spring of 1909 was a time of spectacular difficulty for Carl Jung, and his difficulties were inextricably linked to his involvement with the new field of psychoanalysis. Jung had only recently enjoyed a meteoric rise to psychiatric prominence. From the moment he set foot in the Burghölzli hospital at the end of 1900, it was clear that he was a true intellectual aristocrat – he hailed from a distinguished Basel family – and that he was uniquely gifted to pursue a career in psychiatry. Jung proceeded to win an international reputation at the astonishingly young age of 31, this on the strength of two extraordinary contributions to medical psychology – his volume on the association experiment and his *Psychology of Dementia Praecox* – both of which were published in 1906. For a variety of reasons both personal and theoretical, Jung had elected to give his achievements an unusual cast by unilaterally taking on the burden of appearing in print as a supporter of the controversial Viennese neurologist, Sigmund Freud. Jung's decision, in some ways a benighted one, had led first to a correspondence and then to a friendship with Freud, who could only wonder at his good fortune at securing the support of this unsolicited champion. In short order, Jung made good on the promise of his overtures. In the fall of 1907, he became the first psychiatrist to make a public defense of Freud's theories at an international congress. In the spring of 1908, he took it upon himself to call a Congress for Freudian Psychology, the first such Congress ever held. And, at that Congress, or rather at a private enclave that met immediately afterwards, Jung also agreed to serve as the executive editor of a new journal devoted principally to psychoanalysis, the *Jahrbuch für Psychoanalytische und Psychopathologische Forschungen*. Then things began to come apart.

By making himself Freud's spokesman, Jung had also made himself the target for the anti-Freud sentiment that was just then, in the wake of the scandalous Dora case, beginning to become virulent in German psychiatry and neurology. In Switzerland, where a web of personal and institutional affiliations linked the nation's psychiatrists and neurologists into a close-knit community, interest in psychotherapy and medical psychology was burgeoning. In deference to Jung's position, and that of his mentor Eugen Bleuler as well, the anti-Freud campaign in Switzerland was conducted largely in private. In the fall of 1908, however, the dean of Swiss psychiatrists, the distinguished Auguste Forel, gave the signal for a more trenchant public discussion. Though Jung was not specifically named in Forel's (1908) brief review of the state of contemporary psychotherapy, it was clear that he was the target of remarks that questioned the propriety, and the possible suggestive effect, of inquiring too persistently after sexual complexes. And in case Jung had missed the allusion in Forel's article, Freud thoughtfully pointed it out to him in his letter of November 8, 1908: "Forel's attacks are chiefly on you, probably out of ignorance" (McGuire, 1974, p. 175).

Unfortunately, Jung was at this very time engaged in secret meetings with a former patient, Sabina Spielrein. The Jung–Spielrein relationship is far too complex and far too intimately connected with the events just reviewed for a brief summary. It will suffice to say that the relationship had evolved slowly, with frequent changes of meaning, and that it constituted for Jung a very personal and a very private complement to his public career as Freud's spokesman. We cannot be certain that the relationship was ever consummated; we can be certain, however, that by the late fall of 1908 it had already gone beyond the bounds of Swiss propriety.

At this juncture, either Jung or his wife took the necessary first step toward saving his career by communicating privately with Spielrein's mother. What happened next is well documented in Carotenuto's volume (1982). For our purposes, the crucial event occurred in late February 1909, when disaster struck. Spielrein was unwilling to return to the role of patient. She attacked Jung physically and with sufficient vehemence to draw blood. Jung was now in a position of uncertainty and dread. In the absence of any further communication from the young woman (he would have none until the end of May), Jung did not know whether he would be publicly unmasked and effectively ruined. Worse still, such was the nature of his transgression that a public unmasking would have simultaneously brought the new science of psychoanalysis into instant disrepute, most certainly in Switzerland and quite possibly throughout the German-speaking medical world. Freud, no doubt, would have to disown him. And, as if by a malevolent play of chance, within a matter of days after Spielrein angrily quit his office, the very first issue of the *Jahrbuch*, with Jung, Freud, and Bleuler on the masthead, came rolling off the presses.

If one examines closely Jung's correspondence with Freud during the months of March and April in 1909, the evidence of Jung's terrible predicament is everywhere to be found, beginning with his letter of March 7, 1909. Though he is less than straightforward as to the actual facts of the

Spielrein affair, Jung does take the gentlemanly step of warning Freud that a scandal may be brewing. The letters that follow pitch and yaw terribly as Jung struggles to maintain his composure, while he waits to see what revenge, if any, Spielrein would take. And it is in these very same letters that a resurgent mystical tendency makes its presence felt to a degree unprecedented in the correspondence to date. This mystical tendency reached its climax in the famous "spookery" (McGuire, 1974, p. 216) incident in Freud's home at the end of March when, to Freud's absolute astonishment, Jung correctly predicted that a second loud retort would come resounding from the bookcase. In the letters that immediately followed this incident, moreover, Jung remained largely unrepentant, seemingly determined to see what he called "psychosynthesis" (McGuire, 1974, p. 216) through to the end.

All this is well documented in the Freud–Jung correspondence, in the Carotenuto volume, and in Jung's memoirs (1962). Here let us confine ourselves to a few points with which to round out the context. First, even before disaster had struck and Spielrein had quit his office, Jung had begun trying to contain the potential damage to his reputation by softening his heretofore stringent psychoanalytic line. To Ernest Jones, with whom he was friendly, Jung had written on February 25, 1909:

> We should do well not to burst out with the theory of sexuality in the foreground. I have many thoughts about that, especially on the ethical aspects of the question. I believe that in publicly announcing certain things one would saw off the branch on which civilization rests; one undermines the impulse to sublimation. . . . Both with students and with patients I get on further by not making the theme of sexuality prominent.
>
> (cited in Jones, 1955, p. 139)

Second, both before and after the disaster struck, Jung sought to preserve his own options by assiduously courting the friendship of men other than Freud. These men, in turn, seem to have been used by Jung as a sounding board for those ideas with which he would blanket himself in the cold days after his imagined expulsion from psychoanalysis. The Reverend Oskar Pfister was one such person. Jung's letter to Freud (on January 19, 1909) says of Pfister, "Oddly enough, I find this mixture of medicine and theology to my liking" (McGuire, 1974, p. 197). The young philosopher Paul Häberlin was another new acquaintance. Jung's letter to Freud (March 21, 1909) goes so far as to say of Häberlin:

> He tops Pfister by a head in psychological acuity and biological knowledge, and he has studied theology as well as philosophy and natural science. Nor does he lack a certain mystical streak, on

which account I set special store by him, since it guarantees a deepening of thought beyond the ordinary and a grasp of far-reaching syntheses.

(McGuire, 1974, p. 214)

But the most important of Jung's new acquaintances went unmentioned in the Freud correspondence – Théodore Flournoy. Jung first met Flournoy during this period (Hannah, 1976, p. 98). Flournoy was the grand old man of Geneva psychology and the author of a celebrated work on mediumship that had inspired Jung's own medical dissertation. It was from Flournoy that Jung derived the perspectives that would later inform his mature criticisms of Freud.

It is tempting to see Jung as behaving with a certain panicky calculation in these various maneuvers. And, indeed, there was much in his behavior that a more diligent conscience might have prohibited. But Jung's turn to other men, and most especially his turn to a "mixture of medicine and theology," might perhaps better be seen as a return. With some justice, Jung could say in his own defense that he had strayed too far in Freud's direction and was returning home to views he had held earlier in his career. As well, he could say with some justice – this point must be left undefended here – that he was also championing views held by none other than the young woman whom he had lately been so eager to be rid of, Sabina Spielrein.

As the reader undoubtedly already knows, however, Freud and Jung did *not* break off their relationship at this time. Following his visit to Vienna at the end of March, Jung quit the Burghölzli, vacationed in Italy during mid-April, then returned to Switzerland to establish himself in private practice in the new residence at Küsnacht. During the second week of April, he had a noteworthy dream that helped him clarify, first, his relationship to Freud and, second, the theoretical differences that lay between them. Then in May, to the astonishment of all, Spielrein took the extraordinary step of communicating directly with Freud. By the end of June, to the relief of all, the matter had been finally, and discreetly, settled. By Jung's lights, Freud had earned both his gratitude and his loyalty by standing by him during this difficult time and Jung was moved to continue their personal and political affiliation. Their theoretical differences, meanwhile, went underground, not to surface for another two and a half years.

In the long run, of course, the theoretical differences between the two men were not to be reconciled and the rupture of their friendship had not been prevented, only postponed. But what is principally interesting here is what further light can be shed on Jung's behavior during March and April of 1909 by a consideration of his reading *The Devil's Elixirs*. For it was in early March, during the most acute phase of the crisis, that Hoffmann's novel came into Jung's hands and thence made its appearance in the correspondence with Freud. In reply to Jung's desperate, not quite honest letter of March 7, 1909, warning of a possible scandal involving a patient, Freud had replied in a letter (March 9, 1909) with brave sentiments designed to buck up Jung's courage: "To be slandered and scorched by the love with which we operate – such are the perils of our trade, which we are certainly not going to abandon on their account" (McGuire, 1974, p. 210). But Freud's patience had been tried by Jung's sorry confession – full of references to the Devil – and in the next paragraph he went on to chide Jung for cutting a poor figure. A Jung family legend had it that their line had been begun by an illegitimate child of Goethe three generations before and Freud, knowledgeable of the legend if not quite attuned to the exact genealogical fact, appealed to Goethe-as-ancestor in his rebuke:

> And another thing: "In league with the Devil and yet you fear fire?" Your grandfather [sic] said something like that. I bring up this quotation because you definitely lapse into the theological style in relating this experience.
>
> (McGuire, 1974, p. 211)

The Spielrein affair was still well short of settled, and would remain that way for three more months, but Jung was understandably relieved by Freud's reply and wrote back quickly on March 11, 1909 to thank him for his support. In passing, Jung defended the tone of his confession, "You mustn't take on about my 'theological' style, I just felt that way" (McGuire, 1974, p. 212). In the paragraphs that follow in the letter, one can almost feel Jung regaining his confidence as he mentions his various plans for the future. And, in the process, he returns to the theme of "theology," this time giving it a more whimsical turn:

> I have made a nice discovery in Hoffmann's *The Devil's Elixir* (a good deal of my "theology" evidently comes from there). I am thinking of writing something on it for your *Papers*. A whole tangle of neurotic problems, but all palpably real. Altogether, I have endless plans for work next year, and I look forward so much to the new era of outer (and inner) independence that is so important for me.
>
> (McGuire, 1974, pp. 212–213)

In point of fact, Jung never did write up his thoughts on *The Devil's Elixirs* for Freud's monograph series. The reader will have to decide, after reading further, to what extent Jung's later career might be seen as a gloss on Hoffmann. First, a look at the novel itself is in order so that we can see what Jung found so "palpably real."

Brother Medardus and the archetypes

E.T.A. Hoffmann (1776–1822) was a man of many accomplishments. A jurist by training and profession, he was also a *Kappelmeister* and theatrical producer, as well as a music critic whose essays influenced Wagner and others. His own belief was that he would make his mark on the world as a composer and he left behind a symphony, nine operas, two masses, and numerous shorter compositions. But it is for his idiosyncratic, almost incidental literary output that the world now remembers him. Beginning in 1909, and continuing until his death thirteen years later, working entirely in his leisure, Hoffmann produced a succession of short stories and novels that have since come to define a whole strand of the Romantic movement. His name has become synonymous with the grotesque, the chilling, and the macabre; his influence can be detected in such diverse descendants as Gogol, Poe, and Dostoevsky.

For the English reader unfamiliar with his work, Hoffmann can perhaps best be located somewhere between the Gothic novel and the work of Poe. He is a scion of the Gothic tradition, insofar as the fantastic and the metaphysical are allowed free play in the action, but a worthy ancestor to Poe insofar as each of his creations is informed by an urgently real psychological tension. The reader knows from the outset that what happens in a Hoffmann tale could never have happened; the reader does not for a moment doubt that what is felt in a Hoffmann tale has been felt many times before and will be felt again many times hence.

Hoffmann's themes were ideally suited to be taken up in turn by the first dynamic psychiatry and again by psychoanalysis. Nor was this accidental. Hoffmann familiarized himself with the psychiatry of his day and, among other things, made frequent visits to a nearby asylum in search of inspiration. The intersection with psychiatry shows in his work; as Taylor has put it in his introduction to the English translation (1963) of *The Devil's Elixirs*: "Hypnotism, somnambulism and telepathy are the phenomena which fascinated him; delirium, persecution mania and schizophrenia are the mental states with which he invested his characters; fright, fear and terror are the emotions released by these forces and experiences" (p. vii). To be sure, the category of the "uncanny" pre-existed Hoffmann's works, but it was Hoffmann who gave the uncanny its quintessentially horrible expression, and it was to Hoffmann that Freud turned in 1919 when he thought it necessary to give the definitive psychoanalytic statement on the uncanny.

Die Elixire des Teufels is not thought to be Hoffmann's masterpiece; it is merely the work that fate placed in Jung's hands in March of 1909. Hoffmann wrote the book in two separate parts, the first in 1814, the second in 1815, and the novel reads that way. The first half describes the adventures of one Brother Medardus, while the second half, which begins with a meditation on the afternoon of life, is chiefly concerned with clarifying the mysterious events of the first half and with describing Medardus's reflections on his deeds and his ultimate repentance.

The novel begins with a conceit as the author takes on the guise of an editor presenting a collection of manuscripts he has found. The central manuscript in this collection purports to be the autobiographical confession of an eighteenth-century Capuchin monk, one Brother Medardus. The initial segment of Medardus's account is exquisitely concerned with temptation, especially sexual temptation, and the devices of a tortured conscience. Brother Medardus tells us how he was raised in a monastery, how he mastered a disturbing attraction to the choirmaster's daughter by deciding precipitously to become a monk, and how a serendipitous talent for oratory spread his reputation as a preacher far and wide. Medardus's new-found security is momentarily shattered when a beautiful young woman, unknown to him but the living image of St Rosalia, whose picture hangs in the chapel, comes to him in the confessional and announces that she is in love with him. While he is trying to regain his composure following this incident, Medardus is given as one of his tasks the care of the monastery's relics. Among these relics is a casket of Syracusan wine, said to have been wrested from the devil by St Anthony, and before long Medardus is secretly sampling it. Such are the effects of the elixir, that Medardus finds new eloquence and even greater fame. But the head of the monastery is increasingly displeased – vanity, not piety, is what he hears from the pulpit – and although Medardus feels that he is the victim of jealousy, it is soon plain to all that his position is untenable. Accordingly, he is chosen to take a message to Rome and, with his bottle of the Devil's Syracusan with him, he steps out into the world. Inwardly, he has already planned to go his own way.

Almost at once, Medardus is plunged into a dangerous game of double impersonation. On his way through the mountains he comes across a nobleman resting on a precipice; he startles the man, who promptly falls to his apparent death. Proceeding further, Medardus comes to the castle of a Baron F. Here he discovers that he is taken for the dead nobleman, Count Victor. It had been Victor's plan to pose as a Capuchin so that he could pursue a secret liaison with the Baron's wife, Euphemia. Medardus takes Victor's place in Euphemia's arms, but inwardly he has designs on the Baron's daughter, Aurelia, who is the living image of the woman who had earlier surprised him in the confessional. In a rage of arrogance, Medardus eventually humiliates Euphemia by revealing his true identity, then kills her with the poison she meant for him. He attempts to rape Aurelia, but is surprised by her brother Hermogenes. He kills Hermogenes and flees into the night.

After an interlude in which he stays with a forester, who is boarding a mad monk whom he has found wandering in the forest, Medardus takes up life in a town. He obtains a new wardrobe and a new haircut, largely due to the ministrations of a comic figure, the barber Peter Schönfeld. But just as he has begun to accustom himself to his new life, he is publicly accused of Hermogenes's murder by a mysterious figure, the Old Painter. The Old Painter has appeared before in the story and will appear again – it is plain at this point that he is an apparition and it will be plain shortly that he holds the key to all the strange events that are unfolding.

Helped by Schönfeld, Medardus again makes his escape. Next he comes to a city where he quickly enters the court of the Prince. Here, too, there has been intrigue, but events go well until there is a new arrival at the court: Aurelia. She is both frightened and attracted by this man who so resembles her brother's murderer. They fall in love and their marriage is planned. In a double reversal, Medardus is suddenly unmasked, put in prison, and there visited by both the Old Painter and a mysterious double of himself. Then, equally suddenly, he is acquitted. Another man, the mad monk who had previously appeared at the forester's cabin, has confessed to Medardus's crimes. The real Medardus, however, cannot tolerate his own guilt and in another fit stabs himself in Aurelia's presence. In his delirium he believes he has killed her and again he flees. In the forest he is attacked by the mad monk, who has also escaped, and the barber Schönfeld finds him in a catatonic state and deposits him in an asylum run by his order outside Rome.

Now Medardus enters into a cycle of repentance, self-chastisement, and sanctimoniousness. He becomes caught up in murderous intrigues at the court of the Pope, but makes his escape, and the rest of the novel concerns his journey back through the landscape of his earlier adventures. At each step of the way, he finds more pieces of the puzzle. It becomes clear that Count Victor did not die in the fall from the precipice and that, having gone mad, he has taken up Medardus's identity: Victor is the mad monk who has been pursuing Medardus and confessing to his crimes. Eventually, the real Medardus returns to his original monastery and resumes his former life. By now he has come into possession of a manuscript written by the Old Painter that explains the web of destiny in which he, Count Victor, and Aurelia are all caught up. The Old Painter is a wraith. A student of Leonardo who turned to paganism, he was in his own life bewitched by the very Syracusan that began this tale. It was he who painted the portrait of St Rosalia that hangs in the chapel, but his model for the saint was an apparition of Venus. Then, he sired a child by a witch, herself a double of Venus – St Rosalia, and though he subsequently repented he is condemned to walk the earth until the last of his line has also obtained salvation – or died. The story of the Old Painter's line, contained in his manuscript, is a tale of incest and repentance constantly repeated in each new generation. Victor, Medardus, and Aurelia are the last of the Old Painter's line.

The climax of the novel comes with the appearance of Aurelia at the monastery. Out of repentance for her own sins – the love of a monk – she has decided to enter the convent. But on the day of her investiture, she is murdered by Count Victor, who is intent on completing his criminal career as Medardus's delusional double. Aurelia's death is accompanied by a miracle: the smell of roses, the saint's flower, fills the church. A year later to the day, Medardus, now reconciled to God, himself dies.

Stepping back from the plot, several points are worth addressing. The novel suffers, at least so far as the modern sensibility is concerned, from Hoffmann's determination to keep track of every subsidiary theme and to weave them together at the end. The intent, no doubt, is musical, but the result is that side issues sometimes blot out the main action. And, while some of the revelations of the second half of the book work effectively to clear up the mysteries of the first half, many of them do not. With the figure of the Old Painter, moreover, Hoffmann has irretrievably broken the bounds of reality right from the start; there is thus a limit to the satisfaction the reader can take in the subsequent realistic clarifications of the uncanny, seemingly mad, coincidences that dominate the initial action. And for this reason, the central theme of the novel – the mysterious interconnections of chance, fate, and divine plan – makes less of an impression than Hoffmann intended.

This said, we should hasten to add that the psychological tensions of the novel are surprisingly effective. The myriad juxtapositions of passion and lust on the one hand and pure transcendental love on the other work far better than the reader may suppose from the plot summary. Here Hoffmann was borrowing from his own life and the quality of lived experience comes through clearly. If one has forgotten what it is to conceive a guilty, desperate love, *The Devil's Elixirs* will bring the experience back. Equally effective is Hoffmann's handling of guilt in all its terrible ramifications: pride, posturing, self-destructiveness, and paranoia.

It is not hard to appreciate why this novel appealed to Jung and why he found its problems "palpably real." Himself the son of a Pastor, Jung too had strayed far into the wider world, there to encounter both fame and fantasies of incest. A guilty conscience and a string of evil coincidences were his lot no less than that of Brother Medardus. Moreover, the general outlook of the novel, its mixture of religion, philosophy, and the occult, resembles nothing so much as the point of view Jung had espoused more than a decade earlier in his lectures of 1896–1899 to the Zofingia, a student association, during his years at the University of Basel. The voice was more than amicable – it was familiar.

In one further respect, Hoffmann spoke far more trenchantly to Jung on these subjects than he does to the modern reader. For an essential aspect of the novel, one that tends to elude the modern reader completely, is the multi-generational nature of sin. Count Victor, Medardus, and Aurelia are equally trapped in a web of familial guilt that precedes their own actions. The most they can hope for is that by righteousness they will atone for the sins of their line. The possibilities of ordinary human happiness are denied to them by virtue of the Old Painter's misdeeds generations before. In his way, Hoffmann had anticipated by forty years the doctrine of hereditary degeneration that was to dominate psychiatry for the second half of the nineteenth century. His characters, like those patients who would later be diagnosed as having hereditary taint, are prone to exotic mental states and thus required to observe more stringent moral regimens in their lives than are ordinary people. But here let us observe that Jung had made his entry into the medical world with a work advancing a new perspective on the very issue of hereditary degeneration. Jung's medical dissertation (1902) is principally concerned with the case description of his cousin, who fancied herself to be a medium and incarnated various past lives of herself and of Jung in their seances together. But in the dissertation, he also makes the daring suggestion that perhaps some of the consequences of hereditary degeneration are benign and even desirable.

Specifically, Jung had suggested that one consequence of a psychopathic constitution was a greater psychic sensitivity. This sensitivity typically manifested itself in pathological states, such as the mediumistic trance, but it might also come to the aid of development by allowing the afflicted a glimpse into future adaptations. Thus, Jung implied, the medium's trance-personality, "Ivenes," prefigured her adult identity. This claim is handled gingerly in Jung's text, in part because Jung was mixing French and German sources with regard to the degeneration issue and in part because he had elected to conceal the role of hypnotism in inducing the trance state – an omission that, if discovered, would cast serious doubts on his claim. However, given the nature of the claim, and the fact that, as is now known, the medium was Jung's first cousin, it should not escape notice that Jung partially shared the same inherited tendencies and thus, potentially, the same putative precognitive abilities. Indeed, claims for a special psychic sensitivity, modestly decorated with genial disclaimers, can be found scattered throughout Jung's memoirs.

Beyond the issue of inherited sensitivity, the matter of lineage had other personal meanings for Jung. As his memoirs (1962) make repeatedly clear, Jung had long felt both a mysterious connection with previous generations and a sense that his own personality would necessarily remain incomplete so long as he could not locate his biography in the fabric of history. Thus, to take but one example, not only did he inwardly subscribe to the fancy that Goethe was his great-grandfather, but he also secretly believed, as Ellenberger (1970, p. 378, n. 20) has noted, that his own second self was a veritable incarnation of this forebear. As he wrestled with his terrible predicament in the spring of 1909, then, Jung was undoubtedly tempted by the thought that his great-grandfather's sins were repeating themselves in him. (Freud knew Jung's propensities in this regard – they can be readily deduced from a close reading of his dissertation – and it was undoubtedly for this reason that he elected to quote Goethe in his mild rebuke of March 9, 1909.) How reassuring, then, for Jung to find such exculpating passages as the following in Hoffmann's tale:

> The Pope was silent for a few moments. Then he continued with a serious expression:
>
> "What if Nature were to follow in the realm of the spirit the physical law by which an organism can only reproduce its own kind; if propensity and desire, like the in-dwelling power which makes the leaves green, were to be handed down from father to son, obliterating free will? There are whole families of robbers and murderers. This would then be the original sin, an eternal, ineradicable curse on a guilty house, for which no sacrifice could atone."
>
> (Taylor trans., p. 273)

In the matter of guilt, Hoffmann's nefarious Pope is proposing just that shift of focus – from the individual to the collective – with which Jung himself was later to be associated. Nor should it escape our notice that in March of 1909 such a shift of emphasis served a crucial organizing function for Jung as he wrestled with the persecutions of his "rather too sensitive conscience" (McGuire, 1974, p. 207). What for the individual must be confronted in terms of responsibility and guilt, for the collective can be addressed in terms of the fundamental nature of the psyche, of the inherited structure of "propensity and desire."

Thus Hoffmann crystallized for Jung the manner in which his previous concerns, as manifested in his dissertation, could be resurrected in such a way that he might regain both his composure and the objectivity that is indispensable for a psychotherapeutic viewpoint. By shifting his focus to the realm of the collective, Jung could begin to understand what was typical in his predicament. This is what Freud (who, to be sure, was still ignorant of the facts) was asking him to do; but it was also what he had to do, if he were to survive. Yet, for Jung, such a multi-generational perspective had always been associated with psychosynthesis, with the subconscious apprehension of future possibilities.[1] And so the uncanny coincidences of *The Devil's Elixirs*, which Hoffmann consistently explains by reference to past events with only the merest hint of an unconscious telepathic collaboration between characters, were metabolized by Jung's pre-existent prejudices to generate his own brand of multi-generational tendencies toward precognition. Thus did it happen that, for invoking "grandfather" Goethe in his letter, Freud was soon thereafter rewarded with "spookery" right in his own home.

Again, Jung could be accused of using a shift to the realm of the collective to wall up the moral significance of his own transgressions, but let us remember that the relation of moral responsibility to any objective appraisal of the psyche is a bedeviling topic for anyone. And, let us also remind ourselves, Jung chose to make his career not as a moralist but as a psychologist. This said, it should be noted that when Hoffmann's novel subsequently appeared in Jung's published writings, it was typically in the context of a generalized statement on the relationship of guilt to the unconscious. In Jung's special terminology of the archetypes, that which one wishes to conceal or repress typically becomes personified in dreams as a shadowy companion – the "shadow" in Jung's nomenclature. Of the four later citations of Hoffmann's novel in Jung's work, three are in explicit reference to the archetype of the shadow and the fourth makes essentially the same point. This last citation, which is the first chronologically, occurs in Jung's essay "On the Psychology of the Unconscious" (1943).[2] In this essay, which underwent several revisions as it kept pace with the further evolution of Jung's views, a case description of a hysterical woman serves as the fulcrum for distinguishing between the views of Adler and Freud. Brother Medardus and his *doppelgänger* put in their appearance during the course of an analysis of one of the patient's symptoms:

> The patient, then, had a laughing fit at the death of her father – she had finally arrived on top. It was an hysterical laughter, a psychogenic symptom, something that sprang from unconscious motives and not from those of the conscious ego. That is a difference not to be made light of, and one that also tells us whence and how certain human virtues arise. Their opposites went down to hell – or, in modern parlance, into the unconscious – where the counterparts of our conscious virtues have long been accumulating. Hence for every virtue we wish to know nothing of the unconscious; indeed it is the acme of virtuous sagacity to declare that there is no such thing as the unconscious. But alas! it fares with us all as with Brother Medardus in Hoffmann's tale *The Devil's Elixirs*: somewhere we have a sinister and frightful brother, our own flesh-and-blood counterpart, who holds and maliciously hoards everything that we would so willingly hide under the table.
> (1943, p. 39)

But Jung's long-term debt to Hoffmann would seem to go far beyond an occasional citation. Here we must leap ahead to Jung's later work. It took nearly a decade for Jung to resolve the painful feelings brought about by his eventual break with Freud at the end of 1912, and while most of his scientific work during that decade was devoted to the problem of psychological types, by far the greater part of his energy was spent in intensive self-study. It was only in the 1920s that Jung began publishing the fruits of that self-analysis: the theory of the archetypes. And here we can only report the astonishing fact that *all the major archetypes discovered by Jung in his self-analysis appear in Hoffmann's novel.* In the figure of Aurelia–St Rosalia–Venus we have a clear adumbration of the "anima." The Old Painter can readily be seen behind the archetype of the "wise old man." The archetype of the "persona" has never been better depicted than by Medardus's self-presentation in the court of Baron F., where he was publicly Medardus, but privately, in his joint intrigue with Euphemia, Count Victor pretending to be Medardus. Or rather, Medardus pretending to be Victor pretending to be Medardus. And the complementary archetype of the "shadow" is so well exemplified by the mad monk (Victor) pursuing Medardus that, as mentioned above, Jung three times cited the book specifically as an exemplar of the "shadow" motif. Here let us add that in two of these three citations Jung's reference is ambiguous, as though Brother Medardus, and not the mad monk (Victor), were the pursuing shadow. This, no doubt, reflects simple carelessness of expression, but an unconscious truth may be suspected as well: Jung experienced Medardus, and behind Medardus, the novel as a whole, as *his* "shadow," the first time he read it.

In the matter of archetypes, perhaps we should note the one figure who appears in Hoffmann, but is missing in Jung: the barber Peter Schönfeld. Schönfeld, who repeatedly comes to Medardus's rescue, is a personification of Folly in the best sense – as that whimsical capacity of human nature that is redemptive. Jung's archetypal world lacks an equivalent figure and thus is somewhat staid in comparison to Hoffmann's.[3] And, going beyond the archetypes proper for a moment, there are two other areas where Jung may be indebted to Hoffmann. Jung's later notion of "synchronicity" would appear to owe much to the tangled web of chance and fate that was Hoffmann's main theme. And, as well, Jung's subsequent contention that, following the "afternoon of life," man turns to spiritual issues is explicitly and repeatedly stated as a premise in Part 2 of *The Devil's Elixirs.*

To be sure, Jung's later theory of the archetypes was the fruit of an involved and circuitous intellectual evolution. There is no reason to doubt the sincerity of Jung's own account of his experiences during his self-analysis, and these bear directly on the later theory. Moreover, the general idea of the archetype – the *Ur-Typus* – was not new; as a scientific formulation, it derived from Romantic biology and predated Jung's psychological version by a full century. As for the specific archetypes of Jung's theory, these, too, clearly reflect an interweaving of multiple experiences, intellectual as well as personal. To take but one example, one can find Jung speaking of man's "shadow side," specifically in reference to sexuality, as early as his 1910 review of Wittels's book, *The Sexual Need.* And, if one looks further back, one can find an equivalent phrase, "the psychic shadow side," in an early 1903 paper, "On Simulated Insanity," where it is attributed to Binet as a synonym for the subconscious generally. There can thus be no question of Jung have cribbed his theory from Hoffmann wholesale. Hoffmann was certainly a major influence on him. It is tempting to say that *The Devil's Elixirs* provided the unconscious scaffolding around which the later experiences of the self-analysis, and the theories derived from these experiences, were constructed. But before making such a claim it is important to know just how deeply the novel embedded itself in Jung's psyche when he read it in the spring of 1909. On this last point, there survives one important clue.

A dream in two parts

After visiting Freud at the end of March, 1909, Jung and his wife returned to Zurich and cleaned out his flat at the Burghölzli. Then, in the second week in April, as he planned a bicycle trip to Italy, Jung had a dream that, as he tells us in his memoirs, clarified the essential differences between his outlook and Freud's. The first part of the dream "had its scene in a mountainous region on the Swiss–Austrian border":

> It was toward evening, and I saw an elderly man in the uniform of an Imperial Austrian customs official. He walked past, somewhat stooped, without paying any attention to me. His expression was peevish, rather melancholic and vexed. There were other persons present, and someone informed me that the old man was not really there, but was the ghost of a customs official who had died years ago. "He is one of those who still couldn't die properly. . . ."
>
> I set about analyzing this dream. In connection with "customs" I at once thought of the word "censorship." In connection with "border" I thought of the border between consciousness and the unconscious on the one hand, and between Freud's views and mine on the other hand. . . . As for the old customs official, his work had obviously brought him so little that was pleasurable and satisfactory that he took a sour view of the world. I could not refuse to see the analogy with Freud.
>
> (1962, p. 163)

This part of the dream was followed by "a second and far more remarkable part":

> I was in an Italian city, and it was around noon, between twelve and one o'clock. A fierce sun was beating down upon the narrow streets. . . . A crowd came streaming toward me, and I knew that the shops were closing and people were on their way home to

dinner. In the midst of this stream of people walked a knight in full armor. He mounted the steps toward me. He wore a helmet of the kind that is called a basinet, with eye slits, and chain armor. Over this was a white tunic into which was woven, front and back, a large red cross.

One can easily imagine how I felt: suddenly to see in a modern city, during the noonday rush hour, a crusader coming toward me. What struck me as particularly odd was that none of the many persons walking about seemed to notice him. No one turned his head or gazed after him. It was as though he were completely invisible to everyone but me. I asked myself what this apparition meant, and then it was as if someone answered me – but there was no one there to speak: "Yes, this is a regular apparition. The knight always passes by here between twelve and one o'clock and has been doing so for a very long time (for centuries, I gathered) and everyone knows about it."

(1962, p. 165)

With regard to the knight, Jung did not fail to see the analogy to himself. In his memoirs he goes on to contrast the two figures, the one moribund, the other "full of life and completely real" (p. 165). Unlike Freud, he tells us, he was not content with a psychology that "succeeded in finding nothing more in the depths of the psyche than the all too familiar and 'all-too-human' limitations" (p. 166). He wanted a psychology that allowed for a certain numinous potential within the unconscious, allowed for something that would give meaning to life. This contrast in theoretical orientation, according to his memoirs, is reflected in the differing figures of the customs official and the knight.

Certainly the two dream figures are to be contrasted. But the contrast given in the memoirs has been drawn too sharply. Omitted entirely is a detail that Jung reported to a seminar group in 1925 as the single most disturbing element in the dream: the fact that *both the knight and the customs official were dead and didn't know it.* Not only was Jung puzzled by this parallelism, but he pointedly consulted Freud for his interpretation during their trip together to America during the fall of 1909. Freud, however, as Jung informed his seminar in 1925, could make nothing of this detail either. (Another point revealed to the seminar, to which we will return later, was that the customs official not only reminded Jung of Freud, he *was* Freud. In addition, Jung informed his seminar that the knight was a Crusader, while in the memoirs he allows only that the knight reminded him of stories he'd read in childhood about the search for the Holy Grail.) The theme of "dying but not dying" had multiple references in Jung's life to date – to his father, to Spielrein, to the Old Painter – and they cannot all be sorted out here. Let it be clear, however, that contrary to the overly sharp contrast drawn in the memoirs, the figure of the knight was in his own way as "dead" as that of the customs official. Both figures are superfluous. With respect to the knight, this is clear enough in the dream itself: the knight is a throwback, and he is strikingly out of place amid the bustling commercial life of a modern city.

Here it is important to recall two things. First, Jung was himself an aristocrat of distinguished, even legendary, descent. Jung's ancestry had been one of the traits that had initially impressed Bleuler, himself descended from a peasant background, and thus had contributed to Jung's meteoric rise in the Burghölzli. Second, in April of 1909 Jung was in the precarious position of having given Freud an incomplete account of the Spielrein affair; he was still in considerable danger of being unmasked by the young woman, with unknown consequences to himself and to the new science of psychoanalysis. With these points in mind, the following passage in *The Devil's Elixirs* especially stands out. The action takes place in the court of the Prince. Medardus, posing as a Polish nobleman, has just been miraculously acquitted of Hermogenes's murder; he has not yet convicted himself in a guilty fit before the unsuspecting Aurelia. During the interlude between these two events, he is accosted by the court physician, who thinks it appropriate to deliver a lecture on the declining status of the nobleman in today's society:

In this age when intellectual values are assuming more and more importance, ancestral and family pride has become a quaint, almost ludicrous phenomenon. Starting in the days of chivalry and with the profession of arms, a class arose whose sole task was to defend the other classes, and the subordinated relationship of protected to protector followed naturally. . . .

But the use of brute force is fast diminishing, and the power of the mind is asserting itself in every realm. . . . Each person is thrown back on to his own resources and forced to justify himself in the eyes of the world by his own intellectual achievement, whatever superficial brilliance may attend his position in the state. Ancestral pride, derived from chivalry, reflects a fundamentally opposite ideal, namely my ancestors were heroes, therefore I, too, am a hero. . . .

Where the power of the mind is concerned, things are not like this. Wise fathers often produce stupid sons, and because our age ascribes a nobility of intellect to those who have a nobility of lineage, it is probably more worrying to be descended from Leibniz than from Amadis of Gaul or some ancient knight of the Round Table. The age is moving irrevocably forwards, and the situation of our noble classes is rapidly deteriorating. This may well explain their tactless behaviour towards highly cultured commoners; a mixture of appreciative respect and intolerable condescension, the product of a deep despair that the triviality of their past glory will be exposed to the knowing gaze of the wise, and their insufficiencies held up to ridicule.

(Taylor trans., pp. 209–210)

I believe that this passage in Hoffmann impressed Jung sufficiently in March that it then informed the dream-thoughts and dream-images of April. Medardus's situation at this point in the novel mirrored Jung's own predicament – temporarily acquitted of a charge when really he was guilty. And the physician's speech to Medardus on the precarious state of the nobility would seem to speak to a dawning sense in Jung that his own lineage, no matter how distinguished, was going to be little protection against the impending storm. The sense of this part of the dream, then, is that while he might be different from Freud, and glad of the difference, Jung was still in grave danger of being held up to ridicule by the knowing gaze of the wise.

The connection between the passage just quoted and the Crusader of Jung's dream may seem tenuous at best. But Jung's dream had two parts. There is no customs official *per se* in *The Devil's Elixirs*. There is, however, the following monologue on the subject of "awareness" by the comic barber Peter Schönfeld. Medardus has just regained his sanity at the asylum outside Rome. Schönfeld, who had brought him there, is recounting to him the particulars of his confused state when Medardus interrupts by saying that he counts himself glad to now be sane and wants to hear no more. Schönfeld protests:

Now what is the good of that, reverend Sir? . . . I mean, of that peculiar mental function known as awareness? It is nothing but the miserable activity of some pettifogging toll-keeper, or customs-officer, or assistant chief controller, who sets up a poky little office in his mind and says, whenever any goods are to be sent out: "Oh, no! Export prohibited. They must remain here." The finest jewels are buried in the ground like worthless seeds, and the most that comes up is beetroot, from which, with practice, a quarter of an ounce of foul-tasting sugar can be squeezed by applying a pressure of a thousand tons. Well, well, well. And yet this pitiful exportation is supposed to lay the foundation for trade with the heavenly city, where all is magnificence and splendour. . . .

(Taylor trans., p. 231)

If we grant that this passage in *The Devil's Elixirs* exerted a decisive influence in shaping the dream of the customs official, we can see more clearly the close relation of Jung's "theology" to Hoffmann's. Jung, as he all but tells the reader of his memoirs, was intent on storming the "heavenly city" of the unconscious. He wanted direct access, unencumbered by the limitations of an "all-too-human" reductionism. For Jung, furthermore, such a direct access meant going beyond mere "awareness." It meant finding in the subliminal combinations of the subconscious mind a glimpse into the future. Earlier, I outlined how Hoffmann's multigenerational portrait of fate was redolent for Jung with implicit possibilities of "psychosynthesis." Now I shall go farther and juxtapose Jung's dream of the knight and the customs official with the same theme of "psychosynthesis." Transparently, the knight, construed as either a Crusader or a seeker after the Holy Grail, is someone who wishes to go beyond the humdrum and ordinary, but this of itself does not necessarily imply the "beyond" of precognition. For Jung, however, it did, or at least that is the only conclusion that can be drawn from his letter to Freud a few days after he had the dream.

The letter in question was tentatively begun April 2, but not finished and mailed until April 12, 1909. As it was his first letter to Freud following the visit to Vienna, Jung thought it appropriate to offer his apologies for the incident during his last evening in Freud's home: "When I left Vienna I was afflicted with some *sentiments d'incomplétude* because of the last evening I spent with you. It seemed to me that my spookery struck you as altogether too stupid . . ." (McGuire, 1974, p. 216). But one paragraph later, the letter turns unrepentant and Jung adds ominously: "That last evening with you has, most happily, freed me inwardly from the oppressive sense of your paternal authority. My unconscious celebrated this impression with a great dream which has preoccupied me for some days and which I have just finished analysing" (McGuire, 1974, p. 217). Beyond a doubt, this "great dream" was the dream in two parts depicting the customs official and the knight.[4] The rest of the letter makes it clear that Jung's "theology" is decidedly on the upswing and "psychosynthesis" is more in evidence than ever before. Principally, the letter describes two patients, one new and one old. Of his new patient Jung writes, "First rate spiritualistic phenomena occur in this case, though so far only once in my presence" (pp. 215–216). Of his old patient, who had been discussed with Freud and who had a penchant for repeatedly falling in love with schizophrenic men, Jung writes:

> I had the feeling that under it all there must be some quite special complex, a universal one having to do with the prospective tendencies in man. If there is a "psychanalysis" [sic] there must also be a "psychosynthesis" which creates future events according to the same laws. (I see I am writing rather as if I had a flight of ideas.) The leap towards psychosynthesis proceeds via the person of my patient, whose unconscious is right now preparing, apparently

with nothing to stop it, a new stereotype into which everything from outside, as it were, fits in conformity with the complex. (Hence the idea of the objective effect of the prospective tendency!)

(McGuire, 1974, pp. 216–217)

To make the matter explicit, no sooner had Jung finished analyzing his "great dream" than he was sallying forth with the banner of "psychosynthesis." There was more Hoffmann than Freud in these sentiments, which was as it should have been. For lately there had been more Hoffmann than Freud in Jung's dreams. Spielrein had yet to be heard from at this point, and the ultimate denouement of the Freud–Jung relationship was still years away. But, transparently, the fateful event had already occurred: Jung had drunk very deeply indeed from *The Devil's Elixirs*.

The eclipse of the "poisoning complex"

It would appear to be scarcely accidental that Freud himself took his examples from Hoffmann when, long after the rupture with Jung, he elected to make his own statement on the subject of the "uncanny." What is striking about Freud's (1919) treatment of the subject is how strongly he emphasizes the element of the past. To be sure, Freud's theoretical inclination had always been to emphasize the significance of the personal past, but in "The Uncanny" this inclination hardens into a new theoretical principle. For it is here that Freud introduces his "death instinct" as an instinctive compulsion to repeat earlier events. The past is thus armed with its own terrible power in this revamping of Freud's system; the future is ignored. This makes the strongest possible contrast to Jung's future-oriented views. In the universe of discourse that Freud sets out in "The Uncanny," and again in *Beyond the Pleasure Principle*, such novelties as "psychosynthesis" and "prospective tendency" are systematically rendered impossible. Which, we may suspect, is an essential aspect of the latent polemical intent underlying both works.

For thematic reasons alone one might argue that Jung and *The Devil's Elixirs* were quite probably on Freud's mind when he sat down to work on "The Uncanny." But, as it happens, it is possible to go farther than this and in the process clear up a tiny mystery. For, as Freud warms up for his critique of the "uncanny" as the "constant recurrence of the same thing" (1919, p. 234), he does in fact begin by making reference to *The Devil's Elixirs*, much as though he intended to make it the centerpiece of his study. Shortly, however, in the manner of someone reporting a recent rereading of a work, Freud informs the reader that the plot is too intricate for a short summary and that the accumulation of mysterious repetitions and doublings is aesthetically unsatisfactory, even if it does help one grasp

144

the essential mechanism of repetition. In passing, and somewhat dubiously, Freud alleges that the novel depicts instances of "telepathy," this while making it clear that "telepathy" excites him not at all. Overall, the page and a half on *The Devil's Elixirs* in Freud's essay is cursory to the point where one wonders why it is there at all. Seemingly, all Freud gets for his trouble is to give the reader the tentative impression that the figure of the "double" involves a recurrence of something past.

But Strachey has added a footnote to Freud's discussion of *The Devil's Elixirs* that merits our attention. The note speaks for Strachey's meticulous scholarship – another editor would have missed it entirely – so let us not here complain that the translation (presumably Strachey's own) of a passage from Hoffmann contained within goes unidentified. The note reads in its entirety:

> Under the rubric "Varia" in one of the issues of the *Internationale Zeitschrift für Psychoanalyse* for 1919 (5, 308), the year in which the present paper was first published, there appears over the initials "S.F." a short note which it is not unreasonable to attribute to Freud. Its insertion here, though strictly irrelevant, may perhaps be excused. The note is headed: "E.T.A. Hoffmann on the Function of Consciousness" and it proceeds: "In *Die Elixire des Teufels* (Part II, p. 210, in Hesse's edition) – a novel rich in pathological mental states – Schönfeld comforts the hero, whose consciousness is temporarily disturbed, with the following words: "And what do you get out of it? I mean out of the particular mental function which we call consciousness, and which is nothing but the confounded activity of a damned toll-collector – exciseman – deputy-chief customs officer, who has set up his infamous bureau in our top storey and who exclaims, whenever any goods try to get out: 'Hi! hi! exports are prohibited . . . they must stay here . . . here, in this country.'"

(1919, pp. 233–234)

Freud's gloss is discrepant with the actual situation in the novel. Medardus has regained his sanity, not momentarily lost it; and Schönfeld is not comforting him, but rebuking him for putting so much emphasis on awareness. Let us observe further that Freud breaks off the quotation before the reader would find out that what cannot be exported are the goods of the "heavenly city" of the unconscious. And, stepping back from the text itself, let us add what Strachey was not in a position to know, or rather, to guess. As he warmed up to his study on "The Uncanny," Freud naturally returned to the scene of the crime, to *The Devil's Elixirs*, to see what he could make of it. What he found, as he tells us straightforwardly in his essay, was a novel so intricate and dense that it was not really suitable

145

material for a short discursive essay. In the process of reading the novel, however, Freud came across the passage on consciousness and apparently saw – this is the ostensible point of his note in the *Zeitschrift* – a literary foreshadowing of his own doctrine of the censor. But, I would submit, Freud saw something else as well: the source of Jung's dream image. Freud knew Jung's dream, knew that he had appeared in it, and knew that he had been frustrated in his own attempt to analyze it. Now, just in case Jung was still reading the *Zeitschrift*, Freud made a small point of his recent discovery.

But it is not Freud's later writings on the uncanny with which I wish to concern the reader here. Rather, I would like to offer a tentative suggestion as to the initial impact on him of Jung's invocation of Hoffmann's novel in March of 1909. Freud, of course, had long been familiar with Hoffmann's work in general, and we can take it as given that he had some acquaintance with *The Devil's Elixirs* in particular, though, in point of fact, there is no specific reference to it in any of his writings prior to 1919.[5] Nonetheless, assuming that in 1909 Freud did have some familiarity with the novel's content from a prior reading, he was most likely concerned with that mysterious bottle of Syracusan, the elixir itself, and what it foreboded about Jung's investigations into the "core complex."

Some background is in order here. In the spring of 1909, Freud was approximately one third of the way through a three-year development in which, in collaboration with a small group of favorites, he gradually arrived at a definitive formulation of what he called the "core" or "nuclear" complex. This "core" or "nuclear" complex was to perform two important heuristic functions. It was to unify the burgeoning field of complexes in general and it was to serve as a point of departure for the psychoanalytic investigation of mythology and folktales. Incidentally, either English word faithfully reflects the German "*kerncomplex*," but "core" is perhaps preferable to "nuclear" if only because the alternative translation prejudices the English reader to suppose that right from the start there was an intimate connection with the nuclear family, and thus with the triangular nature of the oedipal conflicts. As Forrester (1980, ch. 3) has shown in some detail, however, it was only very gradually that Freud came to the oedipal and triangular formulation of the "core complex," even if in retrospect this particular version would seem to have been anticipated by his discussion of Sophocles's *Oedipus Rex* in *The Interpretation of Dreams*. During the years 1908–1909, then, the "core complex" was not yet synonymous with the Oedipus complex; it was still an essentially elastic concept that could accommodate a number of subsidiary themes. In particular, a point somewhat minimized by Forrester, Freud consistently supposed that children's sexual researches necessarily played an important role in determining both the timing and the specific content of the "core complex" in any individual's development. The specific theoretical utility of the theme of infantile sexual research is beyond the scope of this paper, but among its virtues was its ready application to the content of various folktales. Toward the end of 1908, Freud repeatedly drew Jung's attention to the theme of children's sexual researches, and Jung responded by undertaking to observe the reactions of his eldest daughter to the birth of her baby brother. Both men understood that whatever Jung discovered through these observations might potentially bear on the doctrine of the "core complex."

What concerns us here is that among the variants of the "core complex" with which Freud was experimenting at the time was one he called the "poisoning complex" (McGuire, 1974, p. 186). Indeed, this particular complex is mentioned in his letter to Jung of December 11, 1908, which is also the first occasion in the Jung correspondence in which the phrase "core complex" (p. 186) occurs. Freud's statement is quite brief and altogether clinical: "A recent observation tempted me to trace the poisoning complex, when it is present, back to the infant's interpretation of its mother's morning sickness" (p. 186). From the remark, one would suspect that no more was in the offing than an interpretation of fears of being poisoned as a fear of sexuality and of pregnancy, the latter being mediated by the infant's perception of its mother's morning sickness. Nonetheless, we know that the idea of the "poisoning complex" was more general still and had lately been much on Freud's mind. On December 8, 1909, three days before this letter to Jung, while discussing a slip of one of Stekel's patients in a Wednesday night meeting, Freud had brought up the idea of "basic complexes" (Nunberg and Federn, 1967, p. 76) and then gone into the specific idea of poisoning. And a month earlier, while discussing Karl Abraham's recent paper on alcoholism and sexuality during the Wednesday night meeting of November 4, 1908, Freud had specifically brought up the "toxic" conception of love and had applied it to his own concept of the libido: "We simply transform the 'love potion' of legend into science. Things of such magnitude can only be rediscovered" (Nunberg and Federn, 1967, pp. 36–37). To be sure, at this time alcoholism was a major psychiatric preoccupation and Freud had good reasons for wishing to link up his theories with this topic. But as his last remark indicates, Freud had also realized by this time that the "toxic" conception of love as a poison bore on his own theory of the libido. The "poisoning complex" thus had the unusual property that it constituted, along the lines of an implicit self-analysis, Freud's comment on his more general theory of the chemical basis of the libido.

Some further background is in order here. Freud had long been persuaded, and had said so repeatedly in his various writings to date, that his concept of the "libido" would eventually be mapped exactly on the action of an endogenous sexual chemical in the brain. In an instructive paper that deserves wider circulation, Swales (1983) has contended that the model for this putative sexual chemical was cocaine. To Swales's detailed argumentation, let me add the thought that it was by virtue of Freud's experiences with this drug that he was readily prepared to outline a "metapsychology" in the emphatic sense that he went beyond the "psychology" of his mentor in these matters, Franz Brentano. This seminal philosopher, as is well known, had no place in his system for an "unconscious" *per se*; for Brentano, the method of psychology was the direct perception of mental states and its object necessarily had to be the product of consciousness. In contradicting the alternative view of Maudsley and others, Brentano noted in passing that although there were physiological processes in the brain that had psychological effects, these effects were readily, if indirectly, detectable by the evidence of conscious awareness. And as an example of such psychologically detectable physiological processes, Brentano (1874, p. 59) listed among other things the effect of "intoxicating beverages." It was, I would contend, the instructive example of cocaine that allowed Freud to extend Brentano's philosophy and make out of it a uniquely profitable new system that made room for unconscious sexual processes, presumed to be physiological, on the basis that their effects were analogously detectable through direct perception.

By conceiving of his libido as essentially a toxic process within the brain, Freud was locating his theory solidly within the traditions of late nineteenth- and early twentieth-century neurology and psychology. But his theory acquired a peculiar epicycle when first Riklin (1908) and then Abraham (1909), the latter working under Freud's direct editorial supervision, began pointing out the frequent recurrence of love-potions in both folktales and the motifs of ancient mythology. Love, it now appeared, had long been conceived of by an analogy to a potent elixir, perhaps derived from the gods. (As Freud put it to Abraham in his letter of June 7, 1908: "the legend of the Soma potion contains the highly important presentiment that all our intoxicating liquors and stimulating alkaloids are merely a substitute for the unique, still unattained toxin of the libido that rouses the ecstasy of love" (Abraham and Freud, 1965, p. 40).) The overall logic of the "core complex," however, demanded that all such mythical conceptions be derived from the conflicts of early childhood, including those arising out of infantile sexual researches. And thus, by this roundabout but quite compelling route, Freud had begun to conceive of something new, the "poisoning complex," with which he would explain the toxic conception of love as a dangerous potion.

The essence of the "poisoning complex" can be stated succinctly. The child watches his mother's morning sickness with perplexity; he is told that a baby is coming and that this is good as it is the result of the "love" between his parents. The child, whose sexual researches are only beginning, thus comes to the conception that "love" is somehow toxic, that it makes people sick in the way poisons do. In this way, the child early comes to formulate the fantasy of a dangerous elixir, precisely the conception that animates countless myths and folktales. Also – an ingenious piece of self-analysis has potentially been constructed here – such a conception, suitably modified to square with nineteenth-century brain physiology, could be found at the heart of Freud's own theory. Nor was the complex without clinical relevance – both fears of being poisoned and the use of substitute poisons such as alcohol and other intoxicants could be meaningfully approached under this interpretive rubric.[6]

Notwithstanding this promising beginning, the "poisoning complex" was not destined for great things in the evolution of psychoanalysis and most readers have undoubtedly never heard of it. Freud was quite serious about it during the period from mid-1908 through May of 1909, only to drop the subject thereafter. Just how serious Freud was can be gauged from his letters to two of Jung's Swiss compatriots, the Reverend Oskar Pfister and Ludwig Binswanger. To Pfister, Freud sent along a critique of a recent contribution on March 18, 1909. The essence of Freud's position is that owing to the "indissoluble connection between death and sexuality" (Freud and Meng, 1963, p. 20) the methods of suicide are always symbolic of sexuality. And among the alternatives in the suicidal endeavor Freud specifically mentions "taking poison" as equivalent to "becom[ing] pregnant" and adds as an explanation, "Poisoning as a consequence of morning sickness is equivalent to pregnancy" (p. 20). The critique sent to Pfister was followed in May by a similar letter to Binswanger commenting on a case report that Binswanger was publishing in two parts in the *Jahrbuch*. In his letter of May 17, 1909, Freud specifically pointed out the lack of any reference to infantile nuclear complexes in Binswanger's report (Binswanger, 1957, p. 11) and then went on to offer his own analysis of the patient's symptoms. Again, among other suggestions, the formula "poisoning = pregnancy" (p. 17) is offered, though here Freud elaborates the concomitant idea that pregnancy may also be symbolized as an infection. In a subsequent letter a week later, Freud suggested that Binswanger publish these glosses as an appendix to the case. Had Binswanger accepted the suggestion, this particular version of the core complex would have gone into print as the first published instance in which the psychopathology of an adult was analyzed through the focusing lens of the doctrine of the "core complex."

But after Freud's attempt to induce Binswanger to publish glosses partially derived from this conception failed, the "poisoning complex" as an important component of the "core complex" rapidly disappeared from sight. It was one of the few ideas that Freud seems to have simply discarded altogether. And here I think the delayed impact of Jung's letter of March 11, 1909 makes itself felt. Initially, after his receipt of the letter, in which Jung promised to write his own study on Hoffmann's novel, Freud's interest in the topic seems to have accelerated. His March critique to

Pfister was mailed within a week after Jung's letter arrived and the glosses to Binswanger were sent out a little more than two months later. But gradually, as he was confronted first by the full flower of Jung's "theology," and then by the revelations of Spielrein in her unsolicited communications of late May and early June, Freud began to realize he was potentially undercutting his own overall theory. As Spielrein's revelations made abundantly clear, the tendency in Zurich was to interpret the new doctrines along rather mystical lines, with mythic personifications and telepathic phenomena in abundance. In such a climate, a view of the libido theory as having been anticipated by ancient myths and folktales, and as being foreshadowed in individual development by a fortuitous conception of childhood, did little to stem the tide of "theology." For, in truth, Freud's idea of the "poisoning complex" was implicitly teleological – the child early gained a conception of love as a dangerous potion that would become highly meaningful later in life. With only a little tinkering, the "poisoning complex" could be given a Romantic twist, as though Nature were preparing the child for its fate by schooling it early in a central myth of mankind.

The matter was especially critical when one understands that Freud's sexual chemistry was the basis of his predominantly reductive view of the psyche, and hence also the basis of his aversion to the kind of teleological conceptions that Jung wanted to introduce. What mattered most here was the general view that a putative sexual chemical was responsible for all significant alterations of consciousness, even if these alterations might disguise themselves with the trappings of the supernatural. Put another way, Freud wanted first of all to make sure that the Devil's elixir was understood as libido in his sense. So long as this was in contention, it did not matter whether or not certain mythic conceptions of love potions were fashioned in childhood by each new generation. The libido theory was the main issue. The niceties of the "poisoning complex," however much they appealed to the systematic nature of Freud's mind, and however much they might accord with the fruits of his own self-analysis, were trivial in comparison. Henceforth, Freud resisted this particular temptation.

Notes

1 The term "subconscious," derived from French psychopathology, is to be preferred here and elsewhere with regard to Jung's nascent theory of "psychosynthesis." In this regard, it is not to be confused with the distinction between "unconscious" and "preconscious" which occurs in Freudian theory.
2 This essay is not to be confused with a number of other essays by Jung with similar titles nor with the first English translation of his *Transformations and Symbols of the Libido* (1911–1912), which was retitled in 1916 by his American translator Beatrice Hinkle as *Psychology of the Unconscious*. Making matters worse, the particular essay at issue began life in 1912 with an altogether

different title, "New Paths in Psychology," and only acquired its present title, and the illustrative citation of Brother Medardus, during its first revision in 1916–1917. For a lucid account of the perplexities of Jung's texts, see Homans's "How to Read Jung" (1979, ch. 2).

3 Hoffmann's Schönfeld has another aspect as well and this may partially explain his failure to win archetypal status. Schönfeld also goes by an Italian name, Pietro Belcampo, and he is as comfortable in the landscape of Rome during the second part of the book as he is in the North German landscape of the first part. No doubt, Hoffmann wished his character to bridge the gulf between the Mediterranean and Teutonic worlds, perhaps with Goethe's *Italian Journey* in the back of his mind. This aspect of the Schönfeld character, as a symbol for that part of the German soul with a penchant for things Italian, would have struck a disquieting note for Jung who, in apparent imitation of Freud, had developed his own Rome neurosis (see McGuire, 1974, p. 346 and Jung, 1962, pp. 287–288). Jung, in fact, never did get to Rome, and when late in life he resolved finally to do so, he became faint at the train station and had to return home. All of which is to say that Schönfeld/Belcampo has achieved a synthesis that Jung could only envy.

4 The dating of Jung's dream to this particular point in time presents some difficulties in light of Jung's statement (1962, p. 163) that he had this dream while he was working on the manuscript of *Transformations and Symbols of the Libido*. As it is clear that Jung only began work on this project in October 1909, the necessary implication is that the dream came either late in 1909 or else during the years 1910–1911. Compounding matters, to his seminar group in 1925, Jung made the same statement – the dream came while he worked on the book – and then went farther and specifically dated the dream to 1912. My supposition in the text, that this is the "great dream" reported in the letter of April 2–12, flies in the face of these statements by Jung.

Nonetheless, there are good reasons for supposing that the supposition in the text is correct and that Jung's dating is wrong. To begin with, both the memoirs and the account given to the seminar group in 1925 contain numerous mistakes with regards to dates. (Frequently, they are the exact same mistakes, as the memoirs repeat the faulty recollections of the seminar.) In the seminar notes Jung's first visit to Vienna is dated to 1906, instead of 1907; in the memoirs his second visit is dated to 1910, instead of 1909; and, also in the memoirs, an important bicycle trip to the northern part of Italy is dated to 1911, instead of 1910. In general, a close scrutiny of the memoirs, the more complete of the two sources with regard to the relationship with Freud, shows it to be a composite of several different accounts, which have been thrown together with only a passing glance at chronology.

5 Freud's prior acquaintance with Hoffmann is attested to by his letter to Martha Bernays of June 26, 1885: "I have been reading off and on a few things by the 'mad' Hoffmann, mad, fantastic stuff, here and there a brilliant thought" (E. Freud, 1960, p. 158).

6 There was another way in which the toxic conception of love figures. At the Salzburg Congress in the spring of 1908, Jung had read a paper in which he advanced his own conception of a non-specific brain toxin in schizophrenia. Against Jung's view, shared in a less constricted form by his mentor Bleuler, Karl Abraham read a paper arguing that the key aspect of schizophrenia was auto-eroticism. Thus began several years of tension between Jung and Abraham. Freud's discussions of the Soma myth, and of love potions generally, in his letters to Abraham has this dispute with Jung as part of their context.

Specifically, Freud and Abraham continued to hold the view that Jung's hypothetical toxin is nothing else but their sexual chemical by another, wrong, name.

References

Abraham, H., and Freud, E. (eds) (1965) *A Psycho-Analytic Dialogue: The Letters of Sigmund Freud and Karl Abraham*. (B. Marsh and H. Abraham, trans.) New York: Basic Books.

Abraham, K. (1909) *Dreams and Myths*. (H. Abraham, trans.) In *Selected Papers of Karl Abraham: Clinical Papers and Essays on Psychoanalysis*. New York: Basic Books, 1955.

Binswanger, L. (1957) *Sigmund Freud: Reminiscences of a Friendship* (N. Guterman, trans.) New York: Grune & Stratton.

Brentano, F. (1874) *Psychology from an Empirical Standpoint*. (L. McAlister, trans.) London: Routledge & Kegan Paul, 1973.

Carotenuto, A. (1982) *A Secret Symmetry: Sabina Spielrein between Jung and Freud*. (A. Pomerans, J. Shepley, and K. Winston, trans.) New York: Pantheon.

Ellenberger, H. (1970) *The Discovery of the Unconscious: The History and Evolution of Dynamic Psychiatry*. New York: Basic Books.

Forel, A. (1908) Zum heutigen Stand der Psychotherapie: Ein Vorschlag. *Journal für Psychologie und Neurologie*, 11.

Forrester, J. (1980) *Language and the Origins of Psychoanalysis*. New York: Columbia University Press.

Freud, E. (1960) *The Letters of Sigmund Freud*. (T. Stern and J. Stern, trans.) New York: Basic Books.

—— and Meng, H. (1963) *Psycho-Analysis and Faith: The Letters of Sigmund Freud and Oskar Pfister* (E. Mosbacher, trans.) New York: Basic Books.

Freud, S. (1919) The "Uncanny." *Standard Edition*, 17: 218–256.

—— (1920) *Beyond the Pleasure Principle. Standard Edition*, 18: 3–64.

Hannah, B. (1976) *Jung His Life and Work: A Biographical Memoir*. New York: Putnam.

Hoffmann, E.T.A. (1816) *The Devil's Elixirs*. (R. Taylor, trans.) London: John Calder, 1963.

Holt, R. (1978) Ideological and Thematic Conflicts in the Structure of Freud's Theories. In S. Smith, *The Human Mind Revisited: Essays in Honor of Karl A. Menninger*. New York: International Universities Press.

Homans, P. (1979) *Jung in Context: Modernity and the Making of a Psychology*. Chicago: University of Chicago Press.

Jones, E. (1955) *The Life and Work of Sigmund Freud* (vol. 2). New York: Basic Books.

Jung, C.G. (1896–1899) *The Zofingia Lectures*. Princeton: Princeton University Press, 1983.

—— (1903) On Simulated Insanity. In *The Collected Works*, 1: 159–187. Princeton: Princeton University Press, 1970.

—— (1910) Marginal Notes on Wittels: *Die Sexuelle Not*. In *The Collected Works*, 18: 393–396. Princeton: Princeton University Press, 1975.

—— (1911–1912) *Transformations and Symbols of the Libido.* (B. Hinkle, trans.) New York: Dodd, Mead, 1947.

—— (1925) *[Analytic Psychology] Notes on the Seminar in Analytic Psychology.* (Compiled by C. de Angulo and approved by C.G. Jung.) Zurich: multigraphed typescript.

—— (1943) On the Psychology of the Unconscious. In *The Collected Works* 7: 1–119. Princeton: Princeton University Press, 1972.

—— (1962) *Memories, Dreams, Reflections.* (R. and C. Winston, trans.) New York: Vintage, 1965.

McGuire, W. (1974) *The Freud/Jung Letters.* (R. Mannheim and R.F.C. Hull, trans.) Princeton: Princeton University Press.

Nunberg, H., and Federn, E. (eds) (1967) *Minutes of the Vienna Psychoanalytic Society (Vol. 2): 1908–1910.* (H. Nunberg, trans.) New York: International Universities Press.

Riklin, F. (1908) *Wish Fulfillment and Symbolism in Fairy Tales.* (W. White, trans.) New York: Journal of Mental and Nervous Disease Monograph Series, 1915.

Rudnytsky, P.L. (1987) *Freud and Oedipus.* New York: Columbia University Press.

Swales, P.J. (1983) Freud, Cocaine, Sexual Chemistry; The Role of Cocaine in Freud's Conception of the Libido. Privately published by author, New York.

6

THOMAS MANN AND
C.G. JUNG

Paul Bishop

Sources: *Oxford German Studies,* 23, (1994) and
The Modern Language Review, 91 (1996).

Biographically speaking, the German novelist Thomas Mann (1875–1955) and C.G. Jung had much in common.[1] For a start, Mann was born 1875, the same year as Jung; for a time they both lived in Küsnacht, near Zurich; and Jung died in 1961 on 6 June, the date of Thomas Mann's birthday. But, as some have begun to suspect,[2] the intellectual affinities and personal contacts between Mann and Jung went much further than just a set of coincidental dates and locations, and Mann's reception of Jung's writings belonged to the creative forces behind his major novels and essays.[3] In this essay I shall, first, survey the scholarly literature on this topic and summarize the main arguments and conclusions reached to date; second, provide new data on Mann's relation to Jung, showing that it was probably closer than has hitherto been recognized; third, on the basis of that survey of Mann's reception of Jung and analytical psychology, consider a Jungian perspective on Mann's works, with particular reference to the *Joseph* tetralogy; and, finally, examine the possible reasons why Mann was reluctant to acknowledge Jung as a source for some of his ideas. Although Mann sought to play down the importance of Jung for his work, I shall argue that understanding this importance is essential to an understanding of the tetralogy's attempted combination of 'myth plus psychology'.[4]

I

Mann's relation to Jung needs to be seen in the context of his interest in psychoanalysis in general and Freud in particular, a subject on which he wrote two major essays, 'Freud's Position in the History of Modern Thought' (1929), and 'Freud and the Future' (1936). According to evidence provided by Manfred Dierks,[5] Mann started to read Freud as early as

1911 with 'Delusions and Dreams in Jensen's *Gradiva*' (1907) and he went on to read *Thoughts for the Times on War and Death* (1915) and the *Three Essays on the Theory of Sexuality* (1905), parodying the ideas of the 'Three Studies' in *The Magic Mountain* (1924). In 1925–1926, at about the same time as he was starting work on his *Joseph* novels, Mann began a more extensive programme of reading Freud's *Collected Works*, which had just been published in Vienna. This time he concentrated on 'On Narcissism: An Introduction' (1914), *Totem and Taboo* (1912–1913), *Beyond the Pleasure Principle* (1920) and 'An Autobiographical Study' (1925). In 1929, the brief but significant correspondence with Freud himself began.

In fact, one of Mann's first observations on the relationship between psychology and mythology, and their joint relationship to art and literature, can be found in his essay 'The Old Fontane' (1910–1919):

> Myth and psychology are two different things: where they dwell together in one bosom, where singer and writer are united in one person, there contradictions emerge. . . . As guardian of the myth, the poet is conservative. But psychology, on the other hand, is the most effective mine-laying tool of democratic enlightenment.
>
> (*E* pp. 305–6)

Similar reflections on the combination of *Mythos plus Psychologie* pepper his writings up to and including the programmatic statements on myth and psychology in his work in his correspondence with the Hungarian philologist, mythologist and classical scholar, Karl Kerényi (1897–1973), particularly in his letters of the 1940s. As Hans Wysling has pointed out, Mann's use of mythical material – and his emphasis on psychology as a means of preserving mythical constructs – became increasingly substantial throughout his literary career.[6]

Thus Mann's interest in psychology in general and his reading of Freud in particular is well documented. There is, however, a major gap in the scholarly literature on Thomas Mann with regard to his reception of C.G. Jung. In 1972, Manfred Dierks posited Schopenhauer as a common source for both men to account for the notably close proximity between certain ideas of Mann and the Jungian notions of the archetypes and the Collective Unconscious.[7] More recently, Dierks was prepared to speak of the 'direct influence' of Jung on Mann in the form of his co-operation with Kerényi on *Das göttliche Kind* (1940) and *Das göttliche Mädchen* (1941),[8] after which 'the trace of direct influence' apparently disappears again.[9] Dierks's schematic comparison of Jung, Mann and Schopenhauer does not, however, necessarily reflect Mann's own attitude towards these two thinkers. In a more recent article, however, Dierks has drawn attention to the similarities in the typological approach of Mann, Jung and Max Weber.[10]

In 1973, Jean Finck went a long way to acknowledging the importance of Jung for Thomas Mann, particularly as far as the novelistic works of the late 1930s and early 1940s are concerned, while holding back from a direct assertion of Jung's significance.[11] And even though Hans Wysling admitted Jung's input among the many other sources of Mann's concept of mythology, and even though he correctly emphasized the most apparently Jungian aspect of Mann's understanding of the mythical role of art, he did not undertake any detailed review of Mann's reception of Jung.[12] In other words, and against their better judgment, these commentators seem to take their cue from Mann's later, demonstrably false denials that he had ever read Jung.

By way of contrast, at least four other commentators have argued that Jung was of fundamental importance for certain developments in Mann's work. First, in two important articles which examined the possible Jungian influence on the *Joseph* tetralogy (1933–1943) and the novel *The Holy Sinner* (1951), Joachim Schulze drew attention to the Jungian psychological schemata which underlie these works and concluded that Thomas Mann must have had a detailed knowledge of Jung's major work, *Symbole und Wandlungen der Libido* ('Transformations and Symbols of the Libido') (1911–1912).[13] Second, Adèle Bloch provided an archetypal interpretation of *Joseph and his Brothers*, albeit one which assumed rather than proved the Jungian background to this work.[14] Third, Koichi Ikeda argued in a more substantiated way that, in addition to the accepted contributions of Freud, there are also structural correspondences, in terms of insight and method, between Jung's psychology and the *Joseph* novels.[15] Finally, entirely independent of the present author, Charlotte Nolte has offered what is virtually a Jungian interpretation of the tetralogy. On this reading, 'in the unifying figure of Joseph' Mann demonstrates 'the interplay between conscious and unconscious elements, whereby myth becomes the factor that turns this interplay into a form of communication which can be understood and interpreted by the conscious mind'. Yet Nolte claims that she had not set out 'to reveal a hidden Jungian influence on Mann', insisting: '[T]here is no underlying intent whatsoever, to show a particular Jungian or other influence.'[16] As this essay seeks to show, such influence did indeed exist.

So if, as Thomas Sprecher has supposed, it was not so much outright rejection as ambivalence that determined Mann's attitude towards Jung,[17] that same ambivalence seems to have affected the critical community. But Mann's diaries and letters, both published and unpublished, will help us to answer four fundamental questions. What did Mann read by Jung? How many contacts did he have in the Jungian community? Did he ever meet Jung? And why did he later decide to play down his connections with Jung? For, contrary to what he later maintained in the 1940s and 1950s, Thomas Mann read at least six texts by Jung, and once met him in person.

What follows is a chronological account of Mann's reception of Jungian psychology.

II

Unfortunately, Mann's diaries between December 1921 and March 1933, which includes the period when Mann was particularly interested in Jung, are no longer available, as they were destroyed by his own hand in May 1945. Thus there is no account of Mann's meeting with Jung, which has always been assumed to have taken place, if at all, during this period. But two letters by Thomas Mann, kept in the C.G. Jung Archive at the *Eidgenössische Technische Hochschule* (ETH) in Zurich, allow us to date this meeting with much greater certainty than hitherto.

In the first of these two letters, dated 17 March 1921, Thomas Mann asked the addressee, August Vetter (1887–1976), to apologize on his behalf to Jung, whose forthcoming lecture – probably on typology – he was going to miss. A mutual acquaintance of Mann and Jung, Vetter was highly interested in aesthetics, and was the author of *Die dämonische Zeit* (1919), *Kritik des Gefühls* (1923) (of which both Mann and Jung possessed a copy) and *Nietzsche* (1926) (of which Mann possessed a copy). In that letter, Mann told Vetter: 'If he [Dr Jung] feels like visiting me on another day for a cup of tea, and it would be best if you came too, then I would be delighted, and perhaps you would be kind enough to telephone me and let me know.' According to this letter, it was Mann who was instrumental in arranging the meeting with Jung. But did the meeting ever take place? Confirmation that it did is provided by Mann's reference to it, albeit very vague, in his letter of 22 February 1945 to Anna Jacobson (see below). Thus in the early 1920s, Mann was already sufficiently interested in analytical psychology to seek a personal audience with its founder.

It is not possible to trace any further personal contacts between Jung and Mann until 1929, but Mann's library contains, among the cuttings he used during the preliminary stages of his work on *Joseph and his Brothers*, a short article published by Jung in the *Europäische Revue* (March, 1926).[18] In 'Archaic Man', Jung discussed the collective identity of primitive man, a theme which Mann explored in the *Joseph* tetralogy, and the relation between the subject and the object of cognition, a topic to which Jung often returned in his writings. Mann was highly interested in the subject–object relation in psychoanalysis, as his letter of 1 March 1930 to H.L. Held (see below), his marginal linings in his copy of Jung's 'Psychological Commentary on *The Tibetan Book of the Dead*' (1935) and his lecture 'Freud and the Future' (1936) all make clear.

The next major contact between Mann and Jung we can document is his letter to Jung of 1 April 1929, also held in the C.G. Jung Archive of the ETH. In this letter, Mann thanks Jung for sending him a copy of his most recent publication, and expresses broad agreement with Jung's ideas. In his letter, Mann wrote:

> Just as you are right to call Freud a destroyer of idealistic illusions about the nature of Man, so confirmation emerges from what you say that the analytic interest for the power of the irrational is not sympathy, not anti-intellectualism, but that this interest is only a method and, in the end, the primacy of reason and of the intellect is maintained.

Two questions immediately arise from this letter. First, what had Jung sent to Mann? Bearing in mind Schulze's conviction that Mann must have read Jung's *Symbole und Wandlungen der Libido* (1911–1912), it would be tempting to think that this was the 'important work' Jung had sent. From internal evidence, however, it is more probable that Jung had sent Mann a copy of his recent paper 'Problems of Modern Psychotherapy', published in the *Schweizerisches Medizinisches Jahrbuch* (1929) (*CW* 16 §114–§174). For the reference to Freud as a destroyer of idealistic illusions about the nature of man echoes Jung's words in that paper:

> The result of the Freudian method of elucidation is a minute elaboration of Man's shadow-side unexampled in any previous age. It is the most effective antidote imaginable to all the idealistic illusions about the nature of Man; and it is therefore no wonder that there arose on all sides the most violent opposition to Freud and his school.
>
> (*CW* 16 §145)

Second, what had Mann just finished writing? Again, dating and context suggest that what Mann in his letter referred to as 'something appropriate' must refer to 'Freud's Position in the History of Modern Thought', delivered as a lecture at the University of Munich on 16 May 1929 and first published in *Die psychoanalytische Bewegung* (May/June, 1929) in Vienna. In this paper, which opened with an exegesis of Nietzsche's aphorism 'German hostility to the Enlightenment' from *Daybreak* (1881)[19] Mann went on to tease out Freud's relationship to German Romantic thought in general and Novalis in particular, identifying psychoanalysis as part of the contemporary trend of irrationalism:

> As a delver into the depths, a researcher in the psychology of instinct, Freud unquestionably belongs with those writers of the nineteenth century who, be it as historians, critics, philosophers, or archæologians, stand opposed to rationalism, intellectualism, classicism – in a word, to the belief in mind held by the eighteenth

and somewhat also by the nineteenth century; emphasising instead the night side of nature and the soul as the actually life-conditioning and life-giving element; cherishing it, scientifically advancing it, representing in the most revolutionary sense the divinity of earth, the primacy of the unconscious, the pre-mental, the will, the passions, or, as Nietzsche says, the 'feeling' above the 'reason'. . . . [Psychoanalysis's] emphasis on the dæmonic in nature, its passion for investigating the night side of the soul, makes it as anti-rationalistic as any product of the new spirit that lies locked in victorious struggle with the mechanistic and materialistic elements of the nineteenth century.

(*PM* pp. 172–3, 191)

Yet Mann came to the conclusion that psychoanalysis, although irrational, was able to resist the reactionary:

It might be called anti-rational, since it deals, in the interests of research, with the night, the dream, impulse, the pre-rational; and the concept of the unconscious presides at its beginnings. But it is far from letting those interests make it a tool of the obscurantist, fanatic, backward-shaping spirit. It is that manifestation of modern irrationalism which stands unequivocally firm against all reactionary misuse.

(*PM* p. 198)

In fact, Freud, to whom Mann sent a copy of *Die Forderung des Tages* (1930), which contains this essay, thanked him for his defence against 'the charge of reactionary mysticism' (letter of 23 November 1929).

In his paper, Jung proposes a four-fold approach to psychological therapy – termed here 'confession, elucidation, education, and transformation' (*CW* 16 §122) – which seeks to supersede the alleged limitations of Freudian and Adlerian analysis and, more importantly, to attend to the rational *and* irrational, biological *and* spiritual needs of man. But it is ironic that, at this stage, Mann was so positive towards a psychology which, later on, he would suspect of propagating a far more malevolent irrationalism. And it is even more ironic that, in his novel *Doctor Faustus* (1947), he would seek to combat such irrationalism within a framework which is, in fact, virtually identical with Jung's own highly irrationalistic analysis of Fascism.

III

One year later, Jung was included on Thomas Mann's reading list during his visit to Egypt from mid-February to mid-March 1930. In a letter of

1 March 1930 to Hans Ludwig Held (1885–1954), the director of the Stadt-bibliothek in Munich, Mann wrote of his impressions concerning the German translation of D.H. Lawrence's *Fantasia of the Unconscious* (1921) and of Jung's introduction to and commentary on the ancient Chinese text *The Secret of the Golden Flower*, translated by the German sinologue Richard Wilhelm (1873–1930) and published in 1929 (*CW* 13 §1–§84):

> Jung's long introduction to the 'Secret of the Golden Flower' [is], for me, the book itself . . . , at any rate it makes the spirituality of his text accessible to me at all – by means of psychology. . . . I was pleasantly surprised to find in Jung the same thoughts that I conjure up in the novel, such as the 'primitive remnant of non-differentiation between subject and object', Lévy-Bruhl's 'partici-pation mystique'. Astonishing! I have a thin skin for such things, it is as if I soak them up.[20]

In his letter to Held, Mann singled out for such high praise two main aspects of Jung's commentary: the recommendation to approach Eastern thought via (Western) European concepts (*CW* 13 §1–§9) and the dis-cussion of the notion of *participation mystique* (*CW* 13 §66), derived from the work of the French sociologist Lucien Lévy-Bruhl (1857–1939). 'Thoughts that I conjure up in the novel' can only refer to *Joseph*, and Jung's contribution to ideas found in the tetralogy are discussed in more detail below. In general, we may say that, at this stage, Mann's enthusiasm for Jung's socio-anthropological assumptions as represented in his com-mentary on *The Secret of the Golden Flower* was apparently unqualified.

By contrast, the first references to Jung in Mann's diary for 1934 are highly negative. On 27 February 1934, Mann reacted very strongly to Jung's controversial decision to assume the editorship of the *Zentralblatt für Psychotherapie und ihre Grenzgebiete*, the official journal of the *Allgemeine Ärtzliche Gesellschaft für Psychotherapie* (General Medical Society for Psychotherapy), whose presidency Jung had simultaneously taken over. The Jewish psychologist Ernst Kretschmer (1888–1964), pre-viously a professor of psychiatry at Marburg, had been president of the society since 1930, but under pressure from the National Socialists resigned from this post on 6 April 1933. As vice-president, Jung stepped in and acted as president until 1940, an action that was widely criticized (and in some quarters still is) as offering support for a Nazi organization.[21] What-ever the rights and wrongs of Jung's apparently dubious decision, Mann for one was not satisfied with Jung's public defence of it. His diary entry of 14 March 1934 records: 'C.G. Jung's response in the N[eue] Z[ürcher] Z[eitung] unpleasant and sneaky, even badly written and unfunny, striking a false pose. He should openly declare his "affiliation".'[22]

Mann's concern about Jung's political affiliations surfaced again in his diary entry for 4 September 1934, probably after reading the essay 'Über einige Bücher' by Herman Hesse in the *Neue Rundschau* (1934) which reviewed a selection of Jung's essays published under the title *Wirklichkeit der Seele* (1934): 'C.G. Jung a dubious character. It is said he has declared himself to be anti-Semitic.' Despite his dismay at Jung's alleged support for National Socialism, Mann read at least one further paper by Jung in the following year, as the diary entry for 16 March 1935 reveals. From this entry, it is clear that Mann had just read Jung's notorious essay 'The State of Psychotherapy Today', published in the *Zentralblatt für Psychotherapie* (1934) (*CW* 10 §333–§370). Mann's condemnation of Jung's alleged political sympathies is mitigated – at least at the beginning – by words of acknowledgement: 'When a man of high intellectual standing such as Jung behaves badly, there are of course elements of truth, which add elements of sympathy to one's disgust.' Mann's diary reflections on Jung's critique of 'soulless rationalism' conclude, however, with a blistering personal attack on Jung:

> He is an example of the need to conform to the times – at a high level; he is *no* 'lone wolf', he is not one of those who remain true to the eternal laws of reason and morality and for that reason have become rebels against the age. He swims with the flow. He is clever, but not commendable.

Whatever his doubts concerning Jung, Mann by no means lost all interest in Jungian psychology. Nothing could be further from the truth. Eleven months later, according to the diary entry for 20 February 1936, he was reading Jung's 'Psychological Commentary', an introduction especially written for the recent German edition (1935) of *The Tibetan Book of the Dead*. Mann's verdict on Jung's psychological commentary was that it was 'interesting', and the extent of this interest may be judged by the marginal linings found in Mann's personal copy in his library at the Thomas-Mann-Archiv in Zurich. The marked sections correspond to passages from §840, §841, §844, §845, §846, §849 and §857 in volume 11 of Jung's *Collected Works*. These reveal at least two reasons why Jung's psychological commentary on *The Tibetan Book of the Dead* was important for Mann. First, it is relevant for the socio-psychological assumptions underlying the *Joseph* tetralogy; and second, it is the text from which Mann extensively quoted in 1936 in his lecture 'Freud and the Future'.

Delivered before several audiences, including at the celebration of Freud's eightieth birthday on 8 May 1936 in Vienna, first published in *Imago* (1936), and even read to Freud in his home,[23] 'Freud and the Future' is, curiously enough, in many ways more about Jung than about Freud.[24] At one point, Mann himself wonders, 'perhaps this is the moment, my friends, to indulge on this festive occasion in a little polemic against Freud himself' (*E* p. 419), but it hardly seems the right moment, and it is certainly not very 'festive'. Right at the beginning of his lecture, Mann declares:

[U]nless I am greatly mistaken, it is just this confrontation of object and subject, their mingling and identification, the resultant insight into the mysterious unity of ego and actuality, destiny and character, doing and happening, and thus into the mystery of reality as an operation of the psyche – it is just this confrontation that is the alpha and omega of all psychoanalytical knowledge.

(*E* pp. 411–12)

'Unless I am greatly mistaken'! The unity of subject and object is an idea that has very little to do with Freudian psychoanalysis but everything to do with Jung's analytical psychology. Mann could have come across the idea, another way of expressing Lévy-Bruhl's notion of 'participation mystique', in at least three works by Jung. First, in the early version of 'Archaic Man' (1926), Jung wrote: 'For archaic man . . . psychic happenings are projected so completely that they cannot be distinguished from objective, physical events' (*CW* 10 §135). Second, in the commentary on *The Secret of the Golden Flower* (1929), in a passage to which Mann alluded in his letter of 1 March 1930, Jung discussed 'the indefinitely large remnant of non-differentiation between subject and object, which is still so great among primitives'. He went on: 'Where there is no consciousness of the difference between subject and object, an unconscious identity prevails' (*CW* 13 §66). And third, in his commentary on *The Tibetan Book of the Dead* (1935), in a passage that Mann marked in the margin of copy with a line, Jung observed: 'There are, and always have been, those who cannot help but see that the world and its experiences are in the nature of a symbol, and that it really reflects something that lies hidden in the subject himself, in his own transubjective reality' (*CW* 11 §849). What Mann described as the alpha and omega of psychoanalysis – the interpenetration of subject and object – returns in *Joseph* as 'the alpha and omega of all our questions' in the 'Prelude' to the tetralogy entitled 'Descent into Hell' (*JAHB* p. 3).

Further on in his lecture, Mann repeats his key theme, that 'the mystery of the unity of the ego and the world, of being and happening, in the perception of the apparently objective and accidental as a matter of the soul's own contriving' constitutes 'the innermost core of psychoanalytic theory' (*E* p. 418). This begs the question: whose theory, Freud's or Jung's? Significantly, Mann then goes straight on to mention Jung directly, referring to him as 'an able but somewhat ungrateful scion of the Freudian school' (*E* p. 418). Yet what Mann has just outlined is, in fact, a Jungian idea. Mann quotes a passage from Jung's commentary on the *Tibetan Book of the Dead* which he had marked in his copy: 'It is so much more straightforward, more dramatic, impressive, and therefore more convincing, to see all the things that happen to me than to observe how I make them happen' (*CW* 11 §841; cf. *E* p. 418). This Mann describes as 'a bold, even an extravagant statement'. Although Mann mentions that Jung was greatly indebted to Schopenhauer and Freud, he passes over these intellectual sources and instead looks elsewhere: '[I]t is in line with my general intention to pause a little longer at the sentence that I quoted from Jung. In this essay and also as a general method which he uses by preference, Jung applies analytical evidence to form a bridge between Occidental thought and Oriental esoteric' (*E* p. 419):

> Nobody has focused so sharply as he the Schopenhauer–Freud perception that 'the "giver" of all "given" things dwells within us. This is a truth which in the face of all evidence, in the greatest things as in the smallest, is never known, although it is so very necessary, indeed vital, for us to know it'.
>
> (*E* p. 419; cf. *CW* 11 §841)

Mann took this overcoming of the subject–object distinction to provide the basis for a theology of immanence, or what he called 'a psychological conception of God, an idea of the godhead which is not pure condition, absolute reality, but one with the soul and bound up with it' (*E* p. 420). This concept of God – which is closely allied with Jung's psychological view of religion – is explicitly linked by Mann to the ideas of his 'mythological novel', *Joseph and his Brothers*, which he now introduces into 'this hour of formal encounter between creative literature and the psychoanalytic' (*E* p. 420). But the psychoanalytic doctrine under discussion is not so much Freudian analysis as Jung's analytical psychology.

The years between 1942 and 1946 saw an extreme fluctuation in Mann's attitude towards Jung: in turn, highly negative, then almost ingratiatory, and finally against him once more. In his handwritten letter of 24 September 1942 from California to the Swiss writer Rudolf Jakob Humm (1895–1977), Mann pulled no punches in an unqualified attack on Jung:

> He was extremely offensive as soon as he opened his political mouth. He understands something about psychology and something about Eastern wisdom and knows how to make quite a clever cocktail out of them. But his views display mindless apathy, and when he, who was always half a Nazi, today declares that disaster befalls us because we have unleashed the drives and turned war into a god, then he deserves to have his ears boxed.

These comments strike exactly the same note as his diary entry for 16 March 1935 (see above), almost as if Mann's reading of 'The Psychology of the Child-Archetype' and 'The Psychological Aspects of the Kore' had never taken place. Mann's reference to Jung's analysis of the causes of the Second World War suggests that he may have been familiar with Jung's essay 'Wotan' (1936), which notoriously interpreted the political phenomenon of National Socialism in psychological terms as an 'outbreak' of the Germanic war-god, Wotan. Mann's own novel, *Doctor Faustus*, is informed by remarkably similar ideas.[25] But if Mann had really thought that Jung was a 'half-Nazi', then why was he building Jungian ideas into the *Joseph* tetralogy which was, after all, written with the intention of wresting myth 'from the hands of the Fascist obscurantists to be "transmuted" for humane ends' (letter to Kerényi of 18 February 1941; see below)?

By contrast, in his letter of 27 June 1944 to the Swiss ambassador in Washington, Mann spoke of Jung in polite and extremely complimentary terms. The ambassador, Alphonse Haettenschwiler, was a Swiss courier who knew C.G. Jung and Kristine Mann (1873–1945) (no relation to Thomas), one of Jung's American followers who set up the Kristine Mann Library in New York.[26] Mann asked the ambassador to pass on Mann's best wishes to Jung following his recent accident (in February 1944, the 69-year-old Jung had slipped on the ice during a walk, broken his leg and subsequently suffered a heart attack), and to congratulate him on his appointment in the previous year to the chair of Medical Psychology at Basle University (due to ill-health, Jung soon resigned the post).

In reply to a series of questions sent to him by Anna Jacobson, Mann wrote to her on 22 February 1945 and played down the Jungian connection:

> I have never seen Jung in Switzerland. He once visited me in Munich together with another gentleman, whom I cannot remember any more. Jung made an exceptionally clever impression on me. His attitude with regard to the Nazis was quite dubious at first, and more than dubious. There have never been literary relations [*literarische Beziehungen*].

Finally, one year later, Mann returned to his political insinuations about Jung in a letter of 15 September 1946 to Karl Kerényi. Apparently, Mann himself had run into trouble, passed off here as 'certain trivial acts of meanness', because of the kind of statements that he had made in the past – such as his support for the invasion of Belgium (2–3 August 1914), for the sinking of the *Lusitania* (7 May 1915), and for the declaration of unlimited submarine warfare (1 February 1917) – and he expressed his gratitude to Kerényi for putting in a good word for him. Mann protested that, whatever he may have said *then*, it was nothing compared to what such people as Jung had said *since*:

> Now certainly it goes a little too far to draw parallels between my position of 1914–1918 and Jung's odious pro-Nazi pronouncements of 1933, and then to find excuses for both one and the other. Really, this pleases me not at all.[27]

Mann's diary records that, on 3 December 1950, he received a copy of the correspondence between Goethe and Schiller, edited by Karl Schmid (1907–1974), professor of German literature at the ETH in Zurich,[28] who later played an active part in the award of Jung's honorary doctoral degree on the occasion of his 80th birthday in 1955. Mann noted in his diary that he was mentioned in Schmid's introduction; in fact, Schmid had presented Mann and Jung as a typological coupling that could be traced back to Goethe and Schiller![29] Nor was Schmid alone in starting to make connections between Mann's work and Jung's. In November 1951, Mann received a letter from the American critic, Hermann J. Weigand, who suggested another such link in the recently completed novel *The Holy Sinner* (1951). Mann's response to the suggestion that he had borrowed anything from Jung was, to say the least, crisp: 'Do I have to have got it *all* from somewhere?'[30] A warning indeed to scholars on the hunt for intellectual sources! Mann's denial of any reference to Jung does not, however, exclude the use of Jungian motifs in the novel. In fact, Schulze's research suggests the very opposite, by showing how that novel returns to precisely the same, highly Jungian mythical scheme of life–death–rebirth that Mann had used in the *Joseph* tetralogy.[31]

Apart from a brief encounter over lunch with an enthusiastic amateur Jungian on 27 September 1952, Mann does not mention Jung again except in a newspaper interview of 13 June 1953. Questioned by Erich Hogestraat for the *Frankfurter Neue Press* after his return to Zurich, Mann claimed that *The Magic Mountain* had as little to do with Freud as the *Joseph* novels with Jung.[32] Yet both Dierks and Wysling have convincingly argued that Mann was already familiar with Freudian psychoanalysis by the time of *Death in Venice* (1912),[33] let alone *The Magic Mountain* (1924).[34] And even Mann himself admitted the influence of psychoanalysis in 'My Relationship to Psychoanalysis' (1925).[35] If Mann's rhetorical question in the interview about the influence of Freud on *The Magic Mountain* conceals the real importance of psychoanalysis for that novel, then by the same token, Mann's perhaps only apparently hypothetical remark about the influence of Jung on the *Joseph* novels heightens the likelihood of such an influence.

Less than a year later, in his letter of 17 May 1954 to Giko Takahashi, Mann made the following highly surprising, and in the light of all the evidence, completely false statement: 'I have never read Jung.'[36] Later that year, Mann thanked Kerényi in a letter of 17 October 1954 for sending him the proof-copy of his contribution to *Der göttliche Schelm* (1954) (*The Trickster: A Study in American Indian Mythology*) (1956), co-authored with Paul Radin and C.G. Jung. Jung's psychological commentary 'On the Psychology of the Trickster-Figure' recapitulates Kerényi's argument and presents it in terms other than myth (*CW* 9/i §456–§488). In three letters – to Kerényi of 17 October 1954; of the same day to the Swiss author Max Rychner (1897–1965), who had also corresponded with Jung; and in his letter of 19 October 1954 to Fritz Strich – Mann reacted with apparently vast surprise about the apparently huge coincidence ('What a peculiar coincidence, 'a strange coincidence', 'a coincidence that strikes me as odd') in the publication of this book and the simultaneous appearance of the continuation of his *Confessions of Felix Krull, Confidence Man*. Forty years ago, he claimed, he had had no idea that he was writing 'a hermetic novel'.[37] Yet in the light of *The Magic Mountain* (published two years after the first part of *Krull* (1922)), which Mann himself described as the story of 'the hermetic bewitchment of its young hero' and an '"alchemical" . . . intensification [*Steigerung*]',[38] this remark appears, to say the least, somewhat disingenuous. In his letter to Rychner, Mann expressed not just apparent surprise but also pleasure at 'discovering' his use of the tradition of 'Rabelais, Spain, Simplicissimus, [Till] Eulenspiegel, Reineke Fuchs': 'One never knows what one is up to, but one likes to find out, particularly one sets great store, as I do, by knowing that one stands in a solid tradition that reaches as far back as possible.'[39] In his letter to Strich, however, he went further and speculated on how this could have happened: 'Only when "Krull" was continued did such associations, no doubt because of the proximity of "Joseph", creep in.'[40] Among the sources consulted during preparation of the *Joseph* tetralogy was, of course, C.G. Jung, who could thus also have been one of the sources of the archetypal 'associations' of the trickster figure, Krull. Whatever Mann might say, the evidence for his constant and profound interest in Jung suggests that he probably was.[41]

In addition to these direct contacts, both personal and 'literary', with Jung, there were numerous indirect contacts with analytical psychology throughout Mann's life. I have already mentioned August Vetter and Karl Kerényi, but further contacts of varying degrees of importance include the Indologist Heinrich Zimmer (1890–1943); Jolande Jacobi (1890–1973), a famous Jungian disciple; the publisher Kurt Wolff (1887–1963); the little known author Bruno Goetz (1885–1954); the German novelist and poet Hermann Hesse (1877–1962), whose work is, subsequent to his undergoing Jungian analysis, saturated with archetypal imagery; the Austrian novelist Hermann Broch (1886–1951); Heinrich Berl (1896–1953), a writer from Baden; and Hermann Graf Keyserling (1880–1946), who founded the

Stiftung für freie Philosophie (otherwise known as the *Schule der Weisheit*) in the city of German *Jugendstil*, Darmstadt.

The extent of a common intellectual background to both Mann's and Jung's thought may further be gauged from the bibliographical resources which each of them shared. Thanks to the catalogue of the C.G. Jung library,[42] the catalogue of the Thomas-Mann-Archiv in Zurich and Herbert Lehnert's two extremely useful articles on Mann's preparatory reading for the *Joseph* tetralogy,[43] it is possible to compare the two men's libraries and thus establish which texts it is likely that they read. Of their wide reading in the fields of anthropology, archaeology, mythology and psychology, three major texts – Alfred Jeremias's *Das Alte Testament im Lichte des Alten Orients* (^{2}1906, owned by Jung; ^{3}1916, owned by Mann); *Urwelt, Sage und Menschheit: Eine naturhistorisch-metaphysische Studie* (1924) by Edgar Dacqué (1878–1945); and the works of Johann Jakob Bachofen (1815–1887)[44] – together with a host of less important works and authors were known to both men. This is to say nothing of their common knowledge, at a much deeper level, of the works of Schopenhauer and Nietzsche,[45] which governed their attitudes towards psychology and mythology to a very high degree. And nowhere do the affinities between Jung and Mann appear to be so central as in Mann's tetralogy, *Joseph and his Brothers*.

IV

The composition of this massive work covered two decades of Mann's writing career, and it was published in four instalments between 1933 and 1943.[46] On the surface, the *Joseph* tetralogy contains several motifs that are obviously informed by Freudian psychoanalysis. First, there are the dreams, a key element in the original Biblical story, of course, and in several places the narrator pauses to reflect on the nature of dreams (*JAHB* pp. 675, 679, 891–2). Second, the novels offer psychoanalytical explanations of the behaviour which they describe. For example, Mut-em-enet's feverish desire for Joseph is a clear expression of her repressed libidinal desire. And the brothers regard their initially hostile reception in Egypt as the return of the repressed, as 'a punishment for guilt long past' (*JAHB* pp. 719–20), because 'Joseph's image and their ancient guilt came to their minds' (*JAHB* p. 1070). Similarly, Jacob's favouritism towards Joseph is explained as a projection of his libidinal attachment to his dead wife on to his son (*JAHB* p. 250), and Mann even offers a psychoanalytical explanation of the brothers' earlier extreme hatred for Joseph: 'For much goes to show that the brethren's hatred for Joseph was nothing but the reverse side of the universal adoration' (*JAHB* p. 263). Finally, the image of the castrating and of the castrated Father is an important and recurring psychological motif (*JAHB* pp. 127, 141, 830). But the psychoanalytical, or rather, analytical psychological (in other words, Jungian, as opposed to Freudian) aspects of these novels go much deeper. Mann's own commentaries on his tetralogy foreground the psychological presuppositions of the work.[47]

In his lecture of 1942, Mann claimed that 'the question as to how I came to select this archaic subject-matter from the dawn of mankind' could be answered, at least in part, by 'something to do with those years, with a stage of life that had been attained'. At 60, this was no 'mid-life crisis', but the product of a shift in sensibility away from the individual and the 'bourgeois' and *towards* 'the mythical', defined as 'the typical, the eternally-human, eternally-recurring, timeless'. As Mann had already observed in 'Freud and the Future': '[I]t is plain to me that when as a novelist I took the step in my subject-matter from the bourgeois and individual to the mythical and typical my personal connection with the analytic field passed into its acute stage' (*E* p. 422). In the context of psychoanalysis, this step also meant a shift away from Freud and towards Jung.

The *Joseph* tetralogy, particularly in the later parts, has as its background the historical scenario of Freud's *Moses and Monotheism* (1939). In that work, Freud discussed in (albeit often inaccurate) detail the growth of monotheism during the reign of the heretic pharaoh, Amenhotep IV (Echnaton), suggesting that Moses had been responsible for introducing an Egyptian theological system into the Hebrew religion. Despite the many superb descriptive passages in Mann's tetralogy, however, this historical setting remains very much in the background and, in fact, fades away at the end, so that the ensuing destruction of Echnaton's reign, vividly described by Freud, is only briefly alluded to by Mann (*JAHB* p. 1200). Instead, the focal point of the tetralogy is a psycho-anthropological theory of the development of human consciousness. There is considerable evidence that this psycho-anthropological theory was borrowed from C.G. Jung.

For the dominant theme of the *Joseph* tetralogy, as Mann himself indicated in his lecture of 1942, is the development of human consciousness. From his comments in that lecture, it is clear that, as a theme, it binds together both his political and his spiritual concerns:

> I dwelled on the birth of the Ego out of the mythical collective, the Abrahamitic Ego which is pretentious enough to assume that Man should serve only the Highest, from which assumption the discovery of God followed. The claim of the human ego to central importance is the premise for the discovery of God, and from the very first the pathos for the dignity of the Ego is connected with that for the dignity of humanity.

At the same time, however, a sense of the importance of the collective is also maintained. In *The Tales of Jacob*, the narrator asks rhetorically:

'[I]s a man's ego a thing imprisoned in itself and sternly shut up in its boundaries of flesh and time? Do not many of the elements which make it up belong to a world before it and outside of it?' (*JAHB* p. 78). Such a view is compatible with the dictum from *The Tibetan Book of the Dead*, to which Jung referred in his psychological commentary on it (1935) and which was in turn quoted by Mann in 'Freud and the Future'. According to this dictum, we must understand 'that the "giver" of all "given" things dwells within us' (*CW* 11 §841; cf. *E* p. 419). In other words, the world is 'given' by the very nature of the psyche. According to a passage from Jung's psychological commentary which is marked in the margin of Mann's copy, *The Tibetan Book of the Dead* vouchsafes

> the ultimate and highest truth, that even the gods are the radiance and reflection of our own souls. No sun is thereby eclipsed for the Oriental as it would be for the Christian, who would feel robbed of his God; on the contrary, his soul is the light of the Godhead, and the Godhead is the soul.
>
> (*CW* 11 §840)

Thus, as Jung had also suggested in his commentary (1929) on *The Secret of the Golden Flower*, for the primitive psyche, the subject–object relationship is one, not of discrete division, but of mutual reciprocity.

On the textual level, Mann's tetralogy demonstrates this tenet by persistently problematizing its own authorship (*JAHB* pp. 32, 552–3, 829) and its narrative technique (*JAHB* pp. 80, 1183).[48] The narrator goes on to attribute agency to History itself, defining 'the original' (*der Urtext*) as 'the first written, or better yet the story as life first told it' (*JAHB* p. 668; cf. pp. 1165–6). Elsewhere, the narrator claims:

> History [*Geschichte*] is that which has happened [*die Geschichte*] and that which goes on happening [*geschieht*] in time. But it is also the stratified record [*das Geschichtete*] upon which we set our feet, the ground [*das Geschicht*] beneath us; and the deeper the roots of our being go down into the layers that lie below and beyond the fleshly confines of our ego, yet at the same time feed and condition it . . . the heavier is our life with thought, the weightier is the soul of our flesh.
>
> (*JAHB* p. 121)

Thus the tetralogy presents myth as the precondition for conscious life but also as the determinant of that consciousness. This conflation of subject and object presages the equation of myth and life Mann highlighted in 'Freud and the Future'.

Throughout the four novels, there is a clear progression in terms of the psychological and religious sophistication of the characters, both on the inter-generational level and on the personal, intra-psychic level of Joseph. Again, we can understand Mann's choice of a Biblical theme, for the original Old Testament narrative often involves a confusion of identity and foregrounds questions of status and the significance of names. These two psychological levels deserve close attention.

To begin with, Jacob is presented as not yet possessing a fully differentiated consciousness of himself (*JAHB* pp. 122–3). Described by Mann in his 1942 lecture as 'a half-detached figure', Jacob and other similar characters are described in that lecture as 'beings whose identity was open in back [*nach hinten offenstand*] and included the past with which they identified themselves' (cf. *JAHB* p. 78). Similarly, the steward who serves both Abraham and Jacob is referred to in *The Tales of Jacob* as '*the* Eliezer altogether' (*JAHB* p. 77), and in 'Freud and the Future', Mann commented: 'For in him time is cancelled and all the Eliezers of the past gather to shape the Eliezer of the present so that he speaks in the first person of that Eliezer who was Abram's servant, though he was far from being the same man' (*E* p. 422). The narrative voice in *The Tales of Jacob* even complains about the difficulty of telling the story of people who don't know who they are (*JAHB* p. 81)!

This characterization is directly in line with Jung's theory that the social and psychological being of primitive or 'archaic' man was marked by his 'collective personality', his inability to divorce himself from what Lévy-Bruhl called *participation mystique*. In a passage of 'The Psychology of the Child Archetype' (1940) which is marked in the margin of Mann's copy, Jung claimed that a major characteristic of the primitive mentality was a state 'when there was as yet no unity of personality' (*CW* 9/i §265). And in 'Archaic Man', Jung argued that religious, symbolic rites had lifted man out of his 'archaic identification with the world' and thereby transformed him into 'a being who stands above it' (*CW* 10 §136).[49] As Mann would have known from his reading of Jung, analytical psychology believes that modern-day, rational consciousness is only a part of man's total psyche, and that below the personal unconscious of each individual there is the Collective Unconscious, a repository of all the collective experiences of earlier mankind. Similarly, in *Joseph in Egypt*, the narrator suggests that if we go back far enough in our individual memory, we can gain access to the collective memory:

How narrow is the span when we look back upon our own lives; how vast when we contemplate the world's abysmal past! And yet we lose ourselves as easily, as dreamily, in the one as in the other; by virtue of our perception of a unity between the two. As little in the small sphere as in the large can we go back to the time of our birth and the beginning of our days, to say nothing of further back. It lies in darkness before the beginnings of the dawn of consciousness or memory. But with our earliest mental life, when we first enter – as primitive man once entered – into civilization, giving and receiving our first little contributions, we are aware of a sympathy, we feel ourselves recognize that abiding unity; with pleased surprise we acclaim our kinship with the larger whole.

(JAHB p. 718)

By contrast, the ideal espoused and achieved by Joseph is the primacy of the individual consciousness.

When we first see Joseph, he is sought by Jacob and responds 'here I am' (*JAHB* p. 40), adumbrating his later statement of psychological identity. He expounds this ideal to Kedma, one of the Ishmaelites (*JAHB* p. 447), and the possible political consequences of this assertion are immediately grasped by the chief of the Midianite merchants (*JAHB* pp. 451–2; cf. 454–5, 463). By contrast with Joseph, Mut-em-enet is a representative of the immature consciousness which cannot but succumb to the temptation to surrender to the Other. She is described as 'a great lady, elegant, superior, proud, worldly, hitherto self-contained within her personal and religious arrogance – and now all at once fallen victim to a you [*dem Du*], and a you – from her own point of view – entirely unworthy and unsuitable' (*JAHB* pp. 730–1). In the affair she attempts to initiate with Joseph, love is conceived of as a confrontation between subject and object, much along the lines of Sartre's conflictual conception of love as an *idéal irréalisable*, consisting of 'the strife between seeking and flight' (*JAHB* p. 730). In her attempts at seduction, Mut-em-enet displays her lack of individual consciousness by identifying herself with Isis (*JAHB* pp. 776, 797). In 'Freud and the Future', Mann puts the phrase 'It is I' (*Ich bin's*) into the mouth of such historical figures as Cleopatra and Christ, labelling this proclamation of identity as 'the formulation of the myth' (*E* p. 424). In *Joseph the Provider*, Joseph first uses this momentous phrase in reply to the chief gaoler, where it is described as 'a formula, old, familiar, and widely appealing from ages past . . . the time-honoured revelation of identity, a ritual statement beloved in song and story and play in which the gods had parts' (*JAHB* p. 863). And he uses it on three further occasions, including that of the famous revelation of his identity to his brothers (*JAHB* pp. 904, 937, 1114).

Having completed the trajectory from collective to individual consciousness, the *Joseph* tetralogy then reverses this process to supersede the dichotomy between the collective and the individual, a point developed in Mann's lecture of 1942:

[I]n Joseph the ego flows back from arrogant absoluteness into the collective, common; and, the contrast between artistic and civic tendencies, between isolation and community, between individual and collective is fabulously neutralized [*hebt sich im Märchen auf*] – as according to our hopes and our will, it must be dissolved in the democracy of the future, the cooperation of free and divergent nations under the equalizing sceptre of justice.

This 'fabulous neutralization' (*Aufhebung im Märchen*) provides the basis of the ethics proposed in the *Joseph* tetralogy. Defending the formula 'It is I' (*Ich bin's*) in his discussion with Pharaoh, Joseph defines it as the pivotal point of the universal and the particular: 'For I am and am not just because I am I. I mean that the general and the typical vary when they fulfil themselves in the particular, so that the known becomes unknown and you cannot recognize it' (*JAHB* p. 937). Joseph goes on: '[I]t is an I and a single individual through whom the typical and the traditional are being fulfilled' and he links individual consciousness, as an expression of 'spirit' (*Geist*), with the divine. The supersession of the dichotomy between universal and particular provides the basis for 'civilized life' (*gesittetes Leben*):

For the pattern and the traditional come from the depths which lie beneath and are what binds us, whereas the I is from God and is of the spirit, which is free. But what constitutes civilized life is that the binding and traditional depth shall fulfil itself in the freedom of God which belongs to the I; there is no human civilization [*Menschengesittung*] without the one and without the other.

(JAHB p. 937)

Earlier, in his afterword of 1925 to *Elective Affinities*, Mann had spoken of the 'ethical culture' (*sittliche Kultur*) displayed by Goethe in that novel. 'We are dealing', Mann wrote, 'with ethical culture, the deepest, most intuitively sympathetic relationship with nature, which is at the same time responsive to the higher command'. And he went on to speak of 'a moral conquest by which tragedy is resolved in love and issues in a transfiguration that instructs humanity to view as holy the unresolved tragedy of its own lot' (*PM* p. 110).

It is precisely this 'sympathy', involving what the tetralogy calls (in a manner reminiscent of the Romantics) 'wit' (*Witz*), with which Joseph is endowed (*JAHB* pp. 996, 1164). Or to put it another way, Joseph has discovered the same knowledge which Hans Castorp learns on the snowy slopes of *The Magic Mountain* (which Mann was completing when he started work on *Joseph*): 'For the sake of goodness and love, Man shall let death have no sovereignty over his thoughts.'[50]

The psychological development of ego-consciousness is accompanied in the sphere of religious affairs by an increase in an attitude of piety towards the divine: 'Piety is the subjectivation [*Verinnigung*] of the outer world, its concentration upon the self and its salvation' (*JAHB* p. 1139). In *Joseph*, the narrator suggests that establishing the primacy of personal consciousness does not by any means abolish the sense for the collective; on the contrary, it is said to preserve the collective and, at the same time, to provide the prerequisite for the highest consecration of human dignity:

> [F]or subjectivation does not mean subjection, nor esteem of self disesteem of others. It does not mean isolation or a callous disregard of the general, the exterior and suprapersonal; in short, of all that reaches beyond the self. On the contrary it therein solemnly recognizes itself. In other words, if piety is the being penetrated with the importance of the self, then worship is piety's extension and assimilation into the eternalness of being, which returns in it and wherein it recognizes itself. That is to depart from all singleness and limitation, yet with no violence to its own dignity, which it even enhances to the point of consecration.
>
> (*JAHB* p. 1139)

When Jacob decides to go and see Joseph, this is described as 'a cosmic procedure; and where the ego opens its borders to the cosmic and loses itself therein, even until its own identity is blurred, can there be any thought of narrowness or isolation?' (*JAHB* p. 1140).

What, then, is the relationship between this archetypal realm, the Collective Unconscious, on the one hand and the realm of individual consciousness, distinctiveness, one might say the *principium individuationis*, on the other? The notion of myth as a bond between these two realms, these two aspects of the psyche, which underpins the psychological developments in the *Joseph* tetralogy, turns out to rely on an ontology which is distinctly Jungian. In two highly enigmatic but immensely important sections of *Joseph and his Brothers*, 'Prelude: Descent into Hell' (*JAHB* pp. 3–34) and 'Prelude in the Upper Circles' (pp. 843–51), Mann turns away from Egyptian and traditionally Judaic mythological elements of the rest of the tetralogy to an explicitly Gnostic or neo-Platonic 'romance of the soul' (pp. 25, 848). It is uncertain whether Mann was influenced in his choice of Gnostic style by Jung's pseudo-Gnostic *Seven Sermons to the Dead* (1916), particularly since that work was initially only printed for private circulation by its author and not published until 1925 (and then in English translation). Nevertheless, Mann's opening 'Descent into Hell' recapitulates the central tenets of that and other Jungian works. And, tellingly, in his lecture of 1942, Mann described this opening descent into hell as 'a journey down into the depths of the past, a trip to the "mothers"'. For his part, Jung made references in his letters to Freud and in his autobiography to his personal descent to the Goethean Mothers, and in *Wandlungen und Symbole der Libido* he used Faust's descent to their shadowy realm to symbolize the descent of the mythical hero to the M/Other of the Collective Unconscious. Following Mann's remarks in 'Freud and the Future', the depths of 'the well of the past' (*JAHB* p. 3) are of a similarly psychological kind: '[T]he primitive foundations of the human soul are likewise primitive time, they are those profound time-sources where the myth has its home and shapes the primeval norms and forms of life' (*E* p. 422).

There is not sufficient space here to go into the intricacies of what such a descent into 'the well of the past' might involve in Jungian terms but, with relation to Thomas Mann, at least this much seems clear. First, the opening 'Vorspiel' operates with a dual ontology which could be expressed in Gnostic/Jungian terms as involving a distinction between the Pleroma/the Collective Unconscious and the Creatura/Ego-consciousness; or, to put it more simply, as a distinction between the realm of the eternal versus the realm of the temporal; or to put it even more simply, as essence versus existence. This duality is reflected in other, similar oppositions in the text, such as the commonplace dichotomy of *Natur* and *Geist*, reflected in the narrator's comment that 'thought and spirit come badly off, in the long run, against nature' (*JAHB* p. 719) or his reference to 'the contradiction between body and soul' (*JAHB* pp. 829–30), while he also reflects that 'life lies deep, not only in the spirit but in the flesh' (*JAHB* p. 765). This same dualism is expressed in Jacob's blessing on Joseph, based on Genesis 49:27 and Deuteronomy 33:13 – 'with a blessing from heaven above and from the depths beneath' (*JAHB* pp. 33, 996, 1155, 1172, 1195) – which forms the basis of the *leitmotiv* of the upper and the lower realms (*JAHB* pp. 124, 281, 389, 430, 937). This dualism running throughout the tetralogy in general and foregrounded in Jacob's blessing on Joseph in particular recalls Jung's principle as set out in *Wandlungen und Symbole der Libido*: 'All that is psychologic[al] has an under and an over meaning.' This principle is itself no more than a restatement of mystical doctrine:

> The heaven above,
> the heaven below,
> the sky above,
> the sky below,
> all things above,
> all things below,
> decline and rise.[51]

Second, this dualism has important existential implications. In 'Freud and the Future', Mann developed, on the basis of an article by Ernst Kris

(1900–1957),[52] the notion of 'lived myth' as 'lived life'; as Mann put it in dogmatic form, 'myth is the foundation of life' (*E* p. 422):

> Life, then – at any rate, significant life – was in ancient times the reconstitution of the myth in flesh and blood; it referred to and appealed to the myth; only through it, through reference to the past, could it approve itself as genuine and significant. The myth is the legitimization of life; only through it and in it does life find self-awareness, sanction, consecration.
>
> (*E* p. 424)

From these remarks, it is clear that what Mann here called 'life in quotation, life in myth' (cf. *E* p. 425) and expounded, novelistically, in *Joseph*, is extremely close to what Jung termed 'the symbolic life' (*CW* 18 §608– §696). In *Joseph*, we see the result of Mann's project to design and execute in artistic terms just such a mythology for his times. For both Jung in his psychological writings and Thomas Mann in the *Joseph* tetralogy, the temporal life of the individual is seen as interpenetrated by an extra-temporal, eternal or archetypal life which, lacking origin, exists by virtue of its self-repetition.[53] In 'Freud and the Future', Mann wrote:

> The feast is the abrogation of time, an event, a solemn narrative being played out conformably to an immemorial pattern; the events in it take place not for the first time, but ceremonially according to the prototype [*Urbild*].
>
> (*E* p. 425)

In his psychological commentary on *The Tibetan Book of the Dead*, Jung defined the archetypes as the 'dominants of the Unconscious', the structures that constitute the Collective Unconscious (*CW* 11 §845), and elsewhere he refers to them as *Urbilder*. Similarly, the *Joseph* tetralogy refers repeatedly and in various ways to 'certain given forms, a mythical frame' (p. 81), 'old lovely fantasies, pictures of beginnings and pre-beginnings' (p. 671), 'images of God, breathing images of the Deity' (p. 876), an 'archetype' (*Urbild*) (p. 123), 'the primitive and symbolic, . . . the timeless and ever revolving sphere' (p. 430), or to 'its own original' (*Urform*) (p. 1165). The dialectical tension between personal present and collective past is described in terms of a rolling sphere (*JAHB* p. 124; cf. p. 281).

In the context of the *Joseph* tetralogy, mythic consciousness is not just knowledge of the interdependence of these two halves of the sphere (*JAHB* p. 18), but also an awareness of the sphere's continuous rolling motion, that is to say, repetition. For those with such a consciousness, says the narrator of *Joseph in Egypt*, life itself becomes like a dream (*JAHB* p. 748). To recognize such repetition is the prerogative of those like Joseph, who tells his father early on: '[T]hat is the profit of these later days, that we know already the course in which the world rolls on, and the tales in which it is fulfilled and which were founded by the fathers' (*JAHB* p. 66).

The image of the sphere reveals, behind the dualism of 'from heaven above and from the depths beneath', the vision of a fundamental unity of Being. In the *Seven Sermons to the Dead*, the Pleroma is identified both with 'the fullness' and with 'nothingness', whereas the Creatura is described as the realm of distinctiveness and effectiveness, the realm of time and space, the *principium individuationis*. In his less mystical and more scientific writings, Jung described Ego-consciousness as being like a chain of islands adrift on the ocean of the Collective Unconscious (cf. *CW* 8 §387). In the symbolically entitled chapter 'Of Light and Darkness' in *Joseph the Provider*, the narrator informs us that '[w]ith the world-whole and its unity the human being has always and ever to do, whether he knows it or not' (*JAHB* p. 909). The basis of this totality is a complementarism, the belief that qualities only exist by virtue of their opposites, which Mann may well have derived from Jung, whose fascination with 'the problem of opposites' and their subsumption under quaternities is a major feature of his thinking. Within the 'revolution of the sphere', pairs of (familial) opposites are united – 'father and son, the unequal, the red man and the bearer of the blessing' – and the Jungian pattern of the quaternity is built up: 'the father–son pair on one hand, the brother pair on the other' (*JAHB* p. 127; cf. p. 745). After he has been thrown by his brothers down into the well, the narrator places such complementaristic thinking at the core of Joseph's personal faith (*JAHB* p. 389).

Turning from the development of Ego-consciousness across the generations as portrayed in the tetralogy to the personal psychological transformations which Joseph undergoes in the novels, an abundance of Jungian motifs can be found. First, as Schulze's two articles have demonstrated, the *Joseph* tetralogy draws on the central mythological motif first discussed by Jung in *Wandlungen und Symbole der Libido* and, in a lecture at the Eranos Conference in 1939, designated the archetype of rebirth. For Jung, the symbols that Freud had regarded as expressions of the incest taboo were, in fact, symbols of the introversion of the libido to a psychic or archetypal Mother, and the solar myth was an expression *par excellence* of the desire of psychic rebirth. This psychological process has its mythico-religious counterpart in what Jung described in *Wandlungen und Symbole der Libido* as the archetype of the dying and rising god. It is evinced, for example, in the religious festival of Tammuz, which is referred to in connection with Joseph's fate on at least three occasions (*JAHB* pp. 43, 58, 1172); in the legend of Adonis, which Joseph relates to Benjamin in 'The Grove of Adonis' (*JAHB* pp. 293–306), and in the Christmas story (*JAHB* p. 19). It is also the basis for the recurring agricultural metaphor of seed sowing and harvest (*JAHB* pp. 57–8, 226, 415, 1005).[54]

In the course of the tetralogy, Joseph undergoes not just one, but two rebirth experiences. The first occurs when his brothers try to murder him and throw him down into the pit, the Hebrew word for which (*Bor*) the narrator glosses as meaning 'well', 'prison', 'underworld', 'the kingdom of the dead'. At this point, Joseph is explicitly identified with 'the mangled god' (*JAHB* p. 390). Symbolically thrown into the underworld, Joseph cries out: 'Mother! Save thy son!' (*JAHB* p. 394), just as Jung thought that the incest taboo warned, not of a sexual desire for the biological mother, but of the descent to the 'matrix of the mind', the birth-giving and devouring Mother, 'the terrible Mother'. This experience of symbolic death and rebirth brings about a change in the identity of Joseph who, as a result of this experience, becomes 'another Joseph' (*JAHB* p. 383) and, following his rescue, changes his name to the more Egyptian-sounding 'Usarsiph' or 'Osarsiph' (*JAHB* pp. 466, 470, 718), thereby emphasizing this transformation.

The second rebirth experience takes place in Egypt, itself thought of by the Hebrews as the 'kingdom of the dead' (*JAHB* p. 460), when he is thrown into prison after Mut-em-enet's accusations (*JAHB* pp. 840, cf. 846–7). Once more, 'the journey into the abyss' is followed by 'renewal of life' (*JAHB* p. 854), and his interpretation of Pharaoh's dreams leads to 'the lifting up of the departed one, so that he was made great in the West' (*JAHB* p. 979), like the sun. Elsewhere, the comparison with the solar myth is made quite explicit: 'Down into the well of the abyss sank Attar-Tammuz as evening star; but as morning star it was certain he would rise' (*JAHB* p. 854). This passage and others like it draw on the pattern of the solar myth schematized by Leo Frobenius (1873–1938) and used extensively in his psychological writings by Jung, particularly in *Wandlungen und Symbole der Libido*.[55]

In that work, Jung subsumed the mythologem of the dying and rising god under the archetype of the hero – 'a hero is he who may again produce himself through his mother'[56] – and the character of Joseph conforms to this archetype in yet another respect. According to Jung, the hero is usually a wanderer, and Joseph's journey from Schechem to Egypt is one of the most important as well as one of the most vividly depicted parts of the tetralogy (*JAHB* pp. 476–7). Furthermore, Joseph's apparent androgyny recalls Jung's complementarism of the sexes, according to which the complete personality would consist of a balance of male and female principles (*CW* 9/i §294). For example, Joseph's discourse to Potiphar on hermaphroditism is highly suggestive of such notions of androgyny (*JAHB* pp. 588; cf. pp. 335, 435, 719). Apropos of Joseph's god, the narrator asks rhetorically: 'Was He not at once Father and Mother of the world, with two faces, one a man's, turned toward the daylight, and the other a woman's, looking into the darkness?' (*JAHB* p. 745). Joseph's androgyny is closely associated with his beauty, and such an association is a persistent theme in Mann's thinking: '[Youth] possesses charm [*Anmut*], a phenomenon [*eine Erscheinungsform der Schönheit*] which of its very nature for ever hovers between the masculine and the feminine' (*JAHB* p. 262; cf. p. 49).

Joseph's characterization as the androgynous hero is equally compatible with his status as what Jung and Kerényi called the 'divine child'. Writing that 'the hermaphrodite has gradually turned into a subduer of conflicts and a bringer of healing' (*CW* 9/i §293) and describing the motif of the child as 'a symbol which unites the opposites; a mediator, bringer of healing, that is, one who makes whole' (*CW* 9/i §278), Jung argued that the synthetic effect of the hermaphroditic child could be symbolized in the '*coniugium solis et lunae*' (*CW* 9/i §295). The 'wit' that Joseph possesses is described by the narrator in the following terms:

> [W]it is of the nature of a messenger to and fro and of a go-between betwixt opposed spheres and influences: for instance between the power of the sun and of the moon, between father- and mother-inheritance, between the blessing of the day and the blessing of the night, yes, to put it directly and succinctly, between life and death.
>
> (*JAHB* p. 1164)

Furthermore, the new theology he introduces supersedes both the religion of Jacob and the Egyptian cults of the sun-gods Amun-Rê and Atôn (*JAHB* pp. 977, 1004).

And there are further correspondences between the archetype of the divine child and Joseph. According to Jung, two particular manifestations of the child archetype, the child god and the child hero, have in common the features of 'the miraculous birth and the adversities of early childhood – abandonment and danger through persecution' (*CW* 9/i §281). Joseph's account to Potiphar of his 'virgin[al] birth' (*JAHB* p. 598) combines these two motifs with those of the Terrible Mother and the Hermaphrodite: 'For as the son is only a youth through death, the mother in the sign of death, but in the morning a man – cannot we then with some justice, considering everything, speak of a virgin birth?' (*JAHB* p. 613). Equally, in *Joseph the Provider* there are numerous correspondences between the figure of Joseph and a particular Jungian archetype, namely the Trickster. For example, Echnaton says to Joseph: 'You seem to be a sort of joker . . . a rascal and horse-thief who can make a man laugh at his tricks' (*JAHB* p. 929; cf. 947–8, 950, 959, 963, 964, 971); Joseph's agrarian policy is described as 'a manifestation of a divinity benign and cunning at once' (p. 1169); and just as Echnaton addresses Joseph as 'not only a prophet but a rogue as well' (p. 976), the narrator defines wisdom itself as 'a shrewdness amounting to guile' (*eine ins Schelmische gesteigerte Klugheit*) (p. 1170). When Jacob adopts Joseph's two sons and blesses them, the narrator reminds us once again that 'his sense of humour [*sein Sinn fürs Schelmische*] was strong' (p. 1182). As Asher's daughter, Serah, sings to Jacob: 'Read it in his laughing features,/All was but a Godlike jest' (*Lies in seinen Schelmenblicken:/ Alles war nur Gottes-Scherz!*) (*JAHB* p. 1137). Although *Der göttliche Schelm* [*The Trickster*], co-authored by Jung, Kerényi and Paul Radin, was not published until 1954 and thus cannot have been an influence on Mann's writing at this stage, Jung drew on such earlier studies of the trickster as Adolf Bandelier's *The Delight Makers* (1890) which may have been known to Mann.

Finally, there are curious references in the tetralogy to the change, not just in Joseph's psychic constitution or that of mankind in general, but to God's. In 'Prelude in the Upper Circles', the origin of Good and Evil is linked with the increasing self-consciousness of the deity: in Gnostic fashion, Abraham is said to be 'a means to His own self-knowledge' (p. 845), for '[t]he God of Joseph's fathers was a God of the Spirit – at least that was the goal of His evolution' (p. 754). In *The Tales of Jacob*, God's apparent jealousy concerning the worship of other gods is explained by the existence of the covenant, 'a bond . . . the existence of which betrays that the sanctification of God and that of Man represent a dual process in which both are most intimately "bound up"' (p. 210). Such statements apparently anticipate Jung's *Answer to Job* (1952), published almost ten years after the last of the *Joseph* novels, which speaks of Yahweh's transformation from an unconscious to an increasingly self-conscious deity, and regards Job's sufferings as the outward occasion for an inward process of dialectics in God (*CW* 10 §587). Although Jung developed this notion far more extensively than did Mann in the *Joseph* tetralogy, the basic premise is identical. At the same time, rather than suggesting a reverse influence of Mann on Jung, that identity points to the common sources of both men, which make questions of influence and reception so difficult to determine.

V

Thomas Mann repeatedly claimed that the *Joseph* tetralogy had, in the words of Ernst Bloch, 'taken myth out of the hands of the Fascists':

> In this book, the myth has been taken out of Fascist hands and humanized down to the last recess of its language – if posterity finds anything remarkable about it, it will be this. In the idea of humanity, the human idea, the sense for the past and that for the future, tradition and revolution form a strange and, to my mind, infinitely attractive mixture.[57]

In his correspondence with Kerényi, Mann made it clear that the tool which he would use to take myth out of the hands of the Fascists would be psychology or, more precisely, 'myth plus psychology':

> I have long been a passionate adherent of this combination, for actually psychology is the means whereby myth may be wrested from the hands of the Fascist obscurantists to be 'transmuted' for humane ends. For me this combination represents no less than the world of the future, a human community that is blessed by a spirit from above and 'out of the depths that lie below'.[58]

As we have seen, in 'Freud and the Future' Mann had already looked to Freud (while citing Jungian ideas) as 'the path-finder towards a humanism of the future', 'a humanism standing in a different relation to the powers of the lower world, the unconscious, the id: a relation bolder, freer, blither, productive of a riper art than any possible in our neurotic, fear-ridden, hate-ridden world' (*E* p. 427).

From Mann's definition of the Id in that lecture, we could describe his New Humanism as a new relationship between the individual and the collective. Psychologically speaking, this means the relationship (in Freudian terms) between the Ego and the Id (at the end of 'Freud and the Future', Mann quoted Freud's programmatic statement 'Where Id was, there shall Ego be') or, in Jungian terms, between the conscious Ego and the Collective Unconscious.

Mann's description in 'Freud and the Future' of 'life in quotation, life in the myth' as 'a kind of celebration' culminates in his praise for 'the feast' (*das Fest*), a notion that recurs in *Joseph* and which itself involves the concept of repetition: 'For a feast is an anniversary, a renewal of the past in the present' (*E* p. 425). Far removed from any Bakhtinian sense of carnival, Mann's notion of *Fest* relies instead on the repetition in time of an archetypal – in other words, timeless, unconscious – event or *Urbild*. In his correspondence with Kerényi, Mann further emphasized how recurrence was an integral part of his concept of 'festival' (*das Fest*), which in turn he described as 'virtually the fundamental theme of my novel'.[59]

Because of its ironic narrator, its structural complexity and its sheer length, the *Joseph* tetralogy is an exceptionally difficult work to interpret. Yet its interpreters have frequently taken at face value Mann's claims that the tetralogy undertakes a single project, to 'take myth out of the hands of the Fascists' and to found a New Humanism. But the tetralogy contains a number of mythical conceptions that are indebted to the work of C.G. Jung and that arguably undercut the apparent political objectives of the work. 'Prelude: Descent into Hell' and 'Prelude in the Upper Circles' posit a timeless, spatial and unconscious realm, in which Mann locates the *Einst*, the 'origin' in the sense Kerényi used it,[60] of events in our world of time and space. The *Urbild* is located, just like Jung's archetype, outside time and space. All events in our world are merely the repetition in chronological time of the timeless *Einst*. And one might look askance at the nature of the collective to which the individual is tied. On one reading of Jung's notion of the Collective Unconscious, it is the universal repository of the memories of the whole of mankind (*CW* 9/i §88–§90); in an earlier version, however, it is more like the collective memory of a particular race. One of the hallmarks of Joseph's character is his individualistic sense of morality, as Mut-em-enet finds out, to her disappointment. Yet the text makes it clear that Joseph's aspiration to be 'a virtuoso of virtue' (*JAHB* p. 757) is motivated, at least in part, as follows: 'A proud tradition of racial purity warned him not to mingle his blood with hers' (p. 752). For example, we are told that Joseph obeys 'the inherited dictate of his blood' (p. 755). And when in Egypt, Joseph's entire physiognomy is affected by his new surroundings (*JAHB* p. 638), just as if – as Jung had notoriously claimed (cf. *CW* 10 §103) – the soil played an important role in determining the constitution of the individual.

Clearly, *Joseph* is much more than a 'Jungian' work, and we have not had time to discuss the playfulness of Mann, 'the ironic German', as evinced in the text. To the extent that it is a 'humanistic' work, and an extremely complex one at that, it also reveals another unexpected affinity with Jung. In certain respects, Mann's immersion in German culture led him to feel responsible for it, perhaps in the way that Jung himself, recorded in *Memories, Dreams, Reflections*, said he did:

> In the days when I first read *Faust* I could not remotely guess the extent to which Goethe's strange heroic myth was a collective experience and that it prophetically anticipated the fate of the Germans. Therefore I felt personally implicated, and when Faust, in his hubris and self-inflation, caused the murder of Philemon and Baucis, I felt guilty, quite as if I myself in the past had helped commit the murder of the two old people. This strange idea alarmed me, and I regarded it as my responsibility to atone for this crime, or to prevent its further repetition.[61]

VI

Why did Thomas Mann wish to deflect attention away from his long-standing interest in and intellectual debt to Jung? There are several possible reasons, some of which have been suggested by critics. First, Hermann Kurzke sees Mann's silence on the influence of Jung as one of the effects of the years in exile, comparable to a similar silence surrounding his interest in Alfred Baeumler, Johann Jakob Bachofen, and Oskar Goldberg.[62] Second, Jean Finck conjectures that, for Mann, Jung was an important means of getting beyond Freud, pointing to Mann's strategy in 'Freud and the Future' of, as Kerényi put it, going beyond the psychologist in honour of whom the celebration had been organized.[63] And in a letter of 18 September 1936, Kerényi paid tribute to *Joseph in Egypt* precisely for having 'overcome the essentially disintegrating mode of analysis of Freudianism'.[64] Jung, too, tried to replace what he saw as Freud's reductive method of analysis with his own synthetic ('constructive' or amplificatory) technique (*CW* 7 §121–§140).

Third, both Kurzke and Manfred Dierks argue that Mann's claim to make use of myth for progressive purposes, the so-called 'transmutation of myth' [*Umfunktionierung des Mythos*], is a notion based on a phrase Mann borrowed from the philosopher Ernst Bloch (1885–1977), with whom Mann corresponded between 1933 and 1940.[65] Bloch notoriously attacked Jung in *The Principle of Hope* (1954/1959) as 'the fascistically foaming psychoanalyst' and, in *Heritage of our Times* (1935), classed him along with Hans Prinzhorn and Ludwig Klages as 'the lovers of dreamdarkness'.[66] Whether Mann's use of myth in *Joseph* is entirely consonant with Bloch's conception of Utopian desire is another matter entirely, but Bloch may well have been at least partly responsible for Mann's silence surrounding his interest in Jung. Fourth, as both Dierks and Finck have alternatively speculated, Jung's alleged compromise with National Socialism would have provided another significant reason why Mann did not wish to be associated with Jung. On the surface, this is the most obvious solution, but it has its difficulties. It does not explain why Mann, while knowing about the rumours concerning Jung's political sympathies, as his diary entries for 1934 and 1935 suggest, none the less in 1936 undertook to read, and moreover express immense enthusiasm for, Jung's psychological commentary on *The Tibetan Book of the Dead*, so much so that, in 'Freud and the Future', he had nothing but praise for Jung. Fifth, one is left with the suspicion, shared for example by Joachim Schulze, that Mann's memory was deliberately defective. Quite rightly, Schulze points to Mann's reluctance to acknowledge his debt in *Doctor Faustus* to the musicology of Arnold Schönberg as an analogous 'memory-lapse'.[67] Finally, Mann might have come to realize that, however insightful Jung's ideas were on the intellectual plane, too much of the mud that had been thrown at Jung on the biographical level had stuck, and that too many of Jung's comments on political events were murky, anyway.

What is clear, however, is the astonishingly large overlap between Mann's and Jung's views on the potential role of myth in bringing about change in human affairs. Even on the most abstract level, Mann's definition in 1920 of 'culture' as 'an integral human whole and harmony . . . the spiritualization of life and the incarnation of the mind – the synthesis of soul and spirit'[68] coincides with Jung's concern for what he called 'the confusions, the conflicts of duty, and the invisible tragedies of the natural

Man in collision with the exigencies of culture' (*CW* 13 §229), a concern which led him to think of the culmination of the 'individuation process', the transformation of Ego-consciousness into the Self, symbolized variously by the hermaphrodite, the alchemical *lapis* and the intricate patterns of the *mandala*, as the highest ideal available to man (*CW* 7 §274, §404; 12 §12 §44). As Jung said in 'Spirit and Life', a lecture given to the Literary Society in Augsburg on 29 October 1926:

> Life and spirit are the two powers or necessities between which Man is placed. Spirit gives meaning to his life, and the possibility of its greatest development. But life is essential to spirit, since its truth is nothing if it cannot live.
>
> (*CW* 8 §648)

Moreover, although Jung thought that the West had never designed a concept, nor even a name, for 'the *union of opposites through the middle path*' (*CW* 7 §327), which he compared to Tao, there is nothing novel about Jung's description of adaptation as a balanced regularity of processes (*CW* 8 §61). Mann would have called this regulated interaction and mutual influence of *Natur* and *Geist* an example of 'measure' (*Maß*) and 'value' (*Wert*): 'Measure is order and light, the music of the creation and everything that is creative; it is also what has been achieved, what has been reclaimed from chaos, the anti-barbaric, the triumph of form, the triumph of Man.'[69] As a result, Jung embarked on establishing the technique of active imagination, encouraging the use of painting, modelling and music in therapy, while Mann outlined an equally important role for art as 'the mediatrix between spirit and life', effecting the 'fusion of matter with humanity, the humanization of life in spiritualizing creation [*Durchdringung des Stoffes mit Menschlichem, Vermenschlichung des Lebens in vergeistigender Gestaltung*]'.[70]

Notes

1 T. Evers, *Mythos und Emanzipation: Eine kritische Annäherung an C.G. Jung*, Hamburg, Junius, 1987, p. 161; and T. Sprecher, *Thomas Mann in Zürich*, Munich, Wilhelm Fink, 1992, pp. 95–7.
2 P. Bishop, '"Literarische Beziehungen haben nie bestanden"? Thomas Mann and C.G. Jung' (*Oxford German Studies*, 1994, vol. 23, pp. 124–72) provides a full bibliography of secondary literature, as well as the original German text of the letters referred to here.
3 I use the following editions for texts by Thomas Mann: *Past Masters and Other Papers*, tr. H.T. Lowe-Porter, London, Martin Secker, 1933 (referred to as *PM*); *Essays of Three Decades*, tr. H.T. Lowe-Porter, London, Secker & Warburg, 1947 (referred to as *E*); *Joseph and his Brothers*, tr. H.T. Lowe-Porter [1956], London, Secker & Warburg, 1981 (referred to as *JHAB*). Jung is quoted from *The Collected Works*, London, Routledge & Kegan Paul,

1953–1979, referred to as *CW*, followed by volume number and a paragraph (§) reference.

4 See Thomas Mann's letter to Karl Kerényi of 18 February 1941 (*Mythology and Humanism: The Correspondence of Thomas Mann and Karl Kerényi*, tr. A. Gelley, Ithaca and London, Cornell University Press, 1975, p. 100).

5 M. Dierks, *Studien zu Mythos und Psychologie bei Thomas Mann* (*Thomas Mann Studien*, 2), Berne, Francke, 1972; and M. Dierks, 'Thomas Mann und die Tiefenpsychologie' and 'Thomas Mann und die Mythologie', in H. Koopmann (ed.), *Thomas-Mann-Handbuch*, Stuttgart, A. Kröner, 1990, pp. 284–300 and 301–6.

6 H. Wysling, *'Mythos und Psychologie' bei Thomas Mann* (*Eidgenössische Technische Hochschule Kultur- und Staatswissenschaftliche Schriften*, 130), Zurich, Polygraphischer Verlag, 1969, pp. 21–2.

7 See the excursus 'Über die Beziehungen Thomas Manns zur analytischen Psychologie C.G. Jungs' in Dierks, 1972, op. cit., pp. 257–60.

8 Translated and published together as C.G. Jung and K. Kerényi, *Essays on a Science of Mythology* [1949], tr. R.F.C. Hull, Princeton NJ, Princeton University Press, 1969. Jung's contributions were 'The Psychology of the Child Archetype' (*CW* 9/i §259–§305) and 'The Psychological Aspects of the Kore' (*CW* 9/i §306–§383). For Mann's marginalia in his copy of *Das göttliche Kind*, see E. Heftrich, *Geträumte Taten: 'Joseph und seine Brüder'*, Frankfurt am Main, Vittorio Klostermann, 1993, pp. 426–7, 560–5.

9 Dierks, 1990, op. cit., p. 296.

10 M. Dierks, 'Typologisches Denken bei Thomas Mann – mit einem Blick auf C.G. Jung und Max Weber', *Thomas Mann Jahrbuch*, 1996, vol. 9, pp. 127–53.

11 J. Finck, *Thomas Mann und die Psychoanalyse*, Paris, Les Belles Lettres, 1982, esp. pp. 298–314.

12 H. Wysling, 'Thomas Manns Rezeption der Psychoanalyse', in B. Bennett, A. Kaes and W.J. Lillyman (eds), *Probleme der Moderne: Studien zur deutschen Literatur von Nietzsche bis Brecht*, Tübingen, M. Niemeyer, 1983, pp. 201–22.

13 J. Schulze, 'Traumdeutung und Mythos: Über den Einfluß der Psychoanalyse auf Thomas Manns Josephsroman', *Poetica*, 1968, vol. 2, pp. 501–20; and J. Schulze, 'Joseph, Gregorius und der Mythos vom Sonnenhelden: Zum psychologischen Hintergrund eines Handlungsschemas bei Thomas Mann', *Jahrbuch der Deutschen Schillergesellschaft*, 1971, vol. 15, pp. 465–96.

14 A. Bloch, 'The Archetypal Influences in Thomas Mann's *Joseph and his Brothers*', *Germanic Review*, 1963, vol. 38, pp. 151–6.

15 K. Ikeda, '"Kunst" und "Analyse": Sinn einer "unwillkürlichen Übereinstimmung" zwischen dem Joseph-Roman von Th. Mann und den tiefenpsychologischen Einsichten von C.G. Jung', *Doitsu Bungaku – Die deutsche Literatur*, 1984, vol. 73, pp. 102–12.

16 C. Nolte, *Being and Meaning in Thomas Mann's 'Joseph' Novels*, Leeds, W.S. Maney & Son, 1996, pp. 22–3, 2, 7–8.

17 Sprecher, op. cit., p. 96.

18 Entitled *Der archaische Mensch* ('Archaic Man'), the text of this article corresponds to §135–§137 and the first part of §138 in volume 10 of the *Collected Works*, part of a much longer paper of the same title which Jung gave as a lecture to the Hottingen Lesezirkel in Zurich in October 1930 and published in full in the *Europäische Revue*, March 1931, vol. 7, no. 3, pp. 182–203 (*CW* 10 §104–§147).

19 F. Nietzsche, *Daybreak: Thoughts on the Prejudices of Morality*, tr. R.J. Hollingdale, Cambridge, Cambridge University Press, 1982, pp. 197–8.

20 H. Wysling and M. Fischer (eds), *Thomas Mann Dichter über ihre Dichtungen*, Munich, Heimeran, 1975–1981, II, p. 108.

21 See the contributions to A. Maidenbaum and S.A. Martin (eds), *Lingering Shadows: Jungians, Freudians, and Anti-Semitism*, Boston and London, Shambhala, 1991; as well as the essay by Grossman reproduced in Part I of this volume.

22 Mann refers here to 'A Rejoinder to Dr Bally', originally two articles published by Jung in the *Neue Zürcher Zeitung* on 13 and 14 March 1934 (*CW* 10 §1016–§1034) in reply to an attack on his connection with the politically suspect General Medical Society for Psychotherapy by the Swiss psychiatrist Dr Gustav Bally in an article entitled 'Deutschstämmige Psychotherapie?', printed in the *Neue Zürcher Zeitung* on 27 February 1934.

23 R.W. Clark, *Freud: The Man and the Cause*, London, Jonathan Cape/ Weidenfeld & Nicolson, 1980, pp. 497–8.

24 One critic has even suggested it might just as logically be titled 'Jung and the Future' (Evans Lansing Smith, 'Descent to the Underworld: Jung and his Brothers', in K. Barnaby and P. d'Acierno (eds), *C.G. Jung and the Humanities: Toward a Hermeneutics of Culture*, London, Routledge, 1990, pp. 251–64 (p. 260)).

25 In *Doctor Faustus* (1947) Mann propounded a mythological understanding of Nazi Germany which is remarkably similar to Jung's. Both Mann and Jung saw the Faust legend as offering insight into what Mann called the 'antiquated and neurotic underground' of the German soul. In exactly the same year (1945), Jung's essay 'After the Catastrophe' used Faust as an almost archetypal representative of the German psyche (*CW* 10 §423, §439). The notion of 'Faustian' culture may have been mediated to both Mann and Jung by Spengler's *Decline of the West* (see H. Koopmann, 'Der Untergang des Abendlandes und der Aufgang des Morgenlandes: Thomas Mann, die Josephsromane und Spengler', *Jahrbuch der Deutschen Schillergesellschaft*, 1980, vol. 24, pp. 300–31; H. Schwerte, *Faust und das Faustische: Ein Kapitel deutscher Ideologie*, Stuttgart, Ernst Klett, 1962, esp. p. 332). In Mann's novel, the central character Adrian Leverkühn is modelled on the life of Nietzsche: the same background, the same brothel experience, and madness and collapse at the same age on the same day; and there are yet further parallels. For his part, Jung claimed in 'After the Catastrophe' that Nietzsche's madness had actually been a 'prophetic example' of the fate of Germany, and that 'Nietzsche was German to the marrow of his bones, even to the abstruse symbolism of his madness' (*CW* 10 §432). And both Jung and Mann saw National Socialism and the Second World War in terms not of political but of *mythical* phenomena, centring around the figure of the Greek god, Dionysos, or his Germanic 'cousin', Wotan. Kerényi was deeply disapproving of Mann's *Faustus*: 'How could he make such a terrible simplification?' (*Mythology and Humanism*, op. cit., p. 21). In a critique of Jung's position in his essays on National Socialism and the Second World War, Robert Haymond has argued that 'by not understanding the dialectic of human nature between internal and social forces, [Jung] was forced into positing an unchanging archetypal essence, ever-flowing beneath the outward manifestations of particular cultures' (R. Haymond, 'On Carl Gustav Jung: Psycho-social Basis of Morality during the Nazi Period' *Journal of Psychology and Judaism*, 1982, vol. 6, pp. 81–112 (p. 106)). This criticism applies, *mutatis mutandis*, to Mann's thinking in *Faustus* but also, above all, to the *Joseph* tetralogy, the mythic optimism of which is, according to Susan von Rohr Scaff, retracted in *Faustus*:

Degradation . . . is what we see in *Doktor Faustus*, the repetition on a debased level of Goethe's Faust myth. In his despair of history after *Joseph*, Mann undoes the optimistic tenets of Goethe's picture of Faust as a fundamentally good man whose god looks upon him kindly and gladly spares him. By identifying Adrian Leverkühn's diabolic pact with Germany's submission to Fascist ideology, Mann portrays modern mythic history in a decline never admitted to his imagination in the tetralogy.

(S. von Rohr Scaff, 'The Dialectic of Myth and History: Revision of Archetype in Thomas Mann's Joseph Novels', *Monatshefte*, 1990, vol. 82, pp. 177–93 (p. 190)).

26 W. McGuire, *Bollingen: An Adventure in Collecting the Past*, Princeton NJ, Princeton University Press, 1982, p. 72.
27 *Mythology and Humanism*, op. cit., p. 146.
28 Not to be confused with the theologian Karl Schmidt (1891–1956), who lectured at the Eranos Conferences between 1945 and 1950.
29 Karl Schmid (ed.), *Der Briefwechsel zwischen Goethe und Schiller*, Zurich, Artemis, 1950, p. 1011.
30 'A Letter from Thomas Mann to Hermann J. Weigand', *Publications of the Modern Languages Association*, 1972, vol. 87, pp. 306–8.
31 Schulze, 1971, op. cit. See also K. Stackmann, 'Der Erwählte: Thomas Manns Mittelalter-Parodie', *Euphorion*, 1989, vol. 53, pp. 61–74 (esp. pp. 72–3).
32 'Rückkehr zur alten Erde: Interview mit Thomas Mann über deutsche und ausländische Literatur', in V. Hansen and G. Heine (eds), *Frage und Antwort: Interviews mit Thomas Mann 1909–1955*, Hamburg, A. Knaus, 1983, pp. 359–62 (p. 361).
33 *Death in Venice* has shown itself to be particularly susceptible to analysis from both a Jungian as well as a Freudian viewpoint. For further discussion, see H. Sachs, 'Das Thema "Tod"', *Imago*, 1914, vol. 3, pp. 456–61; L. Zinkin, '"Death in Venice" – A Jungian View', *Journal of Analytical Psychology*, 1977, vol. 22, pp. 354–66; G. Astrachan, 'Dionysos in Thomas Mann's Novella, "Death in Venice"', *Journal of Analytical Psychology*, 1990, vol. 35, pp. 59–78; A. Cadieux, 'The Jungle of Dionysus: The Self in Mann and Nietzsche', *Philosophy and Literature*, 1979, vol. 3, pp. 53–63; H.M. and R.J. Rockwood, 'The Psychological Reality of Myth in *Der Tod in Venedig*', *Germanic Review*, 1984, vol. 59, pp. 137–41; and C. Paglia, *Sexual Personae: Art and Decadence from Nefertiti to Emily Dickinson*, London and New Haven, Yale University Press, 1990, pp. 595–7.
34 Several articles have illustrated the use of motifs from mythology, alchemy and freemasonry in *The Magic Mountain* (1924). For further discussion, see L. Sandt, *Mythos und Symbolik im Zauberberg von Thomas Mann*, Berne and Stuttgart, Paul Haupt, 1979; U. Benzenhöfer, 'Freimaurerei und Alchemie in Thomas Mann's "Zauberberg" – ein Quellenfund', *Archiv für das Studium der neueren Sprachen und Literaturen*, 1985, vol. 137, pp. 112–21; T.K. Thayer, 'Hans Castorp's Hermetic Adventures', *Germanic Review*, 1971, vol. 46, pp. 299–312; and J. Campbell, 'Mythological Themes in Creative Literature and Art', in J. Campbell (ed.), *Myths, Dreams, and Religion*, New York, E.P. Dutton, 1970, pp. 138–75.
35 T. Mann, *Gesammelte Werke*, Frankfurt am Main, S. Fischer, [2]1974, XI, p. 749.

36 S. Hamakawa, *Thomas Manns Briefe an Japaner*, Tokyo, Dogakusha Verlag, 1960, pp. 24–6; also in Wysling and Fischer (eds), op. cit., II, p. 348.

37 *Mythology and Humanism*, op. cit., p. 210.

38 'Introduction to the "Zauberberg": For Students of Princeton University', *Werke*, XI, p. 612.

39 H. Wysling (ed.), *Briefwechsel Thomas Mann – Max Rychner*, in *Blätter der Thomas Mann Gesellschaft Zürich*, 1967, vol. 7, pp. 23–4. For Rychner's letter of 28 February 1932, see C.G. Jung, *Letters*, ed. G. Adler and A. Jaffé, tr. R.F.C. Hull, London, Routledge, 1973–1976, II, pp. 88–9.

40 Wysling and Fischer (eds), op. cit., I, p. 369.

41 *Felix Krull* (1922/1954) can be read in terms of the Trickster archetype, playing with illusion and indulging in deceit on the level of narrative patterning as well as on the level of stylistic means (see M. Beddow, 'Fiction and Meaning in Thomas Mann's *Felix Krull*', *Journal of European Studies*, 1980, vol. 10, pp. 77–92). Equally, its androgynous and carnivalesque hero is demonstrably assimilable to the figure of Hermes or, as Jung called him, Mercurius (see D. Nelson, *Portrait of the Artist as Hermes*, Chapel Hill NC, University of North Carolina Press, 1971; and H. Wysling, *Narzissmus und illusionäre Existenzform: Zu den Bekenntnissen des Hochstaplers Felix Krull* (*Thomas-Mann-Studien*, 5), Berne and Munich, Francke, 1982, esp. pp. 238–53).

42 *C.G. Jung Bibliothek Katalog*, Küsnacht-Zürich, privately published, 1967.

43 H. Lehnert, 'Thomas Manns Vorstudien zur Josephstetralogie', *Jahrbuch der Deutschen Schillergesellschaft*, 1963, vol. 7, pp. 458–520; and H. Lehnert, 'Thomas Manns Josephstudien 1927–1939', *Jahrbuch der Deutschen Schillergesellschaft*, 1966, vol. 10, pp. 378–406.

44 For Jung's relation to Bachofen, see P. Wolff-Windegg, 'C.G. Jung – Bachofen, Burckhardt, and Basel', *Spring*, 1976, pp. 137–47. For Thomas Mann's, see E. Galvan, *Zur Bachofen-Rezeption in Thomas Manns 'Joseph'-Roman* (*Thomas-Mann-Studien*, 12), Frankfurt am Main, Vittorio Klostermann, 1996.

45 For further discussion of Jung's interest in Schopenhauer and Nietzsche, see Chapters 7 and 8 of this volume.

46 For further bibliographical information on this work, see P. Bishop, '*Jung–Joseph*: Thomas Mann's Reception of Jungian Thought in the *Joseph* Tetralogy', *The Modern Language Review*, 1996, vol. 91, pp. 138–58.

47 See Thomas Mann's article for the 'Berliner Tageblatt' of 26 April 1928 and 'Ein Wort zuvor: Mein "Joseph und seine Brüder"' of the same year, and more substantially in 'Freud and the Future' (1936) and in *The Theme of the Joseph Novels* (a lecture delivered in the Library of Congress on 17 November 1942), Washington, US Government Printing Office, 1942.

48 For further discussion, see A.J. Swensen, *Gods, Angels, and Narrators: A Metaphysics of Narrative in Thomas Mann's 'Joseph und seine Brüder'*, New York, Peter Lang, 1994.

49 In 'Archaic Man', Jung poses the question: 'Is a thing beautiful because I attribute beauty to it? Or is it the objective beauty of the thing that compels me to acknowledge it?' (*CW* 10 §135). In *Joseph in Egypt*, the narrator asks:

A man will often say 'I am urged' to do so and so. But what is it that urges him, which he distinguishes from himself and makes responsible for his act? Certainly it is only himself; himself, together with his desire. Is there any difference between 'I will' and 'Something within

me wills'? Must we say 'I will' in order to act? Does the act come from
the will, or does not rather the will first show itself in the act?

(*JAHB* p. 826)

50 T. Mann, *The Magic Mountain*, trans. H.T. Lowe-Porter [1928], London:
Secker & Warburg, 1945, pp. 496–7.
51 C.G. Jung, *Wandlungen und Symbole der Libido*, Munich: Deutscher Taschen-
buch Verlag, 1991, p. 65; translated by Beatrice M. Hinkle as *Psychology of
the Unconscious*, London, Kegan Paul, Trench, Trubner & Co., 1916.
52 E. Kris, 'Zur Psychologie älterer Biographik', *Imago*, 1935, vol. 21, pp. 320–
44. Mann owned an offprint of this article.
53 See J. Dassin, 'The Dialectics of Recurrence: The Relation of the Individual to
Myth and Legend in Thomas Mann's *Joseph and his Brothers*', *Centennial
Review*, 1971, vol. 15, pp. 362–90.
54

> Joseph too is another such celebrant of life; with charming mytho-
> logical hocus-pocus he enacts in his own person the Tammuz-Osiris
> myth, "bringing to pass" anew the story of the mangled, buried, and
> arisen god, playing his festival game with that which mysteriously and
> secretly shapes life out of its own depths – the unconscious.

(*E* p. 426)

Jung and Mann had probably read about the phallic rites of the kind which
accompanied the religious festival of Tammuz in Herodotus. See A. Grimm,
Joseph und Echnaton: Thomas Mann und Ägypten, Mainz, von Zabern, 1992,
p. 218. For further discussion of the phallic aspect, see G. Bridges, *Thomas
Mann's 'Joseph und seine Brüder' and the Phallic Theology of the Old Testament*, Berne, Peter Lang, 1995.
55

> The sun, victoriously arising, tears itself away from the embrace and
> clasp, from the enveloping womb of the sea, and sinks again into the
> maternal sea, into night, the all-enveloping and the all-reproducing,
> leaving behind it the heights of midday and all its glorious works. This
> image was the first, and was profoundly entitled to become the sym-
> bolic character of human destiny.

(*Psychology of the Unconscious*, p. 390)

56 *Psychology of the Unconscious*, p. 357.
57 Mann, *The Theme of the Joseph Novels*, p. 21.
58 *Mythology and Humanism*, op. cit., p. 100.
59 Letter to Kerényi of 16 February 1939, *Mythology and Humanism*, op. cit.,
p. 88.
60

> 'Origin' means two things in mythology. As the content of a story or
> myth it is the 'giving of grounds' (*Begründung*); as the content of an
> act it is the 'founding' (*Gründung*) of a city or the world. In either case
> it means Man's return to his own origins and consequently the emer-
> gence of something original, so far as accessible to him, in the form of
> primordial images, mythologems, ceremonies.

(K. Kerényi, 'Prolegomena', in Jung and Kerényi, op. cit., p. 14)

61 *Memories, Dreams, Reflections: Recorded and Edited by Aniela Jaffé* [1962], London, Fontana, 1983, p. 261.
62 H. Kurzke, *Thomas Mann: Epoche – Werk – Wirkung*, Munich: C.H. Beck, 1985, p. 251. On Oskar Goldberg, see G. Rose, *The Broken Middle: Out of Our Ancient Society*, Oxford, Blackwell, 1992, p. 152, n. 176.
63 Finck, op. cit., p. 313; K. Kerényi, *Geistiger Weg Europas*, Zurich, Rhein-Verlag, 1955, p. 16.
64 *Mythology and Humanism*, op. cit., p. 72.
65 Kurzke, op. cit., p. 251; Dierks, 1972, op. cit., p. 260; T. Mann, *Briefe*, ed. E. Mann, Frankfurt am Main, Fischer, 1961–1965, II, pp. 262 and 579.
66 E. Bloch, *The Principle of Hope*, tr. N. Plaice, S. Plaice and P. Knight, Oxford, Blackwell, 1986, I, p. 59; and E. Bloch, *Heritage of Our Times*, tr. N. and S. Plaice, Cambridge, Polity Press, 1991, p. 313.
67 Schulze, 1968, op. cit., p. 520. See also F. Zeder, *Studienratsmusik: Eine Untersuchung zur skeptischen Reflexivität des 'Doktor Faustus' von Thomas Mann*, Frankfurt am Main, Peter Lang, 1995.
68 Letter to Hermann Graf Keyserling (1920), *Werke*, XII, p. 603.
69 T. Mann, *Werke*, XII, p. 799.
70 Ibid., p. 800.

Part III

JUNG IN INTELLECTUAL CONTEXT

7

SCHOPENHAUER AND JUNG

James L. Jarrett

Source: *Spring: A Journal of Archetype and Culture* (1981), 193–204.

Suppose a student of the writings of C.G. Jung were given the pedantic task of citing chapter and verse for the following texts:

> As life becomes more and more unconscious, the nearer it approaches the point at which all consciousness ceases, the course of time itself seems to increase in rapidity. In childhood all the things and circumstances of life are novel. . . .[1]

> Up to our thirty-sixth year, we may be compared in respect of the way in which we use our vital energy, to people who live on the interest of their money: what they spend to-day, they have again to-morrow. But from the age of thirty-six onwards, our position is like that of the investor who begins to entrench upon his capital.[2]

> Everything that is really fundamental in a man, and therefore genuine, works, as such, unconsciously; in this respect like the power of nature. That which has passed through the domain of consciousness is thereby transformed into an idea or picture; and so if it comes to be uttered it is only an idea or picture which passed from one person to another.[3]

> I know of no greater absurdity than that propounded by most systems of philosophy in declaring evil to be negative [i.e. privative] in its character. Evil is just what is positive; it makes its own existence felt.[4]

> If only one individual were left in the world, and all the rest were to perish, the one that remained would still possess the whole self-being of the world, uninjured and undiminished, and would laugh

at the destruction of the world as an illusion. This conclusion *per impossible* may be balanced by the counter-conclusion, which is on all fours with it, that if that last individual were to be annihilated in and with him the whole world would be destroyed. It was in this sense that the mystic Angelus Silesius declared that God could not live for a moment without him, and that if he were to be annihilated God must of necessity give up the ghost.[5]

"What bad luck!" the student might utter. "As it happens, I can't think *exactly* where even a single one occurs!" Still, he plunges in bravely enough, and confident, especially if he has access to the general index of the *Collected Works*, that he can rather quickly run down the sources.

But no – not in *those Collected Works*. They are, in fact, all from Schopenhauer.

Indeed, the list of Jungian-sounding quotations from Schopenhauer could be extended almost indefinitely, including the theory of "individuation," Eastern wisdom, the relating of "good consciousness" to the Moral Law and Instinct, citations of Jacob Boehme and the *I Ching*, and so on; though in truth in some cases the similarity would be but superficial. Yet considerable similarity of idea between the two thinkers is demonstrable. Though one must beware of arguing *post hoc*, Schopenhauer indeed was a profound influence, to be ranked alongside of Kant and Freud, and ahead of even Nietzsche and William James.

All his life Jung had a love/hate relationship with philosophy. When the philosophers indulged in verbal acrobatics and logic-chopping, when their speculations cut loose from the moorings of experience, he would cry out, "I'm not a philosopher, I'm an empiricist, a phenomenologist." Yet he was fully aware of the irony of his protest; empiricism and phenomenology are themselves philosophical positions, orientations, schools, methodologies, as are the mechanism and positivism he so despised. Early Jung came to see that nothing is more dangerous to a psychologist than being grounded in a wrongheaded philosophy, but the corrective movement is *not* in eschewing philosophy, becoming a non- or anti-philosopher, for this is to give over criticizing one's own assumptions, one's "personal psychic premises," the great philosophical tasks. A psychologist *is* a philosopher, consciously or unconsciously – but here as everywhere, the influences that remain dark are potentially full of mischief. "Ideas that we do not know we have, have us."[6]

Long before he ever heard of Freud, Jung had encountered a number of theories of the unconscious. From his rather desultory research in the history of philosophy he knew of Leibniz's *petites perceptions*, the subliminal registrations of organisms (even of inorganic substances), and had been thunderstruck by Kant's revelations of the things-in-themselves – spaceless, time-less, cause-less entities within and without the psyche. (He was to remain, in important ways, a Kantian throughout his life.) He knew too some of the speculations of Kant's followers like Schelling and Herbart, and he was impressed with the work of a minor but daring thinker named C.G. Carus, who in 1846 had published *Psyche*, a book in which he discourses on the development of the soul from the unconscious. Eduard von Hartmann's *Philosophy of the Unconscious* (1869) was no doubt much discussed among the intellectuals of his set. Jung, who is open about his intellectual debts, described the study of Kant and Schopenhauer as "mentally my greatest adventure" (*CW* 18: §485). "My ideas of the unconscious," he once told a seminar, "first became enlightened through Schopenhauer and Hartmann."[7] Again, "the great find" was Schopenhauer, for here at last was someone who saw that not all was well in the "fundaments of the universe."

> He was the first to speak of the suffering of the world, which visibly and glaringly surrounds us, and of the confusion, passion, evil – all those things which the others hardly seemed to notice and always tried to resolve into an all-embracing harmony and comprehensibility.[8]

Jung would have had Schopenhauer call that blind will which is at the core of every being *God*, and felt that here for once Schopenhauer's courage failed him, though Schopenhauer, neither theist nor pantheist, saw only obfuscation in the identification. *The World as Will and Idea*, Schopenhauer's great work, epitomizes his philosophy in the very title: Will and Idea (Representation), noumena and phenomena, "things" in their primordial state and as appearance, the Unconscious and the Conscious.

As Jung was to insist against Freud, there are no *ideas* in the unconscious; yet the fountainhead of our deepest ideas and feelings is the unconscious. As Schopenhauer put it:

> But ordinarily it is in the obscure depths of the mind that the rumination of the materials received from without takes place, through which they are worked up into thoughts; and it goes on almost as unconsciously as the conversion of nourishment into the humours and substance of the body. Hence it is that we can often give no account of the origin of our deepest thoughts. They are the birth of our mysterious inner life. Judgments, thoughts, purposes, rise from out that deep unexpectedly and to our own surprise. . . . Consciousness is the mere surface of our mind, of which, as of the earth, we do not know the inside, but only the crust.[9]

Or as he says elsewhere, "Everything that is really fundamental in a man, and therefore genuine, works, as such, unconsciously . . ." [*Parerga and Paralipomena*, vol. 2, chap. 26, §340 – ed.].

"Accordingly, any quality of mind or character that is genuine and lasting, is originally unconscious."[10] Here he speaks of transformation into an "idea or a picture" – the conscious, phenomenal constructs. "Only that which is innate is genuine and will hold water. . . ."[11] What is concocted without coming up from the unconscious is affectation, superficiality.

The unconscious, the primordial part of all being, is the surge of will, desire, want, lust. As with plants and animals, so too with man; but in the latter there emerges that precious function which nearly all philosophers have desperately wanted to make fundamental, even absolute: the intellect. However much our cognitive functions may represent our only hope of escaping the engulfing maw of the will, they are derivative, secondary. "The will is the substance of man, the intellect the accident; the will is the matter, the intellect is the form; the will is warmth, the intellect is light."[12]

Between the abstracting intellect, the reason and will itself stands immediate sensation or feeling. Indeed, Schopenhauer does not always distinguish between willing and feeling. In a linguistic aside not unlike the sort that Jung often indulged, Schopenhauer writes:

A true feeling of the real relation between will, intellect, and life is also expressed in the Latin language. The intellect is *mens, nous*; the will again is *animus*, which comes from *anima*, and this from *anemon. Anima* is the life itself, the breath, *psyche*; but *animus* is the living principle, and also the will, the subject of inclinations, intentions, passions, emotions; hence also *est mihi animus* – for "I have a desire to," also *anima causa, etc.*; it is the Greek *thymos*, the German "Gemüth," thus the heart but not the head.[13]

He adds that our very identity lies in what lies below consciousness:

It rests upon the identical *will* and the unalterable character of the person. . . . In the heart is the man, not in the head. . . . Our true self, the kernel of our nature, is what is behind that, and really knows nothing but willing and not willing, being content and not content, with all the modifications of this, which are called feelings, emotions, and passions.[14]

In an early work he makes the same point, but suggests that a range of will-states is open to our immediate inspection: "Introspection always shows us to ourselves as *willing*. In this *willing*, however, there are numerous degrees, from the faintest wish to passion. . . ."[15] But important as the passage is from lower to higher consciousness, Schopenhauer is far from thinking that development of the intellect demands the attrition of will. "The higher the consciousness has risen, the more distinct and connected are the thoughts [cf. Jungian "differentiation"], the clearer the perceptions, the more intense the sensations. Through it everything gains more depth: emotion, sadness, joy and sorrow."[16]

Jung, who ranks high among the world's thinkers who have been notably imagistic, pictorial, in their cognitive processing, will have found an ally in Schopenhauer in this respect too. The "Vorstellung," sometimes rendered "Idea" in the title of his main book, means literally "placed before," and is perhaps most nearly adequately translated "representation." (In a letter to R.F.C. Hull, his English translator, Jung discusses the difficulties of rendering both *Idee* and *Vorstellung*.)[17] These phenomena, representations emerging from unconscious willing, and known immediately – that is, intuited – are largely pictorial, though we have the ability, of course, to make representations of representations – that is, concepts.[18] "Imagination is an essential element of genius" [WWR, I, §36, p. 168 – ed.]. "Imagination" is presumably meant to include both simple imaging or mental picturing and the extension of the mind beyond the immediately given. The poet (who shares with the nonacademic philosopher Schopenhauer's highest praise) is characterized as one who, starting with mental images, exhibits "the art of bringing into play the power of imagination through words."[19] As writer, Schopenhauer (again like Jung) conjures up pictures continually – in severe contrast to his antithetic rival Hegel.

But the highest function of the artist is to help extend the mind beyond concrete objects and pictures, to the Platonic Ideas. This has two consequences, subjective and objective. In the first, the result is an "enhancement of consciousness to the pure, will-less, timeless subject of knowing."[20] That is, to rescue the will-driven soul from futility one must abandon the phenomenal ego for a state of contemplation. In music we come closest to being presented with the will itself, the Unconscious itself, to regard contemplatively and hence escape for a time being its tool.

Jung recognized early the affinity between his own "primordial images" or "archetypes" and the Platonic Forms, for in both cases they are seen as at once ultimate creative forces in the universe, the engenderers of what boils up into consciousness, and ultimate though ineffable objects of knowledge. "In Plato," he says, "an extraordinarily high value is set on the archetypes as metaphysical ideas, as 'paradigms' or models, while real things are held to be only the copies of these model ideas" (*CW* 8: §275).

Jung speaks variously of the archetypes, calling them "dominants of experience" (*CW* 8: §423), says they "organize images and ideas," are an "inborn disposition to produce parallel images," configurations (*CW* 9, ii: §179), and "forms in which things can be perceived and conceived."[21]

Readers will not have failed to notice Schopenhauer's use of different words to name mental functions, and will have been put in mind of Jung's famous four functions. This needs to be looked at directly.

A most promising statement is this: "The direct opposite of rational knowledge is feeling. . . ."[22] One is struck not only by the differentiation of feeling from thinking, but also his pitting them against each other as "direct opposite(s)." Both Jung (e.g., *CW* 6: §723–9) and Schopenhauer were much struck with the exceptional ambiguity of "Gefühl":

> For the most diverse and even antagonistic elements lie quietly side by side in this concept; for example, religious feeling, feeling of sensual pleasure, moral feeling, bodily feeling, as touch, pain, sense of colour, of sounds and their harmonies and discords, feelings of hate, of disgust, of self-satisfaction, of honour, of disgrace, of right, or wrong, sense of truth, aesthetic feeling, feeling of power, weakness, health, friendship, love, etc. etc. . . . There is absolutely nothing in common among them except the negative quality that they are not abstract rational knowledge.[23]

This, indeed, he makes the definiens of the concept, but he goes on to propose *Empfindung* (sensation) as more precisely designating bodily feelings – and this is exactly what Jung does. One might better say that when Jung uses *Empfindung* to name a distinct function he employs it somewhat broadly; a "sensation type" may be more distinguished by his attention to the account books than by his emphasis on the bodily senses. But what is left over still does not correspond to Jung's notion of "feeling," which for Schopenhauer has nothing to do with emotion and everything to do with sense of *value*. Though rational knowledge, *Wissen*, also does not correspond exactly with Jung's thinking, *Denken*, Schopenhauer wants to distinguish between *reason* and *understanding* in the Kantian manner. "Intuition," a common word in Schopenhauer's vocabulary, appears however only as a translation of *Anschauung*, which means "immediate presentation," in William James's phrase, knowledge by acquaintance, and has little to do with dwelling in the realm of the possible, as in Jung, who stresses the Latin *in-tuire*, to look in.

Another theory that brings to mind the Jungian four categories is found in Schopenhauer's 1813 *On the Fourfold Root of the Principle of Sufficient Reason*. Here the principle "Nothing is without a reason for its being" is found by the young Schopenhauer to take four different forms: the logical, the physical/causal, the mathematical, and the moral. It would be disingenuous to pretend that these correspond to Thinking, Sensing, Intuiting, and Feeling, as Schopenhauer in turn mentioned Aristotle's quadratic analysis of "cause" but made no claim for a correspondence. Still, they do constitute a modification of the Kantian categories (which derive directly from Aristotle), in being *a priori*, necessary ways of interpreting the raw data of experience. And Jung in turn accepts the Kantian (and Schopenhauerian) inbuilt forms without which there can be no movement from the chaos of the unconscious to the relative orderliness of consciousness. We will return to this point of categories and forms presently.[24]

Schopenhauer makes less capital than Jung of the clash of opposites as the source of energy, going in this respect hardly farther than the scattered commonplace that opposites illumine one another.[25] Perhaps Hegel had so thoroughly preempted this anti-thetic way of thinking that it was strictly out of bounds for his rival. Yet some opposites were crucial for Schopenhauer: subject/object, inner/outer, will/body, which overlap significantly. The great point is that he resolves this sort of dualism precisely as Spinoza (not one of Schopenhauer's favorites) did, by a double-aspect theory. "The act of will and the movement of the body are not two different things; . . . they are one and the same, but they are given in entirely different ways – immediately, and again in perception. . . ."[26] The body is the objectification, the outward manifestation, the visible representation of the will. (The intellect is the other, opposite aspect of the brain.)

It may be worth recording the striking similarity of Jung's position:

> For what is the body? The body is merely the visibility of the soul, the psyche; and the soul is the psychological experience of the body; so it is really one and the same thing.
>
> (*CW* 3: §41–2)

Elsewhere he speaks of "the mysterious truth that the spirit is the life of the body seen from within and the body the outward manifestation of the life of the spirit – the two being really one . . ." (*CW* 10: §195).

For Schopenhauer man knows himself as a conscious individual, a phenomenal being; and as thing-in-itself, the unconscious realm that lies below individuation. He liked to cite the authority of Kant for the first, of the *Vedas* for the second.[27] Jung would have said Yea to both the distinction and the documentation. He would also have resonated most affirmatively to Schopenhauer's citation of dreams as best illustrating

> the identity of my own being with that of the external world. . . .
> For in a dream other people appear to be totally distinct from us, and to possess the most perfect objectivity, and a nature which is quite different from ours, and which often puzzles, surprises, astonishes or terrifies us; and *yet it is all our own self.*[28]

Schopenhauer was, indeed, more interested in dreams than most philosophers have been. One other reference may be of interest: mentioning that we sometimes perform certain unusual actions without knowing why,

Schopenhauer says that these are aftereffects of forgotten fate-portending dreams, the dynamics being very much like that exhibited by instinctive behavior.[29]

On the related topic of *differentiation*, for Jung the great *Logos* function which leads out of unconsciousness, there is one important passage in Schopenhauer which may have influenced the budding meta-psychologist:

> Why is our consciousness brighter and more distinct the further it extends towards without, so that its greatest clearness lies in sense perception, which already half belongs to things outside us – and, on the other hand, grows dimmer as we go in, and leads, if followed to its inmost recesses to a darkness in which all knowledge ceases? Because, I say, consciousness presupposes *individuality*; but this belongs to the mere phenomenon. . . . Our inner nature, on the other hand, has its root in that which is no longer phenomenon, but thing-in-itself, to which, therefore, the forms of the phenomenon do not extend; and thus the chief conditions of individuality are wanting, and with these the distinctness of consciousness falls off. In this root of existence the difference of beings ceases, like that of the radii of a sphere in the centre; and as in the sphere the surface is produced by the radii ending and breaking off; so consciousness is only possible where the true inner being runs out into the phenomenon, through whose forms the separate individuality becomes possible upon which consciousness depends. . . .[30]

Withdrawing into the center as "in sleep, in death, to a certain extent in magnetic or magic influences" is becoming part of the undifferentiated will, wherein (as in Aristotle's "active reason") the only claim to immortality resides. Schopenhauer cites the *Bhagavadgita* as authority, explaining that "mystical and figurative language . . . is the only language in which anything can be said on this entirely transcendent theme."[31] Here Schopenhauer anticipates Jung's use of the concept *symbol*, "For when something is 'symbolic,' it means that a person divines its hidden, ungraspable nature and is trying desperately to capture in words the secret which eludes him."[32] The symbol is necessarily paradoxical, its purpose being to synthesize opposites that for the purely rational mind must remain forever apart.

In the same spirit, Schopenhauer says:

> With me the ultimate foundation of morality is the truth which in the Vedas and the Vedanta receives its expression in the established, mystical formula, *Tat twam asi* (This is thyself), which is spoken with reference to every living thing, be it man or beast, and is called the Mahavakya, the great word.[33]

Later he specifically sets the "principle of individuation" over against the *Tat twam asi* principle,[34] and though individuation does not have the same meaning in the two authors, it is fair to say that both see human development as from the undifferentiated unconscious into the light of logic and reason and then farther on to a mystical contemplation of the abiding forms and symbols.

For both thinkers Plato was in this last regard the great exemplar in Western thought – in Schopenhauer he is constantly "the divine Plato" – but they agreed in finding Buddhist and Hindu spiritual wisdom far more advanced than anything in our tradition. But for both the great objects of our contemplative regard are also the great engenderers and shapers of our intelligible life. Schopenhauer called them *Urbilder* or *Musterbilder*, "prototypes" or "archetypes." Speaking of Plato's parable of the cave, he writes: "The real archetypes . . . to which these shadows correspond, the eternal Ideas, the original forms of all things, can alone be said to have true being (*ontos on*), because they *always are, but never become nor pass away*" [*World as Will and Representation*, vol. I, §31 – ed.]. In this instance, Jung specifically notes the similarity of his own thoughts to those of Schopenhauer, prefacing a lengthy quotation from *The World as Will and Idea* with the remark, "I would ask the reader to replace the word 'idea' by 'primordial image,' and he will then be able to understand my meaning" (*CW* 6: §752). "Primordial image," it will be remembered, was the expression which in Jung's development modulates into "archetype." And archetypes are the contents of the collective unconscious, hence innate, the great forms which organize our experience. Interestingly, both authors specifically allow that Locke was right in his attack on innate ideas, since in his context "ideas" are mental representations of material reality, and therefore can be learned only in experience. But they agree further that Locke overdogmatized in saying that nothing is innate. Schopenhauer puts it, "Locke goes too far in denying all innate truths inasmuch as he extends his denial even to our *formal* knowledge – a point in which he has been brilliantly rectified by Kant. . . ."[35] For Jung as for Schopenhauer the archetypes, the primordial images, the prototypical Ideas are the forms into which is poured the material content, with its individual and cultural qualities.[36]

"Night after night," Jung wrote, "our dreams practice philosophy on their own account" (*CW* 12: §247). He meant, of course, that the dreams furnish the raw material of philosophy, but a huge job awaits the conscious reflective mind. Once noting that an "imbecilic locksmith" he encountered had had some marvelous visions that were extraordinarily Schopenhauerian, he quickly adds that the difference was that for the patient in the mental hospital,

> the vision remained at the stage of a mere spontaneous growth, while Schopenhauer abstracted it and expressed it in language

201

of universal validity. . . . A man is a philosopher of genius only when he succeeds in transmuting the primitive and wholly natural vision into an abstract idea belonging to the common stock of consciousness."

(CW 7: §229)

An exhaustive comparison of the two thinkers would reveal other similarities. For instance, both put great stress on personality as a determinant of experience. Both claimed to be empiricists. Schopenhauer made slight anticipations of the concept of *persona*. Neither had much use for "society" as an explanatory concept – and thus were conspicuously outside the Hegelian–Marxian–Weberian tradition that has predominated in the last hundred years. And so on. But enough has been said to suggest the profound similarities.

Influence is a hard matter to prove. No doubt some similarities are little more than coincidences. Others may develop from a common propensity and an attraction for a common tradition (Plato, Kant, the East).

Jung took great delight in finding in his predecessors anticipations of his own ideas – "There is not a single important idea or view that does not possess historical antecedents" *(CW* 9, i: §69), he once wrote – though no doubt it was often the case that Gnostic and alchemical adumbrations of his thought parallel ideas he had independently developed. But Kant and Schopenhauer got to him in his most formative stage, apparently giving direction to some of the concepts which were to prevail throughout his career albeit deepened, extended, and given local habitation in his phenomenological reflections on his clinical practice and perhaps even more on introspection. Jung continually pays tribute to Schopenhauer as an original and great mind who courageously broke free from the crushing weight of the rationalistic tradition, who dared speak of the pre-rational unconscious. We can imagine Jung, after the disappointments of his father's library, coming upon the scandalous Schopenhauer, an unabashed introvert, far more interested in spiritual than material phenomena, a freethinker, a celebrator of Eastern religion, one who knew evil to be real and unrelenting, and who found in contemplation of the great eternal forms some surcease from the will-driven life.

Is it true, as I suspect, that the young analysts who today so eagerly follow Jung's lead into the world of fairytale and myth, adept in horoscopes and the Tarot, stop short when beckoned into the philosophic mansions? If they take as their justifying text Jung's protest that he is "not a philosopher but an empiricist," they are stuck with the letter but remain empty of the spirit; for did not Jung explicitly hold that it is necessary for psychotherapists "to be philosophers or philosophic doctors" *(CW* 16: §181)? This, for the excellent reason that it is often important to enter into philosophical discussions with patients on problems of epistemology, ethics, metaphysics, in making progress toward a *Weltanschauung*. In a late talk to the New York Psychology Club, Jung said quite simply, "I am speaking just as a philosopher."[37]

Notes

1 *The Complete Essays of Arthur Schopenhauer*, trans. T. Bailey Saunders (New York: Wiley Book Company, n.d.), *Counsels and Maxims*, "The Ages of Life," p. 131. (Cited hereafter as *Essays*.)
2 Ibid., p. 128.
3 *Essays, Studies in Pessimism*, "Psychological Observations," pp. 45–6.
4 *Essays, Studies in Pessimism*, "On the Sufferings of the World," p. 1.
5 *Essays, Human Nature*, "Human Nature," p. 28. Cf. *The World as Will and Idea*, trans. R.B. Haldane and J. Kemp (London: Routledge & Kegan Paul, 1883), vol. I, p. 167. (Hereafter *WWI*.)
6 James Hillman, "Anima II," *Spring* 1974, p. 113.
7 C.G. Jung, *Analytical Psychology: Notes of the Seminar Given in 1925*, ed. W. McGuire, London, Routledge, 1990, p. 5.
8 *Memoirs, Dreams, Reflections* (New York: Vintage edition, 1965) p. 69.
9 *WWI*, III, p. 328.
10 *Essays, Studies in Pessimism*, "Psychological Observations," pp. 45–6. Cf. *Schopenhauer's Fourfold Root of the Principle of Sufficient Reason*, trans. E.F.J. Payne (Open Court, 1974), p. 122.
11 Loc. cit.
12 *WWI*, II, p. 412.
13 *WWI*, II, p. 459. Readers of Jung may well fix on "anima" and "animus," but it is evident that Jung's use of these words to designate the contra-sexual soul is not Schopenhauerian.
14 Ibid., p. 460.
15 *Fourfold Root*, p. 168.
16 *WWI*, III, p. 17.
17 *Letters*, II, pp. 460–1.
18 *The World as Will and Representation*, trans. E.F.J. Payne (Falcon Wings Press, 1958, repr. Dover), vol. I, p. 40. (Hereafter *WWR*).
19 *WWR*, II, p. 424.
20 *WWR*, I, p. 199.
21 *Memories, Dreams, Reflections*, p. 347.
22 *WWI*, I, p. 66.
23 Loc. cit.
24 C.A. Meier remarks at the end of a similar comparison that the parallel is best not overdone. *Bewasstsein*, Walter-Verlag, Freiburg im Breisgau, 1975.
25 *WWI*, I, pp. 268, 474.
26 *WWI*, I, p. 170.
27 *Essays, Human Nature*, "Human Nature," p. 27.
28 *Essays*, "Genius and Virtue," p. 86 (emphasis added).
29 *WWI*, ch. 27.
30 *WWI*, III, p. 74.
31 *WWI*, III, p. 75.
32 *Letters*, I, p. 123.
33 *Essays, Human Nature*, "Human Nature," p. 24.

34 *Essays, Human Nature*, "Character," p. 79.
35 *Fourfold Root*, p. 139.
36 See *Memories, Dreams, Reflections*, p. 347.
37 *Spring* 1972, p. 147. On Kant, Jung and philosophy see also Stephanie de Voogd's article in *Spring* 1977, pp. 175–82.

8

C.G. JUNG AND NIETZSCHE

Dionysos and analytical psychology

Paul Bishop

In 'The Psychology of the Unconscious' (1917/1926/1943), Jung wrote that he had been 'well prepared for modern psychology by Nietzsche' (*CW* 7 §199), but the extent of the significance of Friedrich Nietzsche (1844–1900) for Jung can only be gauged through a detailed examination of the reception of the philosopher by the psychologist.[1]

Although Jung never met Nietzsche, he grew up at a time when Nietzsche was still alive (at least, physically) in a mental asylum and when his popularity as a writer was growing. But there were also several personal connections with people who had known him. For example, Ludwig Binswanger (1881–1966), one of Jung's assistants at the Burghölzli clinic who helped him carry out his experiments on word association, was the nephew of Otto Binswanger (1852–1929), the Professor of Psychiatry and head of the psychiatric clinic at the University of Jena (where he treated Nietzsche after his breakdown in 1889–1890). At university, Jung would have known of Jacob Burckhardt (1818–1897), the Swiss cultural critic and historian who was a professor at Basle from 1858 to 1893, and both a friend as well as a professional colleague of Nietzsche. Although there is no evidence that Jung knew Burckhardt personally, it is likely that Burckhardt's views were mediated by a mutual acquaintance, namely Burckhardt's great-nephew, Albert Oeri (1875–1950), a student-colleague and lifelong friend of Jung. Similarly, Jung would have been aware of the presence in Basle of Johann Jakob Bachofen (1815–1887), the historian of law and religion, from whom Nietzsche derived, at least in part, the categories of the Apollonian and the Dionysian. Thus Bachofen forms an important link between Nietzsche's interest in ancient Greek culture and Jung's own fascination with Nietzsche and Dionysos.

The fourth person who formed a direct link between Jung and Nietzsche himself was Lou Andreas-Salomé (1861–1937), a formidable intellectual and erotic presence in the lives of Nietzsche, then Rilke, and Freud. Andreas-Salomé was not only an astute reader of Nietzsche's work and one of the most fervent devotees of Freud's Wednesday evening discussion group, but she was an important psychoanalytic thinker in her own right. Jung met her at the Third International Psychoanalytic Congress in Weimar (21–23 September 1911) (see his letter to Freud of 2 January 1912) and the Fourth Congress (7–8 September 1912). Her posthumously published work *In der Schule bei Freud* (*The Freud Journal*) (Zurich, 1958) provides a first-hand account of the early years of the psychoanalytic movement when the break between Freud and Jung occurred. In an entry dated 2 November 1912, she records Freud's sarcasm directed at the latest apostate of psychoanalysis:

> The present fights have the fascinating effect that Freud sets forth his views about the dissensions on different occasions. This time expressly about Jung's defection. He showed a subtle and ingenious bit of malice in his attempt to make the term 'complex' superfluous, pointing out how it had insinuated itself into the terminology out of convenience, without having grown up on psychoanalytic soil, just as Dionysos was artificially exalted from being an exotic god to becoming the son of Zeus. (At this, Tausk, who was sitting or standing next to Freud, and was still in the white doctor's smock he wore coming from the psychiatric clinic, did not quite stifle a chuckle).[2]

Well might Victor Tausk have laughed at Freud's little joke. But the figure of Dionysos came to the fore in Jung's correspondence with Freud just prior to the parting of their ways.

University

At university, Jung joined and then became the Chairman of the Basle section of the Zofingia Society, a Swiss student fraternity. Between 1896 and 1899, Jung gave four 'lectures' to the society, which reflect his early interest in philosophical questions.[3] In his Inaugural Address in the winter semester of 1897/98, Jung merely mentioned Nietzsche in passing. In 'Thoughts on the Nature and Value of Speculative Inquiry' in summer 1898, however, his use of Nietzsche was more extensive. He quoted on two occasions from the third essay, 'Schopenhauer as Educator', of the *Untimely Meditations* (ZL §166; ZL §186); referred to Nietzsche's phrase 'a philosophy of what lies nearest to hand' (ZL §175); quoted the famous line from *Thus Spake Zarathustra*, 'I say to you, one must yet have chaos in himself in order to give birth to a dancing star' (ZL §235); and concluded his lecture with another quotation from 'Schopenhauer as Educator' (ZL §236). Jung's final lecture, 'Thoughts on the Interpretation of Christianity, with Reference to the Theory of Albrecht Ritschl', given in January 1899, quoted yet again from Nietzsche's essay on Schopenhauer (*ZL* §243). In a less obvious way, Nietzsche is woven into the fabric of Jung's lectures. At one point, he refers to 'the "untimely" non-philosopher', and refers to Nietzsche's 'revaluation of all values' (*ZL* §290), although he does not explore the idea in detail. Walter Kaufmann has, however, suggested that it was probably reading Nietzsche that 'put an end to Jung's Christianity – or drove it underground – and made him ready to embrace Freud'.[4] Yet the matter is more complicated.

For the autobiographical work *Memories, Dreams, Reflections* suggests that Jung had a highly ambivalent attitude towards Nietzsche. Even if the reliability of this work can by no means be taken for granted, it does at least provide us with an account of what Jung (or Aniela Jaffé, or the Jung family) thought we should know. Despite the popularity of Nietzsche at the turn of the century, which is doubtless one of the reasons he was quoted in the Zofingia Lectures, Jung's autobiography records that, when it came to reading Nietzsche, there was a great deal of hesitation on Jung's part: 'Nietzsche had been on my programme for some time, but I hesitated to begin reading him because I felt I was insufficiently prepared' (*MDR* p. 122). For someone who had been perfectly happy to tackle Kant and Schopenhauer, there was clearly a problem here of a more intimate and personal rather than simply intellectual nature. Indeed, Jung himself was prepared to admit as much.

What was this problem? According to Jung, he was afraid of discovering some fundamental similarity with Nietzsche: 'I was held back by a secret fear that I might perhaps be like him, at least in regard to the "secret" which had isolated him from his environment. . . . I feared I might be forced to recognize that I too, like Nietzsche, was "another one in the same mould". . . . I must not let myself find out how far I might be like him' (*MDR* pp. 122–3). This basic similarity can be understood in two ways. First, the idea of the secret runs like a leitmotif throughout his autobiography. Jung wrote:

> It is important to have a secret, a premonition of things unknown. It fills life with something impersonal, a *numinosum*. A man who has never experienced that has missed something important. He must sense that he lives in a world which in some respects is mysterious; that things happen and can be experienced which remain inexplicable; that not everything which happens can be anticipated. The unexpected and the incredible belong to this world. Only then is life whole. For me the world has from the beginning been infinite and ungraspable.
>
> (*MDR* p. 389)

Indeed, one might find in these words a central point of contrast between Jung, who emphasizes *das Geheimnisvolle* ('the mysterious') and its ultimate unknowability, and Freud, who spoke of *das Unheimliche* ('the uncanny') and claimed to find in it confirmation of his theory of infantile sexuality, the Oedipus Complex and castration anxiety.[5] In the case of Jung, the secret is associated with such powerful intuitions of the Dionysian that he had experienced in the course of his childhood years as his dream of the ritual phallus and the vision of God defecating on the roof of Basle cathedral. Correspondingly, Jung believed that 'perhaps – who knows? – [Nietzsche] had had inner experiences, insights which he had unfortunately attempted to talk about, and had found that no one understood him' (*MDR* p. 122).[6]

Furthermore, as a child Jung sensed that he was in fact two different persons, called 'Personality No. 1' (the schoolchild growing up in Klein-Hüningen near Basle) and 'Personality No. 2' (a timeless, eternal counterpart, his own 'Other') (*MDR* p. 62). According to *MDR*, Jung came to believe that Nietzsche, like him, had possessed a dual personality which came into the open when he wrote *Zarathustra*. In his autobiography, Jung wrote that it was when he read *Zarathustra* while a student that he came to see how his personality 'number two' corresponded to Nietzsche's 'number two' – i.e. Zarathustra – which in turn corresponded to Goethe's 'number two' – i.e. Faust. Thus, in his reading of *Zarathustra* (and indeed of *Faust*), Jung felt personally involved: 'This, like Goethe's *Faust*, was a tremendous experience for me. Zarathustra was Nietzsche's Faust, his No. 2, and my No. 2 now corresponded to Zarathustra' (*MDR* p. 123).

While Jung may have felt that his dilemma was very similar to Nietzsche's, he sensed the distance between Nietzsche's fate and his own. For although Jung shared with Nietzsche a sense of double identity, there was a highly significant difference. Whereas, in Jung's view, Nietzsche's dual personality had only come to the fore in *Thus Spake Zarathustra* (in other words, only when it was too late), Jung felt that he had been able to identify and deal with the same problem from an early age and, as a direct result of reading Nietzsche, escaped the fate that had befallen the philosopher. This is how Jung describes Nietzsche's mistake: 'That, I thought, was his morbid misunderstanding: that he fearlessly and unsuspectingly let his No. 2 loose upon a world that knew and understood nothing about such things' (*MDR* p. 123). Alluding to the 'Prologue' of *Thus Spake Zarathustra*, Jung says that Nietzsche's project led ultimately to his own destruction: 'And he fell – tightrope-walker that he proclaimed himself to be – into depths far beyond himself' (*MDR* p. 124).

Jung and Freud

In his dissertation for his Swiss medical doctorate entitled *On the Psy-*

chology and Pathology of So-Called Occult Phenomena (1902) (*CW* 1 §1–§150), Jung drew attention to what seemed to him to be an extraordinary coincidence between an episode of *Zarathustra* and an almost identical occurrence in Kerner's *Blätter aus Prevorst*. Jung discovered that Nietzsche provided him with an example of how the mind can automatically and unconsciously recall large amounts of information with incredible accuracy – in other words, cryptomnesia. Jung found evidence of this phenomenon in the remarkable similarity between a passage in 'Of Great Events' in Part II of *Thus Spake Zarathustra* and an account of an incident originally reported in a ship's log for 1686 and reprinted in the *Blätter aus Prevorst* (1831–1837), a collection of reports of occult and unexplained phenomena by the Swabian physician and Romantic writer, Justinus Kerner (1786–1862). Struck by the close similarity of these passages, Jung maintained that Nietzsche must have read the account in Kerner and then reproduced it almost word for word many years later in *Zarathustra*, without knowing that he was doing so. Jung argued that this was a classic case of cryptomnesia and, as he relates in his dissertation, he even went so far as to contact Nietzsche's sister, Elisabeth Förster-Nietzsche (1846–1935), asking her if she could provide any explanation for this coincidence.[7]

For Jung, this apparent example of cryptomnesia, not to mention the ultimate fate of Nietzsche, were powerful demonstrations of 'the impotence of consciousness in face of the tremendous automatism driving up from the Unconscious' (*CW* 1 §184). In this way, Jung's reading of Nietzsche laid the foundations for one of the most influential concepts of Jungian psychology, the archetype, with its emphasis on the power of the Unconscious as the source of the creative impulse.

At times, Jung seems almost too anxious to involve Nietzsche's life and thought in his own psychological writings, whereas Sigmund Freud, by contrast, maintained that he had hardly read any Nietzsche at all. As a result, Jung tended to play up Freud's ignorance of Nietzsche, even using his obituary of Freud in the *Basler Nachrichten* to attack his deceased opponent's 'apparently total lack of any philosophical premises', backing this allegation up with the claim: 'He once assured me personally that it had never occurred to him to read Nietzsche' (*CW* 15 §61). Jung first made contact with Freud in March or early April 1906, inaugurating a correspondence that lasted a decade and that represents an important source of information not only about the growth of psychoanalysis but also about the reasons why Jung moved away from Freud. More precisely, Jung's letters of the period between 1909 and 1910 clearly reflect his growing interest in mythological motifs in general and the god Dionysos in particular.[8] In his letter of 8 November 1909, Jung excitedly told Freud how his studies of the history of symbolism, particularly Friedrich Creuzer's *Symbolik und Mythologie der alten Völker, besonders bei den Griechen* (*Symbolism and Mythology of the Ancient Peoples, Particularly the Greeks*)

(Leipzig and Darmstadt, 1810–1823) and Richard Payne Knight's *A Discourse on the Worship of Priapus and its Connection with the Mystic Theology of the Ancients* (London, ²1865), had revived his interest in archaeology. It is unlikely that Freud suspected where these mythological investigations would lead his *Kronprinz* nor that Dionysos's feet would soon dance to a different tune from Freud's sexual theory. For as far as Freud was concerned, the 'nuclear complex of neurosis' was the incest fantasy, a key aspect of the sexual theory of libido; but Jung's letters later in 1909 started to link his reading of mythology with Freud's incest theories in a less literal and more symbolic way which presaged the final break between the two men.

Above all, Jung's attention in 1909 became fixed on the image of the god who dies and is reborn, and in a letter of 15 November 1909 Jung explictly associated Dionysos with the Egyptian god Osiris and other (phallic) deities:

> Now to better things – mythology. . . . The dying and resurgent god (Orphic mysteries, Thammuz, Osiris [Dionysos], Adonis, etc.) is everywhere phallic. At the Dionysos festival in Egypt the women pulled the phallus up and down on a string: 'the dying and resurgent god'.
> (*FJL* p. 263; the square brackets round 'Dionysos' are Jung's)

And Jung foregrounded the problem of the Dionysian with even greater clarity a few weeks later in his long letter of 25/31 December 1909. Here, Jung agreed with Freud that the incest taboo is highly significant, but suggested that the importance of the Dionysian elements in previous cultures had not been sufficiently appreciated, claiming that '[w]e shall not solve the ultimate secrets of neurosis and psychosis without mythology and the history of civilization':

> I am turning over and over in my mind the problem of antiquity. It's a hard nut! . . . I'd like to tell you many things about Dionysos were it not too much for a letter. Nietzsche seems to have intuited a great deal of it. I have an idea that the Dionysian frenzy was a backwash of sexuality, a backwash whose historical significance has been insufficiently appreciated, essential elements of which overflowed into Christianity but in another compromise formation. I don't know whether I am writing you banalities or hieroglyphics. An unpleasant feeling!
> (*FJL* pp. 279–80)

Not only does Jung make a clear link between Nietzsche and the Dionysian, but he says that Nietzsche had 'intuited' (*geahnt*) this phenomenon, although he suggests by this that Nietzsche had not grasped its full implications. At this stage, Jung himself was still working towards the position he adopted in *Wandlungen und Symbole der Libido* ('Symbols and Transformations of the Unconscious') (1911/1912), namely that the incest-taboo was responsible for the canalization of libido and the creation of self-consciousness. There is a clear reluctance on Jung's part to discuss all this in the letter, not just because he is deviating from the classic Freudian position stressing sexuality as the unique origin of neurotic disorders, but perhaps also because Jung had still not fully dissociated himself on a personal level from the figure of Nietzsche.

Undoubtedly the most significant letter in the Freud–Jung correspondence from the point of view of the history of analytical psychology is his letter of 11 February 1910. Here, Jung attempted to define the programme of psychoanalysis (which Freud and Jung referred to in their correspondence by means of the two Greek letters 'psi' and 'alpha') in terms of the Dionysian. The immediate context of the letter was a discussion of an organization founded by Alfred Knapp called the 'International Fraternity for Ethics and Culture', an idea Jung rejected. Arguing that 'religion can be replaced only by religion', Jung contrasted the impotence of the ideological vacuum at the heart of any so-called 'ethical fraternity' with the ability of religion to tap into the vital forces of instinct. Instead of committing the intellectual presumption of relying entirely on rationality, Jung proposed to revive religion and, in a passage which equates Christ with Dionysos, he argued that it should be the task of psychoanalysis to create a new Dionysian myth. For rather than aiming like an ethical fraternity to hem in and control man's most basic instincts, Jung believed that the goal of psychoanalysis should be, in the manner of the religions of antiquity, to provide man with a means of making use of these libidinal resources:

> I think we must give it [psychoanalysis] time to infiltrate into people from many centres, to revivify among intellectuals a feeling for symbol and myth, ever so gently to transform Christ back into the soothsaying god of the vine, which he was, and in this way absorb those ecstatic instinctual forces of Christianity for the *one* purpose of making the cult and the sacred myth what they once were – a drunken feast of joy where Man regained the ethos and holiness of an animal. That was the beauty and purpose of classical religion, which from God knows what temporary biological needs has turned into a Misery Institute. Yet what infinite rapture and wantonness lie dormant in our religion, waiting to be led back to their true destination! A genuine and proper ethical development cannot abandon Christianity but must grow up within it, must bring to fruition its hymn of love, the agony and ecstasy over the dying and resurgent god, the mystic power of the wine,

the awesome anthropophagy of the Last Supper – only *this* ethical development can serve the vital forces of religion.

(FJL p. 294)

Not surprisingly, Freud's response to this letter in his reply of 13 February 1910 was terse: 'Yes, in you the tempest rages; it comes to me as distant thunder.' That letter also contained the curt remark: 'I am not thinking of a substitute for religion: this need must be sublimated' (*FJL* p. 295).

Jung's letters to Freud provide evidence for how the foregrounding of Dionysos as a regenerative power formed part of Jung's move away from Freud. The conflict with Freud sharpened over the next few months and culminated eventually in a complete break, whose consequences were profound both for Jung personally and also for his understanding of Nietzsche. By 23 June 1911, it was clear that, as far as Jung was concerned, the symbolism of the incest fantasy had less to do with what happened between Oedipus and Jocasta – in other words, with real, sexual desire – than with the meaning of the mysterious Mothers whom Faust encounters in Part II of Goethe's poetic drama (*FJL* p. 431). In a letter of 3 March 1912, less than a year before the final break with Freud in January 1913, Jung quoted a lengthy passage from *Thus Spake Zarathustra*. The passage comes from the final section of 'Of the Bestowing Virtue' and, bearing in mind Jung's concern with Nietzsche and the Dionysian, it was highly appropriate that he should have presaged the break with Freud in this way:

> Let Zarathustra speak for me:
> 'One repays a teacher badly if one remains only a pupil. And why, then, should you not pluck at my laurels? You respect me; but how if one day your respect should tumble? Take care that a falling statue does not strike you dead!
> You had not yet sought yourselves when you found me. Thus do all believers –. Now I bid you lose me and find yourselves; and only when you have all denied me will I return to you.'
> This is what you have taught me through ΨA. As one who is truly your follower, I must be stout-hearted, not least towards you.

(FJL pp. 491–2)

The final, inevitable break with Freud was followed by Jung's own personal *katabasis* (descent to the underworld), and not simply in the form of intellectual delvings into dusty old tomes on mythology. In his autobiography, Jung relates that, after his break with Freud, he experienced a dream in which frost transformed a leaf-bearing tree – his tree of life –

into sweet grapes, full of healing juices, which he plucked and offered to a waiting crowd (*MDR* p. 200). According to the psychoanalyst John Gedo, the conclusion of this dream symbolizes Jung's desire to fit the role which he had earlier assigned to Freud and psychoanalysis and become *der weissagende Gott der Rebe* ('the soothsaying god of the vine') – his own transformation into Dionysos.[9]

In fact, the problem of the Dionysian is the guiding thread through Jung's (labyrinthine) reception of Nietzsche. As far as that reception is concerned, we can see three main stages of development. First, there is a move away from Nietzsche on the personal level. Second, this is accompanied by an increasingly sophisticated approach to Nietzsche's texts in his psychological writings. Third, at the same time, Jung becomes increasingly aware of the significance of the problem of Dionysos. From its definition in the letter to Freud of 11 February 1910 to the explicit exposition in the essay 'Wotan' of 1936 (*CW* 10 §371–§399), the Dionysian problematic takes on both ethical and political dimensions. Just as Nietzsche's philosophy tells the story of his own self-overcomings and is written, *à la* Zarathustra, in his own blood, so Jung's work represents in many respects his own overcoming of Nietzsche and a coming-to-terms with what Nietzsche called 'the Dionysian'.

The final occasion on which Jung mentioned Nietzsche in his autobiography occurs towards the end of the penultimate chapter. In the context of what amounts to a summary of the existential project which he had undertaken in his life and work, Jung says that his psychology represents an answer to the 'problem' of Faust and the 'problem' of Nietzsche, and the solution to 'the suprapersonal life task, which I accomplish only by effort and with difficulty':

> Could that be why I am so impressed by the fact that the conclusion of *Faust* contains no solution? Or by the problem on which Nietzsche foundered: the Dionysian side of life, to which the Christian seems to have lost the way? Or is it the restless Wotan–Hermes of my Alemannic and Frankish ancestors who poses challenging riddles?
>
> (*MDR* p. 350)

Jung's own solution to this task, which he had discussed in his letter to Freud of 11 February 1910 as the problem of the transformation of Christ back into Dionysos, is referred to again in symbolic terms in the chapter of *MDR* called 'The Tower'. In this passage Jung describes his own coat of arms, consisting of a blue cross in the upper right of the shield and, in the lower left, blue grapes in a field of gold, separated by a blue bar with a gold star:

213

[M]y coat of arms . . . contains . . . a cross azure in chief dexter and in base sinister a blue bunch of grapes in a field d'or; separating these is an etoile d'or in a fess azure. The symbolism of these arms is Masonic, or Rosicrucian. Just as cross and rose represent the Rosicrucian problem of the opposites ('*per crucem ad rosam*'), that is, the Christian and Dionysian elements, so cross and grapes are symbols of the heavenly and chthonic spirit. The uniting symbol is the gold star, the *aurum philosophorum*.

(*MDR* p. 259)

In this device, the Jungian answer to Dionysos is made clear: Dionysos, the creative power of the Unconscious, must be integrated into the conscious life of the psyche. In the face of all opposites (and, in the struggle with Freud, in the face of all psychoanalytical opposition), Jung declares the *coniunctio oppositorum*, the union of the opposites. The uniting symbol of Dionysos and Christ in Jung's coat of arms is the gold star. And as both Jung and Nietzsche knew, 'gold star' is the meaning of the name – Zarathustra.[10]

Jung's reading of Zarathustra

According to *MDR*, Jung's first reading of *Thus Spake Zarathustra*, when he was a student at Basle University, proved to be a dead end: 'Just as *Faust* had opened a door for me, *Zarathustra* slammed one shut, and it remained shut for a long time to come' (*MDR* p. 124). A dead end, that is, in terms of intellectual response, but not in terms of therapeutic benefits, as Jung suggested in his Seminar on *Zarathustra*.[11] For while his autobiography stresses the generally negative consequences of reading Nietzsche, Jung here (on 12 June 1935) emphasized its positive usefulness:

When I read *Zarathustra* for the first time as a student of twenty-three, of course I did not understand it all, but I got a tremendous impression. I could not say it was this or that, though the poetical beauty of some of the chapters impressed me, but particularly the strange *thought* got hold of me. He helped me in many respects, as many other people have been helped by him.

(*SNZ* I p. 544)

In the autumn of 1913 and the spring of 1914, as Europe slowly moved towards war, Jung apparently experienced a series of visions of mass destruction. In his autobiography, Jung related the visions and vivid dreams he experienced in 1913 and 1914 to two key figures of German literature, Hölderlin and Nietzsche. In other words, Jung understood himself as the survivor of those experiences which had destroyed both

Hölderlin and Nietzsche, both of whom subsumed the primal forces behind these experiences under the name of Dionysos. In his seminars of 21 November 1934 and 20 February 1935, Jung referred to this time as the beginning of his first serious engagement with Nietzsche's key text:

> I read *Zarathustra* for the first time with consciousness in the first year of the war, in November 1914, twenty years ago; then suddenly the spirit seized me and carried me to a desert country in which I read *Zarathustra*. . . . I read *Zarathustra* for the first time when I was only twenty-three, and then later, in the winter of 1914–15, I studied it very carefully and made a lot of annotations.
>
> (*SNZ* I p. 259, p. 391)[12]

Although Jung claimed that his second reading was more 'conscious' than the first at university had been, he none the less described it in ecstatic terms which suggest an emotional as well as an intellectual experience.[13] This experience formed part of what is popularly known as Jung's 'confrontation with the Unconscious' (*MDR* p. 194). Stressing how the roots of Jungian theory are to be found in his own personal experience, Jung wrote in his autobiography:

> My own way had a starting point in my intense preoccupation with the images of my own Unconscious. This period lasted from 1913 to 1917; then the stream of fantasies ebbed away. Not until it had subsided and I was no longer held captive inside the magic mountain [*Zauberberg*] was I able to take an objective view of that whole experience and begin to reflect upon it.
>
> (*MDR* p. 233)

The term 'magic mountain' is precisely that which Nietzsche famously used in *The Birth of Tragedy* in connection with the Dionysian experience: 'Now it is as if the Olympian magic mountain [*Zauberberg*] had opened before us and revealed its roots to us.'[14] Not only are the 'roots' of the 'Olympian magic mountain' common to both Nietzsche and Jung, but Jung also adopts the idea that, behind everything, there is one creative source, which Nietzsche called the 'primordial mother' (*Urmutter*) (*BT* §16). This notion lies at the heart of Jung's theories concerning the creativity of the Unconscious.

In 1934, Jung embarked upon his third and, by any standards, his most extensive reading of *Zarathustra*, when he began his Seminar on Nietzsche. The immediate reason for Jung's choice of subject for his seminars, which had been running regularly since 1925, was the collapse of the Vision Seminar (1930–1934). In those lectures, Jung had analysed the visions of Christiana Morgan, but when her identity as Jung's subject was leaked, the seminar was terminated.[15] So it was altogether safer to turn to a written text for source material, and the name Nietzsche was frequently connected with recent political events in Germany. As we have seen, however, Nietzsche and *Zarathustra* had already been a focus of Jung's thinking in the early years of his intellectual development, so it is not surprising that Jung now decided to turn his attention to a work that he had found ceaselessly fascinating and, on occasion, frightening.

In terms of sheer length, Jung's seminar is worthy of comparison with Martin Heidegger's lectures on Nietzsche, given at the University of Freiburg from 1936 to 1940 (thus concurrently with Jung),[16] and Leo Strauss's seminars on *Zarathustra* given at the University of Chicago in 1959.[17] In terms of methodology, however, Jung would have horrified Heidegger, Strauss and such other prominent interpreters of Nietzsche as Karl Jaspers, Karl Löwith and Eugen Fink. Because of the excessive attention paid to parallels in traditions with which Nietzsche was, at best, only loosely connected; the failure to pay close attention to the rhetorical and *aesthetic* qualities of the text; and the almost automatic application of analytical psychological postulates, the seminar runs the risk of saying more about the interpreter than about his ostensible object of interpretation. That said, Jung's approach has two enormous strengths. First, it accepts the text as constituting a meaningful whole – a point on which some Germanists still disagree! Even if, in his seminar, Jung's sense of literary structure lacks a certain sophistication, he paid closer attention than hitherto to the formal aspects of *Zarathustra*. According to Jung, the underlying psychological dynamic in *Zarathustra* is that of enantiodromia, or the emergence of the unconscious opposite in chronological sequence. Indeed, the structure of *Zarathustra* as a whole is said to enact one great enantiodromic moment: 'The book begins with that great spiritual solitude, and at the end come the Dionysian dithyrambs' (*SNZ* II p. 1492). This view is consonant with the world-historical importance which Jung consistently assigned to this work:

> *Zarathustra* . . . is like a dream in its representation of events. It expresses renewal and self-destruction, the death of a god and the birth of a god, the end of an epoch and the beginning of a new one. When an epoch comes to an end a new epoch begins. The end is a beginning: what has come to an end is reborn in the moment when it ceases to be.
>
> (*SNZ* II p. 1132)

Moreover, Jung thought that each chapter represented 'a stage in a process of initiation' (into the archetypal Unconscious) and, more specifically, 'a new image in the process of initiation' (*SNZ* I pp. 459, 461). And, convinced that there was 'a secret logic, a sort of Homeric chain' throughout the work (*SNZ* I p. 462), Jung also sought evidence of the enantiodromic structural principle in the links between various sections of the text, between individual chapters, and even within image clusters: '*Zarathustra* . . . is split up into many chapters very loosely hung together, and the chapters themselves are split up by a multitude of intuitive sparks or hints' (*SNZ* II p. 1133). For example, on 30 June 1937, Jung suggested that the group of three chapters – 'The Night Song', 'The Dancing Song' and 'The Funeral Song' – represent the descent into Nietzsche's inferior function (in other words, the unconscious side of his psyche), while 'The Funeral Song' itself leads to 'the precincts of the Unconscious' (*SNZ* II p. 1189). And on 27 May 1936, he maintained that 'if you carefully study the end of a chapter and compare it with the subsequent title, you discover how he arrives at the particular theme of the next chapter', seeing in the dramatic structure of the 'spiral' a similarity with Goethe's *Faust* (*SNZ* II p. 956; cf. pp.786, 1243).

Second, Jung is excellent at highlighting Nietzsche's use of mythological symbols. To take just one example, Jung discussed in detail the image cluster of the eagle and the serpent/snake (a symbol which also attracted the critical attention of Heidegger). On 2 May and 7 November 1934, Jung interpreted these animals as a premonitory symbol of the union of spirit (eagle) and body (serpent), and hence a 'reconciliation of opposites' (*SNZ* I pp. 18–19):

> Zarathustra sees [the eagle and the serpent] together, representing pairs of opposites, because spirit is always supposed to be the irreconcilable opponent of the chthonic, eternally fighting against the earth.
>
> (*SNZ* I p. 227)

Behind these remarks lies an ancient interpretative tradition which David Thatcher has discussed with reference to Nietzsche. Examination of this tradition shows, in a particularly striking manner, the extent to which Jung and Nietzsche shared such common sources as Creuzer, Ludwig Preller and Schopenhauer.[18]

For Jung, *Zarathustra* was, on one hand, a highly personal work (*SNZ* II p. 1037), an aspect of the unfolding psychological tragedy of an individual, and he believed it marked both the start of Nietzsche's (unresolved) mid-life crisis (*SNZ* I p. 226; SNZ II p. 1070) and the beginning of his mental illness (*SNZ* I p. 695). On the other hand, Jung argued that *Zarathustra* stands in a dialectical relationship to the age in which it was written, because Nietzsche is not only a 'child' of that time but also a 'forerunner of times that have come since and of times that are still to come' (*SNZ* II p. 1037). Because Jung saw *Zarathustra* as an individual as well as an archetypal work, he attached great importance to the account of its composition which Nietzsche provided in the short poem 'Sils-Maria', one of the 'Songs of Prince Vogelfrei' that were published as an appendix to *The Gay Science* in 1897, and whose title refers to the Swiss location where most of *Zarathustra* was written:

> *Sils-Maria*
>
> *Hier saß ich, wartend, wartend, – doch auf nichts,*
> *Jenseits von Gut und Böse, bald des Lichts*
>
> *Genießend, bald des Schattens, ganz nur Spiel,*
> *Ganz See, ganz Mittag, ganz Zeit ohne Ziel,*
> *Da, plötzlich, Freundin! wurde eins zu zwei –*
> *– Und Zarathustra ging an mir vorbei . . .*

> Sils-Maria
>
> Here I sat, waiting – not for anything –
> Beyond Good and Evil, fancying
>
> Now light, now shadows, all a game,
> All lake, all noon, all time without all aim.
> Then, suddenly, my friend, one turned into two –
> And Zarathustra walked into my view.[19]

In this poem, Jung saw the expression both of a real psychological event and of an authentic archetypal experience: '[Nietzsche] said: "Da wurde eins zu zwei und Zarathustra ging an mir vorbei" . . . meaning that Zarathustra then became manifest as a second personality in himself' (*SNZ* I p. 10).[20] Jung was not alone in giving such a relentlessly literalistic reading to this text. For example, the French literary critic René Girard derived the dynamics of Nietzsche's entire *oeuvre* and life from the mysterious encounter presented in the poem. In *Critiques dans un souterrain* (1976), he described this 'expérience du Double' as 'une véritable épiphanie du désir mimétique'.[21] Thus, Jung's own view of the complex relationship between Nietzsche and Zarathustra is best summarized in his own words as follows: 'Zarathustra speaks to Nietzsche, but Nietzsche speaks out of his time' (*SNZ* II p. 831).

In the course of his lecture, Jung developed his understanding of the Nietzschean figure of Dionysos by relating him to his analysis of two larger concerns. First, there is his analysis of the rise of Fascism (implicitly and in some cases explicitly referring to the political drama unfolding around Switzerland in Europe). In this context, Jung spoke not just of Dionysos but of the related figure of Teutonic war-god Wotan (known to the Scandinavians as Odin and to the Anglo-Saxons as Woden), typically depicted as a wanderer or a horseback rider, the god of the thunderstorm.

Second, Jung advanced the prospect of a spiritual renewal that also, but in a different way, relied upon the notion of the Dionysian.

In his first lecture on *Zarathustra* of 2 May 1934, Jung inscribed Dionysos within the very heart of the text he proposed to study, characterizing that work as 'the Dionysian experience *par excellence*':

> *Zarathustra* really led [Nietzsche] up to a full realization of the mysteries of the cult of Dionysos: he had already ideas about it, but *Zarathustra* was the experience which made the whole thing real.
>
> (*SNZ* I p. 10)

And in his lecture on *Zarathustra* of 9 May 1934 (*SNZ* I p. 24), Jung quoted from Nietzsche's account of his *ekstasis* when writing *Zarathustra*; in other words, from that very passage which had prompted him to write to Elisabeth Förster-Nietzsche in 1899.

Another passage that Jung considered particularly Dionysian was *Zarathustra*'s dream in 'The Prophet', in which he saw several Wotanic motifs. On 4 May 1938, Jung interpreted the 'distorted figures' of that dream as a prefiguration of Nietzsche's future mental collapse and, as such, as the quintessential Wotanic experience:

> It is Wotan who gets him, the old wind god breaking forth, the god of inspiration, of madness, of intoxication and wildness, the god of the Berserkers, those wild people who run amok. It is, of course, the shrieking and whistling of the wind in a storm in a nocturnal wood, the Unconscious. It is the Unconscious itself that breaks forth. This is very beautifully described here: doors fly open and out bursts that wind, bringing a thousand laughters. It is a horrible foreboding of his insanity. . . .
>
> (*SNZ* II p. 1227; cf. pp. 1228–9)

On 30 June 1937, Jung asserted that Nietzsche had had a Wotanic experience earlier in his life, as a result of which, he argued, Nietzsche had gained privileged access to a form of 'archetypal' knowledge (*SNZ* II pp. 1205–6). And on 15 June 1938, he reminded his audience that, in his madness, Nietzsche had identified with Dionysos.

Yet there is an even more overtly political dimension to Jung's understanding of the return of Pan/Dionysos which becomes increasingly clear in the course of the lectures. On 22 May 1935, Jung claimed that 'old Pan is again abroad in the woods' (*SNZ* I p. 500), and spoke in this connection of the 'Wotan experience'. And on 26 February 1936, Jung again referred to what he saw as a revival of Wotanism:

Yet it is a fact that old Wotan has to a certain extent come to life
again . . . the myth is *en marche*, old Wotan is going strong again;
you might even include Alberich and those other demons. That
thing lives.

(*SNZ* II p. 868)

Thus the ideas which form the core of Jung's pre- and post-war essays,
notably 'Wotan' (published in March 1936) and 'After the Catastrophe'
(1945), were first discussed in and developed at the same time as his
Seminar on *Zarathustra*.

As far as Jung was concerned, the political and social events of his day
were a consequence of cultural and religious (and thus, for Jung, psychological) changes which he was eager to chart. In terms of Jungian psychology, it is impossible to separate sociological and personal psychological
change since individual psychological developments both reflect and anticipate developments in the collective social sphere. Jung's various under-
standings of Dionysos – both as Wotan in the form of National Socialist
politics and in a different, apparently more theological sense – subsume
diverse areas of interest under one single figure. And as the seminar moved
towards its premature conclusion, so Jung's comments on the political
developments in Germany became increasingly dark and ominous, employing sacrificial metaphors which uncannily anticipate the term 'holocaust',
although never directly discussing the fate of the Jews under National
Socialism.

Shortly before the abrupt conclusion of the Visions Seminar, Jung had
questioned the meaning for the modern age of the gods and mythologies
of antiquity in his thirteenth set of lectures (7 to 21 March 1934). In a
striking passage, Jung made special mention of the German wanderer-god
Wotan as a later manifestation of the Greek god Dionysos. This passage,
with its note of despair, reflects Jung's doubt as to the ability of the
categories of rational thought to deal with such religious or spiritual (that
is, for Jung, psychological) issues. In Jung's view, modernity has alienated
man from his most vital (Dionysian) instincts, and just as gods become
idols, so these repressed desires threaten to return in hollow and insubstan-
tial form:

Who among the living is capable of having more than sentiment in
an old temple? Yes, it is aesthetic, it is beautiful, but do you
understand what an antique God means? How is it possible that
they came to a conclusion that there was such a thing as Apollo
or Ceres? Of course we can be sentimental about it, but it is very
rarely experienced. Old Wotan has now been resuscitated but
what is Wotan to us? He was experienced once, but now it is only
historical sentimentality. Our intellect, our discrimination, has

killed all these things. When the Christian missionaries cut down the oaks of Wotan and destroyed the poles or sacred idols, it was their discriminating minds which said it was impossible for a divine presence to be present in such man-made figures, in such clumsy dirty idols smeared with blood or dirt; their mental knife cut them down and they were obliterated, they crumbled away.[22]

This passage has an unmistakably elegiac note in its lament for the lost rites and deities of paganism and its note of irreparable loss. Equally unmistakable, however, is the political resonance. The poet Theodor Körner, who was killed in the Wars of Liberation (*Beifreiungskriege*), which marked a turning-point in the Napoleonic Wars, was a patriot not just in the manner of his death but also in the style of his lyric output, collected in the appropriately entitled anthology *Lyre and Sword* (*Leyer und Schwerdt*) (1814). In his poem 'The Oaks' ('Die Eichen'), Körner wrote: *Deutsches Volk, du herrlichstes von allen,/Deine Eichen stehn, du bist gefallen!* ('The German people, you are the greatest of all, You have fallen, your oaks stand tall!') Thus the oak, particularly in Germany, does not just imply paganism but it also has patriotic connotations. Awareness of the specific political significance of the iconography of the oak allows one, for example, to see in Caspar David Friedrich's painting *The Hünengrab in Autumn* (1820), not simply a massive stone in a landscape, not merely an expression of the permanence of 'rock-solid' Christian faith, but also an expression of Friedrich's nationalism.[23] In the 1930s, the National Socialist philosopher, Alfred Rosenberg (1893–1946), declared that Christianity had been unable to supplant the pagan cult of Wotan. There is a political echo, perhaps strong, perhaps weak, in Jung's much earlier letter of 23 May 1823 to Oskar A.H. Schmitz (1873–1931), which uses the image of the Wotanic oaks:

> Like Wotan's oaks, the gods were felled and a wholly incongruous Christianity, born of monotheism on a much higher cultural level, was grafted upon the stumps. The Germanic Man is still suffering from this mutilation. I have good reasons for thinking that every step beyond the existing situation has to begin down there among the truncated nature-daemons. In other words, there is a whole lot of primitivity in us to be made good.[24]

In what turned out to be the penultimate seminar, on 8 February 1939, Jung made it clear that he regarded the increasing tension in international relations and the internal situation in Germany as a consequence of the return of hitherto absent or repressed archetypal forces. In his commentary on section 6 of 'Of Old and New Law-Tables', he declared:

221

The state is merely the modern pretence, a shield, a make-belief, a concept. In reality, the ancient war-god holds the sacrificial knife, for it is in war that the sheep are sacrificed. . . . So instead of human representatives or a personal divine being, we now have the dark gods of the state – in other words, the dark gods of the Collective Unconscious. . . . The old gods are coming to life again in a time when they should have been superseded long ago, and nobody can see it.

(SNZ II pp. 1517–18)

Linking the return of the old to a failure on the part of the new to find 'value' in the Jungian sense of a 'leading idea' (cf. *SNZ* I p. 646), Jung argued that the absence of a guiding principle and the failure of the attempt to find values by relating to the archetypes in a positive, unrepressed way had left a vacuum in society which the Collective Unconscious would fill with archaic (and hence often negative) archetypal forms:

Wherever we fail in our adaptation, where we have no leading idea, the Collective Unconscious comes in, and in the form of the old gods. There the old gods break into our existence: the old instincts begin to rage again.

(SNZ II p. 1517)

Yet Jung was at pains to point out the dangers attendant upon political renewal by Dionysian means. In his letter to Schmitz, Jung had retained, along with his respect for, a deep suspicion of, the Dionysian. He asked Schmitz: 'Do you not find it also rather suspect to nourish the metaphysical needs of our time with the stuff of old legends? What would have happened in the 1st century of our era if people had taken the Dionysos legend as the material and occasion for meditation?' Instead, Jung argued that the conflict between the civilized and the barbaric in man can find resolution only in an experience of divine transcendence: 'We need some new foundations. We must dig down to the primitive in us, for only out of the conflict between civilized Man and the Germanic barbarian will there come what we need: a new experience of God.'

Just such an example of 'digging down' could be found, Jung believed, in a song in Part IV of *Zarathustra* (later included in the *Dionysos-Dithyramben*). In the Magician's Song, later called 'Complaint of Ariadne', Jung saw a poetic record of Nietzsche's confrontation with Dionysian *Geist*:

In the latter part of *Zarathustra* there is a beautiful poem where Nietzsche describes how he was digging down into himself,

222

working into his own shaft; there you can see how intensely he experienced the going into himself, till he suddenly produced the explosion of the most original form of spirit, the Dionysian.

(*SNZ* I p. 369)

As far as Jung was concerned, Nietzsche's text was just as much about a psychological response to the existential crisis called the 'Death of God' as it was about politics.

In his third lecture of 16 May 1934, Jung observed that *Zarathustra*'s claim that 'God is dead' was central to the work: 'It is, one could say, the exposition of the whole problem of *Zarathustra*' (*SNZ* I p. 43). Nevertheless, Jung believed that the way in which the work unfolded showed that the problem was much more complex and that, as he put it, God was not so much dead as 'somehow lurking in the background' (*SNZ* I p. 72; cf. *SNZ* II p. 843). Claiming that Nietzsche had 'got the essence of his time' (*SNZ* I p. 69) because he was the son of a pastor, 'the representative of a dying system and a dying spirit', Jung insisted that Nietzsche could not help 'yielding at times to his Christian background' (*SNZ* II p. 1000). Of course, Jung too was the son of a pastor, and had been educated as a Protestant. On 6 May 1936, Jung traced the shift in the conception of God from the fifteenth century to modern-day Protestantism (*SNZ* II pp. 907–8), a development whose outcome was, in his view, the philosophical rationalism and materialism of the nineteenth century (*SNZ* II p. 1248) which Jung presented as the intellectual background to *Zarathustra*: 'Nietzsche's *Zarathustra* is one of the first attempts in modern times to come back to the immediate, individual initiation' (*SNZ* I pp. 460–1). On 28 November 1934, Jung wrote:

Nietzsche was exceedingly sensitive to the spirit of the time; he felt very clearly that we are living now in a time when new values should be discovered, because the old ones are decaying. . . . Nietzsche felt that, and instantly, naturally, the whole symbolic process that had come to an end outside, began in himself.

(*SNZ* I p. 279)

Thus, what Nietzsche called the 'revaluation of all values' (*Umwertung aller Werte*), the rejection of old values and the search for new ones, is understood by Jung as the culmination of an historical process, which Nietzsche at once completed and advanced to a new stage.

Already in his third lecture of 16 May 1934, Jung had anticipated his later exegesis by declaring that the 'Death of God' marked a new psychological point of departure whose goal was described as the archetypal process of 'rebirth':

[W]hen Nietzsche declares that God is dead, instantly he begins to transform. . . . He immediately gets into the process of that archetype of rebirth, because those vital powers in us which we call 'God' are powers of self-renewal, powers of eternal change.

(*SNZ* I p. 54)

The psychological equivalence Jung implied between the return of God and the birth of the Self became one of the key themes of Jung's post-war writings. Throughout his writings, Jung uses Nietzsche in different ways to help unite the various opposites: to unite the sexual and non-sexual aspects of libido in a theory of psychic energy; to unite different psychological approaches through a reconciling symbol; to unite discipline and passion in the production of art; and to unite the psychological opposites in the creation of the Self. His notion of the Self is founded on a Dionysian process of life, death and rebirth: it is thus a Dionysian Self.

The Dionysian Self

Much of analytical psychology, especially in the post-war period, can be read as a response to the religious crisis inaugurated by Nietzsche's claim that 'God is dead.' And although he talks a lot about God, Jung, too, is apparently willing to admit that He is in some sense 'dead'. In 'Psychology and Religion', originally delivered in English as the Terry Lectures at Yale University in 1937 and published in German in revised form in 1940 (*CW* 11 §1–§168), Jung claimed that psychology had become a necessary substitute for faith:

I am not addressing myself to the happy possessors of faith, but to those many people for whom the light has gone out, the mystery has faded, and God is dead. . . . To gain an understanding of religious matters, probably all that is left us today is the psychological approach.

(*CW* 11 §148)

Likewise, in his lecture *Wissenschaft als Beruf* ('Science as a Vocation'), delivered in 1919 in the wake of the Great War in Europe, Max Weber had spoken of the *Entzauberung der Welt* ('disenchantment of the world'), by which he had meant the withdrawal of value from the objective sphere (of society) into the purely subjective spheres of mysticism or personal relationships.[25]

For his part, Jung sketched out the historical context for the disappearance of man's highest value in his numerous lectures on psychology and religion, suggesting that the Death of God could be understood as the culmination of a psychological dynamic which had constituted the development of Western religion. Jung argued that the withdrawal of the deity from the world was nothing new and, indeed, that it was a process which had been going on for centuries (*CW* 11 §141). This neo-Weberian notion of 'the withdrawal of projections', which Peter Homans has correctly identified as one of Jung's most important concepts,[26] was taken up in Jung's post-war essay 'After the Catastrophe', in which he placed what had happened in Germany in the context of an allegedly larger European decline (*CW* 10 §437) and the complete withdrawal of Spirit from the world of Nature (*CW* 11 §431). Jung's psychological diagnosis of modernity echoes Heidegger's declaration in his famous discussion of Hölderlin that the modern epoch is not just bereft of the gods but also full, so to speak, of their absence – a double lack of divinity: 'It is the time of the gods that have fled *and* of the god that is coming. It is the time of *need*, because it lies under a double lack and a double Not: the No-More of the gods which have fled and the Not-Yet of the god that is coming.'[27] In a sense, both Jung and Heidegger's Hölderlin were waiting for the same god to return: Dionysos. And in his infamous interview with the German magazine *Der Spiegel*, under the headline *Nur noch ein Gott kann uns retten* ('Only a God Can Save Us Now'), Heidegger himself showed that he had taken up position in precisely that corner of philosophical despair out of which Jung, with such seeming effortlessness, emerged.[28]

I call Jung's Self a 'Dionysian Self' because, from the beginnings of analytical psychology, Jung turned to the god Dionysos for an image of the psychological patterns and processes he believed he had discovered. In 'Transformation and Symbols of the Libido', Jung's central thesis concerns the return of the libido to an unconscious source of new psychological life (a process Jung called 'introversion'). Thereby, Jung revived in psychological form many of the notions of the classical Mysteries of Dionysos, in which the god was ripped apart and reconstituted. This preoccupation with Dionysos and antiquity was not peculiar to Jung and can be read as continuing an important topos of Romantic literature, the hope for the advent of what Hölderlin, in his poem 'Bread and Wine', called *den kommenden Gott* ('the coming god').

According to Jung, the libido stands in a particular relationship to its ultimate source, the Unconscious. It not only springs from it, but it can flow back into it. To convey his notion of a return to the Unconscious, Jung turns to the astral myth for images of ascent (congruent with the image of the rising phallus), representing the libido striving towards consciousness, and descent (congruent with the image of the phallus resuming flaccidity), representing the return of the libido to the Unconscious. Following Otto Rank in *The Myth of the Birth of the Hero* (1909), Jung took the symbolical figure of the hero to represent a personification of the libido in this process of transformation (*PU* §317). Furthermore, the hero can also be represented by Dionysos (*PU* §297, n. 14). In this respect both Dionysos and Christ can be assimilated into the same figure: 'Dionysos stands in an intimate relation with the psychology of the early Asiatic god who died and rose again from the dead and whose manifold manifestations have been brought together in the figure of Christ into a firm personality enduring for centuries' (*PU* §212).

Jung used other images for the same process of introversion, such as the night sea-journey (*Nachtmeerfahrt*) of Leo Frobenius (*PU* §324–5), and Jung's own subterranean psychic voyages which he experienced after the break with Freud are a perfect example of introversion. The natural cycle of life, death and rebirth, and its physiological and cosmological analogues – the erection, detumescence, and rearousal of the phallus, the rising and setting sun which rises again – are psychologized by Jung into an intra-psychic, archetypal pattern which applies to every individual: the pattern of Dionysian death and rebirth. In *Psychological Types* (1921), Jung elaborated his conception of introversion and extroversion, which provided the basis for the elaborate scaffolding of his theory of typology. At around this time, Jung began to articulate his project to overcome Nietzsche, resurrect the God-concept and turn Christ back into Dionysos in terms of the construction of the Self.

In *MDR*, Jung remembered: 'During those years, between 1918 and 1920, I began to understand the goal of psychic development is the Self. There is no linear evolution; there is only a circumambulation of the Self' (*MDR* p. 222). In fact, Jung probably first mentioned the concept of the Self (the archetype of order and psychic totality) in 'La Structure de l'inconscient', a paper published in 1916 (see *CW* 7 §437–§507). There are further preliminary formulations in the first edition of *Psychological Types* and in the Seminar on Analytical Psychology (given in English in 1925), where Jung said that the Self was 'the totality or sum of the conscious and unconscious processes' and that 'this centre of self-regulation' was 'a postulate that is assumed'.[29] The first detailed definition of the Self – referred to later as 'the totality of Man, the sum total of his conscious and unconscious contents' (*CW* 11 §140) – did not emerge until *The Relations between the Ego and the Unconscious* (1928). In that work, the Self is described as the goal of what Jung calls the 'individuation process':

> There is a destination, a possible goal, beyond the alternative stages dealt with in our last chapter. That is the way of individuation. Individuation means becoming a single, homogeneous being, and, in so far as 'individuality' embraces our innermost, last, and incomparable uniqueness, it also implies becoming one's own Self. We could therefore translate individuation as 'coming to Selfhood' or 'Self-realization'. . . . The Self is our life's goal, for it is the

most complete expression of that fateful combination we call individuality.

(*CW* 7 §266, §404)

According to this definition, the archetype of the Self is 'a quantity that is superordinate to the conscious Ego': 'The Self embraces not only the conscious but also the unconscious psyche, and is therefore, so to speak, a personality which we *also* are' (*CW* 7 §274). But at the same time, Jung imbued this psychological concept with an apparently more religious overtone:

> This 'something' is strange to us and yet so near, wholly ourselves and yet unknowable, a virtual centre of so mysterious a constitution that it can claim anything – kinship with beasts and gods, with crystals and with stars – without moving us to wonder, without even exciting our disapprobation. . . . I have called this centre the *Self*. Intellectually the Self is no more than a psychological concept, a construct that serves to express an unknowable essence which we cannot grasp as such, since by definition it transcends our powers of comprehension. It might equally well be called the 'God within us'.
>
> (*CW* 7 §398–9)

Clearly, the concept of the Self does not so much reject as replace the notion of divine transcendence with the much less clear notion of psychological transcendence. In the psychic economy that Jung proposes, the archetype of the Self replaces the concept of God, and that close affinity – indeed, identity – of the God-concept and the concept of the Self is suggested by the transposition of the definition of God attributed by Jung to Alanus de Insulis in 'Transformation Symbolism in the Mass' (1942/ 1954) and in 'A Psychological Approach to the Dogma of the Trinity' (1942/1948), *Deus est circulus cuis centrum est ubique, circumferentia vero nusquam* ('God is a circle whose centre is everywhere and the circumference nowhere') (*CW* 11 §92, §229), to the Self: 'The Self is not only the centre but also the whole circumference which embraces both conscious and unconscious' (*CW* 12 §44).[30] And in a letter to M. Leonard of 5 December 1959, Jung not only used that Latin phrase but, venturing what he termed 'the illegitimate hypostasis of my image', actually spoke of '*a God beyond Good and Evil*'.[31]

The chief characteristic of the Jungian Self is its capacity for creation and self-transformation, a striving for an ever more complete union of the two great opposites, consciousness and the Unconscious. In the process of creating the Self, the libido (conceived by Jung as a stream of psychic energy) descends into the depths of the Collective Unconscious (the great psychic M/Other), dying unto the conscious world as it introverts, to re-emerge stronger, bolder, more creative, born anew: like a god which dies and is reborn. This is the Dionysian Self, and the Self as Jung conceives it is *dionysisch* in precisely the sense in which Nietzsche had defined the term in his notes for *The Will to Power*:

> The word '*Dionysian*' means: an urge to unity, a reaching up beyond personality, the everyday, society, reality, across the abyss of transitoriness: a passionate-painful overflowing into darker, fuller, more floating states; an ecstatic affirmation of the total character of life as that which remains the same, just as powerful, just as blissful, through all change; the great pantheistic sharing of joy and sorrow that sanctifies and calls good even the most terrible and questionable qualities of life; the eternal will to procreation, to fruitfulness, to recurrence; the feeling of the necessary unity of creation and destruction.[32]

In 'Transformation Symbolism in the Mass', originally delivered as an Eranos lecture in 1941, Jung specifically related the legend of Dionysos to the archetype of the Self. In a long and complicated passage written entirely in the spirit of Nietzsche's *Die Geburt der Tragödie*, Jung argued that the unity of the *principium individuationis* must be replaced by a higher unity, symbolized by Dionysos:

> The Logos is the real *principium individuationis*, because everything proceeds from it, and because everything which is, from crystal to Man, exists only in individual form. In the infinite variety and differentiation of the phenomenal world is expressed the essence of the *auctor rerum*. As a correspondence we have, on the one hand, the indefiniteness and unlimited extent of the unconscious Self (despite its individuality and uniqueness), its creative relation to individual consciousness, and, on the other hand, the individual human being as a mode of its manifestation. Ancient philosophy paralleled this idea with the legend of the dismembered Dionysos, who, as creator, is the ἀμέριστος (undivided) νοῦς, and, as the creature, the μεμερισμένος (divided) νοῦς. Dionysos is distributed throughout the whole of nature, and just as Zeus once devoured the throbbing heart of the god, so his worshippers tore wild animals to pieces in order to reintegrate his dismembered spirit . . . The psychological equivalent of this is the integration of the Self through conscious assimilation of the split-off contents. Self-recollection is a gathering together of the Self.
>
> (*CW* 11 §400)

By smashing the *principium individuationis*, the Dionysian experience takes place outside time and space so that we can know nothing of it: the Dionysian moment requires Apollonian form before we can experience it in tragedy. The Jungian concept of the Self is equally unknowable. Indeed, the achievement of the Self is posited as an ideal, unrealizable in the reality of history, society or human existence.

Like Nietzsche's, Jung's notion of the Self is dynamic, implying not simple stasis but complex activity, and it is thus best understood in terms of the image which Jung used in 'On the Psychology of the Trickster Figure' (1954) and in *Mysterium Coniunctionis* (1955/56) – the living unity of a waterfall which dynamically mediates between the two symbolic opposites of above and below (*CW* 9/i §484 and *CW* 14 §674, §705–§706).

Unlike Nietzsche, however, who always speaks of *creating* the Self, Jung sometimes talks instead about *discovering* the Self. The title of the English translation of *Gegenwart und Zukunft* (1957), 'The Undiscovered Self', makes this point quite clear. Elsewhere, Jung wrote: 'Conscious realization or the bringing together of the scattered parts is in one sense an act of the Ego's will, but in another sense it is a spontaneous manifestation of the Self, which was always there' (*CW* 11 §400). By contrast, in one of *Nachlaß* notes directed primarily at Christianity, Nietzsche declared:

> It is mythology to believe that we will find our true self after we have left behind or forgotten this and that. In this way we unravel ourselves back into infinity: but *to make ourselves*, to *shape* a form out of all the elements – that is the task! Always the task of a sculptor! Of a productive man!'[33]

As far as the doctrine of the Self is concerned, however, the most significant point of coincidence between Nietzsche and Jung is their conception of the Self as a totality. In a famous passage of encomium from *Twilight of the Idols* (1889), Nietzsche offered Goethe as an example of just such totality, and he baptized Goethe's *credo* as the Dionysian faith:

> *Goethe* – not a German event but a European one: a grand attempt to overcome the eighteenth century through a return to nature, through a going-*up* to the naturalness of the Renaissance, a kind of self-overcoming on the part of that century. . . . What he aspired to was *totality*; he strove against the separation of reason, sensuality, feeling, will (– preached in the most horrible scholasticism by Kant, the antipodes of Goethe); he disciplined himself to a whole, he *created* himself. . . . A spirit thus *emancipated* stands in the midst of the universe with a joyful and trusting fatalism, in the *faith* that only what is separate and individual may be rejected,

that in the totality everything is redeemed and affirmed – *he no longer denies*. . . . But such a faith is the highest of all possible faiths: I have baptised it with the name *Dionysos*.[34]

Coda

In *Psychological Types*, Jung offered one of his most important commentaries on Nietzsche.[35] Following a lengthy discussion of Schiller's *Letters on the Aesthetic Education of Man* (1795), Jung concentrated here on *The Birth of Tragedy* (1871):

> This early work is more nearly related to Schopenhauer and Goethe than to Schiller. But it at least appears to share aesthetism [*Ästhetismus*] and Hellenism with Schiller, pessimism and the motive of deliverance in common with Schopenhauer, and unlimited points of contact with Goethe's *Faust*.
>
> (*CW* 6 §223)

By talking about *der Ästhetismus* instead of *der Ästhetizismus*, Jung makes it clear he is talking about a doctrine of the aesthetic, not the style of *l'art pour l'art*. According to Jung, there was a fundamental difference in the views of art proposed by Schiller on the one hand and Nietzsche on the other:

> Whereas Schiller, almost timidly and with faint colours, begins to paint light and shade, apprehending the opposition in his own psyche as 'naïve' versus 'sentimental', while excluding everything that belongs to the background and abysmal profundities of human nature, Nietzsche's apprehension takes a deeper grasp and spans an opposition, whose one aspect yields in nothing to the dazzling beauty of the Schiller vision; while its other side reveals infinitely darker tones, which certainly enhance the effect of the light, but allow still blacker depths to be divined.
>
> (*CW* 6 §224)

Here, Jung appears to be echoing Nietzsche's description in section 19 of 'the highest and, indeed, the truly serious task of art – to save the eye from gazing into the horrors of night and to deliver the subject by the healing balm of illusion [*Schein*] from the spasms of the agitations of the will'. Jung is, however, misled into perceiving the difference of emphasis between Schiller and Nietzsche as a difference of 'standpoint'.

As Jung points out, the fundamental pair of opposites in Nietzsche's account of art in general and tragedy in particular is that, found in Bachofen and, before him, the German Romantics, of Apollo and Dionysos. In

The Birth of Tragedy, Apollo and Dionysos represent 'art deities' (*Kunst-gottheiten*), 'artistic energies' (*künstlerische Mächte*), the 'Apollonian art' of sculpture and the 'Dionysian art' of music, and the 'art worlds' (*Kunst-welten*) of dreams and intoxication (*BT* §1). Whereas, in his earlier lecture 'A Contribution to the Study of Psychological Types' (1913), Jung incorrectly equated the Dionysian with a striving for the multiplicity of objects (*CW* 6 §876–§877), here he correctly identifies Apollo with the multiplicity of objects in the world of time and space (the *principium individuationis*). By contrast, Dionysos stands for 'the freeing of unmeasured instinct, the breaking loose of the unbridled *dynamis* of the animal and the divine nature; hence in the Dionysian choir Man appears as *satyr*, god above and goat below' (*CW* 6 §227; cf. *BT* §8). Quoting directly from *The Birth of Tragedy*, Jung wrote that, under the effect of the Dionysian, 'Man is no longer an artist, he has become a work of art [*Kunstwerk*]: in these paroxysms of intoxication the artistic power of all nature reveals itself . . .' (*CW* 6 §227; cf. *BT* §1). On Jung's account, the Dionysian is clearly a psychological process, '[w]hich means that the creative *dynamis*, the libido in instinctive form, takes possession of the individual as an object and uses him as a tool, or expression of itself' (*CW* 6 §227). At this point, Jung intervened in Nietzsche's argument to make a clarification and to raise an objection:

> If one might conceive the natural being as a 'product of art' [*Kunstwerk*], then of course a man in the Dionysian state has become a natural work of art; but, inasmuch as the natural being is emphatically not a work of art in the ordinary meaning of the word, he is nothing but sheer Nature [*bloße Natur*], unbridled, a raging torrent, not even an animal that is restricted to itself and its own laws. I must emphasize this point both in the interests of clarity and of subsequent discussion, since, for some reason Nietzsche has omitted to make this clear, and has thereby shed over the problem a deceptive aesthetic veiling, which at certain places he himself has instinctively to draw aside.
>
> (*CW* 6 §227)

Nietzsche unclear? In fact, Jung has misunderstood a distinction central to Nietzsche's argument and, more important, overlooked the significance attached by Nietzsche to the category of the aesthetic.[36]

To begin with, Jung overlooks the distinction made by Nietzsche between the Dionysian barbarian and the Dionysian Greek:

> From all quarters of the ancient world – to say nothing here of the modern – from Rome to Babylon, we can point to the existence of Dionysian festivals, types which bear, at least, the same relation to

the Greek festivals which the bearded satyr, who borrowed his
name and attributes from the goat, bears to Dionysos himself'.

(*BT* §2)

It is these festivals of which Nietzsche wrote that 'the most savage natural
instincts were unleashed, including even that horrible mixture of sensuality
and cruelty which has always seemed to me to be the real "witches' brew"'
(*BT* §2). Moreover, *The Birth of Tragedy* makes use of a mode of argumentation known as 'binary synthesis'. In binary synthesis, the name of one of
the antitheses is also applied to the synthesis, which thus represents both a
richer concept but one that tends towards one of the original antitheses.[37]
In section 21, Nietzsche makes it clear that the union of Apollo and
Dionysos represents the highest goal, not just of tragedy, but of art as a
whole. As far as Nietzsche is concerned, tragedy acts as a cipher for the
aesthetic and what he calls 'this metaphysical intention of art to trans-
figure' (*BT* §24). In the following passage, it looks as if Apollo is going to
lose out to Dionysos; but, in the end, both are combined. And that combination is itself placed under the sign of Dionysos:

> In the total effect of tragedy, the Dionysian predominates once
> again. Tragedy closes with a sound which could never come from
> the realm of Apollonian art. And thus the Apollonian illusion
> reveals itself as what it really is – the veiling during the perfor-
> mance of the tragedy of the real Dionysian effect; but the latter is
> so powerful that it begins to speak with Dionysian wisdom and
> even denies itself and its Apollonian visibility. Thus the intricate
> relation of the Apollonian and the Dionysian in tragedy may
> really be symbolized by a fraternal union of the two deities:
> Dionysos speaks the language of Apollo; and Apollo, finally the
> language of Dionysos; and so the highest goal of tragedy and of
> all art is attained.
>
> (*BT* §21)

Thus Dionysos as the outcome of binary synthesis is identical with what
Walter Kaufmann described as Nietzsche's mature concept of the Dionysian but restricted to his later writings.[38]

Having declared that 'it is only as an *aesthetic phenomenon* that existence
and the world are eternally *justified*' (*BT* §5; cf. §24; 'Attempt at a Self-
Criticism' §5), in the final section of *The Birth of Tragedy* Nietzsche
explains how music and myth constitute that aesthetic justification, by
saving every 'moment' and enabling us to move to the next:

> Thus the Dionysian is seen to be, compared to the Apollonian,
> the eternal and original artistic power that first calls the whole

world of phenomena [*Erscheinung*] into existence – and it is only in the midst of this world that a new transfiguring illusion [*Verklärungsschein*] becomes necessary in order to keep the animated world of individuation alive. If we could imagine dissonance become Man – and what else is Man? – this dissonance, to be able to live, would need a splendid illusion [*Illusion*] that would cover dissonance with a veil of beauty [*Schönheitsschleier*]. This is the true artistic aim of Apollo in whose name we comprehend all those countless illusions of the beauty of mere appearance [*Illusionen des schönen Scheins*] that at every moment make life worth living at all and prompt the desire to live on in order to experience the next moment.

(*BT* §25)

Jung's failure to grasp Nietzsche's mode of argumentation skews the pitch for his own critique of Nietzsche's argument. For Jung regards the combination of Apollo and Dionysos in Greek culture as, far from an actual state of affairs, a cultural goal for which to strive:

Nietzsche considers the reconciliation of the Delphic Apollo with Dionysos as a symbol of the reconciliation of this antagonism within the breast of the civilized Greek. But here he forgets his own compensatory formula, according to which the Gods of Olympus owe their splendour to the darkness of the Grecian soul. The reconciliation of Apollo with Dionysos would, according to this, be a 'beauteous illusion' [*schöner Schein*], a desideratum, evoked by the need of the civilized half of the Greek in the war with his barbaric side, that very element which broke out unchecked in the Dionysian state.

(*CW* 6 §228)

Here, Jung fails to comment on the significance of the expression *schöner Schein*. Yet the concept of *schöner Schein* lies at the core of Schiller's thinking on aesthetics, which Jung discusses in the previous chapter of *Psychological Types*, and, by the same token, it lies at the core of Nietzsche's aesthetics, too.

In the *Kallias Letters* (1793), Schiller defined Beauty as freedom in appearance (*Freiheit in der Erscheinung*). Thus the essence of Beauty lies in its *appearance*. In Weimar aesthetics, the image of the veil came to symbolize the transforming effect of the aesthetic moment. In *The Birth of Tragedy*, Apollo is repeatedly identified with *schöner Schein* (*BT* §1). In section 4, Nietzsche defined the Apollonian dream as 'the appearance of appearance [*Schein des Scheins*]'. In other words, the Apollonian in its aesthetic modality is the representation ([*schöner*] *Schein*) of the phenomenal world (*Erscheinung*). And, according to Nietzsche, Apollonian *Schein*, the object's merely phenomenal modality (mere appearance), constitutes one half of the poetic experience (*BT* §1). Like Goethe and Schiller, Nietzsche also used the image of the veil to symbolize aesthetic illusion and, in section 2, he identified the Apollonian consciousness – in both its aesthetic and its phenomenal modalities – with a veil, covering up a Dionysian reality. And in section 8, he spoke of the Apollonian dream as a trans-forming veil. This use of the image must, however, be also distinguished from its use in his association of Apollo with Schopenhauer's image of the veil of Maya, in contrast to which Dionysos is said to represent the destruction of this veil, leaving it as if in tatters and revealing – beneath the phenomenal world of appearance (*Erscheinung*) – the fundamental noumenal unity of Being. In other words, it is important to distinguish between Nietzsche's two uses of the word *Schein*: on the one hand, the 'as if' (*als ob*) of aesthetic appearance (*Schein* or *der Dichtung Schleier*) and, on the other, the phenomenal 'veil' (*Er[schein]ung*). It is the aesthetic sense of 'appearance' that Nietzsche wrote in the foreword to the second edition of *The Gay Science* that 'those Greeks were superficial – *out of profundity*', for they knew how 'to stop courageously at the surface, the fold, the skin, to adore appearance [*Schein*], to believe in forms, tones, words, in the whole Olympus of appearance [*Scheins*]'.[39]

Or to put it another way, Apollo and Dionysos are analogous to the two drives identified by Schiller in his *Letters on the Aesthetic Education of Man*. There, Schiller made a distinction between two basic drives he called the sensuous drive (*Stofftrieb*) and the formal drive (*Formtrieb*). The reciprocal co-ordination of these two drives resulted in what he called the ludic drive (*Spieltrieb*). Out of the ludic drive, Schiller argued, there arises the aesthetic. This model of synthesis is reworked by Nietzsche in the form of a binary-type synthesis (used elsewhere by Schiller). For, taken separately, neither Apollo nor Dionysos – neither the form drive (the Apollonian phenomenal form) nor the material drive (the Dionysian passion) – constitute the aesthetic moment proper of the ludic drive (the Apollonian aesthetic form that contains the Dionysian), which arises out of a reciprocal co-ordination of the two. Significantly, in *Psychological Types* Jung recognized the significance of *play* to stimulate the creativity of the *imagination* (*CW* 6 §93) – thereby giving prominence to two key concepts in Schillerian aesthetics.

It is no idle digression to consider the aesthetic theories of Schiller and Nietzsche, for it is with vocabulary from precisely those theories that Jung conducts his argument. He sets up a distinction between the psychological and the aesthetic, arguing that what Nietzsche called the metaphysical was really to do with the Unconscious. Yet what Jung says about the Unconscious has far more to do with the aesthetic, the category which, in *Psychological Types*, he rejected, as careful analysis will show. In section 1 of *The Birth of Tragedy*, Nietzsche writes: '[The] antagonism [between Apollo and Dionysos] [is] only superficially reconciled by the common term "art"'; and that 'eventually, by a metaphysical miracle of the Hellenic "will", they appear [*erscheinen*] coupled with each other.' For Jung, these two statements are to be read as contrastive. Let us examine his commentary on these statements in further detail.

As regards first the statement, Jung wrote: 'This utterance . . . must be kept clearly in mind. It is as well to remember this sentence in particular, because Nietzsche, like Schiller, has a pronounced inclination to ascribe to art the mediating and redeeming role' (*CW* 6 §230). Jung called this position 'aesthetism':

> Aesthetism is a modern glass, through which the psychological mysteries of the cult of Dionysos are seen in a light in which they were certainly never seen or experienced by the ancients. With Nietzsche, as with Schiller, the religious point-of-view is entirely overlooked, and its place is taken by the aesthetic.
>
> (*CW* 6 §231)

It is a position, however, that Jung rejected: 'In adopting this view, therefore, that the conflict between Apollo and Dionysos is purely a question of antagonistic art-tendencies [*Kunsttriebe*], the problem is shifted onto aesthetic grounds in a way that is both historically and materially unjustifiable' (*CW* 6 §231). In particular, Jung thought that the aesthetic approach disregarded the problems of ugliness and of evil. Jung wrote:

> The result is that the problem remains stuck in the aesthetic [*im Ästhetischen*] – the ugly is also 'beautiful'; even the evil and atrocious may wear a desirable brilliance in the false glamour of the aesthetically beautiful [*im trügerischen Schimmer des Ästhetisch-Schönen*].
>
> (*CW* 6 §230)

What Jung says is not quite true; in section 24, Nietzsche argued that the ugly and the disharmonic could indeed stimulate aesthetic pleasure, and that

> it is precisely the tragic myth that has to convince us that even the ugly and disharmonic are part of an artistic game [*ein künstlerisches Spiel*] that the will in the eternal amplitude of its pleasure plays with itself [*mit sich selbst spielt*].

In other words, the aesthetic approach does not ignore, but 'justifies', ugliness and evil. On Jung's account:

the aesthetic estimation immediately converts the problem into a picture which the spectator considers at his ease, admiring both its beauty and its ugliness, merely reflecting the passion of the picture, and safely removed from any actual participation in its feeling and life.

(*CW* 6 §232)

What Jung offers here, however, is a caricature of the aesthetic approach. For if any approach seeks to engage 'actual participation in its feeling and life', then it is the aesthetic one, as that was understood by Goethe, Schiller and Nietzsche.

Ironically enough, Jung rejected the aesthetic approach and opted for what he called the 'psychological' one. The irony resides in the fact that almost everything that Jung says about the 'psychological' approach can be applied, more accurately, to the aesthetic approach, which Jung, mistakenly, rejected. To put it another way, Jung's psychology makes most sense when read as aesthetics. And that would mean it would be a psychology without 'miracles'.

As regards the second of Nietzsche's two statements about the union of Apollo and Dionysos, Jung wrote:

Even at that time, in spite of the aesthetic viewpoint, Nietzsche had an intuition [*Ahnung*] of the real solution of the problem; as, for instance, when he wrote that the antagonism [between Apollo and Dionysos] was not bridged by art, but by a 'metaphysical miracle of the Hellenic "will"'.

(*CW* 6 §233)

In fact, Jung argued, 'metaphysical' can be read in a 'psychological' way:

'Metaphysical' has for us the psychological significance of 'unconscious'. If, then, we replace the 'metaphysical' in Nietzsche's formula by 'unconscious', the desired key to this problem would be an unconscious 'miracle'. A 'miracle' is irrational; the act itself therefore is an unconscious irrational happening, a shaping out of itself without the intervention of reason and conscious purpose; it just happens, it grows, like a phenomenon of creative Nature, and not as a result of the deep probing of human wits; it is the fruit of yearning expectation, faith and hope.

(*CW* 6 §233)

At this point, Jung broke off, promising to return to this problem (*CW* 6 §234). Further on in *Psychological Types*, Jung claimed: 'The solution of the problem in *Faust*, in the *Parsifal* of Wagner, in Schopenhauer, even in

236

Nietzsche's *Zarathustra*, is *religious*' (*CW* 6 §524). Yet from Jung's remarks about the reconciling function of the symbol, it would appear that, far from being religious, the solution is aesthetic. Indeed, by this stage in *Psychological Types*, Jung had already invoked Schiller's definition of the symbol as 'living form' and alluded to Goethe's *Faust* in his discussion of the specific life-promoting significance of the symbol (*CW* 6 §202).

Finally, Jung returned to his typological intentions at the end of Chapter 3 of *Psychological Types*. According to Jung, the Dionysian represented the psychological function of sensation (*Empfindung*) and the psychological process of extroversion. Equally, the Apollonian is said to represent intuition (*Intuition*) and introversion. In contrast to the logico-rational functions of thought (*Denken*) and feeling (*Fühlen*), these categories were, Jung claimed, quite different and, indeed, could be regarded as prior to thinking and feeling. Astonishingly, Jung called them *aesthetic* functions:

> But there is also quite a different standpoint, from which the logical-rational elaboration is not valid. This other standpoint is the aesthetic [*Dieser andere Standpunkt ist der ästhetische*]. In introversion it stays with the *perception* [*Anschauung*] of ideas, it develops intuition, the inner perception [*Intuition, die innere Anschauung*]; in extraversion it stays with *sensation* and develops the senses, instinct, affectedness. Thinking, for such a standpoint, is in no case the principle of inner perception of ideas, and feeling just a little; instead, thinking and feeling are mere derivatives of inner perception [*der inneren Anschauung*] or outer sensation.
>
> (*CW* 6 §239)

Jung called these types 'intuitive' and 'sensation' types. The surprise, however, is not just because Jung claimed to derive these principles from Nietzsche's ideas (*CW* 6 §240). Rather, it is because Jung's presentation of these categories, while actually having very little to do with the aesthetic, none the less makes use of such key terms of Weimar Classicism as *Anschauung*. For Goethe, Schiller and Nietzsche, it is the co-ordination of all the faculties to which the adjective 'aesthetic' is applied. For his part, Jung also subscribed to that goal, yet rejected the terminology of German aesthetics, while nevertheless redeploying it in his own 'psychological' sense. What Schiller described as Man in the aesthetic mode and Jung called the Self, was precisely that totality Nietzsche declared to be the Dionysian faith of Goethe.[40]

Despite the confusion in *Psychological Types* over whether Nietzsche was an introverted intuitive type (*CW* 6 §242) or an introverted thinking type (*CW* 6 §632), Jung (who regarded himself as an introverted thinker) characterized Nietzsche's achievements in the final paragraph in terms that could also be applied to himself:

In his initial work he unwittingly sets the facts of his own personal psychology in the foreground. This is all quite in harmony with the intuitive attitude, which characteristically perceives the outer through the medium of the inner, sometimes even at the expense of reality. By means of this attitude he also gained deep insight into the Dionysian qualities of his unconscious. . . .

(CW 6 §242)

By paying closer attention to Jung's intellectual sources, particularly Nietzsche and the tradition that Nietzsche mediated to Jung, we become better able to appreciate Jung's position in the history of German ideas. Furthermore, by reading Jung's psychological theories in the light of German aesthetics, we begin to understand how a *coniunctio oppositorum* may be possible without having recourse to miracles.

Notes

1 For further discussion of the central argument of this essay, see P. Bishop, *The Dionysian Self: C.G. Jung's Reception of Nietzsche*, Berlin and New York, Walter de Gruyter, 1995. Jung's works are referred to by volume number and paragraph number from the *Collected Works* (*CW*). *Wandlungen und Symbole der Libido* ('Transformations and Symbols of the Libido', translated by Beatrice Hinkle in 1915 as *Psychology of the Unconscious*) is quoted by paragraph number from the recent reprint of the Hinkle translation (London, Routledge, 1991) (*PU*). Jung's autobiography is quoted by page number from *Memories, Dreams, Reflections, Recorded and Edited by Aniela Jaffé*, London, Collins/Routledge & Kegan Paul, 1963 (*MDR*).
2 L. Andreas-Salomé, *The Freud Journal*, tr. by Stanley A. Leavy, New York, Basic Books, 1964, pp. 38–9.
3 C.G. Jung, *The Zofingia Lectures* [*The Collected Works, Supplementary Volume A*], tr. J. van Heurck, London, Routledge & Kegan Paul, 1983 (hereafter referred to as *ZL*); and C.G. Jung, *Die Zofingia-Vorträge* (*Gesammelte Werke, Ergänzungsband* I), ed. H. Egner, Zurich and Düsseldorf, Walter, 1997.
4 W. Kaufmann, *Discovering the Mind*, New York and London, McGraw-Hill, 1980, III (*Freud versus Adler and Jung*), p. 426.
5 Freud, 'The "Uncanny"' (1919), in *The Standard Edition of the Collected Works of Sigmund Freud*, London, Hogarth Press, 1953–1974, XVII, pp. 217–56.
6 That the 'secret' consists of such visions is far more likely than that Jung is alluding to covert homosexuality. (In his letter to Freud of 28 October 1908, Jung mentioned that as a boy he has been the victim of a sexual attack by a man; and in the records of a meeting of Vienna Psychoanalytic Society of 28 October 1908, Freud is recorded as mentioning that, according to Jung, Nietzsche had contracted syphilis in a homosexual bordel). Yet it is interesting that Jung mentions that of the only two of his friends who 'openly declared themselves to be adherents of Nietzsche', both were homosexual: 'one of them ended by committing suicide, the other ran to seed as a misunderstood genius' (*MDR* p. 124).

7 For further discussion, see P. Bishop, 'The Descent of Zarathustra and the Rabbits: Jung's Correspondence with Elisabeth Förster-Nietzsche', *Harvest: Journal for Jungian Studies*, 1997, vol. 43, pp. 108–23.

8 W. McGuire (ed.), *The Freud/Jung Letters: The Correspondence between Sigmund Freud and C.G. Jung*, tr. Ralph Manheim and R.F.C. Hull, Cambridge MA, Harvard University Press, 1988. Hereafter referred to as *FJL*.

9 J.E. Gedo, *Magna est vis veritatis tuae et praevalebit: Comments on the Freud–Jung Correspondence* (unpublished m.s., 1974); quoted by Peter Homans in *Jung in Context: Modernity and the Making of a Psychology*, Chicago and London, University of Chicago Press, 1979, p. 79.

10 See Nietzsche's letter to Peter Gast of 23 April 1883: 'Today I learnt by chance *what* "Zarathustra" means: it means "Gold-Star". This coincidence made me happy. One might think that the whole idea of my little book was rooted in this etymology – but until today I knew nothing about it' (Friedrich Nietzsche, *Briefwechsel: Kritische Gesamtausgabe*, ed. G. Colli and M. Montinari, Berlin, Walter de Gruyter, 1975–1984, III, 1, p. 366). Cf. Jung: 'According to a surmise by Kern, Zarathustra may mean "golden-star" and be identical with Mithra' (*PU* §687).

11 See C.G. Jung, *Nietzsche's 'Zarathustra': Notes of the Seminar given in 1934–1939*, ed. J.L. Jarrett, London, Routledge, 1989 (hereafter referred to as *SNZ*, followed by volume number and page reference). For a shorter version, see *Jung's Seminar on Nietzsche's 'Zarathustra'*, ed. and abridged J.L. Jarrett, prefaced W. McGuire, Princeton NJ, Princeton University Press, 1998.

12 See P. Bishop, 'Jung's Annotations of Nietzsche's Works: An Analysis', *Nietzsche-Studien*, 1995, vol. 24, pp. 271–314.

13 It is interesting to note that, at about the same time (1916), and also in his thirties, the German theologian Paul Tillich (1886–1965) had his own 'Zarathustra-Erlebnis' which is reported in his biography in very similar terms. See W. and M. Pauck, *Paul Tillich: Sein Leben und Denken*, Stuttgart and Frankfurt am Main, Evangelisches Verlagswerk, 1977, I, pp. 63–4. For further discussion, see J.P. Dourley, *C.G. Jung and Paul Tillich: The Psyche as Sacrament*, Toronto, Inner City Books, 1981.

14 F. Nietzsche, *The Birth of Tragedy*, §3, in *Basic Writings of Nietzsche*, ed. and tr. W. Kaufmann, New York, The Modern Library, 1968 (hereafter referred to as *BT*). The image was also taken up by Thomas Mann in his novel, *The Magic Mountain* (1914).

15 See C. Douglas, *Translate this Darkness: The Life of Christiana Morgan*, New York, Simon & Schuster, 1993, pp. 214–15.

16 M. Heidegger, *Nietzsche*, tr. D.F. Krell, San Francisco, Harper, 1991.

17 For further discussion, see L. Lampert, *Leo Strauss and Nietzsche*, Chicago and London, University of Chicago Press, 1996.

18 See D. Thatcher, 'Eagle and Serpent in *Zarathustra*', *Nietzsche-Studien*, 1977, vol. 6, pp. 240–60.

19 F. Nietzsche, *The Gay Science*, tr. W. Kaufmann, New York, Vintage Books, 1974, pp. 370–1.

20 See P. Nill, 'Die Versuchung der Psyche: Selbstwerdung als schöpferisches Prinzip bei Nietzsche und C.G. Jung', *Nietzsche-Studien*, 1988, vol. 17, pp. 250–79 (p. 263).

21 See R. Girard, *Critiques dans un souterrain*, Paris, Grasset, 1976, pp. 23 and 93. See also K. Löwith, *Nietzsches Philosophie der ewigen Wiederkehr des Gleichen*, Hamburg, Felix Meiner, [3]1978, pp. 186 and 188–9.

22 C.G. Jung, *The Visions Seminars*, ed. J.A. Pratt and P. Berry, Zurich, Spring Publications, 1976, II, p. 502.
23 See J.C. Jensen, *Caspar David Friedrich: Leben und Werk*, Cologne, DuMont, [4]1977, pp. 129–31.
24 C.G. Jung, *Letters*, ed. G. Adler and A. Jaffé, tr. R.F.C. Hull, London, Routledge & Kegan Paul, 1973–1976, I, pp. 39–40.
25 M. Weber, 'Science as a Vocation', in H.H. Gerth and C. Wright Mills (eds), *From Max Weber: Essays in Sociology*, London, Routledge, 1991, pp. 129–56.
26 Homans, op. cit., pp. 26–44.
27 'Hölderlin and the Essence of Poetry', tr. D. Scott, in M. Heidegger, *Existence and Being*, London, Vision Press, 1949, pp. 293–315 (p. 313).
28 '"Nur noch ein Gott kann uns retten"': *Spiegel*-Gespräch mit Martin Heidegger am 23. September 1966', *Der Spiegel*, Nr. 23, 1976, pp. 193–219.
29 C.G. Jung, *Analytical Psychology: Notes of the Seminar Given in 1925*, ed. W. McGuire, London, Routledge, 1990, p. 120.
30 In his letter of 8 February 1946 to Max Frischknecht, Jung wrote: 'I too slipped up over the source of "Deus est sphaera". The dictum does not come from Alanus de Insulis either, but from a Hermetic treatise entitled *Liber Hermetis* or *Liber Trismegisti*, which exists only in manuscript form. (Codd. Paris. et Vatic.) Cf. M. Baumgartner, in *Beiträge zur Geschichte der Philosophie des Mittelalters*, 2nd. ed., IV, 118: *Deus est sphaera infinita, cuius centrum est ubique, circumferentia nusquam*' (Letters, I, p. 412). In *Mysterium Coniunctionis* (1955–1956), Jung attributed the phrase 'God is an intelligible sphere whose centre is everywhere and whose circumference is nowhere' to St Bonaventura (*CW* 14 §41, n. 42). According to Brian Copenhaver, the maxim 'God is an infinite sphere whose centre is everywhere, whose circumference is nowhere', can be found in a late twelfth-century work called the *Book of Propositions or Rules of Theology, said to be by the Philosopher Termigistus* (*Hermetica*, ed. B. Copenhaver, Cambridge, Cambridge University Press, p. xlvii).
31 Jung, *Letters*, II, p. 526.
32 F. Nietzsche, *The Will to Power*, tr. W. Kaufmann and R.J. Hollingdale, New York, Vintage Books, 1968, §1050, p. 539.
33 F. Nietzsche, *Nachlaß*, end of 1880, in F. Nietzsche, *Werke: Kritische Gesamtausgabe*, ed. G. Colli and M. Montinari, Berlin, Walter de Gruyter, 1967ff., V/1, p. 691, 7 (213).
34 F. Nietzsche, *Twilight of the Idols/The Anti-Christ*, tr. R.J. Hollingdale, Harmondsworth, Penguin, 1968, pp. 102–3.
35 Here, I have decided not to use Hull's revision of Baynes's translation in the *Collected Works*, but the original Baynes translation: C.G. Jung, *Psychological Types or The Psychology of Individuation*, tr. H.G. Baynes, London, Kegan Paul, Trench, Trubner & Co., 1946, pp. 170–83. I have, however, included paragraph references to the *Collected Works* (which are different from those in volume 6 of the *Gesammelte Werke*).
36 I draw here on ideas developed in numerous discussions and conversations, formal and informal, with my Glasgow colleague, R.H. Stephenson, to whom I am greatly indebted.
37 See E.M. Wilkinson and L.A. Willoughby, 'Introduction', in F. Schiller, *On the Aesthetic Education of Man in a Series of Letters*, Oxford, Clarendon Press, [2]1982, p. lxxxvi.
38 'The later Dionysus is the synthesis of the two forces represented by Dionysus and Apollo in *The Birth of Tragedy* – and thus Goethe, certainly not an anti-Apollonian, can appear in one of Nietzsche's last books [see above] as the

perfect representative of what is now called Dionysian' (W. Kaufmann, *Nietzsche: Philosopher, Psychologist, Antichrist*, Princeton NJ, Princeton University Press, [4]1974, p. 129.

39 Op. cit., p. 38. Elsewhere in that work (§54), Nietzsche wrote: 'What is "appearance" [*Schein*] for me now? Certainly not the opposite of some essence. . . . Appearance [*Schein*] is for me that which lives and is effective and goes so far in its self-mockery that it makes me feel that this is appearance and will-o'-the-wisp and a dance of spirits and nothing more . . .' (p. 116). And in a section entitled 'Our ultimate gratitude to art' (§107), Nietzsche emphasized the importance of seeing the world as an aesthetic phenomenon as follows: 'As an aesthetic phenomenon existence is still *bearable* for us, and art furnishes us with eyes and hands and above all the good conscience to be *able* to turn ourselves into such a phenomenon' (pp. 163–4).

40 See the following by P. Bishop, 'Über die Rolle des Ästhetischen in der Tiefenpsychologie: Zur Schiller-Rezeption in der Analytischen Psychologie C.G. Jungs', *Jahrbuch der Deutschen Schillergesellschaft* (vol. 42, 1998); 'Epistemological Problems and Aesthetic Solutions in Goethe and Jung', *Goethe Yearbook* (vol. 9); 'Affinities Between Weimar Classicism and Analytical Psychology: Goethe and Jung on the Concept of the Self', *Forum for Modern Language Studies* (1999); and 'C.G. Jung and Goethe: Intellectual Affinities, With Special Reference to *Faust*', *Publications of the English Goethe Society* (2000).

9

FROM SOMNAMBULISM TO THE ARCHETYPES

The French roots of Jung's split with Freud

John R. Haule

Source: The Psychoanalytic Review, 71 (1984), 635–59.

According to the common view of Jung as the rebellious crown prince of psychoanalysis, his doctrine of the archetypes appears, at worst, a light-headed fascination with occultism or, at best, a way to overcome the historical and personalistic reductionism of the Freudian doctrine of sexual stages. Against the background of German thought and East-of-the-Rhine psychiatric interests, one is inclined to discuss whether the neuroses are bred in a biographical or an archaeological matrix, or whether we have genes or culture to thank for universal patterns. Quite another field of discussion opens up if we begin by noting the geographical fact that Zurich lies *West* of the Rhine. Jung's connections with Geneva and Paris are far more important than usually assumed; his French heritage is almost suppressed as some kind of secret. Probably the explanation for this is in the overwhelming success of psychoanalysis, as a result of which the earlier French psychologists have been largely forgotten. Now, due to their rediscovery by Ellenberger (1970), Jung's dissent from the doctrines of psychoanalysis appears in a new light. As we gain new appreciation for the psychological investigations being conducted at the turn of the century by the French hypnotists and their English-speaking followers, it is difficult to avoid the impression that the doctrine of the archetypes emerged in Jung's thought as a means to wed the best of Freud with the best of Janet.

Dissociation psychology

The story begins in the seventeenth century with Descartes, who set the course for pre-psychological philosophy with his disciplined naiveté in asking what we can really be sure we know. Succeeding philosophers doubted progressively more and were able to be sure of progressively less until the development culminated in the "radical associationism" of David Hume. Introspection alone being trusted as an investigating tool, associationists divested themselves of metaphysical presuppositions to limit themselves to the bare facts: the conscious stream of images and ideas. These they conceived on the model of Newtonian physics, as something akin to tiny spheres of matter in motion, determined by laws of attraction and repulsion. The problem was to explain how simple ideas combined to form complex ideas, as Hume points out in his opening remarks in *A Treatise of Human Nature* (1739):

> Were ideas entirely loose and unconnected, chance alone would join them; and 'tis impossible that some simple ideas should fall regularly into complex ones (as they commonly do) without some bond of union among them, some associating quality by which one idea naturally introduces another.
>
> (p. 1)

Self-observation led Hume to the conviction that there were three associating qualities: resemblance, contiguity in time or place, and cause and effect. Others held that anything but contiguity was too subjective.

Although sober and close to everyday experience – especially in comparison with the romantic German system builders – this tradition provided a rather narrow and mechanistic foundation for psychology. Hence the enthusiasm with which the French psychologist Alfred Binet (1892) greeted the publication of Frédéric Paulhan's *L'activité mentale et les éléments de l'esprit* (1889). The sterile doctrine of associationism had finally been overcome. "Paulhan has considerably reduced the part attributed to the association of ideas, and shown that these associations are only workmen in the service of the higher influences that direct them" (p. 352). Paulhan was the philosophical spokesman for a movement of vast proportions which, in its clinical interests, concerned itself primarily with what was known at the time as hysteria and with the therapeutic and experimental tool of hypnosis. Closely associated with these was the passionate popular interest in the phenomena of spiritualism, which had spawned both parlor games and conscientious investigating bodies. (The London Society of Psychical Research and its American counterpart were both formed in the early 1880s.)

The old philosophical associationism was transformed into the experimental and mystical movement known as "dissociationism" – by no means as opposed to the first as the name might imply. Dissociationism accepted the notion that ideas and images tend to combine into complexes, but conceptualized the process very differently. Rejecting (forever) the concept of mental Newtonian forces, they held that every aggregation of ideas and images possessed, in some measure or other, its *own personality*. The guiding image for this was the phenomenon of multiple personality, for which there was already a hundred-year-old therapeutic tradition, going back to Mesmer, Puységur, Despine, Azam, and the people Janet calls the "French alienists." In the most spectacular of their cases, such as Despine's Estelle (the late 1830s) and Azam's Félida X (principally during the 1860s), a second "personality" emerged which was free of the neurotic symptoms of the first. Janet (1907) calls Félida "the educator of Taine and Ribot," without whom "it is not certain that there would be a professorship of psychology at the Collège de France" (his own chair; p. 78).

Dissociationism replaced Newtonian causality with a principle of teleology, summarized in Paulhan's book (1889) by three laws:

1. The Law of Systematic Association. "Every psychic fact tends to enter into partnership with and to give rise to psychic facts which can harmonize and cooperate with itself toward a common goal or toward compatible goals which can comprise a system." (p. 88)

2. The Law of Inhibition. "Every psychic phenomenon tends to impede the manifestation and development of or to banish from sight the psychic phenomena which it cannot assimilate according to the law of systematic association, that is to say the phenomena which it cannot assimilate in the interests of a common goal." (p. 221)

3. The Law of Contrast. "A psychic state tends to be accompanied (simultaneous contrast) or followed (successive contrast) by a state which opposes it or which at least in some respects is its contrary." (p. 315f.)

More simply expressed, the first law describes how the subpersonalities of multiple personality arise; the second describes their mutual animosity; and the third their alternating or simultaneous appearance in the consciousness and behavior of the individual.

Interest in *dédoublement de la personnalité* has risen and fallen with time. Its greatest period of scientific and popular favor, however, was the last two decades of the nineteenth century, between the year (1882) Jean-Martin Charcot convinced the French Academy of Science that hypnosis was not beneath its dignity as an object and tool for research, and the year (1900) Sigmund Freud revealed psychoanalysis to the world in his book, *The Interpretation of Dreams*. During this time, the main tool of psychological research and therapy was hypnosis; the main psychological phenomenon of interest was somnambulism, of which multiple personality and spiritualism were varieties; and the main psychological disorder was hysteria. Hypnosis, hysteria, and spiritualism are all variants of somnambulism, which, in psychological parlance at the turn of the century, referred to *any* rather complex act performed while asleep, in trance, or in some other "altered state of consciousness" – to use the expression in vogue today.

Dissociationism was never "disproven." It merely fell out of favor for a few decades because the sexual stages of psychoanalysis and the reflex arc of behaviorism were found to be sufficiently satisfying models by a sufficiently large number of psychologists. Yet, the heuristic image of multiple personality never disappeared entirely from psychological discussion. People such as Pierre Janet, Morton Prince of Boston, and the Harvard psychologist, William McDougall – not to mention Jung – continued to favor it during the decades of its eclipse. Since the late 1950s, dissociation psychology has re-emerged in several areas of investigation: research in hypnosis (Frankel, 1976; Gill and Brenman, 1959; E. Hilgard, 1977; J. Hilgard, 1970); the anthropological study of altered states of consciousness (Bourguignon, 1965, 1968, 1973, 1974, 1976; Crapanzano, 1973; Crapanzano and Garrison, 1977; Figge, 1972, 1973a, 1973b; Goodman, Henny, and Pressel, 1974); and the psychological study of altered states in which new theories about psychic complexes are being developed, sometimes in apparent ignorance of the older ones (Fischer, 1970; Goodwin, Powell, Bremer, Heine, and Stern, 1969; Grof, 1977; Leuner, 1962; Overton, 1968). In addition there have been many reports of cases of multiple personality in recent years, the number of published reports being a rough index of the scientific acceptability of multiple personality as heuristic image. Finally, popular interest in spiritualism of all kinds runs very high again today, as it did then. Just as the dissociationism of a hundred years ago appeared to be a recovery from the two centuries in which scientific zeal had attempted to force the facts of our psychic life into the Procrustean bed of Newtonian mechanics, so the recent rise of dissociationism may be a response to several decades of psychoanalytic and behavioristic reductionism.

As an alternative to the associationists' Newtonian model, dissociation psychology recommended itself for at least three reasons. First, it replaced the impersonal, atomic level mechanisms more appropriate to psychics and astrology with a kind of holistic personalism, which appears more adequate for understanding the experience and behavior of human individuals. Second, it seemed even more "scientific" in that it relied on what seemed to be pure observation; for even the untrained observer could see that two or more trains of thought may run simultaneously (as in conversing while driving a car). But a compelling adjunct to this was the fact that there exist lower life forms, well-known in biology, in which larger individuals are comprised of colonies of simpler individuals. Many dissociationists gave prominent mention to this fact; Sidis and Goodhart (1904) provide a whole chapter, with pictures. The third advantage of dissociationism is that it formed a natural basis for understanding pathology. A generally accepted theory of psychopathology had not yet been advanced, particularly not one involving the neuroses. The image of multiple personality filled this void by speaking of the degree of amnesia separating one stream of images from another. Hysteria appeared to be understood for the first time; perhaps other psychological disturbances could be seen as variants on hysteria.

Janet: dissociation and exhaustion

Pierre Janet wrote the definitive work in the field of dissociation psychology, *L'automatisme psychologique* (1889, his doctoral thesis in philosophy, completed before he began work on his medical degree). In the book he carefully articulates a description of hysteria on the basis of several case histories. One of the most important of these is that of Lucie, a twenty-year-old woman who had had convulsions in her early childhood and attacks of blindness around the age of nine. When Janet first saw her, she suffered from hysterical crises of five hours' duration, marked by convulsions and periods of rigid posturing in which she appeared horror-struck with her unseeing eyes fixed on the curtains of the room. She also had periods of somnambulism in which she would be talkative, have an appetite and eat, or do her bookkeeping. While bookkeeping, she would be able to see only the ledger book and its figures, remaining oblivious to all other stimuli. She could keep books only in her somnambulic state.

Through hypnosis, Janet discovered three states of consciousness, labeled Lucie 1, Lucie 2, and Lucie 3. Lucie 1 depended almost entirely on the visual sense, although her visual field was considerably smaller than normal; she was totally anaesthetic over her entire body. Lucie 2 was dependent primarily upon the tactile sense and fairly blind, though her hearing was somewhat better than that of Lucie 1. Lucie 2 was the one who assumed the posture of terror. Lucie 3, attainable only after a great deal of intense hypnotic induction, had both tactility and vision, and more completely than either of the other two states. Lucie 3 remembered the trauma at age nine which appears to have conditioned at least the attitudes of terror. She had been frightened by some men who had hidden behind a curtain. The other two personalities did not remember this event. To put the conclusions of *L'automatisme* simply, Lucie 1 and Lucie 2 both suffered from a restriction of their fields of consciousness. These two restricted fields, furthermore, did not overlap, either in sensation or in memory. Thus the two states were neatly dissociated. Lucie 3 is their integration. When her memories were made available to the other two states, Lucie's hysterical condition was cured.

The evidence of several such cases inclined Janet to place heavy emphasis on the fixed idea: for example, that men will be hiding behind curtains to do Lucie harm.

> To have one's body in the posture of terror is to feel the emotion of terror; and if this posture is determined by a subconscious idea, the patient will have the emotion alone in his consciousness without knowing why he feels this way. "I'm afraid and I don't know why," Lucie can say at the beginning of her crisis when her eyes take on a wild look and her arms make gestures of terror. *The unconscious is having its dream; it sees the men behind the curtain and puts the body in a posture of terror.*
>
> (p. 409, emphasis added)

As the dissociated idea seemed to hold the secret of hysteria, Janet undertook a series of studies on the characteristics and functions of the fixed ideas of his patients. Several of these papers, collected in the first volume of *Névroses et idées fixes* (1898), led to the conclusion that hysteria is unique among the neuroses in its propensity for complete and enduring dissociation. Consequently a new theory of psychopathology was required and appeared in 1903 as the two-volume work, *Les obsessions et la psychasthénie*.

The patients Marcelle (Janet, 1891) and Justine (Janet, 1894) both appeared to change their pathology under the influence of Janet's treatment. Both manifested distinguishable states of consciousness (like the dissociation in hysteria), and in both cases the somnambulic state could be duplicated by hypnosis (again like hysteria). But in both cases, when the fixed ideas were made conscious, they did not become integrated with the dominant personality (as in the cure for hysteria); rather both patients became obsessive. Their fixed ideas persisted as absurd images and fears. But instead of being completely dissociated, they were present in consciousness and appreciated as absurd though they could not be managed. Janet states:

> These obsessions have, at least in the present case, their origins in a very deep state; in this state, they would be clear and affirmative and have the form of fixed ideas and hallucinations. But now the state which gave them birth has disappeared and they subsist half effaced but tenacious and enter into conflict with consciousness and common sense.
>
> (1894, p. 31)

Neurosis can therefore not be identical with dissociation, nor can the severity of neurosis be an index of the degree of dissociation. For the severe obsessive suffers no less than the severe hysteric, although his or her dissociation is less complete. Furthermore, Marcelle also manifested "abulia." Given the task of picking up an object from the table before her, she would hesitate 1 to 2 minutes before picking up her own crocheting needle or 10 to 12 minutes before picking up Janet's pencil. With practice, she could manage to pick up the pencil as "quickly" as the needle, though when presented with a new object, she had the same difficulties all over again. (Janet apparently did not recognize the probable importance of "transference" issues in such cases.) But when *distracted*, she could pick up any such object without hesitation. Janet concluded from this that the neurotic's voluntary (conscious) functions are weak. The act of picking up a pencil proceeds smoothly when it is performed "automatically" (unconsciously) or when it has been laboriously integrated into consciousness by practice. The difficulties begin when the subject has to *voluntarily* decide upon a *new* action and then to carry it out. What is lacking to Marcelle in her abulia is the "mental synthesis" required to represent to herself the act of picking up the pencil (Janet, 1894). ("Mental synthesis" is the composite whole made up of the objects comprising the conscious field as well as the notion of an ego capable of acting upon those objects.)

Examination of the fixed ideas, therefore, brought Janet to the conclusion that their presence and activity is independent of the phenomenon of dissociation. Sometimes the patient's symptoms went beyond the fixed ideas (such as Marcelle's abulia), and sometimes fixed ideas may be replaced by others without essential change in the patient's condition (such as Justine's panic fear of cholera giving way to an hilarity over the comic Chinese military general, "Cho-lé-ra"). The fixed idea, Janet concluded, is a secondary symptom of mental weakness. Neurosis is this weakness – generally a constitutional weakness which develops into neurosis when the individual "exhausts" himself with overwork, emotional shocks, or illness (Janet, 1930). In hysteria the mental synthesis is weakened so that whole blocks of functions become dissociated (e.g., paralysis and anaesthesia of an arm). In abulia it is weakened so that decisions cannot be reached or acted upon. In an obsession it is weakened so that fixed ideas cannot be criticized or integrated.

Consequently, by the turn of the century, the dominant theme in Janet's works was that of exhaustion (*épuisement*) or of lowering the mental level (*abaissement*). This theme had at least four advantages. First, it did not conflict with the well-documented phenomena of dissociation (in all degrees from normal to severely disturbed). Second, it was a superior principle on which to base a psychopathology, for all neurotics suffered from exhaustion although not all were abnormally dissociated. Third, the theory did not excuse the psychologist from studying each patient separately and appreciating his individuality. "For those who, like me, claim not to understand very well the general theories of fixed ideas, each patient is interesting in himself and demands to be analyzed in isolation" (1898, p. xiv). Fourth, and probably most important, the theory of exhaustion was "objective" in two senses. It is objectively verifiable in its effects (feelings of fatigue, uncompleted actions, etc.), and it is a universal principle – quite unlike a fixed idea – the content of which is peculiar to the individual. In contrast, a dissociation theory based on the fixed idea as identifier presents the psychologist with a great difficulty. Understanding occurs when generals (concepts) are applied to particulars (individuals), but fixed ideas are always particular.

Freud: dissociation and causality

Freud's roots in French dissociationism are indisputable. In 1885–1886, he spent some months listening to Charcot's lectures in Paris at the Salpêtrière. Shortly thereafter, he published German translations of two books of the Nancy hypnotist and outspoken critic of the Paris school, Hippolyte Bernheim. He was also rebuffed in Vienna for his too enthusiastic report on the work of Charcot. In 1895, Breuer and Freud made the researches of Binet and the brothers Janet (Pierre and Jules) the starting point in their *Studies on Hysteria*:

> We have become convinced that the splitting of consciousness which is so striking in the well-known classical cases under the form of *le dédoublement de la personnalité* is present to a rudimentary degree in every hysteria, and that a tendency to such a dissociation, and with it the emergence of abnormal states of consciousness . . . is the basic phenomenon of this neurosis. In these views we concur with Binet and the two Janets, though we have had no experience of the remarkable findings they have made on anaesthetic patients.
>
> (p. 12)

Already in 1895, however, Freud was diverging in a major way from the thinking of Janet. In place of Janet's skepticism about the diagnostic value of the fixed idea, Freud made the assumption that it *defined* the dissociation. For example, in Breuer's paradigmatic case, Anna O suffered from paralysis of the right arm, amnesia for her mother tongue, German, and the obsessive image (fixed idea) of a black snake. Aside from the hallucinatory image, these symptoms represent losses of function; the functions of speaking German and exercising the right arm have been dissociated from the ego. The only thing which remains as an *addition* to consciousness is the unassimilated image of the black snake. As the "talking cure" moved backward through the events of Anna's life, it reached the moment when she sat beside her father's sickbed with her right arm "asleep," as it hooked over the back of the chair.

> She fell into a waking dream and saw a black snake coming towards the sick man from the wall to bite him. . . . She tried to keep the snake off, but it was as though she was paralyzed [particularly the right arm]. . . . When the snake vanished, in her terror she tried to pray. But language failed her . . . till at last she thought of some children's verses in English.
>
> (p. 38f.)

The hallucination of the snake is the sole memory of an event which Anna has unconsciously banished from memory. The paralysis and amnesia for German are linked to this fixed idea as important elements of the incident in which the hallucination first occurred. The symptoms are a vestige, a "reminiscence" of an event dissociated from consciousness. The cause for the whole procedure is the emotional shock which brought it on.

Janet had been aware that such traumatic events could occasion an hysterical condition and had published several cases demonstrating it. What distinguished Freud's approach was his insistence on a necessary link whereby the content of the fixed idea explained the dissociation. This left a new problem – how to explain the patient's fascination with this *particular* fixed idea. The cases discussed in *Studies on Hysteria* all seem to support the hypothesis that the fixed ideas were "reminiscences" of the traumatic event which caused the dissociation. Causality became for Freud an Archimedean point outside the morass of neurotic thinking and behavior. By 1895 Janet had already concluded that traumata were not the only causes of hysteria. He was beginning to gravitate to the exhaustion theory as *his* Archimedean point. In contrast, Freud *assumed* the existence of traumata and even "found" them in cases where he later had to admit they could not have been. When he could no longer maintain the trauma theory, he proposed a theory of sexual stages. In so doing, he retained the fixed idea as definitive of the patient's neurosis, but abandoned the image of multiple personality. The discontinuity between the idiosyncratic fixed idea and the universal pattern of infantile sexuality is retained in the manifest/latent doctrine: the fixed idea (image, symptom) is always manifest, while its meaning (in the events of infantile life) is always latent.

Certain passages from his dream book (1900) and letters (cf. Roazen, 1976) show that Freud was not wholly antipathetic to dissociationism. But according to Stepansky (1977), Freud accepted the formulation, "we concur with Binet and the two Janets . . ." only at Breuer's insistence (pp. 28ff., 37). Once the sexual theory was established, dissociation theory became superfluous. Only "reminiscences" remained in the form of the

notion of intrapsychic conflict and the tripartite divisions of the topo-
graphical and dynamic theories.

Freud's insistence on the sexual theory may have included a large
component of good public relations. It lent the image of psychoanalysis a
distinct form as the image of multiple personality had done for dissociationism, and it had certain strengths where the other was weak. For
example, it claimed physiological foundation in the reflex arc – which,
according to Miller, Galanter, and Pribram (1960, p. 46) was the only way
to be "scientific" in psychology until the 1940s – and in the notion of
dammed-up sexuality. Freud's statement to Jung (Jung, 1961, p. 150) that
the sexual doctrine was to be a bulwark "against the black tide of occultism" seems to have been justified in that psychoanalysis has never been
weakened by the spiritualistic taint which clung to the image of multiple
personality. This may be one reason "Freud and his disciples have
abstained from any attempt to reconcile the facts of multiple personality
with the Freudian psychology" (McDougall, 1926, p. 523). Finally, Freud's
method of listening to everything the patient has to say (even the apparent
nonsense which billows forth in "free association"), was a kind of solution
to the dilemma which the hypnotists had, wondering whether and when
they should believe the patient (cf. Prince, 1929; Sidis, 1902). According to
Freud, everything is to be listened to and yet everything is more or less
deceptive, for "manifest" symptoms are a compromise with "latent" truth.
Certainty comes from the doctrine of interpretation.

In reality, Breuer's and Freud's tribute to French dissociationism simultaneously announced its decline. The image of multiple personality was
important to them only because it seemed to explain the effects of "traumata." In taking this approach, they assumed that the "normal" psyche
was unified and that "dissociation" is synonymous with "pathology" – all
very much in contrast with the school of dissociationism, on behalf of
which Morton Prince (1914) argues:

> The dissociated and multiple personalities are not novel and freak
> phenomena, but are only exaggerations of the normal and due to
> exaggerations of normal processes, and it is for this reason that
> they are of interest and importance. For, being exaggerations, they
> accentuate and bring out into high relief certain tendencies and
> functional mechanisms which belong to normal conditions and
> they differentiate mental processes one from another, which
> normally are not so easily recognized.
>
> (p. 562)

Secondly, Breuer and Freud imposed a causal schema upon dissociationism's essentially teleological image of complex formation. But more
importantly than this, the development of Freud's thought generated a

new image of the psyche. In dispersing the alleged causal moment over the several years of infantile sexual development, Freud replaced a spatial metaphor (the "co-conscious" subpersonalities of dissociationism) with a temporal metaphor (the sexual stages).

Jung: dissociation and the archetypes

The dissociationism of a hundred years ago, under the leadership of Pierre Janet, is what I refer to as Jung's French heritage. When we keep it in focus, Jung's career very much deserves the label he liked to give it, Complex Psychology, and agrees with his sense of history (Jung, 1935a): "My own course of development was influenced primarily by the French school and later by Wundt's psychology. Later, in 1906, I made contact with Freud, only to part company with him in 1913" (par. 1737). Even Jungians have read this with skepticism. It sounds too much like an attempt to diminish Freud's role in Jung's development, to deny that he was ever (outside of Freud's imagination) the crown prince of psychoanalysis. Similarly his remark in the foreword to the second Swiss edition (1924) of *Symbols of Transformation* (1911), "my respected and fatherly friend, the late Théodore Flournoy," may be read as an attempt to declare that he had never been Freud's "son," having always been Flournoy's. However, Barbara Hannah (1976) tells us that Jung often travelled to Geneva to visit Flournoy during the years immediately after his break with Freud and that he found his French-speaking countryman a much more compatible conversationalist (p. 98).

Furthermore, two of Jung's important early publications (1902, 1911) were modelled on or organized around works of Flournoy. That the first of these (*On the Psychology and Pathology of So-Called Occult Phenomena*) is often dismissed with a scratch of the head reveals how little the historical situation at the turn of the century is appreciated. Psychology and spiritualism were intertwined. Societies for psychical research were applying dissociation theories to parapsychology. Charcot had studied the phenomena of faith cures at Lourdes. Janet (1898) had integrated parapsychological phenomena in his study of dissociation and had depicted psychotherapy as having gradually differentiated itself from religious practices and beliefs (1919). Furthermore, the model for Jung's dissertation was Flournoy's controversial book, *From India to the Planet Mars*, a study of the Geneva medium, Hélène Smith, who claimed to relive former lives while in trance: one as a queen in fifteenth-century India and the other as an important lady on Mars.

This book, more than any other, claimed the phenomena of spiritualism as legitimate territory for effective psychological research. Flournoy, in a five-year-long virtuoso performance as psychologist and detective, had managed to track down all the extravagant claims of the medium and demonstrate their probable origins in cryptomnesias. Furthermore, by studying the content of Mlle Smith's several "romances," Flournoy determined that Indian, Martian, Arabian, and European "incarnations" were all variations on a single theme, guided by the same complex. Although Jung's *Occult Phenomena* diverges from Janetian skepticism over the content of the fixed ideas, it is very much in harmony with Flournoy's brand of dissociationism, and refers to *India to Mars* several times. Apparently lacking the time or patience to reveal a comprehensive system of cryptomnesias in his medium, Fräulein SW, Jung strenuously asserts the importance of this unconscious device and includes, quite gratuitously, a passage from Nietzsche's *Zarathustra* side by side with an almost identical passage from Kerner's *Blätter aus Prevorst*. It is a stunning discovery of cryptomnesia in a great writer, but has little directly to do with Fräulein SW, in whom Jung detected influence from Kerner's more famous work, *The Seeress of Prevorst*.

The heart of Jung's thesis, however, is that SW's mediumistic fantasies played an important function in the girl's adolescent development. The semisomnambulic figure of Ivenes appeared to be her "healthy personality" (a little like Félida X's "number two"), a kind of trial project for what she might become in twenty years' time. "One cannot say that she deludes herself onto the higher state, rather she dreams herself into it." This recognition of a teleological component in fantasy, while foreign to Freud, had indeed been recognized by Paulhan, Janet, and Flournoy. However, Jung went further than they dared (or wanted) to go, in speculating that his own case may not have been unique, and that the classic cases of multiple personality ought to be reinterpreted in its light.

> It is therefore conceivable that the phenomena of double consciousness are simply new character formations, or attempts of the future personality to break through. . . . In view of the difficulties that oppose the future character, the somnambulisms have an eminently teleological significance, in that they give the individual who would otherwise inevitably succumb, the means of victory.
>
> (par. 136)

After his high-spirited dissertation, Jung immersed himself in a prolonged empirical study of the fixed ideas, or complexes, as he preferred to call them. The great mass of data assembled in the first part of his *Experimental Researches*, "Studies in Word Association" (1906) demonstrated that the component memories, ideas, and images of a complex, all sharing a distinct emotional tone, could be identified by such objective means as measuring the time between administration of a stimulus word and the subject's response. Jung believed and Freud seems to have accepted that these studies provided "empirical demonstration" of the truth of psychoanalytic theory, but the careful reader discovers only the loosest connection between these articles and the contemporary works of Freud. What the studies do demonstrate is that each individual's psychic life arranges itself into an idiosyncratic group of complexes, largely reflective of significant events and periods of his life. The emotional "tone" of a complex invariably brings about hesitations and "mistakes" in the style of what Freud called "the psychopathology of everyday life." But there is nothing to indicate that sexuality determines all complexes or lurks "latently" behind the "manifest" responses of the patient. Rather, Jung takes the responses quite literally. The complexes do, very often, conceal closely guarded secrets, but the association experiment reveals them directly without need for such psychoanalytic interpretive doctrines as condensation, displacement, and the like. The image guiding Jung's thought is that of multiple, simultaneously active, subpersonalities. Jung is thinking spatially (centers of aggregation) while Freud thinks temporally (sexual stages), teleologically rather than causally.

The same may be said for the monograph on schizophrenia, published the following year (1907), where Jung demonstrates in great detail that the word-salad of a hopelessly deteriorated woman makes sense, being organized by complexes. In interpreting the material, he again employs the notion, shared by Flournoy and Freud, that all fantasies are meaningful and bear close investigation of their content, but eschews the rigorous detective work characteristic of psychoanalysis. He does allude to the manifest/latent theory of Freud: "We see only the dream-image but not the thought-complex behind it" (par. 256). But he does not at all mean by this phrase what Freud means by the distinction dream image/unconscious thought. Rather Jung's meaning is much closer to the Janet of *L'automatisme*, where conscious, discursive thinking is opposed to the stereotypy of the subconscious "automatism." The passage in Jung (1907) continues:

> the patient takes her dream products as real and claims that they are reality. She acts just as we do in dreams, when we are no longer capable of distinguishing between logical and analogical connections; . . . she speaks as if she were still in the dream, *she is involved in the automatic machinery*, with the result that all logical reproduction naturally ceases.
>
> (par. 256, emphasis added)

This language from the strict dissociationist Janet may be found side by side with the Janetian language of *Obsessions* (1903): exhaustion, the lowering of psychological tension (*abaissement*), sentiments of incompleteness, and so on.

The abundance of such evidence inclines me to suspect that in 1907 Jung was reading Freud with Janetian, or French dissociationist, eyes. The suspicion is supported by the argument of the first chapter of the book, where Jung depicts Freud as having *continued* the work of Janet and the French school. French psychology determined the dissociable nature of the psyche; Freud's contribution was to recognize the *purpose* (!) of dissociation, namely "to find out what is not available in reality" (par. 60–71). Here, Jung refers to Freud's writing in *Studies on Hysteria* (1895), when Freud had not yet distinguished himself decisively from French dissociationism. The section contains no references to later works of Freud.

Jung's next major publication was the monumental and labyrinthine *Symbols of Transformation* (1911) which resulted in his break with Freud. The precipitating reason for the break appears to be that, through the mythological preoccupations of the book, Jung finally and irrevocably talked himself out of the psychoanalytic doctrine of incest. Before the crucial second (and last) installment of the book appeared, Jung had already accepted an invitation from Fordham University in New York to give a series of lectures. He used these (1912) to redefine his relationship to psychoanalysis. He argues that oedipal issues in themselves cannot account for neurosis; for everyone has an oedipus complex, yet not everyone is neurotic. Only those *predisposed* to neurosis run aground on the oedipal shoals. "Drawing back from certain tasks cannot be explained by saying that man prefers the incestuous relationship, rather he falls back into it because he shuns exertion" (par. 470). Neurosis is due to an innate sensitiveness or weakness (par. 390–401). Jung becomes an exponent of Janet's theory of psychic exhaustion. Having rejected the causal, temporal foundations of psychoanalysis, he falls back on the logic of the image which has guided him all along.

In succeeding years, Jung regularly reminds his audience of the complex (dissociation) theory. He writes (1924): "The psychic double is a commoner phenomenon than one would expect, although it seldom reaches a degree of intensity that would entitle one to speak of a 'double personality'" (par. 227); he recommends (1939) the writings of Janet, Flournoy, Prince, and others so that his readers will understand the image of multiple personality and the premises on which he is working (par. 490); he traces (1951b) his own psychological heritage from Paracelsus through Mesmer, Charcot, Janet, and Freud (par. 231); and he cites (1954) cases of double personality, *automatisme ambulatoire*, and the researches of Janet to illustrate what the "complexes" are (par. 383). He gives the fullest description of a complex in his Tavistock Lectures (1935b):

Complexes are autonomous groups of associations that have a tendency to move by themselves, to live their own life apart from our intentions. I hold that our personal unconscious as well as the collective unconscious, consists of an indefinite, because unknown, number of complexes or fragment personalities.

(par. 151)

In the same lecture, Jung enumerates the following characteristics of a complex: (1) it has a sort of body with its own physiology so that it can upset the stomach, breathing, heart; (2) it has its own will power and intentions so that it can disturb a train of thought or a course of action just as another human being can do; (3) it is in principle no different from the ego which is itself a complex; (4) it becomes dramatized in our dreams, poetry, and drama; (5) it becomes visible and audible in hallucinations; and (6) it completely victimizes the personality in insanity.

Finally, the doctrine of the archetypes appears in Jung's work as the completion of the complex theory, its first indications appearing already in 1911. Flournoy had published a fifteen-page pamphlet of dreams and visions from a "Miss Frank Miller," an American student, who had added her own cursory detective work, tracking the origins of the fantasies back to her own memories – somewhat in the style of Flournoy's *India to Mars*. Jung's (1911) interpretation of the pamphlet is a five-hundred-page journey through world mythology which, it might be said, turns Flournoy "on his head." Synopsis of the central argument may be given without reference to anything foreign to the complex theory as found in the word association studies. Led by Miss Miller's emotionally charged associations, Jung investigates *Cyrano de Bergerac* and *The Song of Hiawatha* (among other sources), to learn more about the dreamer's complex, which shows a propensity for one romantic death after another and, finally, as the fantasy figure, Chiwantopel, is understood to have departed for "ten thousand moons," until he and the one woman in all creation who can appreciate him (Miss Miller) will finally meet. In Jung's view, this complex was the one psychic factor which might have been able to pull Miss Miller out of her dreamy adolescence and into effective contact with the world. Its emphatic death means that it was about to sink so far from consciousness that schizophrenia could be the only result. Jung's diagnosis proved correct, and Miss Miller's American psychiatrist wrote to say that personal acquaintance with his patient had not taught him more about her than had Jung's book (Jung, 1911, p. xxviii).

But Jung's method of analysis goes beyond a purely French-school complex theory. He did not limit himself to the associative material mentioned by the dreamer herself, but concerned himself with mythological and literary parallels of which she may have been entirely ignorant. This is the beginning of the conceptualization which eventually acquires the name "archetype" (Jung, 1919).

There are at least six partly complementary, partly contradictory, meanings of *archetype* in Jung's writings. In the first place, used as a substantive, archetype properly refers to the hypothesized "source" of typical images. It is not itself an object of experience, but is the ultimate form-giving principle in human experience. Although he frequently deplores the misunderstandings by which readers have come to believe that archetypes are inborn images, in fact Jung himself contributes to this confusion by using archetype in a second sense to refer to typical images, themselves. Thus, for instance, he writes of the "mother archetype," the "child archetype," or the "trickster archetype" in which mythological patterns are cited in order to elucidate the psychology of an individual.

In a third sense, archetype may be called the teleological component in instinct. Jung (1919) provides the following parallel definitions:

> Instincts are typical modes of action, and wherever we meet with uniform and regularly recurring modes of action and reaction we are dealing with instinct, no matter whether it is associated with a conscious motive or not.
>
> (par. 273)

> Archetypes are typical modes of apprehension, and wherever we meet with uniform and regularly recurring modes of apprehension we are dealing with an archetype, no matter whether its mythological character is recognized or not.
>
> (par. 280)

Fourth, the archetype may be discussed as a dynamic/structural component of the psyche, somewhat analogously as Freud speaks of id, ego, and superego. In this vein, Jung speaks of precisely five "archetypes": ego, persona, shadow, anima or animus, and self. Each has its own function within the psyche as a whole: discrimination and conscious making (ego); adaptation to the social world (persona); dissociation and integration of the repressed (shadow); encounter with and transformation of the "other," both without and within, both fleshly and spiritual (anima or animus); guidance of psychological development toward "wholeness" or "individuation" (self) (Jung, 1951a, pp. 3–35).

Fifth, the archetypal may designate a quality of experience, alternatively described as powerful, fascinating, or "numinous." Homans (1979) relies heavily on this meaning of archetype in his Kohutian interpretation of Jung.

Finally, a sixth meaning of archetype may be discovered insofar as the archetype is a complex, but a typical one. I refer primarily to this meaning in discussing the French roots of Jung's split with Freud. Because he had discerned something typical in Miss Miller's romantic hero complex, Jung was emboldened to explicate it through two of his own favorite literary works, Goethe's *Faust* and Nietzsche's *Zarathustra*. Having read these classics in his youth, Jung recognized in each of them a documentation of the experience of having a second personality, ageless, remote from the everyday world, but close to nature. He called this his "No. 2" personality, and recognized Faust as Goethe's "No. 2" and Zarathustra as Nietzsche's "No. 2" (Jung, 1961, p. 102). Thus it is apparent why Faust and Zarathustra play such important roles in the interpretation of the Miller fantasies. Christian de Neuvillette (from *Cyrano*) and Chiwantopel are two of the symbols by which Miller's "No. 2" shows himself; and Jung "dreams himself into" her mentality (to use the language of Jung, 1902) by repeated appeal to the two paradigms for his own "No. 2."

What appears here, *in nuce*, is an extension of dissociationism to make possible a new theoretical construct and a new approach to therapy. Janet's exhaustion theory had enabled him to retain his physician's persona and "apply" treatments, such as hypnotic alterations of the patient's imagery and tasks to help recover memories.

> My treatment of the patient was something more than a suggestion; it was an excitation. . . . I demand from Irène attention and efforts; I insist that she shall have an increasingly clear consciousness of her feelings. All these things are means for enhancing the nervous and mental tension, for obtaining, if you like to phrase it in that way, the functioning of the higher centers. . . . I often had to scold her, to discover the directions in which she was impressionable, to shake her morally in various ways, in order to "buck her up" to make her rediscover memories and actions.
> (Janet, 1919, p. 848, citing an article of his own from 1904)

Freud's theory of sexual stages leads to an entirely different model. Despite the fact that most psychoanalysts have first been trained as physicians, the theory and treatment process of interpretation require that the analyst relinquish the persona of the physician as detached agent and respond to the ongoing drama of relationship between analyst and analysand (transference/countertransference). The relationship becomes a "transference neurosis" to be conquered by aiding the analysand in getting "insight" into the "repetition compulsion." The analyst, however, must never lose his or her position as analyst/interpreter. The analyst straddles the fence of involvement, accepting the analysand's projections (one foot inside the relationship) but relentlessly interpreting them (one foot outside the relationship).

Jung relinquishes his physician's persona even more radically than does Freud. Indeed, interpretation is no longer even of primary importance, particularly the kind of interpretation which reduces phenomena to their alleged causes.

In the transference all kinds of infantile fantasies are projected. They must be cauterized, i.e., resolved by reductive analysis, and this is generally known as "resolving the transference." Thereby the energy is again released from an unserviceable form, and again we are faced with the problem of disposability. Once more we shall put our trust in nature, hoping that, even before it is sought, an object will have been chosen which will provide a favourable gradient.

(Jung, 1917, par. 96)

This passage, taken from another of Jung's transition essays, when he was trying to define himself in contrast to Freud and Adler, articulates what might be called a dual theory of interpretation. "Reductive interpretation" in the style of Freud or Adler is to be used to break through the vicious circle of the neurosis. After this, the workings of "nature" are to be respected, and the analyst "interprets" only in the sense of commenting on and helping to make conscious a process already moving toward maturity or "individuation." Even "the resistance" is "part of nature" and to be "respected." Jung (1937) describes one spectacular and successful case in which he understood and was able to interpret nothing at all of the patient's dreams. In his *Psychology of the Transference* (1946), he interprets a series of alchemical woodcuts in which a queen and king (the analyst's anima and the analysand's animus) *dissolve together* in the alchemical bath. This is the symbolic equivalent of his "dreaming himself into" Miss Miller's incipient schizophrenia.

Whereas the dissociation theory of the French school described purely idiosyncratic splitting, Jung begins to argue in *Symbols of Transformation* (1911) that there are typically human patterns discernible in these splits: thus the employment of Goethe's *Faust* as a bridge between Miss Miller's "No. 2" and his own "No. 2." Jung (1911) cites a letter of the historian Jacob Burckhardt to a student:

What you are destined to discover in *Faust*, you will have to discover intuitively. . . . *Faust* is a genuine myth, i.e., a great pri-mordial image, in which every man has to discover his own being and destiny in his own way.

(p. 32, n. 45)

Just as every person discovers his own being in the primordial image (later called archetype) so the analyst discovers the being of the analysand – that is, a partially lived possibility in himself.

The same may be said of the figure of Zarathustra in Nietzsche's work, but Jung had special hopes for this archetypal figure. He tells us in his seminar on *Zarathustra* (1934–1939) that he had studied Nietzsche's book carefully while on military duty in World War I, hoping to find evidence for what an "autonomous complex" of such central importance could do. Coming after this "Nekyia" or undersea journey, as he calls it (or his "creative illness" as Ellenberger, 1968, calls it) this study of *Zarathustra* had profound personal meaning for Jung. But more than that, it constitutes his own search for a *Kernkomplex*, as ten years earlier Freud (Freud and Jung, 1908) had described his metapsychological search for an Archimedean point by which the multitude of individuals could be understood against a universal pattern.

Conclusion

The three metapsychologies (oedipal, archetypal, and economic) epitomize relations between psychoanalysis, analytical psychology, and psychological analysis. All three know something about the patient in advance: Freud that psychosexual development is disturbed; Janet that there is something wrong with the availability and tension of psychic energy; and Jung that a human pattern will manifest itself which at some time or other has been delineated in mythology. All three approaches appeal, therefore, to some aspect of the universally human in order to understand the individual. But whereas Janet's "metapsychology" enables him to retain his physician's persona and treat the patient as a patient, Jung follows Freud in relinquishing that persona in order to strike a partnership with the client whereby the two jointly investigate the analysand's psyche. On the other hand, Freud's metapsychology necessitates discarding everything the client dreams and says as mere husk, concealing the sexual *Kernkomplex*, while Jung follows Janet in believing the analysand and accepting the client's world view as the primary given. Regarding the complexes, tendencies, or fixed ideas, Janet abandons their contents, considering only the economics of their arousal and discharge while Jung follows Freud in devoting nearly all of his attention to the investigation and analysis of these contents. On the other hand, Freud's metapsychology admits of only one conflict pattern (the oedipal) and only one stereotyped splitting (conscious/unconscious/preconscious censor or ego/id/super-ego) whereas Jung and Janet agree that each psyche splits in its own idiosyncratic manner.

The doctrine of the archetypes enables Jung to walk this narrow ridge, availing himself of the advantages of both schools. First of all, it appeals to the universally human ("collective") to attain interpretative distance from the individual. Second, because it can only be employed *upon* psychic contents, it leaves the analyst entirely at the service of the analysand. The analyst can only follow or accompany the analysand into the wilderness of the latter's psyche. Third, because the number and configuration of the archetypes has been deliberately left indefinite, the doctrine enables a constantly shifting flexibility whereby any dissociated condition may be explicated by models continuously in a state of redefinition. Fourth, as a consequence of this flexibility, the psychologist who thinks archetypally can afford to take the analysand at his word and in his own world, as there is no necessity to translate the "manifest" into some therapeutic formulation of the "latent." Fifth, Jung remains closer to the "French school" than even Janet, as Janet forsakes the uniqueness of the fixed idea in order to speak of its economics.

Finally, the doctrine of the archetypes formulates the means and method by which the analyst relates "analytically" to the analysand. On the basis of these universal patterns, the analyst is able to "dream himself into" the condition of the analysand. The analyst uses his or her own dissociability to understand that of the client. Janet did not come close to this insight. Freud approached it in his doctrine of the transference, but there an oedipal parent–child relationship is expected, where the analyst is the senior figure. In archetypal psychology, however, the analyst enters the alchemical bath with the analysand: both are wounded, both are healers, and both are transformed.

Solve et coagula (dissolve and coagulate), the motto of alchemy, has the psychological significance of "dissociate and integrate." Although it is beyond the scope of this paper to discuss the role of dissociationism in Jung's alchemical studies, their very existence demonstrates two important facts about dissociationism. The French hypnotists by no means invented dissociationism; they merely recognized and explicated a universal human possibility which had been under discussion symbolically and in projected form for centuries. Also, Jung's development of the theory of the archetypes does not imply that he had "transcended" dissociationism or lost interest in the complex theory. Rather, what has been transcended is the almost Cartesian concern with the mind's shuffling of ideas. Like psychoanalysis, Jungian psychology is a "praxis" of relationship, but it is the archetypal form of dissociationism, while psychoanalysis represents an alternative to dissociationism. As Shoenberg (1975) has pointed out, Freud's true adversary was never Adler or Jung, but has always been Janet.

References

Binet, A. (1892) *Alterations of Personality* (H.G. Baldwin, trans.). London: Chapman & Hall, 1896.

Bourguignon, E. (1965) The Self, the Behavioral Environment, and the Theory of Spirit Possession. In M.E. Spiro (ed.), *Context and Meaning in Cultural Anthropology* (pp. 39–60). New York: Free Press.

——— (1968) World Distribution and Patterns of Possession States. In R. Prince (ed.), *Trance and Possession States* (*Proceedings of the Second Annual Conference of the R.M. Bucke Memorial Society, 4–6 March 1966*, pp. 3–34). Montreal: R.M. Bucke Memorial Society.

—— (ed.) (1973) *Religion, Altered States of Consciousness, and Social Change*. Columbus: Ohio State University Press.

—— (1974) Cross-Cultural Perspectives on the Religious Uses of Altered States of Consciousness. In I.I. Zaretsky and M.P. Leone (eds), *Religious Movements in Contemporary America* (pp. 228–243). Princeton: Princeton University Press.

—— (1976) *Possession*. San Francisco: Chandler & Sharp.

Breuer, J. and Freud, S. (1895) Studies on Hysteria. *Standard Edition*, 2. London: Hogarth Press, 1978.

Crapanzano, V. (1973) *The Hamadsha: A Study in Moroccan Ethnopsychiatry*. Berkeley: University of California Press.

Crapanzano, V. and Garrison, V. (eds) (1977) *Case Studies in Spirit Possession*. New York: Wiley.

Ellenberger, H.F. (1968) The Concept of Creative Illness. *Psychoanal. Rev.*, 55: 442–56.

—— (1970) *The Discovery of the Unconscious: The History and Evolution of Dynamic Psychiatry*. New York: Basic Books.

Figge, H.H. (1972) Heilpraktiker und Kurpfuscher "aus dem Jenseits": Therapeutische Behandlungsmethoden im Rahmen der brasilianischen Umbanda. *Therapie der Gegenwart*, 111: 96–112.

—— (1973a) *Geisterkult, Bessenheit und Magie in der Umbanda Religion Brasiliens*. Freiburg i. Br.: K. Alber.

—— (1973b) Zur Entwicklung und Stabilisierung von Sekundärpersönlichkeit im Rahmen von Bessenheitskulten. *Confinia Psychiatrica*, 16: 18–37.

Fischer, R. (1970) Ueber das Rhythmische-Ornamentale in Halluzinatorisch-Schöpferischen. *Confinia Psychiatrica*, 13: 1–25.

Frankel, F.H. (1976) *Hypnosis: Trance as a Coping Mechanism*. New York: Plenum.

Freud, S. (1900) The Interpretation of Dreams. *Standard Edition*, 4, 5. London: Hogarth Press, 1978.

Freud, S. and Jung, C.G. (1908) *The Freud–Jung Letters: The Correspondence between Sigmund Freud and C.G. Jung* (W. McGuire, ed.; R. Manheim and R.F.C. Hull, trans.). Princeton: Princeton University Press, 1974.

Gill, M.M. and Brenman, M. (1959) *Hypnosis and Related States: Psychoanalytic Studies in Regression*. New York: International Universities Press.

Goodman, F.D., Henny, J.H., and Pressel, E. (1974) *Trance, Healing, and Hallucination: Three Field Studies in Religious Experience*. New York: Wiley.

Goodwin, D.W., Powell, B., Bremer, D., Heine, H., and Stern, J. (1969) Alcohol and Recall: State-Dependent Effects in Man. *Science*, 163: 1358–1360.

Grof, S. (1977) The Implications of Psychedelic Research for Anthropology: Observations from LSD Psychotherapy. In I.M. Lewis (ed.), *Symbols and Sentiments: Cross-Cultural Studies in Symbolism* (pp. 144–173). New York: Academic Press.

Hannah, B. (1976) *Jung: His Life and Work: A Biographical Memoir*. New York: Putnam.

Hilgard, E.R. (1977) *Divided Consciousness: Multiple Controls in Human Thought and Action*. New York: Wiley.

Hilgard, J.R. (1970) *Personality and Hypnosis: A Study of Imaginative Involvement.* Chicago: University of Chicago Press.

Homans, P. 1979 *Jung in Context: Modernity and the Making of a Psychology.* Chicago: University of Chicago Press.

Jaffé, A. (1968) *From the Life and Work of C. G. Jung* (R.F.C. Hull, trans.). New York: Harper Colophon.

Janet, P. (1889) *L'automatisme psychologique: Essai de psychologie experimentale sur les formes inférieures de l'activité humaine.* Paris: La Société Pierre Janet, 1973.

—— (1891) Etude sur un cas d'aboulie et d'idées fixes. *Revue Philosophique,* 34: 384–407. (Reprinted "almost without modification" in Janet, 1898, pp. 1–68.)

—— (1894). Histoire d'une idée fixe. (In Janet, 1898, pp. 156–212. Reprinted with the addition of "only a few details" from *Revue Philosophique,* 37: 121–168.)

—— (1898) *Névroses et idées fixes* (vol. 1), *Etudes experimentales* (4th edn). Paris: Alcan, 1925.

—— (1903) *Les obsessions et la psychasthénie* (vols 1 and 2). (Vol. 2 in collaboration with F. Raymond.) New York: Arno, 1976.

—— (1907) *The Major Symptoms of Hysteria.* New York and London: Hafner.

—— (1919) *Psychological Healing: A Historical and Clinical Study* (E. Paul and C. Paul, trans.). New York: Arno, 1976.

—— (1930) Pierre Janet [Autobiography]. In C. Murchison (ed.), *A History of Psychology in Autobiography* (vol. 1, pp. 123–133). Worcester: Clark University Press.

Jung, C.G. (1902) On the Psychology and Pathology of So-Called Occult Phenomena. *Collected Works,* 1: 3–81. Princeton: Princeton University Press, 1970.

—— (1906) Experimental Researches. *Collected Works,* 2. Princeton: Princeton University Press, 1972.

—— (1907) The Psychology of Dementia Praecox. *Collected Works,* 3: 1–151. Princeton: Princeton University Press, 1960.

—— (1911) Symbols of Transformation: An Analysis of the Prelude to a Case of Schizophrenia. *Collected Works,* 5. Princeton: Princeton University Press, 1967.

—— (1912) The Theory of Psychoanalysis. *Collected Works,* 4: 83–226. Princeton: Princeton University Press, 1961.

—— (1917) On the Psychology of the Unconscious. *Collected Works,* 7: 3–119. Princeton: Princeton University Press, 1966.

—— (1919) Instinct and the Unconscious. *Collected Works,* 8: 129–138. Princeton: Princeton University Press, 1960.

—— (1924) Analytical Psychology and Education. *Collected Works,* 17: 63–132. Princeton: Princeton University Press, 1954.

—— (1934–1939) *Nietzsche's Zarathustra: Notes of the Seminar Given in 1934–1939* (J.L. Jarrett, ed.). London: Routledge, 1989.

—— (1935a) Foreword to von Koenig-Fachsenfeld: *Wandlungen des Traumproblems von der Romantik bis zur Gegenwart. Collected Works,* 18: 773–775. Princeton: Princeton University Press, 1976.

—— (1935b) The Tavistock Lectures: On the Theory and Practice of Analytical Psychology. *Collected Works.* 18: 1–182. Princeton: Princeton University Press, 1976.

—— (1937) The Realities of Practical Psychotherapy. *Collected Works*, 16: 327–338. Princeton: Princeton University Press, 1966.

—— (1939) Conscious, Unconscious, and Individuation. *Collected Works*, 9i: 275–289. Princeton: Princeton University Press, 1969.

—— (1946) The Psychology of the Transference. *Collected Works*, 16: 163–323. Princeton: Princeton University Press, 1966.

—— (1951a) Aion: Researches into the Phenomenology of the Self. *Collected Works*, 9ii. Princeton: Princeton University Press, 1959.

—— (1951b) Fundamental Questions of Psychotherapy. *Collected Works*, 16: 111–125. Princeton: Princeton University Press, 1966.

—— (1954) On the Nature of the Psyche. *Collected Works*, 8: 139–158. Princeton: Princeton University Press, 1960.

—— (1961) *Memories, Dreams, Reflections* (A. Jaffé, record. and ed.; R. and C. Winston, trans.). New York: Pantheon.

Leuner, H. (1962) *Die experimentale Psychose, ihre Psychopharmakologie, Phänomenologie und Dynamik in Beziehung zur Person: Versuch einer konditional-genetischen und funktionalen Psychologie der Psychose.* Berlin: Springer.

McDougall, W. (1926) *An Outline of Abnormal Psychology.* London: Methuen.

Miller, G.A., Galanter, E., and Pribram, K.H. (1960) *Strategien des Handelns: Pläne und Strukturen des Verhaltens* (P. Bärtschi, trans.). Stuttgart: Klett, 1973. (Original: *Plans and the Structure of Behavior.*)

Overton, D.A. (1968) Dissociated Learning in Drug States (State Dependent Learning). In D.H. Efron, et al. (eds), *Psychopharmacology: A Review of Progress, 1957–1967*, No. 1836. Washington: Public Health Service.

Paulhan, F. (1889) *L'activité mentale et les éléments de l'esprit.* Paris: Alcan.

Prince, M. (1914) *The Unconscious: The Foundations of Human Personality, Normal and Abnormal.* New York: Macmillan.

—— (1929) *Clinical and Experimental Studies in Personality.* Cambridge, MA.: Science-Art.

Roazen, P. (1976) *Freud and His Followers.* New York: Knopf.

Shoenberg, P.J. (1975) Symptom as Stigma or Communication in Hysteria. *Internat. J. Psychoanal. Psychother.*, 4: 507–517.

Sidis, B. (ed.) (1902) *Psychopathological Researches: Studies in Mental Dissociation.* New York: Stechert.

Sidis, B. and Goodhart, S.P. (1904) *Multiple Personality: An Experimental Investigation into the Nature of Human Personality.* New York: Greenwood Press, 1968.

Stepansky, P.E. (1977) A History of Aggression in Freud. *Psychological Issues*, 10 (3), Monograph 39. New York: International Universities Press.

10

BERGSON AND JUNG

Pete A.Y. Gunter

Source: *Journal of the History of Ideas*, 43 (1982) 635–52.

I

To date there has not been an extensive analysis of the parallels between Henri Bergson's philosophy and Carl Gustav Jung's analytical psychology. Such an analysis can prove useful. The parallels between Jung and Bergson are thoroughgoing and can cast a revealing light on the thought of each. There is, moreover, a line of influence running from Bergson's philosophy to Jung's dynamic psychiatry. The psychiatrist was able to use models developed by the philosopher to help shape and broaden his own ideas. This should not be surprising, for Bergson intended philosophy to be a fruitful, catalytic agency, not a sterile scholastic game. It is highly instructive that in Jung's case Bergson was able to have such a fruitful, constructive effect.

II

It has been a long while since Bergson's *L'Evolution Créatrice* (Paris, 1907) made him world-famous overnight, calling forth an enthusiastic public response such as is rarely encountered by a philosopher. (When he came to Columbia University to lecture in 1913, Bergson through his popularity created what one authority describes as the first traffic jam in the history of the new world.)[1] The eclipse of the Bergsonian movement after World War I and the diversion of philosophy into quite different channels have, however, caused the impact of his ideas in the first two decades of this century to be largely forgotten.

Basic to the philosophy of Bergson is his distinction between time as spatialized and time as experienced. "Spatialized" time is mathematical, a "clock time" all of whose parts are alike and all of whose instants are static. When analyzed, such a time turns out to be not time at all but a "fourth dimension of space."[2] By contrast, experienced time is a qualitative duration, no new parts of which are identical or capable of being repeated. In his first book (*Essai sur les données immédiates de la conscience*

(1889), translated as *Time and Free Will; an Essay on the Immediate Data of Consciousness* (1910), Bergson limits duration to the human stream of consciousness: "Pure duration is the form which the succession of our conscious states assumes when our ego . . . refrains from separating its present state from its former states" (*TFW*, 100). In such circumstances we form "both the past and the present states into an organic whole, as happens when we recall the notes of a tune, melting, so to speak, into one another" (ibid). Duration is thus experienced as a melodic continuity, a flow. Unfortunately, Bergson complains, our ordinary thought breaks up this organic becoming into atomized fragments.

This is, in fact, the essential function of a spatialized, mathematical time. It presents us with a fixed, stable, neatly segmented world in which we can safely go about our practical affairs. But while such a schema is useful, it is liable to prejudice the philosopher and the psychologist who may forget what it leaves out. While an atomized, fragmented world contains nothing that should not be, in principle, predictable, the experienced world of "inner duration" exhibits the emergence of novelty: the appearance of the really surprising, the ontologically new. In other words, for Bergson inner duration provides a paradigm of creativity; spatialized time provides a paradigm of predictable repetition.[3]

As Samuel Alexander said, Bergson was perhaps the first philosopher to "take time seriously."[4] While to take time seriously may be to make a distinction between duration and space, there are problems connected with this distinction. Bergson sometimes speaks as if inner duration and spatialized time constitute two entirely distinct worlds. Thus, it seems as if he has created a new dualism every bit as radical as the Cartesian dualism which preceded him. While numerous passages in *Time and Free Will* might be called on to support this Cartesian interpretation, Bergson's second book, *Matière et Mémoire* (1896) dispenses with sharp dualisms. In this work, so difficult and yet so central to Bergson's philosophy, duration is renamed and also partially reconceived as "memory," while memory is shown to be in constant and fertile interaction with matter. In exploring this interaction Bergson develops a theory of the unconscious and of mental pathology which was to have a significant effect on subsequent dynamic psychiatry.

In Bergson's psychological duration there is no clear-cut distinction between present and past: the past shades into the present without precise boundaries. It is only a slight extension of this idea to conclude that there is no clear-cut distinction between our present and the *totality* of our past, that is, between our present state and the totality of our personal memory. Thus, Bergson (like Freud) postulates that all of our memories are conserved and make up our unconscious mind.[5] It is this unconscious mind which constitutes the basis of our character and nourishes our free acts:

The whole of our past psychical life conditions our present state, without being its necessary determinant; whole also, it reveals itself in our character, although no one of its past states manifests itself explicitly in character.

(*MM*, 191)

It may appear that in recollection we return in thought from the present to the past, but the truth is quite different: in recollection our memories return to us, often involuntarily. Our brains operate so as to screen out most of this forgotten background, else we would be inundated by reminiscences. As it is, our lives are a sort of dialectical tension between our unconscious, perpetually seeking expression, and our present, practically oriented action which, thanks to the focal power of our neural system, enables us to "attend to life."

In *Creative Evolution* the psychology of *Matter and Memory* becomes a metaphysics on the grand scale. The contrast between memory and matter is transformed into the contrast between life and entropy: life proceeding toward higher and higher levels of creativity, matter receding toward thermodynamic dissolution and, in the process, opposing the upward thrust of evolution.[6] Just as in human consciousness contemporary states interpenetrate, so in evolution, Bergson holds, each of the three main directions in which life has diverged (vegetative, instinctive, intelligent) contains aspects of the others. Man, the most "intelligent" vertebrate, possesses unsuspected "instinctive" capacities; social insects, though instinctive, possess vestigial capacities for intelligence. Vertebrates and insects both possess the plant's capacity to ingest and store energy, and plants (as the behavior of climbing vines and insectivorous plants testifies) can mimic animal behavior (*CE*, 108–9).

The preceding is a highly schematic picture of Bergson's evolutionism. It omits consideration of the life force (*élan vital*) that he describes as impelling evolution on its course. That consideration will arise in comparison with the Jungian notion of *libido*. It also fails to mention the concept of *intuition* which Bergson describes as a refinement of "instinct," a way of grasping the flux of duration "from within."

For our purposes the important thing to note in all this is that with *Creative Evolution* the human unconscious becomes suprapersonal. There is in each of us the memory of a biological past which far antedates our individual lives. Though Bergson does not speak of a human collective unconscious, his search for supraindividual elements in man's unconscious mind will certainly appear remarkably familiar to students of Jung.

III

Ascribing intellectual influence is often tricky. Did Freud, or Pierre Janet, or Charcot create the concept of the unconscious? Or should we reach further back to Eduard von Hartmann and Arthur Schopenhauer, to Benedict Spinoza, Gottfried Leibniz – even to Plato? One thing is certain: the complex of assumptions referred to by historians of ideas as "dynamic psychiatry"[7] was very much in the air around the turn of the century. The climate of opinion beginning to precipitate itself in Zurich, Paris, and Vienna contained many ideas which might plausibly be ascribed to Jung, Bergson, Janet, Adler, Freud, or others. Luckily, Jung had much to say about Bergson. It is to Jung's own assertions, therefore, that we must turn.

Jung has stated clearly the similarities he perceived between his views and Bergson's. In 1914, he confided:

> I realize that my views are parallel with those of Bergson, and that in my book (*The Psychology of the Unconscious*) the concept of the libido which I have given is a concept parallel to that of *élan vital*; my constructive method corresponds to his intuitive method. I, however, confine myself to the psychological side and to practical work. When I first read Bergson a year and a half ago I discovered to my great pleasure everything which I had worked out practically, but expressed by him in consummate language and in wonderfully clear philosophical style.[8]

The date of this admission is important because it locates Jung's acquaintance with Bergson at the time he was struggling to free himself from his collaboration with Sigmund Freud. As is widely known, it was the libido-concept which increasingly divided the two: for Freud, libido was primarily sexual, but Jung increasingly insisted that sexuality is only one component of psychic energy.

Was Bergson's *élan vital* really similar to Jung's post-Freudian *libido*? E.A. Bennet denies it:

> Mental energy is a much-debated concept in psychology and philosophy. Bergson's *élan vital*, for instance, is a specific theory of mental energy and is different from Jung's view. It is mentioned here because the two have been confused. Those who seek a complete exposition of Jung's viewpoint are referred to his paper "On Psychic Energy"....[9]

But when we turn to Jung's "On Psychic Energy" (begun 1912–1913, completed 1927), we discover that *Jung himself draws a parallel here between élan vital and Jungian libido*.[10] Nor was this his last such comparison. In "On Psychoanalysis" (1913)[11] and "A Contribution to the Study of Psychological Types" (1913)[12] the parallel is again extended. In "The Content of the Psychoses: Part II" (1914)[13] and "Psychological Understanding" (1914)[14] the equation is restated *twice in each essay*. The comparison in question lost no significance for him, for Jung proposed it again twenty years later in "The Meaning of Psychology for Modern Man" (1934).[15]

A detailed comparisons of Bergson's and Jung's notions of life-energy would not be without interest. It would reveal a nucleus of agreement as well as peripheral differences. I suggest, however, that comparisons be cut short by simply admitting that Jung, who was certainly in a position to know, was right about the close similarity of the two ideas. If he did not think so, it would have been strange indeed for him to say so, in print, at least nine times.[16]

Parallelism, however, is not influence. Did Bergson's conception of *élan vital*, a life-force containing sexuality as only one of its expressions, aid Jung? The answer depends in part on when Jung first encountered Bergson and, equally, on when he began to diverge from Freud.

The dates of Jung's conclusive divergence from Freud have been amply documented. Liliane Frey-Rohn concludes:

> Although the first hints of a new concept of energy could already be seen in *The Psychology of Dementia Praecox*, the breakthrough to an abstract concept of energy took place in the years 1911– 1913.[17]

By 1906 Jung was familiar with certain of Bergson's basic ideas. A reader of the *Journal of Abnormal Psychology*, he would probably have come across J.W. Courtney's brief discussion (August 1906) of Bergson's theory of false recognition.[18] Jung's *The Psychology of Dementia Praecox*, written in 1906, refers to Bergson's theory of dreams.[19] More significantly, it contains numerous references to Pierre Janet's *Les Obsessions et la psychasthénie* (1903) which contains references to and important quotes from *Matter and Memory*. The relations between Janet, Bergson and Jung are interesting subjects for speculation, and I shall discuss them again near the end of this study.

In the 1909–1910 issue of *The Journal of Abnormal Psychology*, James Jackson Putnam published an article, which Jung and Freud both read, titled "Personal Impressions of Sigmund Freud and His Work."[20] Putnam was an avid Bergsonian who persisted in trying to convert Freud to certain of Bergson's views. In his journal article Putnam mentions Bergson's account of the part played by memory in perception and his theory of the role played by memories as living forces in our daily lives.

Putnam was not the only source from which Jung might have learned about Bergson. Ernest Jones noted that Jung had completed the first part of *The Psychology of the Unconscious* by June, 1910.[21] In this work (*Wandlungen und Symbole der Libido*, referred to below as *Wandlungen I* and *II*), Jung refers to Bergson's concept of creative duration in a footnote to a passage in which Jung describes "the driving force of the libido."[22] In this footnote Jung briefly thanks Dr Adolph Keller of Zurich, whom he had known for several years, for calling his attention to this idea. In March 1909, he had mentioned to Freud that Keller (who later published a study of Bergson)[23] was "busily at work in psychoanalysis."[24]

In 1911 Jung again was in a position to ponder the ideas, if not of Bergson, then at least of Bergsonians. Beatrice M. Hinkle, converted to dynamic psychiatry through a reading of Breuer's and Freud's *Studies in Hysteria* and "a book by Bergson,"[25] set out for Europe in 1911 to see Bergson and Jung. She was to be present at the Third Psychoanalytic Congress in September 1911, as were Keller and Putnam whose ideas Freud asked Jung to probe during Putnam's stay.[26] Jung need not have troubled himself. Putnam's paper ("A Plea for the Study of Philosophic Methods in Preparation for Psychoanalytic Work")[27] does not mention Bergson, but its reiteration of the place of creativity in evolution and in human life are thoroughly Bergsonian. Nor is it likely that Jung would have failed to learn of Putnam's philosophical sympathies through Freud.

In *Wandlungen II*, written in 1912, Jung uses Bergson's *durée* to describe creation through time. His description appears in the context of a mythological investigation:

> In the Egyptian Book of the Dead, Tum is even designated as a he-cat, because as such he fought the snake, Apophis. The encoiling also means the engulfing, the entering into the mother's womb. This time is defined by the rising and setting of the sun, that is to say, through the death and renewal of the libido. The addition of the cock again suggests time, and the addition of implements suggests the creation through time. ("Durée créatrice," Bergson.) Oromazdes and Ahriman were produced through Zrwanakarana, the "infinitely long duration."[28]

The purely formal concept of time is, Jung concludes, expressed in mythology by transformations of the creative libido.

By 1910, then, Jung had connected Bergson's concept of creative duration with the concept of libido. Two years later he had restated the connection, extending it to include symbolic expression. Can we go further? To answer this question we would have to know either how extensive were Jung's conversations with Adolph Keller or exactly when he read Bergson (presumably *Creative Evolution*). *Wandlungen II* – which Jung had great difficulty finishing – was completed in September 1912.[29] If Jung were writing in *early* 1914 when he reported having read Bergson a year and a half before, this would push back the reading of *Creative Evolution* to the middle months of 1912 – early enough to aid him in broadening his concept of psychic energy and with time to provide him with positive reinforcement in his struggle with Freud.

Although these factors are not conclusive, there are three arguments which indicate that something more than parallelism was at work. The first is the essential convergence of the two concepts, as Jung describes them. Coincidences certainly do occur in the history of ideas, but the more convergence becomes identity, the more we ought to consider the possibility of influence. (Basic agreements of the two thinkers on the concept of life-energy will become more apparent as we proceed.) The second is the language which Jung uses in describing the positive force of libido. When he speaks of an "onward urging, living libido"[30] or of an "active fructifying (upward striving) form of the libido,"[31] we find ourselves in the presence of an *élan* not to be found in Freud, Schopenhauer, or even Nietzsche.

Finally, orthodox psychoanalysts saw Bergson's influence at work in Jung's defection. Thus, Ernest Jones confides:

> As early as 1909 Jung was complaining to Freud about his difficulty in explaining to his pupils the concept of libido and begged him for a fuller definition. Freud tersely replied that he could give no clearer one than he had already. Only two years later Jung equated the concept with Bergson's *élan vital*, with life energy in general, and thus robbed it of its distinctive sexual connotation.[32]

Freud evidently perceived Jung's apostasy similarly. Writing to Putnam in 1915 he complained:

> What I have seen of religious-ethical conversion has not been inviting. Jung, for example, I found sympathetic so long as he lived blindly, as I did. Then came his religious-ethical crisis with higher morality, "rebirth," Bergson and at the same time lies, brutality and antisemitic condescension towards me.[33]

One would like to know more about Freud's view of Bergson's influence. Unfortunately, the published record says little more on this point.

If the period 1911–13 marks the emergence of Jung's new psychiatry and his break with Sigmund Freud, the years 1913–20 have been called his "fallow period." Henri Ellenberger points out, however, that in this period, which culminated in Jung's *Psychological Types* (1921), his system of psychological analysis achieved definitive form.[34] In *Wandlungen II* one finds anticipations of concepts for which Jung was later to become famous, but anticipations are not yet doctrines. Jung's reading of Bergson in mid-1912 to mid-1913 occurred at a time when important components of Jung's conceptual scheme were still taking form. During the period 1913–20 Jung specifically equates Bergson's ideas with his own concepts of instinct,[35] intuition,[36] the (limited) function of the human intellect,[37] reaction-formation,[38] and introversion-extroversion.[39] His treatment of mechanism and finalism during these years is notably similar to Bergson's (though here the common source is probably Kant),[40] as is his closely related insistence that the difficulties of the present, and not of the past or future, are the key to mental illness.[41] Nor can it be purely a matter of accident that Jung includes the intuitive personality among his four basic psychological types and, like Bergson, connects intuition with future-oriented speculation.[42] There can be no question, then, that the philosophy of creative evolution had by 1913 become an integral part of Jung's reflections. One can easily imagine that it played a role in the development of such Jungian concepts as the archetypes, individuation, the collective unconscious, and intuition. I shall argue that this likelihood becomes increasingly strong as one moves from the first of these concepts (the archetypes) to the last (intuition).

The concept of the unconscious developed by Bergson in *Matter and Memory* (1896) is limited, as we noted above, to the individual's experience. On this point Bergson agreed with Freud: there is nothing in the unconscious that was not first in the conscious mind. In *Creative Evolution* (1907) this position is revised through the inclusion in man of the memory of his evolutionary past:

> Is it not plain that life goes to work . . . exactly like consciousness, exactly like memory? We trail behind us, unaware, the whole of our past; but our memory pours into the present only the odd recollection or two that can in some way complete our present situation. Thus the instinctive knowledge which one species possesses of another on a certain particular point has its roots in the very unity of life, which is, to use the expression of an ancient philosopher, a "whole sympathetic to itself."
>
> (*CE*, 167)

This passage demonstrates the analogy and the connection between the individual unconscious and what I call Bergson's collective "biological unconscious." Each living creature, he holds, contains within itself dormant potentialities, "memories" of a common past which it shares with all other living creatures. We thus share *via* an inherited and universal unconscious what Bergson claims are unsuspected capacities for the understanding of modes of life other than our own. Other creatures are also endowed with such capacities which, however, they use in very practical, if often unedifying, ways. A wasp like the sphex seems to have an almost *a priori* instinctive knowledge of its prey, the cricket, and is able to sting the cricket precisely on the three nerve centers which paralyze its legs, transforming it into a suitable living meal for the sphex's larvae.[43] We will return to the sphex when we consider Bergson's concept of instinct in connection with the Jungian archetypes.

Man is not, in Bergson's terms, primarily an instinctive animal. He is a vertebrate, hence a creature of intelligence. In man, however, can be found potentially compensatory instinctive capacities which, if extended and made reflective, might give us the key to many puzzles. These insights Bergson calls "intuitions." Unlike the primitive substratum from which they are drawn, intuitions are "disinterested, self-conscious, capable of reflecting upon [their] object and enlarging it indefinitely" (*CE*, 176). But, however disinterested and reflective they may become, for Bergson our intuitions have their roots in modes of knowledge and action of which we are ordinarily unaware.

This all too brief résumé of Bergson's concepts of biological memory, instinct, and intuition provides the basis for a comparison with Jung's notions of the collective unconscious, archetypes, and intuition. In *Creative Evolution* (1907) Bergson does not discuss his collective unconscious in terms of anthropology and myth, although he does so specifically in *The Two Sources of Morality and Religion* (1932). Rather, he applies that concept to biological problems. Jung was cautious in dealing with the natural sciences but was quite capable of approaching the unconscious from a biological viewpoint. In "Instinct and the Unconscious," a talk delivered in July 1919, he begins by criticizing the neo-Darwinian account of instinct:

> But such an explanation is far from being satisfactory. Bergson's philosophy suggests another way of explanation, where the factor of "intuition" comes in. Intuition, as a psychological function, is also an unconscious process. Just as instinct is the intrusion of an unconsciously motivated impulse into conscious action, so intuition is the intrusion of an unconscious content, or "image" into conscious apperception.[44]

Instinct and intuition are analogous but by no means identical: instinct, an impulse toward action, and intuition, an unconscious apprehension, are "counterparts." The one is no less difficult to understand than the other. But Jung cautions in language which is almost a direct quote from *Creative Evolution*:

> we must never forget that things we call complicated or even miraculous are only so for the human mind, whereas for nature they are just simple and by no means miraculous. We always have a tendency to project into things the difficulties of our understanding and to call them complicated, while in reality they are very simple and do not partake of our intellectual difficulties. Intellect

273

is not always an apt instrument; it is only one of several faculties of the human mind.[45]

A few pages further on he credits the French intuitionist with having rediscovered an archetype in his "durée créatrice."[46]

The family resemblance between Jung's collective unconscious and Bergson's collective biological memory is thus undeniable. Even so, it might be thought that the *contents* of these two universal memories differ completely. The Bergsonian collective unconscious would appear to contain the amorphous flux of the life-force with its intermingled potentialities, while Jungian racial memory would appear to contain a set of fixed, clearly distinguishable forms (archetypes). Unquestionably the two men chose to present their ideas in those terms; under closer examination, however, the contrast is attenuated.

Jung regarded his archetype or "primordial image" as a "crystallized form": a crystallization of the libido which lacks the libido's pregnant dynamism.[47] For Jung dynamic life-energies are the ultimate source of the primordial images. The underlying "dynamis" must be cast in the form of a fixed symbol. We experience, Jung explains: "an ever-growing resistance against the purely shapeless and chaotic character of sheer *dynamis* . . . the unquenchable need for reform and law. The soul, which dives into the stream, must also create the symbol, which embraces, maintains, and expresses this energy."[48] Such is the task of the poets and artists "whose chief creative source is the collective unconscious,"[49] but the artist's ultimate source is the stream, not the crystallized contents, the raw developmental potential and not the finished symbol. Similarly, the mystic's insights derive from a common basis: "the primordial foundation of primitive mentality, with its primitive energetic notion of God, in which the impelling *dynamis* has not crystallized into the abstract idea of God."[50] When a mystic or an artist is "seized by an archetype" we do not have to conceive him in the grip of an abstract form. Rather, he is grasped by fundamental energies *which it is his task to express in novel forms*. Like Bergson, then, Jung describes creativity as the crystallization of an underlying psychic flux or stream.

It can be argued that though one can find an *élan* in Jung's archetypes, one can find nothing like an archetype in Bergson's evolutionism, but this is not true. There are specific developmental potentials in Bergson's *élan vital*. Evolution by no means excludes the emergence of distinguishable types or even a sort of preexistence of these types in the original evolutionary thrust. Hence, the capacity of the sphex to recognize the basic structure of its prey lies in a biological memory which the sphex retains long after having developed along a quite different evolutionary path. Bergson gives several examples of such biological memories: the sitaris bettle, which utilizes the life cycle of the anthrophora (a bee) as if it were a learned entomologist (*CE*, 146–7); the scolia, which stings the motor ganglia of the rose beetle so as to cause paralysis but not death (*CE*, 172); the ammophila hirsuta, which, stinging the nine nerve centers of its caterpillar, then squeezes its head so as, again, to cause not death but paralysis (*CE*, 172). Such instinctive behavior, Bergson contends, involves not complicated reflexes but a kind of knowledge,[51] and this knowledge depends upon a biological memory which is remarkably specific. Just how specific this memory is becomes even clearer when we recall Bergson's example of the human eye and that of the pectin, a shellfish whose eye is almost identical with our own even to the point of having an inverted retina. In this case, Bergson holds, biological memory is specific enough to produce identical organs in very different organisms on widely divergent evolutionary pathways.

It is surprising that the similarity between Jung and Bergson at this point has rarely, if ever, been stressed. For both thinkers, possibility is not "ahead of" us in a set of clearly marked ideal characteristics, a view rejected by both thinkers as an unrealistic form of "finalistic" teleology. Rather, for Jung and Bergson, possibility is "behind us" in biological conditions stemming from the past. When we meet, Bergson says, "on one line of evolution, a recollection, so to speak, of what is developed along other lines, we must conclude that we have before us dissociated elements of one and the same original tendency" (*CE*, 118). When Bergson stresses the manner in which these tendencies originally "coalesce" (*CE*, 117), "interpenetrate" (*CE*, 135) or are "blended" (*CE*, 99), he is emphasizing their internal relatedness in an un-Jungian manner. But in stressing the reality of a collective unconscious and its specific developmental potentials, Jung and Bergson are speaking very nearly in the same voice. Nor was this near identity lost on Jung who liked to refer to his archetypes using the Bergsonian phrase "les éternels incréés."[52]

A similar agreement emerges when Jung's notion of differentiation is compared with Bergson's concept of evolutionary divergence. Like the concept of the archetype, the concept of differentiation is not explicitly worked out in *Wandlungen I* and *II*, though it is implicit in Jung's account of the individual's journey toward self-realization through the struggle with the "mother-libido" and his analysis of the concept of The Hero. In *Psychological Types*, however, the concept of differentiation is made into a technical term and used to explain individuation[53] which, Jung holds, is differentiation since by means of it the individual is more and more separated from the mass of his fellows. With characteristic optimism, he sees the human race, like the human individual, as engaged in this process which separates man from his archaic past while rendering him truly civilized.

We have already seen that Bergson lays great emphasis on evolutionary differentiation or divergence. He thus differs from, for example, Pierre

Teilhard de Chardin for whom convergence, not divergence, is the essence of evolution.[54] For Bergson, however, the end result of these evolutionary "divergent directions" (*CE*, 101, 135) is the creation of distinct species and ultimately distinct individuals. While individuality is never perfect, life "manifests a search for individuality, as if it strove to constitute systems naturally isolated, naturally closed" (*CE*, 14–15). Bergson uses the human process of individuation as a metaphor for evolutionary divergence. Life, he teaches, is tendency:

> and the essence of a tendency is to develop in the form of a sheaf, creating, by its very growth, divergent directions among which its impetus is divided. This we observe in ourselves, in the evolution of that special tendency which we call our character.
>
> (*CE*, 99–100)

Self-realization is for Bergson differentiation, the divergence from shared traits to the development of traits uniquely defining an individual. Like Jung, Bergson sees human history as a process of differential self-realization:

> Man, then, continues the vital movement indefinitely, although he does not draw along with him all that life carries in itself. On other lines of evolution there have traveled other tendencies which life implied, and of which, since everything interpenetrates, man has, doubtless, kept something, but of which he has kept only very little. *It is as if a vague and formless being, whom we may call, as we will,* man *or* superman, *had sought to realize himself, and had succeeded only by abandoning a part of himself on the way.*
>
> (*CE*, 266)

Implicit in this description is the belief – also found in Jung – that a compensatory move toward intuition is needed in the modern world if man is to realize himself as a complete being.

In developing his concepts of the archetypes and the collective unconscious, Jung would have found it helpful to utilize Bergson's similar ideas with their broad background of biological and philosophical reflections. He certainly would have been encouraged by Bergson's conclusions. But when it comes to the concept of intuition, Bergson's influence is decisive. Jung is the first psychologist to introduce the "intuitive" person as a distinct character type. Intuition, to be sure, has meant different things to different thinkers. Throughout the history of Western philosophy it has traditionally connoted recourse to eternal forms: the meaning of Alfred North Whitehead's claim that Western philosophy is just so many footnotes to the philosophy of Plato. Bergson, however, denied the Platonic concept of intuition. Where for Plato direct knowledge (intuition) has as its object timeless forms, for Bergson intuition probes the dynamics of reality. Plato's "knowledge" of change is at best opinion, but Bergson inverts this claim, contending that "knowledge" of static forms is merely "symbolic." It is clear that Jung's intuitive type stands in the Bergsonian, and not in the Platonic, tradition. By equating intuition with future-oriented speculation, by finding its substratum in the dynamic unconscious, Jung transforms our notion of intuition into a species of dynamism.

Jung shows a curious ambiguity toward Bergson's notion of intuition. In *Psychological Types* he is at pains to explain that it is Nietzsche, not Bergson, who truly understands intuition.[55] German philosophy, Jung asserts, grasped the notion of intuition in the late nineteenth century, well before the philosopher across the Rhine.[56] Jung's denial is remarkably weak, however. Leaving aside his barely veiled nationalism, there is the odd fact that less than a year before, in "Instinct and the Unconscious," Jung himself had equated his concept of intuition with Bergson's. This sudden about-face is nowhere explained. It is equally hard to square the position which Jung takes in *Psychological Types* with his remarks in 1916 at the Zurich School for Analytical Psychology:

> Special thanks are due to Bergson for having broken a lance for the right of the irrational to exist. Psychology will probably be obliged to acknowledge and to submit to a plurality of principles, in spite of the fact that this does not suit the scientific mind.[57]

Only in this way, Jung concludes, can psychology be saved from shipwreck.

There is an element of conjecture in the suggestion that Bergson's ideas on psychic energy played a role, at a crucial time, in separating Jung from Freud. (The evidence here is admittedly circumstantial.) There is a less pronounced element of conjecture in the assertion that the Jungian concepts of the archetypes, the collective unconscious, and individuation were broadened and, in part, crystallized through a reading of *Creative Evolution*. That Jung should have taken up intuition, in his special sense, as a fundamental way of viewing reality and a fundamental character-type, is a move clearly influenced by Bergson, though there is certainly room for conjecture about the exact manner in which Bergson's influence made itself felt. There is another point of influence, however, about which there can be little doubt but about which Jung was probably not aware. It stems from the work of Pierre Janet.

Like Bergson's philosophy, Janet's psychological analysis has gone into eclipse. Around the turn of the century Janet was the acknowledged leader of dynamic psychiatry. Jung studied for a semester with him in Paris in 1900[58] and took from him several key ideas which can be traced to later, post-Freudian features of Jung's psychology. Two of Janet's central concepts clearly worked their way into Jung's thought: "fonction du réel" and "tension psychologique." The hardest conceivable task, Janet held, is that of coping with present reality. This effort he termed the function of reality – renamed the ego by later psychiatrists. "Psychological tension" is closely related to the function of reality. In a healthy mind psychological tension is maintained and developed, and the function of reality is sustained. But when, through the encounter with insuperable obstacles, the tension of personality is broken, we have regression, "l'abaissement du niveau mental." In *Wandlungen II* and in *Psychological Types* Jung returns repeatedly to these ideas, reshaping them in terms of his own theory of psychological energy, using them against Freudian theories of the self.[59] Janet terms the activity through which the function of reality is made effective by confronting the present, *présentification*. Jung recurs to this notion repeatedly, insisting against Freud that mental illness often springs from a failure to deal with *present* problems and that the illness can by no means be traced simplistically to early childhood traumas. He recurs often also to the decay of psychological tension and its accompanying regression, insisting that regression in many cases results from the fear of life, not from crippling childhood conflicts. It can also, he holds, result from an injury to the ego itself.

The extent to which Janet's concepts of "attention to life" and "psychological tension" were derived by him from Bergson's *Matter and Memory* ought to be more widely known to historians of psychology. In 1911, in an introduction written for the English translation of *Matter and Memory*, Bergson states that these two concepts, at first considered paradoxical, were found indispensable by Pierre Janet in developing a theory of "psychasthenic" mental illness[60] (which Jung would later term "introverted schizophrenia"). Bergson refers to Janet's major work *Les Obsessions et la psychasthénie* (1903), citing passages in the first volume (474–502) as verification for his claim.[61] One does not find in these pages an explicit admission by Janet of the influence of Bergson's ideas, but Janet's phrase "psychological tension" is precisely the phrase used by Bergson in *Matter and Memory*, while the manner in which Janet employs it is scarcely distinguishable from Bergson's usage. The similarity between Bergson's "attention to life" and Janet's "function of reality" is conspicuous. When Jung, therefore, uses these and other closely related concepts to distinguish his dynamic psychiatry from Freud's, he owes (probably without being aware of it) a real debt to Bergson. Perhaps had he been aware of this, certain similarities which he later discovered between analytical psychology and the philosophy of creative evolution would have appeared less surprising to him.

There is no attempt here to deny Jung's creativity or to hold that he "derived his dynamic psychiatry from Bergson." What I have tried to establish is, first, that there is an extraordinarily close agreement between these two thinkers on many basic points – an agreement historians of ideas have overlooked. This fundamental agreement should be useful in understanding creativity in Jung's thought. But a second point is that there is a line of influence running from Bergson's thought to Jung's analytical psychology. As a rule this function appears to have been "catalytic" in a special way, that is, it helped Jung in directions in which he was already going. In the case of indirect influence (exerted through the person and writings of Pierre Janet), Bergson's ideas were almost certainly more decisive in providing Jung with root assumptions. But the credit here must be shared with Janet, not only because he applied the philosopher's insights to specific cases, and thus developed ("crystallized") them, but because in other respects Bergson was indebted to Janet.[62] Theirs was a complex, problematic, and highly fruitful collaboration.

IV

I conclude by posing a general question suggested by the content and conclusions of this paper: Does Jung really have a concept of creativity, or does his recourse to a fixed set of timeless archetypes limit him to a cyclic, repetitive concept of man and of history? Many of Jung's assertions would support this conclusion. Thus, in *Psychological Types* he states, concerning the human knowing process:

> These adjustments are not merely accidental or arbitrary happenings, but adhere to strictly preformed conditions, which are not transmitted, as are perception-contents, through experience but are *a priori* conditions of apprehension. . . . This explains why even fantasy, the freest activity of the mind, can never roam in the infinite (albeit, so the poet senses it), but remains bound to the preformed possibilities, the *primordial images or archetypes*.
>
> (378)

If, as James A.C. Brown and others have noted, there is a "generally static impression conveyed by the Jungian system,"[63] the priority of the archetypes would be its source.

But in *Psychological Types*, at least, Jung is ambivalent on precisely this point. While there is, he intimates, a fixed set of archetypes, these archetypes achieve new, creative expression and can thus be said to evolve. Thus there is room in Jung's thought during this period for a static, Kantian rendering of the archetypes as sheer *a priori* determinants of thought and behavior as well as for a dynamic, process-oriented explanation of the archetypes as specific tendencies toward development. However, the second, more Bergsonian tendency in Jung's thought provides a more fruitful, and hopeful, beginning.

Notes

1 Geraldine Jonçich, *The Sane Positivist: A Biography of Edward L. Thorndike* (Middletown, Connecticut, 1968), 334.
2 Henri Bergson, *Time and Free Will*, authorized translation by F.L. Pogson (London, 1950), 109. (Hereafter *TFW*.)
3 *Time and Free Will* did produce, however, an anticipation of Jung's person–persona contrast. Bergson states (*TFW*, 231): "Hence there are finally two different selves, one of which is, as it were, the external projection of the other, its spatial and, so to speak, social representation." This social self may be "parasitic" upon the fundamental self. "Many live this kind of life, and die without having known true freedom" (*TFW*, 166).
4 S. Alexander, *Space, Time and Deity* (New York, 1950), I, 44.
5 Bergson, *Matter and Memory*, authorized translation by W. Scott Palmer and Nancy Margaret Paul (London, 1950), 94–5. (Hereafter *MM*.)
6 Bergson, *Creative Evolution*, authorized translation by Arthur Mitchell (New York, 1911), 246–51. (Hereafter *CE*.)
7 Henri Ellenberger, *The Discovery of the Unconscious* (New York, 1970), 932.
8 Carl Gustav Jung, "The Content of the Psychoses, Part II, 1914," trans. M.D. Elder, in *Collected Papers on Analytical Psychology* (authorized translation), ed. C.E. Long (London, 1922), 351.
9 E.A. Bennet, *C.G. Jung* (London, 1961), 31. For a similar opinion, cf. Thomas F. Graham, *Parallel Profiles: Pioneers in Mental Health* (Chicago, 1966), 147.
10 Jung, "On Psychical Energy," in *Contributions to Analytical Psychology*, trans. H.G. and Cary F. Barnes (New York, 1928), 32.
11 Jung, "On Psychoanalysis," in *Collected Papers on Analytical Psychology*, 230–1.
12 Jung, "A Contribution to the Study of Psychological Types," trans. C.E. Long, in *Collected Papers on Analytical Psychology*, 293.
13 Jung, "The Content of the Psychoses, Part II, 1914," 348, 351.
14 Jung, "On Psychological Understanding," *Journal of Abnormal Psychology*, 9 (1914–1915), 396, 399.
15 Jung, "The Meaning of Psychology for Modern Man," *Collected Works*, 2nd ed., eds. Herbert Read, Michael Fordham, Gerhard Adler, and William McGuire, trans. R.F.C. Hull (Princeton, NJ, 1960–79), X, 147. Jung includes Aristotle's *hormé* here as another possible candidate, and denies that any such notion (even, apparently, his own) can fully explain mental dynamics.
16 Jung's paralleling of his libido and Bergson's *élan vital* is accompanied after 1920 by previously unstated reservations. Translations of passages concerning Bergson are also changed in Jung's collected works so as to distance Jung from Bergson. In "On Psychic Energy" (completed in 1928) the paralleling of Jungian libido with *élan vital*, *hormé*, and (Schopenhauer's) will is followed by a demurrer: "From these concepts I have borrowed only the concrete character of the term, not the definition of the concept. The omission of the detailed explanation of this in my earlier book is responsible for numerous misunderstandings, such as the accusation that I have built up a kind of vitalistic concept" (Jung, *Collected Works*, VIII, 30). But Jung, prior to the 1920s, was in a position to express himself accurately and to examine carefully the work of his English-language translators. The *meaning* of statements made concerning Bergson by Jung and translated prior to 1920 is often not consistent with later versions of the same statements.
17 Liliane Frey-Rohn, *From Freud to Jung* (New York, 1974), 158.

18 J.W. Courtney, "Review of 'A Propos de Déjà vu' by Pierre Janet," *Journal of Abnormal Psychology*, **1** (August 1906), 149–50.
19 Jung, "The Psychology of Dementia Praecox," in *Collected Works*, III, 66n. Bergson is referred to here in conjunction with Edouard Claparède though Bergson's "Le Rêve" is not included in Jung's bibliography. Claparède's "Esquisse d'une théorie biologique du sommeil" (*Archives psychologique de la Suisse Romande*, IV, 1904–1905, 245–349) is footnoted.
20 James Jackson Putnam, "Personal Impressions of Sigmund Freud and his Work," *Journal of Abnormal Psychology*, **4** (1909–1910), 293–310. Cf. 297–8 for Putnam's remarks on Bergson. Jung's comments on the article are contained in a letter to Sigmund Freud (10 Jan. 1910); Freud's mention of Putnam's article appears in a letter to Jung (13 Jan. 1910). *The Freud/Jung Letters*, ed. William McGuire, trans. Ralph Manheim and R.F.C. Hull (Princeton, 1974), 286.
21 Ernest Jones, *The Life and Work of Sigmund Freud*, vol. II: *Years of Maturity* (New York, 1961), 143.
22 Jung, *Psychology of the Unconscious*, Part I, authorized translation and introduction by Beatrice M. Hinkle (New York, 1965), 295–6.
23 Adolph Keller, *Eine Philosophie des Lebens* (Jena, 1914), 46.
24 Jung, "Letter to Sigmund Freud, March 7, 1909," *The Freud/Jung Letters*, 209.
25 John C. Burnham, *Psychoanalysis and American Medicine: 1894–1918, Medicine, Science, and Culture* (New York, 1967), 131–2.
26 *The Freud/Jung Letters*, 444–5. Cf. Sigmund Freud, "Letter to Carl Gustav Jung, September 1, 1911," in ibid., 441–2.
27 James Jackson Putnam, "A Plea for the Study of Philosophic Methods in Preparation for Psychoanalytic Work," *Journal of Abnormal Psychology*, **4** (Oct.–Nov. 1911), 249–64.
28 Jung, *Psychology of the Unconscious*, 314.
29 Ernest Jones, *The Life and Work of Sigmund Freud*, II, 143.
30 Jung, *Psychology of the Unconscious*, 335.
31 Ibid., 416.
32 Ernest Jones, *The Life and Work of Sigmund Freud*, II, 383.
33 Sigmund Freud, "Letter to James Jackson Putnam, July 8, 1915," trans. Judith Bernays Heller, in Nathan G. Hale, Jr., ed., *James Jackson Putnam and Psychoanalysis* (Cambridge, Mass., 1971), 188–91. This passage was omitted from previously published versions of Freud's letter (191n.).
34 Henri Ellenberger, *The Discovery of the Unconscious*, 698–703.
35 Jung, "Instinct and the Unconscious," *Contributions to Analytical Psychology*, 274.
36 Ibid., 274.
37 Ibid., 275.
38 Jung, "On Some Crucial Points in Psychoanalysis," *Collected Papers on Analytical Psychology*, 274–5. This insight is contained in a letter of March 1913.
39 Ibid., 293.
40 Jung, "The Psychology of Dreams," *Collected Papers on Analytical Psychology*, 309–10. Prepared in 1914, this talk was given after World War I.
41 Jung, "On Psychoanalysis," ibid., 229.
42 Jung, *Psychological Types*, trans. H. Godwin Baynes (New York, 1944), 461–7, 508–13, 567–9.
43 Critics have held that Bergson drew an unwarranted conclusion from Henri Fabre's (1823–1915) research by suggesting that the sphex's attack on the

cricket is unerring. (See Jean Henri Casimir Fabre, *The Mason-Wasps*, trans. Alexander Teixeira de Mattos (New York, 1919).) Whether Bergson in fact committed this error is a matter that deserves a lengthy and careful analysis that cannot be undertaken here. It should be noted, however, that in the same passage in which he describes the behavior of the sphex Bergson also describes errors made by wasps which result in killing rather than paralyzing their prey. Like intelligence, he concedes, instinct is "fallible" (*CE*, 172–3). For more recent treatments of this issue see Raymond Ruyer, "Bergson et le sphex ammophile," *Revue de Métaphysique et de Morale*, 64 (1959), 165–79; Loren Eisely, "The Coming of the Giant Wasps," *Audubon Magazine*, 77 (September, 1975), 36–9.

44 Jung, "Instinct and the Unconscious," *Contributions to Analytical Psychology*, 274. This passage is retranslated in Jung's *Collected Works* so as to distance Jungian from Bergsonian intuition. As late as 1928, however, Jung published it unchanged.

45 Ibid., 274–5; cf. *Creative Evolution*, 89–91, 217.

46 Jung, "Instinct and the Unconscious," in *Contributions to Analytical Psychology*, 280. Jung reiterated this claim in 1935. *Collected Works*, XVIII, 121.

47 Jung notes that Bergson also uses the term "crystallization" to "illustrate the essence of intellectual abstraction." Jung, "A Contribution to the Study of Psychological Types," *Collected Papers on Analytical Psychology*, 293.

48 Jung, *Psychological Types*, 318.

49 Ibid., 318–39.

50 Ibid., 316.

51 For a recent account of the instincts of the paralyzing wasps, see Loren Eiseley, loc. cit., note 43 above. *All the Strange Hours* (New York, 1975), 243–54.

52 Jolande Jacobi, *Complex/Archetype/Symbol in the Psychology of C.G. Jung*, trans. Ralph Manheim (Princeton, 1959), 52.

53 Jung, *Psychological Types*, 534–40.

54 Nicholas Core, *Pierre Teilhard de Chardin: His Life and Spirit* (New York, 1960), 10.

55 Jung, *Psychological Types*, 398–9.

56 Ibid., 400.

57 Jung, "The Conception of the Unconscious," *Collected Papers on Analytical Psychology*, 464.

58 "I studied with Janet in Paris and he formed my ideas very much. He was a first-class observer, though he had no dynamic psychological theory. It was a sort of physiological theory of unconscious phenomena, the so-called *abaissement du niveau mental*, that is, a certain depotentiation of the tension of consciousness" *C.G. Jung Speaking: Interviews and Encounters*, ed. William McGuire and R.F.C. Hull (Princeton, 1977), 283.

59 Present in abundance in "The Psychology of Dementia Praecox," they remain largely "repressed" during Jung's collaboration with Freud.

60 Bergson, *Matter and Memory*, xix. The other of Janet's chief works is *L'Automatisme psychologique* (Paris, 1889).

61 Pierre Janet, *Les Obsessions et la psychasthénie* (Paris, 1903), I, 474–502.

62 See esp. Claude M. Prévost, *Janet, Freud et la psychologie clinique* (Paris, 1973). On 203n. Prévost calls for a systematic study of the relationships between Janet and Bergson, a study which will be extremely difficult.

63 James A.C. Brown, "Assessments and Applications," *The Freudian Paradigm*, ed. Md. Mujeeb-ur-Rahman (Chicago, 1977), 379.

INDEX